D0282463

ALSO BY TIMOTHY SHENK

Maurice Dobb: Political Economist

REALIGNERS

FARRAR, STRAUS AND GIROUX

New York

REALIGNERS

PARTISAN HACKS,
POLITICAL VISIONARIES,
AND THE STRUGGLE
TO RULE
AMERICAN DEMOCRACY

Timothy Shenk

Farrar, Straus and Giroux
120 Broadway, New York 10271

Copyright © 2022 by Timothy Shenk
All rights reserved
Printed in the United States of America
First edition, 2022

Illustration credits can be found on page 449.

Library of Congress Control Number: 2022023646
ISBN: 978-0-374-13800-4

Our books may be purchased in bulk for promotional, educational, or business
use. Please contact your local bookseller or the Macmillan Corporate and
Premium Sales Department at 1-800-221-7945, extension 5442, or by email at
MacmillanSpecialMarkets@macmillan.com.

www.fsgbooks.com
www.twitter.com/fsgbooks • www.facebook.com/fsgbooks

1   3   5   7   9   10   8   6   4   2

For Renu, for everything

CONTENTS

Introduction: The Golden Line *3*

1. Guardians *13*

2. Partisans *43*

3. Liberators *81*

4. Organizers *119*

Interlude: The Party of Everyone *163*

5. Prophets *171*

6. Insiders *213*

7. Insurgents *255*

8. Politicians *295*

Conclusion: The Road to Freedom *341*

Notes 351

Acknowledgments 427

Index 431

REALIGNERS

Introduction: The Golden Line

It turns out that success has a sound. I heard it a few years ago, shortly after moving to Washington, D.C., when I booked a table at the city's most popular French restaurant. Le Diplomate—or Le Dip, as you were supposed to call it—had been making cameo appearances in Washington's scandal du jour, this one starring a high-ranking politico who was being forced out of office because, among other sins, he had ordered his motorcade to use its sirens so that he wouldn't miss a reservation at his favorite brasserie.[1]

Drawn in by the publicity, I decided to splurge on a meal. I expected to see waiters in crisp aprons gliding between tables, dispensing a never-ending supply of baguettes and foie gras mousse so light that it floated off the plate. Instead, I walked off the street into a wall of sound, paused for my eyes to adjust to the murky lighting, then glanced over tables filled with VIPs waiting for their beef bourguignon.

The noise was the result of a packed crowd and dreadful acoustics. But you could hear a thrum of self-satisfaction running underneath, a contented rumble that accompanied the clattering of silverware. Le Dip was the place where the middling ranks of the Washington establishment—lobbyists, consultants, journalists, congressional staffers, denizens of the administrative state—relaxed after a long day of power brokering. Now they were rewarding themselves with a night out, savoring a glass of red while scanning the room to see if any boldface names were in attendance.

A few months later I came across a document that brought me back to my evening at Le Dip. It was a petition written in the fall of 1776 by the "freemen of Albemarle county"—home of Charlottesville and Thomas Jefferson's Monticello—to the Virginia General Assembly, where legislators were drafting a new state constitution. The authors explained that they were writing because, under Virginia's system of government, "all power is radically in the people." That is, in them.[2]

But as the message went on, it became clear that even if the people were the root of the government's power, in practice they couldn't do much. If they could, the freemen of Albemarle would be designing a constitution themselves, not sending letters. A line ran between the public and the governing class, a line that set them apart even as it bound them together: "the GREAT GOLDEN LINE," the petition-ers called it, "between the Rulers and the Ruled."[3]

The history of American democracy is a history of arguments over where to draw the golden line between the rulers and the ruled. Think-ing back to my glimpse of life on the other side of the golden line at Le Dip, I kept wondering: How did we get here?

———————————

Let me explain. As you might have noticed, the twenty-first century hasn't been going terribly well for the American political elite: a string of disastrous interventions abroad, the Great Recession and anemic recovery, the serialized outrages of the Trump era, then the bungled response to a pandemic that cost more American lives than the Civil War. Each failure is processed through a media infotainment complex that treats politics as part battle for the national soul and part blood sport. Add it all together, and you might decide that the country is careening toward a full-blown legitimacy crisis.

Except politics has also fallen into a grinding routine. For all their differences, Barack Obama and Donald Trump each campaigned on a political revolution they failed to deliver. The murder of George Floyd sparked the largest mass demonstrations in U.S. history, but the movement for police reform ran into a congressional buzz saw. Rioters intent on overturning an election stormed the Capitol, only to discover that they couldn't do more than delay the certification of Joe Biden's victory by a few hours. And when Biden took power, Democrats learned the dangers of promising a second New Deal without FDR-size majorities.

Which leaves us with the worst of two worlds, a system that feels like it's both sliding into stagnation and teetering on the brink of a total meltdown.

Make America Hope and Change Again?

That's not the only strange fact about the contemporary political scene. For most of American history, one party has tended to dominate: Jeffersonians in the early republic; Democrats in the age of Jackson; Republicans during the era of the Civil War and Reconstruction, then again from the 1890s down to the Great Depression; and Franklin

Roosevelt's Democrats in the Depression and postwar years. But neither party has been able to put together an enduring majority since the collapse of the New Deal coalition. The last authentic landslide in the popular vote—defined as winning by more than ten points—occurred when Ronald Reagan carried forty-nine states in 1984, and Reagan's personal popularity didn't do his party much good. While the president was cruising to reelection, Democrats retained control of the House and picked up seats in the Senate.

Today, victories at FDR's scale are unimaginable, and revolts against the incumbent party are the norm, making it impossible for either coalition to form a stable majority.[4] With national elections decided by wafer-thin margins, it becomes much more likely that control of Washington will fall to a party that didn't win a numerical majority—a president taking office without carrying the popular vote, a Senate chosen by a minority of the country. Meanwhile, the losing party's best shot at winning next time is to grind the system to a halt, betting that voters will blame the people running the show. More often than not, it's a bet they'll win.

The peculiarities of American politics make the failure to win by decisive margins especially consequential. Almost every other democracy has more than two major parties.[5] If nobody wins outright, elected officials bargain among themselves to form a coalition government. American politicians have to forge their majorities at the polls, and the numbers have to be huge if a campaign platform is going to survive the legislative gauntlet.

So the United States is unusual compared with the rest of the world because of its two-party system, and the country today is unusual compared with its historical norm because no coalition has a lasting hold on power.

This book starts from the premise that you can't understand American democracy—from its origins in the eighteenth century down to the impasse it has reached today—without taking a close look at the people who have walked the golden line between the rulers and the ruled. They are the democratic elite, the portion of the ruling class whose authority derives, at least in theory, from the public's consent. And they have a power that's unique to modern democracies: the ability to form electoral coalitions that bind millions of people together in a single cause.

The rest of this book is about what the American democratic elite has done with that extraordinary power. It's a biography of American democracy told through its majorities, and the people who made them. The subject is worth paying attention to now because, over the long arc of American history, creating a new majority has been the single most effective way of breaking through political logjams of the kind we're facing.[6] There are plenty of visionary proposals out there for remaking society. What's missing is a plan for building a coalition that could turn those dreams into reality.

Realignments are usually analyzed by political scientists brandishing precinct-by-precinct breakdowns of the electorate. This account shifts the focus to a part of the story that's easy to lose track of between all the data sets: the narratives, policies, and symbols—in short, the ideas—that produce coalitions.[7] It views American democracy through the eyes of a small number of people who tried to remake the country, not just with one decisive victory, but by stitching together a majority over decades. It runs from the dawn of the republic, when the founders discovered the unique power of appealing to a national electorate, down to the twenty-first century, with Barack Obama straining to hold together a fracturing system. In between, it includes such partisan operatives as Martin Van Buren and Mark Hanna—architects, respectively, of the Jacksonian Democratic coalition and of the Republican majority that emerged out of the Gilded Age—who were concerned above all with winning the next election. But it also features activists intent on transforming American life through mass politics, ranging from the abolitionist Charles Sumner to Phyllis Schlafly, founding mother of the conservative movement. And it has space for intellectuals such as W.E.B. Du Bois and Walter Lippmann, who explored the inner logic of modern democracy while keeping a close eye on real-world politics.

These lives are studies in the character, limits, and promise of the American democratic tradition. At their most effective, realigners combine a brutally frank assessment of the political system with a vision for how they might still change the country. Rejecting the moderate's dream of unanimity, they accept—and often celebrate—conflict. But they can't afford a radical insistence on moral purity. Driven by the imperatives of coalition building, realigners accept two principles that seem contradictory at first glance: the inevitability of disagreement and the virtues of persuasion.

It's a difficult balancing act, and realigners often fall into one of two more familiar roles: party hacks on one side, prophets denouncing a fallen world on the other.[8] This book considers what it takes to walk this tightrope. I mean "takes" in both senses of the term: the skills it requires, and the price it exacts.

Unavoidably, the following pages concentrate on a narrow sliver of the population, a political class that even today is mostly wealthy, white, and male. But that doesn't make it a tribute to great men altering the course of nations with a flick of their wrists. Coalitions unite figures up and down the social scale—party leaders, outside activists, and the wider public—around a shared project. By linking diverse groups together in a single cause, they can provide a democratic corrective to tribalism, just as a healthy democracy is the best antidote to populism. And by forcing elites to reckon with the views of the masses, they can offer something close to a loophole in the iron law of oligarchy, the inexorable tendency for democratic institutions to wind up being run by small cadres of insiders.[9] When ordinary citizens have a voice—and the power to restrain their ruling class—then democracy has real meaning.

But even in this rosy scenario, there's no escaping the democratic elite. They do the work that crystallizes the inchoate mass of public opinion into lasting change, from writing platforms to drafting legislation.[10] Like the creative team behind a summer blockbuster, their success ultimately depends on public approval. But they're the people making the movie.

The history of the American democratic elite begins at specific time and place, with the drafting of a Constitution designed to bring thirteen fractious republics under the control of a centralized political class. To curb state legislatures, the framers created a government founded, as Alexander Hamilton put it, "on the solid basis of THE CONSENT OF THE PEOPLE."[11] Power in the new regime flowed from elections, allowing the framers to dismiss accusations that they were imposing aristocracy by another name. And because the executive and legislature were chosen by a national electorate, their democratic bona fides trumped mere states. The resulting system—a federal government overseen by an elite cloaked in the authority that came from speaking for the country as a whole—supplied what James Madison described as "the only defence against the inconveniencies of democracy consistent with the democratic form of government."[12] The people and the democratic elite were twins, brought into the world by the same parents at the same time. "We the people" voted, while the democratic elite ruled.[13]

But even when suffrage restrictions kept most of "we the people" from actually voting, winning the public's consent proved far more difficult than the founders envisioned. And more important. Because just a few years into the life of the new government, a civil war erupted inside the democratic elite. With the political class split in two, the battle to win political power by assembling an electoral majority was launched.

It has never stopped. During centuries filled with fraud, violence, and demagoguery—along with quadrennial proclamations that the next election is the most significant of our lifetimes—there have also been moments when skilled political leaders turned popular majorities into agents of sweeping transformation that altered the balance of power in American life. If democracy is worth loving, as opposed to grudgingly accepting as a least-bad alternative, it's because we've had those moments before. And if there's an escape from the doom loop that American politics has become, it's because we might have those moments again.

Hard to believe, I know—and not just because the present is so grim. When historians consider the broad sweep of the American past, they often reach for a single overarching story to hold the narrative together. These skeleton-key histories have taken various forms over the years. A century ago, they tended to feature a struggle between the many and the few, pitting a virtuous public against its capitalist over-lords.[14] Attention pivoted from conflict to consensus in the long economic boom that followed World War II, with historians depicting a middle-class nation inoculated against ideological extremes by a distinctive mixture of individualism and conformism.[15] Today, it's more common to underscore the centrality of white supremacy, drawing a straight line from slavery in the seventeenth century to systemic racism in the twenty-first.[16]

Skeleton-key histories of all kinds—whether they emphasize class conflict, liberal consensus, or racial domination—by their nature highlight continuity. That's the source of their power, showing the same patterns repeating themselves time and again, finding the center in a story that might otherwise devolve into a disconnected string of events.

Looking at history from a realigner's perspective brings a different picture into focus. Assembling a national coalition in a large and diverse country is like putting together a puzzle with pieces that are constantly changing shape. And so, rather than stressing continuity, a study of re-alignments has to underline the importance of breaking with the past. Because there's no one thread tying the history of American democracy together, no abiding center, no single answer. But there is a recurring question: How can you build an electoral majority?[17]

Realignments take place one conversion at a time, shattering old alliances and forging new ones. American history is filled with pronouncements that a party is on its deathbed, only to see its resurrection a few years later as the champion of a new majority. In the 1924 presidential election, Democrats lost every state outside the Jim Crow South and barely scraped together a quarter of the popular vote.[18] Had a farsighted Democratic strategist announced that within a decade the party would assemble the largest majority in America by uniting white supremacists and Black communists, Great Plains populists and polyglot urban ethnics, backcountry Jacksonians and dissident Ivy Leaguers, the unlucky prophet would have been laughed out of politics.

Even when electoral upheavals aren't quite so drastic, campaigns are still decided on the margins.[19] The difference between political hegemony and perennial minority status often comes down to boosting turnout with core supporters just a bit, or losing a handful of key groups by a little less. With converts at a premium, realigners are forced to believe in change.

Looking at how coalitions take shape over time offers a useful reminder that in politics there are no permanent friends or enemies.[20] It's easy in a polarized age to project today's partisan divisions onto the past. But turning history into a never-ending feud between the red and blue teams, where everyone knows their side in advance, guarantees that the only lesson you'll learn is how right you always were. And it sets you up to turn against voters the instant they deliver a verdict you don't like. Which they inevitably will.

There's a warning here for anyone who fears that American politics has entered dangerous territory, where antidemocratic forces are preparing to seize control of the government by any means necessary. Even if you think that fending off this challenge requires a fundamental overhaul of the political system, the path to reform starts with building a majority under the current rules of the game. Because you can't save democracy without first winning some elections.

I am by no means above the partisan fray. I spent the Trump presidency working as an editor at the left-wing journal *Dissent*, and if you want to know how I felt on election night 2016—not happy!—it's in our archives. But I came by my addiction to politics by growing up in a family that loves to argue about this stuff, including true-blue Democrats and Trump-loving Republicans.

Over long hours at the dinner table I learned that even if you can't agree, it helps to know what you're fighting about. And so the chapters ahead, without airbrushing away the uglier parts of the picture, try to explain why each of these characters saw themselves as the heroes of their own stories.

Pick a problem in the United States today, and you can find its counterpart abroad: populist revolts, mounting economic inequality, ferocious battles over both cultural identity and basic human rights, a hollowing out of democracy as authority flows to technocrats shielded from public accountability.[21]

The issue, in short, is structural. But these structures didn't descend from above. The American political system was created—every piece of it—by us. Or, to be more precise, and as we'll see, it was created by a governing class whose power derived from its ability to speak for "we the people." Our democratic elite has done a lot of speaking over the centuries, and we all live with the consequences.

Let's listen.

1

Guardians

Publius Valerius served the people. A Roman aristocrat, Publius helped lead the revolution that overthrew the last king of Rome in 509 B.C.[1] Rather than seizing power for himself, Publius worked to establish the first Roman republic. Grateful citizens rewarded him with the surname Poplicola: "friend of the people."

Early American history was filled with pseudonymous scribblers dressing up their arguments in costumes borrowed from antiquity—Catos, Agrippas, even the occasional Caesar. Alexander Hamilton was especially fond of Publius. He first used the name in 1778, then brought it out again during the ratification debates over the Constitution in the fall of 1787.[2] It struck the right balance for a statesman who would serve the public without succumbing to the mob, another friend of the people.

Writing at a furious pace—about a thousand words a day over seven months—Publius mounted a comprehensive defense of the proposed government. "In decency he should now rest on his arms, and let the people draw their breath for a little," one critic of the Constitution grumbled two months into the campaign.[3] First published in New York, the eighty-five essays found a wider audience in 1788 when they were collected in a two-volume book titled *The Federalist*. Most were written by Hamilton, a handful by his fellow New Yorker John Jay, and the remainder by James Madison.

At the beginning, the authors tried to ensure that Publius spoke in one voice, though as the deadlines piled up, coordination quickly became impossible. But a set of common themes ran through Publius's writings. Together they provided the blueprint for a new political order built out of three interlocking parts: a central government strong enough to bring unruly state legislatures to heel, a political elite that Publius insisted would be "pre-eminent for ability and virtue," and a national electorate whose approval would legitimize the entire system.[4]

Take one leg away from this stool, and the whole thing collapsed. A weak government would tip the country into chaos. A corrupt political class could do the same. And even the best regime could not survive without a semi-plausible foundation in the will of the people; the democratic elite needed the *demos*. More than anything else in the Constitution—more than the separation of powers, more than checks and balances—this three-part system was the basis for Publius's appeal to the country, and ultimately for the Constitution's remarkable longevity.

But Publius missed something crucial about the new government. According to *The Federalist*, elections would fracture the public into a kaleidoscopic array of competing interest groups. Narrow factions might temporarily form a majority in a single state, but never in a large and diverse country. With the masses divided, statesmen would be free to pursue the true interests of the country.

That, of course, is not how events played out. Instead of breaking into ever-shifting factions, the public split in two.[5] Not even Publius could resist the lures of partisanship. Just a few years after uniting to defend the Constitution, Hamilton and Madison became leaders of rival political parties—Hamilton's Federalists, Madison's Republicans—each convinced that the other was leading the country back toward monarchy.

Republicans won because they were the first to grasp the power of an electoral majority and master basic techniques for winning office.

But they wanted to use the tools of partisan politics to destroy political parties, freeing statesmen from their dependence on fleeting majorities.

And they succeeded. When Madison left public life after two terms as president, the Federalist Party was imploding and Republicans were learning to accept crucial elements of Hamiltonian orthodoxy. In the Era of Good Feelings, Publius was reborn.

The rise, fall, and resurrection of Publius is, in miniature, the story of the American political elite in its formative years, as republican statesmen careened toward democracy. It shows them writing fundamental rules of American politics, and then discovering new ones as they began to grasp the purpose and power of elections. And to understand this larger history, it helps to begin with a peculiar friendship.

In almost every way that counted in the narrow circles they traveled, James Madison and Alexander Hamilton were opposites—except for politics, which is what they both cared about most.

The eldest of eleven children, Madison grew up on four thousand acres of the Virginia Piedmont.[6] Madison's family plantation, later named Montpelier, was home to more than one hundred slaves. The bookish young master stayed indoors, fashioning himself into a proper gentleman. He blitzed through his undergraduate education at Princeton in two years, leaving with a working knowledge of French, Latin, Greek, and Hebrew. In 1776, at the age of twenty-five, he participated in the convention that declared Virginia's independence. Too sickly for combat—he blamed his absence from the battlefield on "discouraging feebleness"—Madison instead opted for politics.[7] He had a talent for picking up influential mentors, including Thomas Jefferson and George Washington, and in 1780 he became the youngest member elected to the Continental Congress.

Nobody denied Madison's genius, but he was far from a natural politician. Short and frail, with chestnut hair that, in his early thirties, was already thinning, he mumbled his way through speeches and tended to fall silent in crowds. "A gloomy, stiff creature," wrote the wife of one of Madison's colleagues. "They say [he] is clever in Congress, but out of it there is nothing engaging or even bearable in his manners—the most unsociable creature in existence."[8]

Hamilton was . . . not that.[9] The illegitimate child of a Scottish merchant, he was a self-made aristocrat who, after coming of age in the British West Indies, left the Caribbean behind as a teenager and never looked back. He dropped out of King's College (later Columbia) to join the Revolution, serving as George Washington's aide-de-camp and leading a bayonet charge at the Battle of Yorktown. In 1782 Hamilton joined Madison as a representative in the Continental Congress. By then, Hamilton had married a wealthy heiress and fathered the first of his eight children (though rumors suggested that he had another out of wedlock). Madison was courting a fifteen-year-old girl who soon broke off their relationship.

George Washington's two young protégés were an unlikely but effective duo.[10] From their first meeting until the ratification of the Constitution, one problem overshadowed their discussions. Benjamin Franklin described it this way: "We have been guarding against an evil that old states are most liable to, *excess of power* in the rulers; but our present danger seems to be the *defect of obedience* in the subjects."[11]

This was a dilemma more than a hundred years in the making. By the middle of the seventeenth century, the colonies that later became the United States already allowed for more popular participation in government than anywhere in Europe.[12] At the onset of the Revolution, about a quarter of England's white men could vote; in the thirteen colonies about to declare independence, the total was closer to two-thirds.[13]

But suffrage alone did not make a democracy. Americans were expected to know their place in a deferential political culture that recognized the inevitability—and desirability—of hierarchy. Campaigns typically featured contests between competing members of the colonial elite, turning elections into mechanisms for validating the status quo. Most of those who could vote usually chose not to, with participation rates fluctuating between highs around 50 percent and lows bottoming out around 10 percent.[14]

Dismal voter participation reflected the low priority of politics in colonial life. As one writer put it in 1776, "The rich, having been used to govern, think it is their right; and the poorer commonality, having had hitherto little or no hand in government, seem to think it does not belong to them to have any."[15] Real power belonged to distant authorities—a king, a parliament, an aristocracy, an entire world that kept on turning without any assistance from the masses.

The Revolutionary War knocked that world off its axis. The years between the signing of the Declaration of Independence and the drafting of the Constitution witnessed an outpouring of democratic energy on an unprecedented scale. Popular conventions rewrote state constitutions to consolidate power in legislatures, which were seen as the branch of government most accountable to the people. The Articles of Confederation left most of the work of governing up to the (presumably more democratic) states. Turnout for elections jumped. More important, the character of the typical elected representative changed, as farmers and other men of humble background claimed a place in government.[16]

The new legislators took office in the midst of a crisis. Colonial Americans had been some of the wealthiest people in the world. Average incomes were significantly higher than in England, and economic inequality much lower. But then came the Revolution, an economic disaster that sent per capita income plunging by at least 20 percent. The total damage might have exceeded that of the Great Depression.[17] Small landowners struggled to keep up with rising interest rates, and veterans complained of unpaid wages. In protests up and down the country, demonstrators burned courthouses and assaulted government officials. (Tax collectors were especially popular targets.) Legislatures from Georgia to Rhode Island addressed these grievances by passing measures catering to their voters—for instance, printing paper money that inflated away the debts of their rural constituents. To the men—and, occasionally, women—who profited from the payment of these debts, grassroots rebellions and legislative reforms looked like incipient class war.[18] Elite nerves were especially frayed because, despite the public outroar, losses from the economic downturn were concentrated at the top, where the loss of British trade hit the hardest.

"Our whole system is in disorder," fretted Hamilton.[19] Madison was just as anxious, telling Jefferson in 1784, "confusion indeed runs through all our public affairs."[20] In his private notes, Madison wrote that the turmoil brought "into question the fundamental principle of republican Government, that the majority who rule in such Governments are the safest Guardians both of public Good and of private rights."[21]

After liberating themselves from a monarch, Americans had been afraid to trust the government with too much power. Hamilton and Madison thought it was time for a correction. Their mentors— Washington, Jefferson—had won a revolution. But the spirit of 1776 had curdled after a decade of mismanagement. Incompetent state legislators and rioters in the streets were two sides of the same problem—an absence of strong, centralized authority that would correct for "the *defect of obedience* in the subjects." With the cynicism of youth, they wanted to move from leading a revolution to running a government.

They got their chance in 1787. A convention had been called in Philadelphia to revise the Articles of Confederation. The men who would be Publius wanted to scrap the whole thing and start over. "This is the critical opportunity for establishing the prosperity of this country on a solid foundation," Hamilton told Washington, warning that the delegates in Philadelphia must not "let slip the golden opportunity of rescuing the American empire from disunion, anarchy, and misery."[22] Speaking bluntly, he said that Americans were "gradually ripening in their opinions of government—they begin to be tired of an excess of democracy."[23] Now it was time to save the people from themselves.

Always the diligent student, Madison arrived in Philadelphia eleven days before the convention was scheduled to begin. His outline for an entirely new government called for a system divided into three branches—executive, legislative, and judicial—each possessing the ability to check the others. Congress would be split into an upper and lower house, with representation in both branches determined by population. Voters would directly elect members of the lower house, who in turn would choose members of the upper house. The plan also gave the legislature the ability to veto state laws, a point that Madison considered essential.[24]

At Philadelphia, Hamilton was as unreliable as Madison was studious. Madison spoke often, took copious notes, and later said, rather priggishly, that he "was not absent a single day, nor more than a casual fraction of an hour in any day."[25] Hamilton was quiet for the first three weeks, then broke his silence with a six-hour address detailing his own blueprint for the government, including an executive so powerful that, he acknowledged, it would be called "an *elective Monarchy*."[26] The delegates praised Hamilton for his genius, then ignored his suggestions. He soon left the convention, spending much of the summer back in New York and returning full-time only in September.

But at a crucial moment he rose in support of Madison. One month into the convention, a debate broke out after South Carolina's Charles Pinckney told the delegates that they did not have to worry about a class war, saying, "The people of the United States are more equal in their circumstances than the people of any other Country."[27]

Madison disagreed. Although he granted that the United States did not have an inherited aristocracy, he said that "the distinction of rich and poor" was already present and would grow more pronounced with time. "An increase of population will of necessity increase the proportion of those who will labour under all the hardships of life, and secretly sigh for a more equal distribution of its blessings," he said.[28] Hamilton seconded his friend. "It was certainly true that nothing like an equality of property existed," he said, adding that "inequality of property constituted the great and fundamental distinction in Society."[29]

By accepting economic division, Madison and Hamilton hoped

to transcend it. In Madison's case, this meant establishing a political system that could serve as an impartial arbiter between factions. Hamilton, less confident in society's tendency toward equilibrium, believed that a strong government would have to step in to maintain balance. Madison spoke about harmony and neutrality, Hamilton about efficiency and power. One focused on curbing local democracy, the other was already thinking about how a national government could flex its muscles. Madison said that the House of Representatives would be the seat of authority in the new government; Hamilton set his eyes on the presidency. But those differences sounded abstract in 1787, when the two were desperate to restore order to a country they feared was spiraling into anarchy.

And they both thought it could be done by handing power to the people—indirectly. To the founders, untrammeled democracy stood for mob rule.[30] But they needed a justification for taking power away from states that wouldn't spark a revolt from citizens accustomed to choosing their leaders. So they established a higher authority, a national electorate whose elected leaders could tame the state legislatures. "The great fabric" of this new government, Madison said, "should rest on the solid foundation of the people themselves."[31] That's why Madison, like Hamilton, insisted that at least one branch of the legislature should be chosen by popular vote.

Compelled by political necessity, Hamilton and Madison were stumbling toward a third way between democracy and aristocracy.[32] Elections had been—and still are—a tricky subject for advocates of pure democracy. Casting a ballot for the candidate of your choice looks like the essence of democracy to contemporary eyes. But when the founders thought of democracy, they pictured the ancient Athenians, who had a much more nuanced view of elections. Democratic Athens relied on lotteries to fill most public offices, preferring to leave the decision to chance, rather than to a process that could lead to the rich and well connected monopolizing government—and locking out ordinary citizens.[33] If you're looking to empower the masses, then a system rigged in favor of the wealthy probably wouldn't be your first choice.

That's why, according to Aristotle, it was "democratic for officials to be chosen by lot, and oligarchic by election."[34]

A dose of oligarchy is just what the framers wanted. They saw elections as a check against the dangers of democracy, a way of supplying the political class with the authority that came from representing the public while keeping power in the hands of the right sort of rulers. "Guardians of the people," Madison called the democratic elite, "selected by the people themselves."[35]

Today, we describe this kind of government as a representative democracy, a term that seems to have been coined in 1775 by a young Alexander Hamilton.[36] Americans did not invent the concept of political representation, but they were the first to make it—as Madison noted with pride—"the pivot" of their politics, with all power derived from the consent of voters.[37]

You can see this reasoning at work in Madison's preferred method for selecting a president. Although he eventually came around to the Electoral College, he first argued that the president should be chosen by "the people at large"—that is, by popular vote.[38] "Elections," he explained, would "extract from the mass of the Society the purest and noblest characters which it contains."[39] The wider the field, the easier it would be for statesmen to distinguish themselves. A national election would be the widest field of all and therefore produce the best candidate, a complete inversion of ancient democracy's assumption that true self-government was possible only in a small community.

Pure democracy seeks to abolish the elite; representative democracy is designed to legitimate one. Thomas Jefferson captured the logic in a letter to John Adams. "There is a natural aristocracy," Jefferson wrote. "That form of government is the best which provides the most effectually for a pure selection of these natural aristoi into the offices of government."[40] Think of the Constitution as a machine, full of clanking pistons and churning gears, engineered to create a democratic elite by sifting out natural aristocrats from the public at large.

The founders had a specific image in mind when they pictured a natural aristocrat. A gentleman like themselves, he was by definition white, male, and well-to-do, with the independence and education that money could buy. He was supposed to wear the right clothes (lace ruffles, silk shirts), have the right hobbies (dancing, fencing), and have the right hair (powdered, or a wig). More important, he was supposed to think in the right way—free from local prejudices, with his eyes on the common good, a master of what Hamilton called "the science of politics."[41]

Before natural aristocrats could approach the many, however, they had to reach consensus among themselves. Out of the many divisions in Philadelphia, one issue was so explosive that the Constitution's final text avoided mentioning it by name. The delegates were more candid when they were talking among themselves. "The security the Southern states want," South Carolina's Pierce Butler explained, "is that their negroes may not be taken from them."[42]

———————

"In all ages one half of mankind have been slaves," Charles Pinckney observed two months after his paean to American equality.[43] Although Pinckney's math was off for the United States, where just under a fifth of the population was enslaved, he was correct that slavery had existed throughout history.[44] But racialized slavery was something new—and so, in the eighteenth century, was the concept of race.[45]

Early American colonists recognized, of course, that the Africans they enslaved had darker skins than their own. Like other elites before and since, they developed prejudices about the people whose labor they exploited. But their depictions of African inferiority centered on culture, not race. Belief that humanity could be categorized into races based chiefly on skin color, that Black people and white people belonged to distinct races, and that the white race was innately superior to the Black—all that belonged to a later era. It was the difference between a hazy prejudice and a (purportedly) scientific classification.

What changed to make the idea of race thinkable—and, as the

eighteenth century wore on, increasingly popular? In the United States, the answer was bound up with the intertwined histories of slavery and democracy.[46] Slavery had required no special justification in the thousands of years it had flourished. By the time the framers gathered in Philadelphia, however, slavery was on the road to extinction in most of the North. Faced with an unprecedented assault, slavers were forced to justify a way of life that had once seemed beyond question.

Societies founded on explicit hierarchies could depict slavery as one more link in the great chain of being. Some people were masters, others were slaves, and the rest fell somewhere in between. That was how the world had always been and always would be.

A nation committed to the principle that all men were created equal needed a stronger justification for so blatant a denial of liberty. In the wake of the American Revolution, race increasingly provided this defense. All men could still be created equal if Africans and their descendants weren't the same kind of men, exactly.

This notion was still controversial when the framers were deliberating in Philadelphia, especially among the gentlemanly class. "Educated Americans in the early republic," notes the historian Nicholas Guyatt, "found it far harder to be outright racists than we usually imagine."[47] Their Bible told them that all humanity shared a common heritage, and the bulk of Enlightenment science backed up scripture's authority.

Madison was familiar with the debate over race because two of the most prominent advocates on opposing ends of the argument happened to be among his oldest friends.

On one side stood Jefferson. In *Notes on the State of Virginia*, published in 1785, Jefferson moved easily between speculations on the origins of differences in skin color to aesthetic reflections on the alleged superiority of white skin to "that immoveable veil of black which covers all the emotions of the other race." He deemed Black people "equal" to white people in memory, "much inferior" in reason, and even further behind in imagination, where they were "dull, tasteless, and anomalous." Summarizing his research, he wrote, "I advance it therefore as a suspicion only, that the blacks, whether originally a distinct race, or made distinct by time and circumstances, are inferior to the whites in the endowments both of body and mind."[48]

Within a few decades, Jefferson's conclusions would be common sense in much of white America. At the time, even a cautious endorsement of racial difference—"I advance it therefore as a suspicion only . . ."—led critics to charge him with everything from sloppy science to blasphemy. The sharpest reply came from Samuel Stanhope Smith, a professor and Presbyterian minister who had known Madison since the two were students together at Princeton. Smith delivered his first rejoinder to Jefferson at a 1787 meeting of the American Philosophical Society (coincidentally, also held in Philadelphia). It was published the following year under the title *An Essay on the Causes of the Variety of Complexion and Figure in the Human Species.*[49]

Disparities that Jefferson attributed to race, Smith credited (or blamed) on environment. "Color," he wrote, "may be justly considered as an universal freckle."[50] Smith even speculated that better living conditions would transform the features of Africans brought to the United States—straightening hair, thinning lips, and perhaps whitening skin. The argument captured the essence of Smith's approach to race. Whiteness was his ideal, but perhaps everyone could be white.

When Jefferson looked to the future, he saw only one solution to the problem of American slavery: first abolition, then colonization. Unless Black people and white people were moved "beyond the reach of mixture," he warned, emancipation would "produce convulsions which will probably never end but in the extermination of the one or the other race."[51] Smith did not call for the immediate abolition of slavery—and he probably owned at least one slave—but he thought it was a mistake to rule out integration.[52] He proposed setting aside a "large district" in the West where interracial couples would be rewarded with free land. He hoped the program would "obliterate those wide distinctions which are now created by diversity of complexion," re-creating in the United States the single race that had existed at the dawn of humanity.[53]

There was one point, however, on which Jefferson and Smith agreed.

Slavery, as Smith put it, was "a volcano which sleeps for a time only to burst at last upon the unsuspecting tranquility of the country with a more terrible destruction."[54] It must end. They just didn't know how.

———————

At Philadelphia, Madison looked at slavery with what he elsewhere called the "naked eye of the ordinary Politician."[55] He lamented that in an enlightened age "the mere distinction of color" had become grounds for "the most oppressive dominion ever exercised by man over man," but he doubted that Americans could overcome this "mere distinction."[56] Integration was impossible, he later insisted, because "the prejudices of the Whites . . . must be considered as permanent and insuperable."[57] Caught between a moral wrong and a political impossibility, he followed Jefferson in pinning his hopes on colonization.

Despite increasing opposition to slavery in the North, most of the delegates from free or soon-to-be-free states were not inclined to press Southerners on their peculiar institution. There were only three direct attacks on slavery at the convention, two of which came from slave owners. (One was from Madison, who might have added it to the record years afterward.)[58]

Hamilton's experience was representative. Though he was a founding member of the New York Society for Promoting the Manumission of Slaves, his wife had grown up in a family that owned some two dozen slaves, and evidence suggests that Hamilton might have purchased slaves for himself.[59] At Philadelphia, he was happy to put aside his philosophical objections to slavery in order to hold the nation together.

Slavery's threat to the union was already obvious. "The States were divided into different interests," Madison told the convention, "principally from the effects of their having or not having slaves."[60] Madison's vision for the new government assumed that competing minorities would cancel each other out, allowing the natural aristocracy to step in and protect the interests of the nation as a whole. The system broke down if the people split in two, each convinced that the other posed an existential threat.

Northerners and Southerners needed a compromise that both sides could take back home. The final product was a masterpiece of strategic ambiguity: a document that both slaveholders and abolitionists would later claim as their own, and a Constitution that enabled the spread of racialized slavery without ever referring directly to either race or slavery. The slave trade could be banned, but not until 1808. Careful wording allowed the framers to say that the Constitution did not recognize a right to (in Madison's words) "property in men," but slave owners had a right to reclaim fugitives who escaped to a free state.[61] The three-fifths compromise, based on a ratio that Madison introduced in 1783, counted slaves as three-fifths of a person for representation and taxation, boosting the South's influence in government at the potential cost of subjecting it to a higher tax burden.[62]

The bargain over representation was one of Madison's few outright victories at the convention. He lost the veto over state legislatures that he thought essential. After pushing for proportional representation in the Senate—as a Virginian, he wanted large states to carry more weight—he lost that argument, too. He gave up on direct election of the president without a fight, acknowledging that Southerners would refuse to accept a system in which they could be outvoted by the North. (The Electoral College, by contrast, turned a disenfranchised Black population into an advantage.) There would be no explicit protections for property holders. At times, Madison couldn't even tell what the major arguments were. While other delegates fenced over the structure of the executive branch, Madison told Jefferson he thought the conversation "tedious."[63]

Neither Madison nor Hamilton left Philadelphia with much confidence in their work. Madison feared that the government would be too weak to restrain the states. Hamilton predicted that "dissolution of the Union" was "the most likely result."[64] Yet they both swallowed their objections. The compromises had been dexterous enough—and the fear over what would happen if they failed deep enough—to produce a document both could endorse, albeit reluctantly.

But what about everyone else?

Early on, the framers agreed to keep their deliberations secret. They wanted to speak candidly, and they believed that speculating about public opinion was a fool's errand. Instead of trying to reflect majority will, Madison urged the convention to produce a document that would win the backing of "all the most enlightened and respectable citizens" and trust that "the unreflecting multitude" would fall in line.[65]

Now that there was a proposal to defend, the unreflecting multitude would have their say. It was another step in the dance between aristocracy and democracy: elites could draw up a new government behind closed doors, but they could not move ahead without the public's consent. Attention shifted to state ratifying conventions, where delegates selected by voters would determine the Constitution's fate.[66]

Hamilton laid out the state of play in notes to himself written shortly after the Philadelphia convention adjourned. The Constitution's greatest asset was the eminence of its supporters: creditors, major commercial interests, the framers themselves (especially Washington), and "men of property . . . who wish a government of the union able to protect them against domestic violence and the depredations which the democratic spirit is apt to make." On the other side were debtors, state legislators, and anyone who feared "institutions that may seem calculated to place the power of the community in few hands." To Hamilton's jaundiced eye, the balance of forces was too close for comfort.[67]

Almost 250 years later, it's still unclear how many Americans supported the Constitution. According to one historian of the early republic, "If there had been a modern poll taken in 1787–1788, most people in the country probably would have opposed it."[68] In the absence of reliable data, all we can say for certain is that ratification was a squeaker, and that elite backing was almost as much of a burden as a strength. As a Massachusetts Antifederalist explained, the mere fact that "lawyers, and men of learning, and moneyed men that talk so finely" were lining up behind the Constitution was proof to many that natural aristocrats were scheming "to make us poor little people swallow down the pill."[69]

Like Madison and Hamilton, most Antifederalists—as opponents of the Constitution became known—assumed that society would always be divided into classes. But they were much less confident in their elites. "The great consider themselves above the common people," said New York's Melancton Smith, one of the Constitution's most incisive critics. "They cannot have that sympathy with their constituents which is necessary to connect them closely to their interest."[70]

Not even the natural aristocrats were uniformly enthusiastic. "If the Constitution be adopted it will be a grand point gained in favor of the aristocratic party," observed a twenty-year-old John Quincy Adams. "There are to be no titles of nobility; but there will be great distinctions; and those distinctions will soon be hereditary, and we shall consequently have nobles, but no titles." JQA, as he called himself to avoid confusion with his celebrated father, was assured of a place in the new aristocracy. But as the young man watched the debates over ratification, he grieved over what was being lost. "It is hard to give up a System which I have always been taught to cherish," he said, "and to confess that a free government is inconsistent with human nature."[71]

Publius was born to counter precisely this kind of skepticism. And the act of defending the government over several months gave Hamilton and Madison a newfound respect for the Constitution. Instead of cowering before the masses, Publius shrugged off the accusation of elitism. "The idea of an actual representation of all classes of the people, by persons of each class, is altogether visionary," explained one of Hamilton's contributions. Society was divided into different spheres of influence, each with its own hierarchy. In the cities, artisans and manufacturers would defer to merchants. In the countryside, the gentry could represent everyone from "the wealthiest landlord down to the poorest tenant." Members of "the learned professions" would be trusted by all sides. Anyone could be elected, but in practice this would be a government of lawyers, merchants, and planters.[72]

Hamilton didn't see anything wrong with that. State and local governments could take care of the ordinary business of life—keeping the peace, upholding public morals, and all the other "minute interests, which will necessarily fall under the superintendence of the local administrations." National representatives would be "speculative men" who concerned themselves with loftier matters: waging war, making peace, and managing the nation's finances.[73]

Ancient democracy had been a local affair, a matter for city-states, not empires. By giving up on direct democracy, Americans could spread across the continent—"extend the sphere," in Madison's words, writing as Publius.[74] With more land to go around, the country could support an independent yeomanry, avoiding the sharp divides between rich and poor that were toxic in a republic. Instead of crowding together in cities riven by class conflict, white men would find equality and freedom out on the frontier. And as the population expanded, interests would continue to multiply, providing a crucial safeguard against majority tyranny.

The battle over ratification was hard-fought, and the Federalists did not always win. In Rhode Island, the only state to submit the Constitution to a popular referendum, they received less than 10 percent of the vote. In Virginia's convention, they squeaked by with ten votes to spare, 89 to 79. New York, the last major state to decide, looked to be even closer.

Hamilton entered New York's convention with arguments honed during his months as Publius. When Antifederalists charged the framers with conspiring on behalf of an American aristocracy, Hamilton replied, with perfect pseudo-sincerity, "Who are the aristocracy among us?" Turning the accusation on its head, Hamilton insisted, "The true principle of a republic is, that the people should choose whom they please to govern them." If voters selected natural aristocrats of their own free will, what was the problem?[75]

The historical record doesn't tell us what Hamilton's face looked like while he lectured his opponents on the meaning of self-government. But it's easy to imagine him smiling.[76]

———

The summer of 1789 was a happy time for both halves of Publius. Madison was serving in Congress, Hamilton preparing to become the first treasury secretary. They lived near each other in New York, the nation's temporary capital, and took frequent walks together around the city. Many years later, a woman recalled seeing them "turn and laugh, and play with a monkey that was climbing in a neighbor's yard."[77]

Between the monkeyshines, they both established themselves as key figures in the new government. Madison had the more difficult path to power. While Hamilton slid into Treasury with Washington's blessing, Madison had to fight his way into office. First he hoped to join the Senate, but Antifederalists in the Virginia state legislature blocked his way. Then he settled on the House of Representatives, only to discover that Antifederalists had persuaded James Monroe to run against him. A scion of the Virginia gentry, Monroe was a longtime friend of Madison's and a fellow protégé of Thomas Jefferson's. Unlike Madison, he was also tall, handsome, a veteran of the Revolution—and an Antifederalist.

Busy in New York, where he was still serving in Congress, Madison resisted the idea of doing anything that would have "an electioneering appearance, which I always despised and wish to shun."[78] He relented after hearing repeated warnings that Monroe could win, arriving back in Virginia less than two months before the election.

Though he had spent most of his adult life in politics, Madison hadn't delivered a major public speech until earlier that year, when he was campaigning for a place in the Virginia ratifying convention. Now he threw himself into the race, traveling the district, writing letters to newspapers and individual supporters, and holding debates with Monroe. Decades later, he looked back fondly on a night he spent jousting with his opponent in front of "a nest of Dutchmen . . . whose votes might tip the scales."

> We met there at [a] church. Service was performed, and then they had music with two fiddles. They are remarkably fond of music. When it was all over we addressed these people and kept them standing in the snow listening to the discussion of constitutional subjects. They stood it out very patiently—seemed to consider it a sort of fight, of which they were required to be spectators. I then had to ride in the night, twelve miles to quarters; and got my nose frost-bitten.[79]

Madison paused at this point in the story and touched his nose, where the mark was still visible. He called it a battle scar.

A slight blemish wasn't the only sign of the campaign's effect on Madison. The framers had not included a bill of rights with the Constitution. Madison supported the decision, arguing that no "parchment barriers" could stand in the way of determined majorities.[80] He reversed his position after hearing multiple reports that the campaign was slipping away from him. Reaching out to the sizable number of voters still wary of the Constitution, he pledged to support a bill of rights in the first Congress and claimed (falsely) that at Philadelphia he had called for "several of the very amendments" now being discussed.[81]

Madison won by a solid fifteen points, but the number of votes was small enough—just under 2,300 total—that a few nests of Dutchmen could have tilted the outcome to Monroe.[82] After clawing his way into power, Madison returned to the capital ready to work.

"His person is little and ordinary," observed the Massachusetts congressman Fisher Ames, but "he is our first man."[83] After helping Washington write his inaugural address, Madison composed the reply from the House and then assisted the president in drafting his response. He introduced his first piece of legislation two days after the House and Senate reached a quorum. During the first seven months in session he delivered more than 150 speeches. And by the end of the year he had delivered on his most important campaign promise by shepherding a bill of rights through Congress.

Hamilton was one of the few people in the government whose influence exceeded Madison's. Treasury was the largest department in the infant executive branch, and within the administration Hamilton was second only to George Washington. At State, Thomas Jefferson had four clerks at his service; the attorney general had none. Hamilton started with a staff of almost forty, plus more than two thousand other employees under his supervision—postmasters, customs officials, revenue agents—scattered around the country.[84]

He entered office with a plan to remake the government, and the country, by uniting "the interest and credit of rich individuals with those of the state."[85] Prosperity to Hamilton was a means to a nobler end—national greatness, a glory that couldn't be measured on a balance sheet. Before long, the United States would be a thriving empire, with a powerful state capable of defending itself in a hostile world.

The capstone of his program was a national bank that would bring order to the nation's chaotic financial system. Interest rates would fall, commerce would thrive, and the people would discover that shared economic interests were an ideal basis for political union. Rich and poor, slaveholders and merchants, men and women, even adults and children—all had a part to play in his program. (According to Hamilton, increased child labor was one benefit of encouraged manufacturing.)[86] The nation would be tied together with threads of gold, watched over by an economic elite whose fortunes were bound to the republic.

With Washington's backing, Hamilton moved from success to success. "Congress may go home," wrote the Pennsylvania senator William Maclay. "Mr. Hamilton is all powerful and fails in nothing which he attempts."[87]

"The true test of a good government," Hamilton had written as Publius, is its "tendency to produce a good administration."[88] He saw his Treasury Department as a case study in good administration and a natural extension of the program he'd laid out in *The Federalist*. It was

Publius in practice. But he was about to discover that his old partner disagreed.

———

At first, Hamilton attributed Madison's resistance to naïveté. "He has the same end in view as I have," he said, but "is very little acquainted with the world."[89] In the spring of 1792 Hamilton reached a more disturbing conclusion. "Madison's true character is the reverse of that *simple, fair, candid one,* which he has assumed," he fumed in a six-thousand-word letter detailing his former friend's betrayals. After starting with the *"same point of departure"* in their politics, some mysterious force—perhaps ambition, jealousy, or a desire to please Jefferson—had put Madison *"at the head of a faction decidedly hostile to me and my administration."* (Note: *my* administration—this was personal.) Hamilton claimed that he never would have accepted the position at Treasury if he had known that Madison would turn against him. But with the battle joined, he announced "my determination to consider and treat him as a political enemy."[90]

Hamilton's list of grievances was long. Madison had resisted the administration's plan to repay state debts accumulated during the Revolution, yielding only after Hamilton agreed that the nation's permanent capital would be located in the South, along the Potomac River. Next, he opposed the national bank. Then he argued that Hamilton's plan to spur manufacturing was unconstitutional. Slowly, cautiously, his shy and diminutive friend had become the public face of a nascent opposition movement.

Madison did have self-interested motives for the split. The biggest beneficiaries of Hamilton's agenda were elite merchants and manufacturers, not the Southern planter class. At home, Madison had to deal with onetime Antifederalists, who remained a force in Virginia politics. But he insisted that Hamilton had gotten the chain of events backward. "Hamilton deserted me," he claimed. "In a word, the divergence between us took place—from his wishing . . . to administer the Government into what he thought it ought to be."[91]

After years of worrying about demagogues in state legislatures, Madison decided that the centralizers gathering around Hamilton posed an even greater danger to liberty. Writing to Jefferson in the summer of 1791, he warned that Hamilton's program was turning private capital into "the pretorian band of the government—at once its tool and its tyrant; bribed by its largesses, and overawing it."[92] At the same time, diverging opinions of the French Revolution—Hamilton feared anarchy, Madison was more sympathetic—drove them even further apart.

Publius's identity crisis was more a case of time surfacing previously buried differences than of either undergoing a political conversion. Hamilton thought more about power than about restraint. Madison was more concerned with political theory than with political economy. One was an immigrant who found it easy to "think continentally"; the other was rooted in Virginia.[93] The most acute commentary on Congress in *The Federalist* had come from Madison, but everything Publius said on the presidency was written by Hamilton.

Experience turned hairline fractures into a clean break, making Hamilton a master of administration and Madison a reluctant student of popular politics. As treasury secretary, Hamilton had a constituency of one—George Washington. Madison had to worry about voters, those peculiar folks who watched him debating Monroe as if it were "a sort of fight of which they were required to be spectators."[94] One wanted to yoke financial interests to the government, the other had to appease Antifederalists. Out of Hamilton's experience came a plan for turning the United States into a commercial empire; out of Madison's came the Bill of Rights.

Both sides agreed that the other posed a fatal threat to the republic. Madison thought the logic of Hamilton's program pointed toward monarchy. Hamilton flipped the accusation back at him, depicting Madison as an unwitting accomplice in a scheme to overthrow the government. Certain that the fate of the nation hung in the balance, they

turned on each other. The natural aristocracy was at war with itself—
and a new kind of politics was lurching to life.

———————

Madison claimed that he didn't have a choice. "Parties are unavoidable," he wrote in 1792. "The great object should be to combat the
evil"—including the evil posed by Hamilton.[95] And so the scourge of
parties teamed up with Jefferson to summon one into existence.

Madison's vision of party organization consisted mostly of coalition building within Congress, supplemented by occasional appeals to
a vaguely defined public. He recruited Philip Freneau, a friend from his
Princeton days, to edit a newspaper that could serve as a mouthpiece for
the embryonic movement. Writing anonymously for the paper, Madison published a series of articles—shorter than Publius's essays and
presented in a more colloquial style—that gave his party a name and an
intellectual backbone.

"The Republican party, as it may be termed," Madison announced,
was the natural party of the majority—"the mass of people in every part
of the union, in every state, and of every occupation."*[96] With coalition
building on his mind, he reached out to former Antifederalists, describing them as well-meaning friends of liberty. He depicted public opinion as the true sovereign in a free government, called yeoman farmers
unique repositories of civic virtue, and for the first time denounced "an
immoderate . . . accumulation of riches." All of that contrasted with
the Hamiltonians, a party of "the opulent," who believed that ordinary
people could not govern themselves and therefore relied upon "the pag-
eantry of rank, the influence of money and emoluments, and the terror
of military force."[97]

Although Hamilton was a more skilled polemicist than either Jef-

———

* To avoid confusion with the later Republican Party, historians often call Jefferson
and Madison's faction "Democratic-Republicans."

ferson or Madison, the party of the opulent—or Federalists, as they preferred to be called—was on the whole less likely to make use of the press than were the Republicans. With George Washington as a shield, Hamilton didn't need to experiment with public outreach. He continued to believe that politics was mostly a question of winning influential patrons, and there was no better patron to have than Washington.

Even Jefferson and Madison begged the president to run again in 1792, not yet willing to concede that Hamilton had won over the national patriarch. Washington was reelected with unanimous support in the Electoral College and barely a whisper of a campaign. It was a textbook example of how the founders thought a president should be chosen. But the model was starting to look decidedly old-fashioned.

———————

Americans were novices in party warfare, and their initial efforts appear clumsy when judged by later standards—held back by antique prejudices against reaching out to voters, yet overwrought in their conspiracy theorizing about secret monarchists plotting to destroy the republic. The underlying issue was that neither Republicans nor Federalists accepted that the other side had a right to exist. They were parties against parties, cures for the temporary insanity that had overtaken the country.

Reverence for Washington held off the spirit of faction for a while, but as his second term dragged on, the growing partisan divide could no longer be ignored. Consistent voting blocs emerged in Congress, signs of division within the governing class. With the specter of revolutionary France haunting both parties, political debate took on a paranoid, fevered quality, as if Americans were just a few wrong turns away from seeing guillotines in the streets.

Away from the capital, the wildfire spread of "Democratic-Republican societies" underlined the mounting discontent with the administration.[98] First appearing in the spring of 1793, the societies were soon holding meetings from Vermont to South Carolina. They became de facto branches of the Republican Party, sites where mechanics, farmers, and other members of the middling sort could debate issues and plan campaigns. A distinct tone of class resentment pervaded the meetings, animated by the sense—shared by Madison—that Federalists were creating a monied aristocracy of financial speculators leeching on the common man.[99]

The idea of an unelected group of citizens claiming to represent the public struck conservatives as an instance of democracy run amok. The societies, fumed a Massachusetts Federalist, "arrogantly pretended sometimes to be the people, and sometimes the guardians, the champions of the people."[100] Republicans kept them at a distance, uncertain of what to do with political organizations that had no clear place inside the constitutional framework. (It wasn't always easy to hold them at arm's length: one South Carolina society named itself "Madisonian.")

The societies vanished as quickly as they had appeared. Although a few local groups clung to life, their moment had passed by the end of 1795. But they left behind a pathbreaking example of political organizing outside government, along with tantalizing suggestions of what a Republican coalition might look like after Federalists could no longer hide behind George Washington.

Spurred by a mix of principle and fear, power and weakness, Republicans stumbled toward a more democratic politics. The presidential election of 1796 offered an early test case. Although Jefferson did not even acknowledge that he was running, his supporters worked alongside veterans of the Democratic-Republican societies, arranging public events and distributing ballots. It wasn't enough to win the presidency, but it hinted at the future: a combination of top-down leadership and bottom-up mobilization, less freewheeling than the Democratic-Republican societies but far more open than Publius had envisioned.[101]

Jeffersonians had better luck four years later, when their coalition was bound together—and expanded—by hatred of Adams. Some were driven by their fears that the Alien and Sedition Acts of 1798 were preludes to tyranny, others by opposition to Adams's conciliatory policy toward the former slaves in the newly independent Haiti, still others by the federal army's crackdown on a tax revolt in eastern Pennsylvania. In 1800, Jeffersonians swept the South, as well as Pennsylvania and New York. Thanks to tireless campaigning from his running mate, Aaron Burr, Jefferson even carried New York City, buoyed by strong performance in its poorest wards. (Republicans also won the popular vote in New Jersey, but the Federalist state legislature awarded its electoral votes to Adams.)[102]

It was a strange majority, the product of grassroots organizing, elite management, and inflated representation for slave states produced by the three-fifths compromise. Though turnout varied widely, participation rates in some counties climbed up to 70 percent of the eligible population.[103] This was American democracy in action, a party loudly proclaiming its obedience to the people while being overseen by the grandees of Virginia's planter class, including Madison, whom Jefferson selected as secretary of state. But it was enough to carry through the first peaceful transfer of power as the result of an election in world history, bringing a measure of calm to a political culture that had entered into perilous terrain.

Meanwhile, Hamilton seethed. Part of him loathed the country's democratic turn. Contrasting his politics with "the disciples of the new creed," he called himself a patriot "of the OLD SCHOOL," who "would rather risk incurring the displeasure of the people, by speaking unpalatable truths, than betray their interests by fostering their prejudices."[104]

In less self-pitying moments, Hamilton tried reconciling himself to the changing times. "We must consider," he wrote in 1802, "whether it be possible for us to succeed without in some degree employing the weapons which have been employed against us." Stealing a page from the Democratic-Republican societies, he called for a "Christian Constitutional Society" that would deploy "all lawful means in concert to promote the election of *fit men*."[105] As the name implied, the party's two overarching principles would be support for Christianity and the Constitution, both of which the Francophile Jefferson supposedly endangered—the seeds, potentially, of a Federalist majority.

Hamilton's plan went nowhere. Increasingly disillusioned with politics, he turned away from public life. "Mine is an odd destiny," he observed.

> Perhaps no man in the UStates has sacrificed or done more for the present Constitution than myself—and contrary to all my anticipation of its fate, as you know from the very beginning I am still laboring to prop the frail and worthless fabric. Yet I have the murmurs of its friends no less than the curses of its foes for my rewards. What can I do better than withdraw from the scene? Every day proves to me more and more that this American world was not made for me.[106]

"Our real disease . . . is DEMOCRACY," he wrote to a Massachusetts Federalist in July 1804.[107] The next morning, he traveled across the Hudson River to Weehawken, New Jersey, arriving late for his duel with Aaron Burr.

———

Republicans had pulled off the first realignment in American history, creating a strong and durable majority that kept the party in power while slowly choking the life out of the Federalists. In all but one of the next five elections, Republicans nominated a Virginian for president and a New Yorker for vice president. It worked every time, winning two terms each for Jefferson, Madison, and Monroe. The War of 1812—"Mr. Madison's War," as Federalists derisively referred to it— dealt the final blow to the Hamiltonians. Although the military conflict ended in a stalemate, Americans won a major symbolic victory by holding their former masters to a draw. After a feeble 1816 campaign, Federalism collapsed. "Never was there a more glorious opportunity for the Republican party to place themselves permanently in power," thrilled the New Englander (and onetime Federalist) Joseph Story.[108]

But as the Federalists slipped into oblivion, Hamilton's agenda was taken aboard by his onetime enemies. It began under Jefferson, when Republicans made their peace with banks and tariffs so long as they were used to help the producing classes. Although Madison allowed the charter on Hamilton's bank to expire, he came to regret the decision during the War of 1812, when the government was forced to muster an army and navy, raise taxes, and manage a ballooning public debt. At the end of the war, he urged Congress to reinstitute the bank, pass tariffs to protect domestic manufacturing, and invest in a network of roads and canals that would bind the nation together.[109]

In 1817 Madison left the White House to his chosen successor, James Monroe. (The unpleasantness of the 1788 campaign was a distant memory.) Formally, the process that put Monroe in the White House was more democratic than anything the country had yet witnessed. In 1820, for the first time, the majority of states chose the winner by popular vote rather than through state legislatures.[110] But the result looked more like a return to the Washington era than a reconstituted Athens. Without any real opposition, Monroe carried every state and won 80.6 percent of the vote, all in an election where participation rates were lower than at any time since Washington's reelection.[111] Americans continued to show up at the polls for state and local races, but with consensus reigning in the capital, the spirit had gone out of national politics.

The system was working just as Madison had predicted thirty years earlier. By crushing the Federalists, Republicans had liberated Americans from the burden of partisanship. Elites would fight among themselves without breaking into two warring tribes, and the public could go about the ordinary business of life. And thanks to an influx of European capital—another Hamilton legacy—business was doing quite well indeed, fueling an economic recovery that finally undid the damage from the Revolution.[112]

The fourth president to come out of Virginia, Monroe was closer to a Washington than a Madison: imposing, authoritative, and more than a little dull. Although he was an archetypal example of the gentleman in politics, Monroe didn't have anything like Washington's unique standing as father of the country—which, to Madison, was all the more evidence that the system worked. Any government could secure consensus when it piggybacked off a figure like George Washington. To produce near unanimity in a presidential election that combined former Hamiltonians and Jeffersonians in a single party led by a standard-issue member of the Virginia squirearchy and former Antifederalist—*that* was an accomplishment.

After thousands of years where democracy had been synonymous with anarchy, an exuberantly democratic political culture had emerged—and it turned out that there was nothing to be scared of. The word "democracy" lost its unsavory connotations, turning into a point of national pride. "What bodings, what anxieties, were experienced during this long agony of Conservatism," recalled a child of Yankee Federalists reflecting on the turbulent politics of his youth. "And yet society survived. The old landmarks, though shaken, still remained, and some of them even derived confidence, if not firmness, from the agitation. Nay, strange to say, in the succeeding generation, democracy cast its slough, put on clean linen, and affected respectability."[113]

Publius couldn't have asked for more.

2

Partisans

Light glinted off the president's bejeweled fingers. It was 1849, early in Martin Van Buren's fourth term. Through political guile and military force, Van Buren had seized control of the government. Now he was contemplating the next steps in a plot to crush the last, desperate revolt against his empire. After a glorious beginning, the American democratic experiment was heading toward a bloody conclusion.

With that dire image, *The Partisan Leader* came to an end. An unfinished novel that had been rushed to print for the 1836 election, *The Partisan Leader*'s dystopian vision fit neatly within an expanding catalogue of Van Buren hate literature.[1] Van Buren had been a loyal member of Andrew Jackson's administration for eight years, the last four as vice president. Although Jackson had inspired plenty of ominous predictions, there was a frantic quality to the warnings about Van Buren. Jackson's enemies saw him as an old-fashioned demagogue. Van Buren belonged to a new, more frightening species. He was—*shudder*—a politician.

The rise of the professional politician was part of a revolution in American democracy: the establishment of the first mass, national parties in modern history.[2] Campaigns became popular spectacles, the centerpiece of a political culture that turned electioneering into mass entertainment. Voter participation rates soared, regularly exceeding

80 percent of the eligible population. Summarizing the transformation, a Richmond newspaper howled in 1835, *"The Republic has degenerated into a Democracy."*[3]

Van Buren thought of it more as a logical progression.[4] He viewed American history as one long argument between Republicans and Federalists, a battle where his three great heroes—Jefferson, Madison, and Jackson—all lined up on the side of the common (white) man battling against "the establishment of a moneyed oligarchy."[5] Where Jeffersonians treated political parties as an emergency deviation from the norm, Van Buren considered partisan struggle essential to a functioning democracy.[6] Parties channeled the inevitable conflicts in a democracy toward productive ends, taming oligarchs without unleashing destructive class warfare and diverting attention from the growing divide between free and slave states.

Van Buren was both a student and a practitioner of the new partisan politics, a Madison for American democracy's next chapter. His greatest achievement was the creation of the Democratic Party—or, as it was known at the time, "the Democracy."[7] If Jackson was the Democracy's soul, then Van Buren was its mind.

He was given many nicknames over the decades: the Sly Fox, the Careful Dutchman, King Matty, the Great Manager, the Master Spirit, and, eventually, Van Ruin. The best one was the Little Magician. It seemed, for a time, as if he had the country under his command, until his single, disastrous term as president ended with a failed reelection campaign.

But Van Buren's story had a twist ending. After leaving the White House, he became an inadvertent architect of a *second* political revolution, helping point the way toward the antislavery coalition that transformed a fringe movement into an electoral majority. Accidentally, he built a bridge between the Republican Party of Thomas Jefferson and the Republican Party of Abraham Lincoln.

"The life of Van Buren, if it receives the consideration it deserves, if the people will give it the close thinking it needs, will be the most useful lesson they have ever read since they began the A, B, C of our government," declared another entry in the canon of Van Buren hate-lit, a scabrous biography ghostwritten for Davy Crockett, the frontier icon turned congressman.[8] Faux-Crockett was more right than he knew. Through Van Buren's eyes, we can see the making and breaking of Jacksonian democracy—and the story of a magician undone by his own spells.[9]

———

With Van Buren, everything came down to politics. Looking back on his career, he boasted in 1854 that he might have held more public offices than any other American of his generation: "Surrogate of his County, State Senator, Attorney General of the State of New York, Regent of the University, Member of a Convention to revise the Constitution of the State, Governor of the State, Senator in Congress for two terms, Secretary of State of the United States, Minister to England, Vice President, and President of the United States."[10]

The achievements were all the more impressive given the unpromising material Van Buren had to work with. Short and squat, with not a hint of greatness about him, he was a middle child in a family of twelve. Born in 1782, he came of age in Kinderhook, a sleepy village in New York's Hudson Valley. Part of a tight-knit Dutch community whose roots stretched back to the seventeenth century, he is still the only president to have learned English as second language. He was also the first one born after the Revolution, and therefore the first with no memories of life as a British subject.

Much about Van Buren's childhood still looked distinctly old-world. The Hudson Valley was an almost feudal society, with a minuscule landowning elite at the top and landless tenants underneath. A handful of wealthy families dominated state politics, constituting an aristocracy in all but name. Almost half of white men were excluded from the franchise; the young Van Buren had his own voting qualifications challenged, an embarrassment he never forgot.[11]

But New York was changing, its population surging because of immigration, and its white men emboldened by the Revolution. Abraham Van Buren, father of Martin, was swept up by the age's leveling spirit. His modest tavern became a Republican meeting place, catching Jeffersonians (including Aaron Burr, later inspiring rumors that Martin was his illegitimate son) as they traveled between New York City and Albany.[12]

Decades later, John Quincy Adams described Van Buren as a better socialized version of James Madison. "They are both remarkable for their extreme caution in avoiding and averting personal collisions," Adams noted—a great talent for a coalition builder. But unlike the painfully shy Madison, Van Buren had a gift for putting people at ease. Adams called him *"l'ami de tout le monde"*—everyone's friend—and said, not without jealousy, that it was "the great secret of his success in public life."[13]

Van Buren subscribed in full to the Jeffersonian party line—small government, states' rights, and strict construction of the Constitution. He loathed royalty and feared government power. But all those nights at Abraham's side taught him the dangers of crankery, leaving him with a lifelong skepticism of ideologues.

Restraint became a virtue to him, maybe the highest in the world of politics. His greatest loyalty was to the system itself. He would bend, plead, cajole, equivocate, capitulate, and do whatever else it took to keep the peace. "Whatever weaknesses I may be subject to," he observed, "dogmatism, I am very sure, is not one of them."[14] He was, to use an expression that became popular during his adulthood, "Van Buren-ish."[15]

That flexibility helped him overlook the denial of liberty taking place under his own roof. Abraham Van Buren, in addition to his tavern, had six slaves to his name. Young Martin owned at least one slave, a Black man named Tom, until 1814. In the ease with which he blended devotion to liberty with trafficking in human property, Van Buren was once again a model Jeffersonian.[16]

Van Buren was self-conscious about his meager formal education, later bemoaning the "disinclination to mental efforts which has thro'

life been my besetting infirmity."[17] After a few years in a one-room
schoolhouse, he began studying to be a lawyer, eventually moving to
New York City to work in the law firm of William Van Ness. A loyal
Republican, Van Ness was Aaron Burr's second in the fatal duel with
Hamilton. When Van Ness was charged with being an accessory in Hamilton's murder, he asked Van Buren to defend him in court. Van Buren
won the case.

The law profession was a natural choice for Van Buren. "Lawyers,"
Alexis de Tocqueville would soon explain, "belong to the people by
birth and interest, and to the aristocracy by habit and taste; they may
be looked upon as the connecting link between the two great classes of
society."[18] Tocqueville could have been talking about the eager young
man from Kinderhook who accumulated a tidy nest egg catering to
New York's old elite and a rising class of merchants and financiers.

The democratic dandy.

Van Buren's legal practice left him plenty of time for politics, and in 1812 he won election to the state senate. As he strode through Albany, the Jeffersonian warrior looked every bit the bourgeois gentleman: thinning hair and expanding waistline, with a dandyish wardrobe of pearl vest, orange cravat, white duck trousers, and yellow kid gloves.

The foppish exterior concealed one of the country's shrewdest political minds. Federalists were on the decline in New York, but Republicans were too busy fighting among themselves to present a coherent alternative. Looking at the landscape, Van Buren saw the makings of a new political order. Part of him loathed the aristocracy; part of him yearned to join it. But he knew that coming from the *demos* had its advantages.

———

Organization was the key to Van Buren's politics and his one great departure from Republican orthodoxy. He believed that simple majority rule inevitably degenerated into oligarchy. Only a political party could restrain the forces of aristocracy, giving the public a champion in the battle to preserve self-government.

A *party*, singular. In the eternal battle between Jeffersonians and Hamiltonians, Van Buren never quite accepted the legitimacy of the other side. The people could be misled from time to time, but he thought Republicans would always win if they stuck together. He established one of the country's first political machines, a top-down enterprise called the "Albany Regency." Caucuses of party officials set the party line, newspapers disseminated their positions to the public, and a patronage network kept the whole operation funded with donations from government employees who owed their jobs to the machine. Party discipline, a party press, and party patronage: here was the holy trinity of partisan politics.[19]

The typical Regency man was a self-made Republican lawyer. He had a stable income but hadn't joined the charmed circle of New York's elite. Politics gave him a creed, a calling, and a place in the world; it gave him a reason to live. He saw himself as a protector of the common good, and he relished beating patricians in the struggle for power. He might also have developed a taste for the finer things along the way; one could defend the people without wanting to live like them.

The typical Regency man, in short, was Martin Van Buren.

Even after he was elected to the U.S. Senate in 1821, Van Buren kept a firm grip on Albany. When protests over New York's stringent voting requirements grew too loud to ignore, he belatedly signed on to a movement to draft a new state constitution. The resulting convention was a classic Van Buren operation. He started by ensuring that the meeting would unfold on his terms. Of the 126 delegates, 98 were either affiliated with or sympathetic to his wing of the party, turning the convention into a debate between radical and moderate Republicans. Van Buren inclined toward the moderates, and he set to work expanding suffrage without endangering the propertied class. While the Federalist minority ranted about "the evil genius of democracy," Van Burenites extended the vote to more than 80 percent of white men.[20]

What to do with the state's almost thirty thousand "free persons of color" was a trickier issue.[21] Under the old constitution, Black men who satisfied the property requirements could vote on the same terms as white men. With slavery in rapid decline—the legislature had approved a gradual emancipation law ending slavery by 1827—the number of potential Black voters was set to expand. (Five counties in New York City and the Hudson Valley had the greatest concentration of African Americans anywhere in the country outside South Carolina.)[22] If the state kept its race-blind policy, it could soon have a significant Black voting bloc that, historically, leaned toward the Federalists.

Racial prejudice and partisan calculation pointed Republicans in the same direction: to abolish barriers of class, they had to create new ones based on race. If Federalists lived in fear of leveling mobs, Republicans dreaded a future where, as one delegate put it, racial "distinctions that now prevail shall be done away—when the colors shall intermarry—when negroes shall be invited to your tables—to sit in your pew, or ride in your coach."[23]

Under New York's existing regulations, property qualifications were higher for the state senate than for the assembly. Federalists accepted Black voting, but they also wanted to impose the senate's higher property requirement—owning $250 worth of real estate—on all elections. A small number of radicals endorsed universal male suffrage. (There was no chance that the convention would have supported enfranchising women of any color.)

Most Republicans followed a third path. With Van Buren's support, the convention abolished the two-tiered system for white people while slashing property requirements. But they kept the old $250 standard for African Americans *and* extended it to assembly elections, shrinking the Black electorate to a fraction of its former size. By 1826, a total of sixteen African Americans could vote in New York City, from a population of more than ten thousand.[24]

New York's experience was repeated across the North. Although a majority of Northerners opposed slavery, they were not at all prepared for racial equality. The comparative tolerance of the post-Revolutionary years melted away as white people confronted the fact that freed slaves wouldn't simply disappear. White racial prejudice swelled, and Northerners began developing their own precursors to Jim Crow, forbidding interracial marriage, segregating schools, and denying Black people the right to serve on juries.[25]

Master-race democracy was the price Northerners paid for combining gradual emancipation with suffrage expansion. Martin Van Buren was happy to pay it.

Washington was more difficult for him to manage. He moved to the capital in 1821, during the palmy days of the Era of Good Feelings. He thrived in the city, mingling with ex-Federalists (he lived with several at Georgetown's Peck Hotel), charming Southerners (his first day in Washington included a meeting with South Carolina's John Calhoun), and courting power brokers (he took a special trip to Philadelphia to meet with Nicholas Biddle, president of the Bank of the United States).[26]

Socially, he could not have asked for more. Politically, it was a nightmare.

What was so bad about good feelings? For Van Buren, almost everything. The death of the Federalist Party did not mean the end of the Hamiltonian menace. Under the guise of consensus, Federalism was taking over the Republicans. Monroe was bad enough, and the 1824 campaign to replace him was even more dispiriting. A four-man race where all the candidates ran as Republicans—a close approximation to Madison's ideal—culminated with John Quincy Adams taking power despite running behind Andrew Jackson in both the popular and electoral vote.

Adams had long ago overcome his qualms about the Constitution and followed his father into politics. Although the younger Adams entered office as a Federalist, he was first and foremost a nationalist, and he was drawn toward the Republicans after winning election to the U.S. Senate from Massachusetts at the ripe age of thirty-six. He was also a model natural aristocrat, groomed for statesmanship from childhood by his father.

But Adams was trained to lead a world that no longer existed. Deaf to the music of democratic politics, the new president urged lawmakers not to be "palsied by the will of our constituents."[27] He conjured a vision of the United States as a land of perpetual improvement, bound together by federal roads and canals, enlightened by a national university, ruled by "talents and virtue alone."[28] A pleasing image to some, but in Van Buren's eyes a high-minded justification for American oligarchy.

There was another, still graver threat to consider. When the framers were drafting the Constitution, the divide between North and South had almost derailed the entire project. Into the 1790s, it could be plausibly argued that slavery was headed toward a peaceful death. But instead of slipping into irrelevance, slavery was reborn in the new century. A booming international market for cotton sent demand for slave labor skyrocketing, and the Louisiana Purchase opened vast swaths of territory for expansion.[29] While one section was abolishing slavery, the other was celebrating the rise of King Cotton.

And that's when Missouri asked to join the union as a slave state. The ensuing crisis lasted for more than a year, ending in 1820 with a compromise that also allowed Maine to enter as a free state and drew a line that (supposedly) prohibited slavery above the 36°30' parallel. Following the controversy from Monticello, Thomas Jefferson observed, "A geographical line, coinciding with a marked principle, moral and political, once conceived and held up to the angry passions of men, will never be obliterated; and every new irritation will mark it deeper and deeper."[30] John Quincy Adams agreed, writing in his diary that the debate "revealed the basis for a new organization of parties . . . terrible to the whole Union, but portentously terrible to the South—threatening in its progress the emancipation of all their Slaves."[31]

Van Buren had a solution. If the choice came down to slavery or freedom, Americans might resolve the debate with bullets. But if the country was divided between rival political parties, they could settle their differences at the polls.

He laid out his strategy in an 1827 letter to Thomas Ritchie, a leader of the "Richmond Junto," Virginia's counterpart to the Albany Regency. "We must always have party distinctions and the old ones"—between Republicans and Federalists—"are the best." "It would take longer than our lives (even if it were practicable) to create new party feelings to keep those masses together. If the old ones are suppressed, geographical divisions founded on local interests or, what is worse prejudices between free and slave holding states will inevitably take their place."

The answer was simple: restoring the Jeffersonian coalition between "the planters of the South and the plain republicans of the North."[32]

In concrete terms, it meant putting together a party that could win both Virginia (the largest state in the South, and in Jefferson's time the largest in the country) and Van Buren's New York (the largest state in the North and soon to be the largest in the country). When backed up by an organized political machine, this party would bind the sections together and crush Adams's neo-Federalism. Jeffersonian principles, political machines, and a national coalition—to Van Buren, it added up to American democracy.

But who would lead the party? According to Van Buren, the only choice was Andrew Jackson.

This was a change of heart for Van Buren. He had crossed paths with Jackson when they both served in the Senate, and neither had left much impression on the other. In the 1824 presidential race, Van Buren opted for the old-line Republican William Crawford. But Jackson's impressive showing convinced Van Buren that Old Hickory could beat Adams in a rematch.

Van Buren had not forgotten his earlier reservations. "Genl Jackson has been so little in public life," he told Ritchie, "that it will be not a little difficult to contrast his opinions on great questions with those of Mr. Adams." He was, politely, calling the older man an empty suit. The trick, then, was to give him a Jeffersonian spine.

> His election, as the result of his military services without reference to party and so far as he alone is concerned, scarcely to principle, would be one thing. His election as the result of a combined and concerted effort of a political party, holding in the main to certain tenets and opposed to certain prevailing principles, might be another and a far different thing.[33]

Van Buren looked at Jackson the same way he looked at the American electorate: as a partisan waiting to be born.

⸻

Jackson was just one piece of the puzzle. He brought along the West, an essential part of the neo-Jeffersonian coalition. Van Buren trusted that he could take care of New York. But neither represented the Deep South, base of the old Republican Party.

So Van Buren turned to John Calhoun, resulting in a fateful pairing
that defined the contours of the embryonic anti-Adams coalition. The
South Carolinian was widely regarded as one of the leading statesmen in
his generation, which was also Van Buren's (Calhoun was four months
older). Still in his forties, Calhoun had served in the House and as secretary of war under Monroe, where he was the youngest member of the
cabinet. And now, awkwardly, he was Adams's vice president.[34]

Calhoun was everything that Van Buren wasn't: hailed as a serious
political thinker, celebrated for his independence, an embodiment of
principled politics. "What I think I see, I see with so much apparent
clearness as not to leave me a choice," he said. "[It] has always given me
the impression that I acted with the force of destiny."[35]

Van Buren, on the other hand, was just so . . . Van Buren-ish.

He looked, it was said of Calhoun, "as if he had never been born."[36]
Functionally illiterate for most of his childhood, he underwent an intellectual awakening as a teenager. He graduated Phi Beta Kappa from
Yale, where he delivered a commencement address on "the qualifications necessary to constitute a perfect statesman."[37] Elected to Congress in 1810, Calhoun positioned himself as a moderate Republican,
a child of the South who tempered Jeffersonian politics with just the
right amount of Yankee Federalism. He supported higher tariffs, a national bank, internal improvements, and a flexible interpretation of the
Constitution. "Calhoun is a man of fair and candid mind; of honorable
principles: of clear and quick understanding: of cool self-possession; of
enlarged philosophical views, and of ardent patriotism," swooned John
Quincy Adams in 1821. "He is above all sectional, and factious prejudices, more than any other Statesman of this Union, with whom I have
ever acted."[38]

This embodiment of damn-the-consequences devotion to principle
soon embarked on a long journey toward a sectionalism that made him
the intellectual godfather of the Confederacy. In 1824 Calhoun was
a protean enough figure that both Jacksonians and Adams supporters
wanted him as vice president, and he had been willing to serve under
either man. But politics below the Mason-Dixon line were changing,

and when Jackson carried seven Southern states—including South Carolina—Calhoun's choice was made for him. He turned against his own administration and enlisted with the nascent Jacksonian opposition.

It was a coup for Van Buren. If he was going to restore the alliance between the planters of the South and the plain republicans of the North, there was no substitute for Calhoun. The two represented different regions and stood for different kinds of politics. Both suspected that one day they would be fighting for the same job. For now, however, their interests were aligned.

Jackson wasn't close with either man, but he recognized their strengths. He selected Calhoun as his running mate and made Van Buren his de facto campaign manager. Jackson was the head of the operation, balanced out by his two deputies, one a Southerner and statesman of impeccable reputation, the other a Northerner and peerless partisan operator. A deal was struck—for the moment.

John Quincy Adams watched the movement taking shape against him as if he were a spectator at his own execution. "A great effort has been made in both Houses to combine the discordant elements of the Crawford and Jackson and Calhoun men into a united opposition, against the Administration," he noted early in 1826.[39] "Van Buren is now the great electioneering manager for General Jackson," he observed one year later, then predicted that the New Yorker had "every prospect of success."[40] Adams saw what was coming; he just couldn't figure out how to stop it. A lifetime of training for statesmanship hadn't prepared him for the Albany Regency gone national.

As the 1828 election approached, state and local pro-Jackson committees sprang up around the country, organizing rallies, lining up support from local party machines, and turning out voters at the polls. The campaign's two headquarters—one near Jackson in Nashville, another supervised by Van Buren in Washington—implemented a coherent national strategy. Van Buren was also the campaign's unofficial treasurer, funneling donations toward newspapers, pamphlets, and campaign memorabilia. "A stranger would think that the people of the United States have no other occupation than electioneering," Adams groaned.[41]

Jackson took almost every state outside of New England, obliterating Adams in the South while narrowly carrying New York.[42] The electoral map looked like a sequel to 1800, the last time an Adams had been thrown out of the White House. Jackson's vote total quadrupled from four years earlier, making him the first president to win an election in which a majority of the adult white men in the United States participated. Despite Van Buren's talk about Republican principles, Jacksonians kept the details of their agenda vague, relying on hazy calls for reform that allowed voters to fill in the blanks for themselves.

The founders thought they had designed a system that would reward natural aristocrats. Now it belonged to partisan operators mobilizing a mass electorate—not to Adams, but to Van Buren.

The new president was sworn into office on March 4, 1829. Adams did not attend the ceremony.

———————

Early in the administration, Jackson and Van Buren struck up a habit of riding through Washington on horseback, discussing politics as they wound along the Potomac. Jackson had chosen Van Buren as secretary of state, and their partnership of convenience blossomed into a real friendship.[43] Together, they worked through responses to the unfolding crises of their years in power, responses that turned the antiestablishment rebellion of 1828 into the basis of a coherent political party. By trying to re-create Jeffersonian Republicanism, Jacksonians invented "the Democracy."

The Democracy, its partisans tirelessly proclaimed, stood for a people—*the* people—under constant threat from a shifting cast of outsiders: a parasitic elite leeching off the productive majority; extremists on both sides of the slavery question; snotty reformers who wanted the government to control the lower sorts; Indians occupying land that by right belonged to white men; and members of the fairer sex who forgot that a woman's place was in the home. Underpinning all this was the belief that the federal government should have, in the words of the Democratic platform of 1840, "limited powers, derived solely from the Constitution."[44] Animated by a passionate but constricted egalitarianism, the Jacksonian persuasion was part policy checklist, part tribal war cry, and part political philosophy.

Indian removal—more accurately, expulsion—dominated the administration's early years. It was a reward for Southerners and westerners who had cast a ballot for Jackson, with critical votes provided by Northern Democrats, especially Van Burenites in the New York delegation.[45] By the end of Jackson's first term, however, the president was focused on a different threat—a fearsome enemy called "the money power."[46]

An updated version of the Hamiltonian nemesis, the money power gave concrete expression to a fear that coursed through Jacksonian democracy—a dread that, lurking in the shadows, a secretive cabal of financial oligarchs was conspiring to seize control of the government, fusing economic and political power to sustain a parasitic ruling class. The Bank of the United States, the reborn version of Hamilton's greatest triumph, was an obvious vessel for these anxieties. When Jackson vetoed the BUS's recharter, he acted like the laissez-faire populist he was. His enemy was a particular group of nefarious elites, not an overarching system: the money power, not capitalism, or even capitalists as such.[47] (As the proprietor of a plantation with 150 slaves, Jackson was in no position to complain about the influence of the wealthy over government.)[48]

The war against the money power was only one element of the Jacksonian worldview. Although it played well in the North, it had less appeal in the South and West. And so Democrats supplemented their talk about the few and the many with appeals to racial solidarity and promises of territorial expansion. Slavery, of course, had to be kept out of the national debate. But so did nativist grumbling about the country's growing Irish population. Democrats believed in Herrenvolk diversity. Catholic and Protestant, immigrant and native born—all deserved respect in the white man's Democracy.

—————

As a populist revolt matured into the Democracy, the question of whether Calhoun or Van Buren would succeed Jackson resolved itself. Van Buren did not put himself at the forefront of the president's crusades, but he didn't stand in their way, either. "You will say I am on my old track—caution—caution," he wrote to Jackson during one of the administration's battles.[49] Jackson was the great man, divinely certain that he embodied the will of the people. Van Buren was his faithful lieutenant, helping Jackson avoid traps laid by his enemies.

Calhoun was a different story. It had become clear that, in Calhoun's words, the South was destined to become "a fixed and hopeless minority."[50] Defending the region—meaning, above all, its slaveholding elite—became his obsession. He broke publicly with Jackson in 1830, becoming the leading champion of nullification, the doctrine that states had the right to block federal laws they deemed unconstitutional. Calhoun resigned in 1832 when a position opened up for him in the Senate. John Quincy Adams, in a rare moment of agreement with the Jacksonians, pronounced himself "deeply disappointed" in Calhoun. "I anticipated that he would prove an ornament and a blessing to his country . . . [but] now expect nothing from him but evil," Adams wrote in his diary of the man who became "the embodied Spirit of Slavery."[51]

Slavery, yes, but also the particular kind of democracy that grew around slavery, like a vine wrapped around a gnarled oak. Rather than counting on simple majority rule—a game the South would always lose—Calhoun argued for a system of "concurrent majorities," giving veto power to representatives of different social interests. Slavery would be protected, and politicians would be forced to seek consensus. "Instead of faction, strife, and struggle for party ascendancy," he predicted, "there would be patriotism, nationality, harmony, and a struggle only for supremacy in promoting the common good of the whole."[52] The will of the people didn't emerge naturally from an election; it was manufactured by statesmen.

He felt the same way about equality. Men were not born equal, but with the right social arrangements they could be made so—as, he argued, was happening for the white men of the South. "With us the two great divisions of society are . . . white and black," he said. "And all the former, the poor as well as the rich, belong to the upper class, and are respected and treated as equals."[53]

It was a model Calhoun thought the rest of the nation could learn from. His critique of Northern society had both a radical and a conservative edge. In attacking the money power, he was even more pointed than Jackson. Let capitalists have their way, he warned, and the rich would become richer while the common man was reduced to bare subsistence. But he also feared a revolt of the laboring masses—the ignorant, the poor, "the lowest and most worthless portions of the community."[54]

Slavery provided his way out. Properly understood, he argued, capitalists and slaveholders shared a common interest. The Southern ruling class, wiser than its Northern counterpart, would restrain the excesses of both capital and labor, guarding against both the money power and revolution from below.

Unless politicians got in their way. If one figure embodied Calhoun's fears for American politics, it wasn't a rebellious slave or a firebreathing abolitionist. It was Martin Van Buren. The New Yorker said he had no intention of undermining slavery, but to Calhoun this simply proved that Van Buren didn't grasp the explosive potential of partisan politics. Party organization led inevitably to the creation of a political class that cared only about winning the next election. The logic of majority rule would take over, splitting the nation into two parties divided along geographical lines. "By the necessary course of events, if left to themselves, we must become, finally, two people," he insisted. "Abolition and the Union cannot coexist."[55]

For now, however, the union held. Van Buren was the inevitable choice to replace Calhoun as Jackson's running mate in 1832. Competing against a multicandidate field, Jackson received a slightly smaller percentage of the popular vote than in 1828. But the raw total increased from some 640,000 in 1828 to just over 700,000 in 1832. There was a new coherence to his coalition of urban workers, western frontiersmen, and Southerners of all sorts. (Jackson won 100 percent of the vote in Missouri, Mississippi, Alabama, and Georgia.) He did not, however, carry South Carolina, where Calhoun exercised a control that the Albany Regency could only dream of.[56]

Calhoun had independence; Van Buren had power. The Little Magician won the presidency in his own right four years later with a coalition that stretched from Maine to Louisiana. "The people are for him," a distraught opponent lamented in the run-up to Van Buren's election. "Not so much for him as for the principle they suppose he represents. That principle is Democracy."[57]

The first president to come of age after the Revolution, Van Buren wasn't a statesman in the grand style, not a great orator, not an important thinker. A furious critic called him "secret, sly, selfish, cold, calculating, distrustful, treacherous" and described him as "one little man without talents, and what is worse, without honesty." Worst of all, he was a politician who in 1836 earned more votes than any other candidate in American history to date.[58]

It almost looked like destiny.

———

"To yield to necessity," Van Buren wrote to himself as a young man, "is the real triumph of reason and strength of mind."[59] His ill-starred turn in the White House was a lesson in how strict necessity could be. Jackson's administration had been consumed with crises that were often of the president's own making. Van Buren's troubles were outside his control—a party grown too comfortable with power; Southerners who doubted any Northerner's pro-slavery bona fides; and, worst of all, a brutal economic downturn that began in 1837 and persisted throughout his entire term in office.[60]

The slump brought the limitations of the Jacksonian revolution into focus. Americans had enjoyed decades of prosperity, but the rewards were concentrated among the wealthy, sending economic inequality soaring. Jackson's bank war barely slowed the emergence of a financial elite, and it did even less for a swelling underclass of poor white people.[61]

Just as troubling, for Van Buren, was a shift in the regional balance of power. In 1800, the South had been the wealthiest region of the country. It also had the lowest levels of income inequality, even after accounting for the enslaved population. For a white man, it was arguably the best place to live in the world. By 1840 it was both poorer and more economically stratified than the industrializing North. The trend lines were moving in a dangerous direction for the union—and for politicians who staked their careers on preserving sectional harmony.[62]

The South's decline shouldn't be overstated: the region was still growing, albeit at a slower clip than the North; it was also home to most of the country's wealthiest men.[63] But this strength only made it harder to maintain sectional equilibrium. A still powerful Southern elite was becoming angrier and more frightened as it faced down challenges from poor white people at home and emboldened Yankees in Washington. And with a comparatively weaker South becoming more aggressive in its demands, Northerners began asking why they should take orders from an ungrateful planter class.[64]

To keep a splintering coalition together, Van Buren made himself more Jacksonian than Jackson, ratcheting up the campaign against the money power at the same time he cracked down on antislavery dissent.

On economics, he moved toward radicals calling for "separation of bank and state." Van Buren's ultimate proposal—an "Independent Treasury" that kept federal funds away from banks—was not the pure shot of laissez-faire that radicals thirsted for, but it was strong enough that when he signed the measure into law (on July 4, 1840), Democrats called it a second Declaration of Independence.[65]

As usual, the bank war did best in the North, but Van Buren made sure that the white men of the South and West received their due. Jackson crusaded for the Indian Removal Act, but Van Buren presided over the Trail of Tears.[66] One month after Calhoun called slavery a "positive good" on the floor of the Senate, Van Buren became the first president to mention slavery in an inaugural address, where he promised to defend the South against the "dangerous agitation" of abolitionists.[67] He was true to his word, opposing attempts to end slavery in D.C. and supporting a gag rule to block discussion of antislavery petitions in Congress.

Radicalism against the money power; white supremacy everywhere else. Van Buren was once again yielding to necessity, following Jacksonian Democracy to a logical conclusion.

Logical, but not unchallenged. For a reminder of the complexity of balancing the Democratic Party's factions, Van Buren only had to look around his administration.

On one side, there was his friend and secretary of the navy James Kirke Paulding.[68] A native New Yorker, Paulding was a playwright, novelist, and poet. He was also a thoroughgoing racist. "The government of the United States, its institutions, and its privileges belong of right wholly and exclusively to the white men," he explained in his 1836 tract, *Slavery in the United States*.[69] Distilling Jacksonian democracy into a single phrase, he celebrated "the great aristocracy of the white man."[70] Paulding was repulsed by interracial marriage, warning about "traitors to the whiteskin" who tarnished their bloodlines by mixing with a race that "anatomists and physiologists have classed . . . as the lowest in the scale of rational beings."[71]

Fiery stuff. But one of the country's most notorious "traitors to the whiteskin" was Van Buren's own vice president, Richard Mentor Johnson.[72] A former Kentucky senator, Johnson never legally married, but he lived openly with his slave Julia Chinn. The couple had two daughters, Imogen and Adaline. As an outraged Democratic paper in New York later reported, Johnson treated his children "as in all respects equal to those of his free white neighbors."[73] Scandalously, he allowed them to marry white men. And so, with Johnson as vice president, under Van Buren the United States was literally a heartbeat away from having an interracial First Family.

Van Buren—cautious, cautious Van Buren—had selected Johnson because the Kentuckian was revered in the West for killing the Shawnee chieftain Tecumseh, and he was a hero to urban workers for spearheading an effort to abolish federal imprisonment for debt. (Jackson, too, thought this was the right choice.)

Eventually Van Buren came to regret the decision. The politics of race were changing, and criticism of Johnson kept escalating. In 1840, Democrats dropped Johnson from the ticket, running Van Buren for reelection without a vice presidential nominee.

The turn against Johnson was part of a larger cultural shift. Jacksonians provided early and enthusiastic audiences for minstrel shows ridiculing the familiar catalogue of Democratic villains: overeducated reformers, wealthy snobs, kooky abolitionists, and free Black people.[74] Mob violence surged in the 1830s, often targeting African Americans. The year of Van Buren's election, 1836, saw some of the worst racial violence of the entire antebellum era.[75]

As Johnson fell out of favor, Northern workers discovered a new hero: John Calhoun.[76] Convinced that Van Buren's bid for reelection would fail, Calhoun began laying the groundwork for a presidential run by assembling his version of Van Buren's alliance between "the planters of the South and the plain republicans of the North."

Left-wing Calhounism was especially popular in New York City. "The radical portion of the Democratic party here," Calhoun was informed, "is the very portion most favorable to you."[77] They shared common principles (free trade, small government) and common enemies (the money power, highbrow humanitarians). And they agreed, with the Yankee Jacksonian Theophilus Fisk, that the truly oppressed had "*pale* faces"—the white wage slaves of the North.[78]

In 1840, however, Calhoun put his ambitions on hold. Van Buren's frantic maneuvering kept the Democratic coalition together—just.

The president entered his reelection campaign hopeful that the people would stand by him. He soon learned that voters saw things differently.

———————

On April 14, 1840, the Pennsylvania congressman Charles Ogle rose to speak on a routine measure allocating $3,665 in funding for repairs and upkeep for "the President's house"—which, Ogle charged, Van Buren had turned into "a PALACE as splendid as that of the Caesars, and as richly adorned as the proudest Asiatic mansion."[79] Ogle spent the next three days detailing Van Buren's lavish spending—the French lamps, Grecian baths, and private gardens with paired hills, each shaped like "AN AMAZON'S BOSOM, with a miniature knoll or hillock on its apex, to denote the nipple." A pamphlet of his remarks ran to thirty-two pages, in minuscule font. It became the antebellum equivalent of a bestseller, providing Van Buren's opponents with the cornerstone of their campaign to drive the Little Magician out of his Washington palace.[80]

Ogle's diatribe was lurid, outrageous, and a total fabrication. Compared with other presidents, Van Buren was a frugal spender. But the lies about nippled hills revealed an important truth. Conjuring up the image of an evening with "the *elite* of the court," Ogle asked, "how would a plain, frank, intelligent republican farmer *feel*—how would he *look*, if he were caught at a table like that?" The answer was obvious: "He would feel as if he knew that *that* was not exactly *the place* for him."[81]

After twelve years in power, the Democracy resembled its own kind of aristocracy. In opposition emerged a new breed of conservatives who dropped Federalist lamentations about mob rule and claimed to speak for the many against the few. They called themselves Whigs, after the English party born out of rebellion against James II. The American Whigs targeted "King Andrew I" and his courtiers, none more nefarious than the Little Magician.[82] Their target wasn't the money power; it was a political elite who whipped up a class war so they could keep cushy government jobs.

Davy Crockett's hatchet job of a Van Buren biography was a representative illustration of the emerging opposition's worldview. "Statesmen are gamesters," the book announced, "and the people are the cards they play with."[83] It dismissed the assault on the money power as "a mere trickery, . . . a humbug, . . . a scarecrow."[84] According to Crockett, Democrats had mastered the art of fabricating controversies for their own gain: "They lash the people up into a perfect fury; they inflame them into madness; they make them feel all the concern and excitement that they could possibly do if their life depended upon it . . . all to put *Mr. Love-leisure* into a comfortable office."[85]

There was always a tinge of the absurd in the Whigs' coonskin-cap conservatism. Although both parties had coalitions that cut across class lines, Whigs tended to draw support from merchants, planters, and industrialists. They denied the existence of class conflict and idolized the self-made man (a phrase coined by the Whig journalist Calvin Colton).[86] But in a nation filled with self-made men—or, at least, men who liked to think of themselves as self-made—the Whig program had authentic popular appeal.

And their message wasn't just about economics. Whigs were also the party for evangelicals looking to improve the country's moral character (and wary of Democratic acceptance of Catholics). They picked up votes from critics of the Jackson–Van Buren Indian removal policy and racial moderates disturbed by the unruly white supremacy coming from certain quarters of the Democracy.* Whigs could be innovators, too, giving important roles as organizers and speakers to women.[87]

By 1840, moreover, the country was three years into an economic slump, with no end in sight. The time was ripe for a revolt against "Van Ruin." Whigs settled on William Henry Harrison, like Jackson a for-

---

* Not that the party was above playing the race card. In 1840, an article in an Illinois Whig newspaper, composed in a mock-Black dialect, announced that in a second Van Buren administration "de nigger all shall vote, and dat oder man in Kentucky state [Richard Mentor Johnson], is goin to make all the nigger women's children white." Although unsigned, it was probably written by a young Abraham Lincoln. Quoted in Michael Burlingame, *Abraham Lincoln: A Life*, vol. 1 (Baltimore, 2008), 109.

mer general with a reputation as an Indian killer. Party newspapers described Harrison as a man of the people, unlike his effete Democratic opponent and his even more suspect vice president. In reality, Harrison was a product of the Virginia gentry, and Van Buren close to a self-made man, but no matter. A Whig paper gloated, "THE AVALANCHE OF THE PEOPLE IS HERE!"[88]

AN INTERESTING FAMILY.

Whig caricature of the Democracy, with an opossum Van Buren carrying Thomas Hart Benton and John Calhoun in his pouch.

From a narrowly democratic perspective, the election was a triumph. 2.4 million voters turned out, more than had ever participated in a single election, and just over 80 percent of the total electorate.[89] For the Democracy, it was a disaster. New voters stormed to the polls—and most of them were Whigs. Harrison carried states in every region of the country, including Van Buren's New York, while the Whigs took control of Congress. The party had rerun 1828, with Harrison as Old Hickory and Van Buren as the hapless Adams. A Democratic newspaper screamed, "We have taught them how to conquer us!"[90]

———————

Van Buren did not plan on staying conquered for long. He blamed his defeat on a temporary bout of insanity brought on by "the debaucheries of a political Saturnalia."[91] Americans had been led astray, but they would come back to the Democracy. And he would be there, a president in exile, waiting for the people to return to their senses.

He rode out his banishment in style. Ogle would have had a field day with Van Buren's new home, a palatial mansion located on 137 acres in the elms and pines of the Hudson Valley. (He traded notes on country life with James Paulding, who lived in nearby Hyde Park.) From these luxurious headquarters Van Buren kept close tabs on developments in Washington: Harrison's shocking death after thirty-one days in office; the debacle that ensued when the new president (and former Democrat), John Tyler, all but declared war on the Whigs; and the steady stream of updates from Democrats who assumed that the nomination would be his for the taking next time. Deliciously, he watched as Calhoun entered the presidential race, only to have Van Buren supporters trounce him at Democratic conventions from Massachusetts to Alabama.

Just as Van Buren's path to the White House was opening up, a roadblock the size of Texas landed in his way. He had spent four years as president maneuvering around the question of whether Texas—then an independent republic—would be admitted to the union. But with the Tyler administration pushing for annexation, the country was once again dividing along sectional lines.[92]

The problem was easy to explain. All the available evidence suggested that most American voters wanted three things: to expand across the continent, to keep the union intact, and to maintain their democracy. Each desire was reasonable in itself, but there was no way to accommodate all three at once.

Every time a new state was added, it pushed slavery back into the national debate. Giving up on expansion would keep the sectional peace, but both Southerners and Northerners saw the territories as a safety valve that kept their own regions stable (it was either more land for potential slave owners or an escape from of a lifetime of wage labor for workingmen in the free states). Expansion might have gone forward if it had somehow been removed from domestic politics, but that would have made a mockery out of the notion that the people ruled.

Democracy, union, expansion—more and more, it looked like Americans would have to choose two out of three. It was the great trilemma of antebellum politics.

Van Buren's problems didn't stop there. More Southerners were coming around to Calhoun's way of thinking, defending slavery as a positive good. Abolitionists were still marginal figures in mainstream politics, but they were harder to ignore.[93] At the same time, the balance of power within the Whigs and Democrats was shifting. Slavery's fiercest defenders were clustering with the Democrats, and its most aggressive critics were moving toward the Whigs (including John Quincy Adams, enjoying a second life as a Massachusetts congressman and unrelenting critic of slavery, completing an arc from nationalist to sectionalist that perfectly mirrored that of his ex-friend Calhoun). And it didn't help that Calhoun himself became the public face for Texas annexation in 1844 after John Tyler selected him as secretary of state. (Calhoun's predecessor, Abel Upshur, had died in a freak naval accident.) Fresh off his losing presidential bid, Calhoun seized the opportunity to give a boost to the slave power while dealing a mortal wound to his old rival.

All this left Van Buren searching for a compromise while the middle ground was eroding by the day. He decided to stick with the status quo, announcing his opposition to annexing Texas. By coincidence, the news became public on the same day that the arch-Whig Henry Clay came out against statehood for Texas, creating the impression of a bipartisan elite trying to keep a deadly pathogen out of the political bloodstream.

It was the bravest decision of Van Buren's career, and it cost him the Democratic nomination. He won a majority of votes in the first ballot at the convention but fell short of the two-thirds total that party rules required of a nominee. Southerners had a veto, and after Texas there was no chance they would accept Van Buren. In private, even Andrew Jackson gave up on his old lieutenant. After nine ballots, Democrats settled on the Tennessee governor James Polk, a Van Buren supporter who had earlier pinned his hopes on a vice presidential nomination.

Van Buren wrote 1840 off as a mistake; 1844 was a betrayal. Not even Polk's victory in the election dulled the pain. The Tennessean won by restoring the Jacksonian coalition of planters and plain republicans, but Northerners were looking more like junior partners in the relationship. If the Democracy didn't yet belong to Calhoun, it wasn't Van Buren's party anymore, either.

Back in Kinderhook, Van Buren mulled over what to do next. He would never be president again, but he thought he could still save his party. A new chapter had opened up in the eternal struggle between aristocracy and the people. First it had been Jeffersonians against Hamiltonians, then Jacksonians against the money power. Now an insidious enemy was attacking the Democracy from within—*the slave power.*

———

The concept of a "slave power" entered American politics courtesy of Thomas Morris, an Ohio senator and one of the rare antislavery Democrats.[94] Morris first suggested that Southerners were conspiring against Northern liberty while debating Calhoun's proposed gag rule in 1836. He kept up his attacks after the controversy subsided, winning himself support from abolitionists but infuriating his fellow Democrats. In 1838 Ohio's Democratic legislature voted to replace him with a less combative successor. Freed from his obligations to the Democracy, Morris took to the Senate floor with his fiercest attacks yet.

"The slave power of the South and the banking power of the North are now uniting to rule this country," Morris announced.[95] His anti-slavery was thoroughly Jacksonian. He depicted the slave power as the heir to the money power, and cast himself as a defender of the aristocracy of the white man. "I am not now contending for the rights of the negro," he emphasized. "No, sir! I am contending for the rights of the white person in the free States."

Replacing the "slave power" for the "money power" was a simple move, just a matter of viewing Southern planters through the same lens that Jacksonians used for Northern capitalists. Like parasitic financiers, slave owners were corrupting democracy itself, exploiting their political and economic influence to take over the government. Abolitionists condemned slavery as a sin against God; Morris called it a plot against the workingman.

Somewhere between sociological analysis and conspiracy theory, the idea of a slave power had bite because there was plenty of evidence to substantiate the claim that the planter class had the country wrapped around its little finger. The United States was on its way to becoming the wealthiest slave society in world history, with almost four million enslaved people valued at more than three billion dollars, greater than the total for all the country's railroads, banks, and factories combined.[96] Far from dying out, slavery was a greater force than at any time in human history.

The South's economic might was both cause and consequence of its tight grip on political power. Slave owners dominated Washington. With their numbers inflated by the three-fifths clause, the Southern political elite united in defense of their peculiar institution, overpowering a divided North. Van Buren's capitulations to the planters had been Exhibit A in the case for Southern influence, and even that hadn't been enough to protect him. Now the argument made itself: slavers controlled the South; the South controlled the Democracy; and, most of the time, the Democracy controlled the government.[97]

But could they hold on to it? By 1845, Van Buren feared that slave-holder extremism was breaking the Democratic compact between

North and South. Anticipating, correctly, that Polk would launch a war against Mexico, he warned that a bloody conflict to extend slavery would compel Northern Democrats to turn against the South or risk "encountering political suicide with their eyes open."[98]

After war broke out, a proposal from the Pennsylvania congressman David Wilmot crystallized the burgeoning antislavery sentiment within the Northern wing of the Democracy. The Wilmot Proviso would have excluded slavery from all territory acquired during the Mexican-American War. Though Southerners killed the measure in the Senate, it marked the arrival of an antislavery politics compatible with white supremacy.[99]

Wilmot was straightforward about his motivations. Addressing a New York audience, he explained that it should be called "the White Man's Proviso." If present trends continued, he warned, African Americans would soon outnumber white people. When that terrible day arrived, the white minority would be forced to "either abandon the country to them, or cut their throats." To avert the choice between exile and genocide, they had to act now. "The negro race already occupy enough of this fair continent," he said. "Let us keep what remains for ourselves, and our children—for the emigrant that seeks our shores—for the poor man, that wealth shall oppress—for the free white laborer."[100]

Wilmot was speaking in New York because the state had become the center of antislavery Democracy. Van Buren's supporters had already been sharpening their knives against Polk, first for stealing the nomination and then for shortchanging them in the distribution of spoils after the election. The New York Democracy broke in two, with one faction ("the Hunkers") backing the administration, and another ("the Barnburners") loyal to Van Buren.

If anything, Barnburners were the stauncher defenders of racial hierarchy. They had denounced an 1846 effort to lower restrictions on Black voting and attacked Whigs as the "Nigger Party."[101] They also tended to be the more committed Jacksonians, opposed to state banks and big government. But they refused to accept that slave owners had a right to bring their human property into the western territories, and they were even clearer about the dangers of the slave power.

Led by the charismatic John Van Buren—Martin's son—four thousand Barnburners met in the village of Herkimer, New York, in October 1847. By the end of the convention, they had distilled the essence of antislavery Democracy into a slogan that would transform American politics: "Free Trade, Free Labor, Free Soil, Free Speech, and Free Men."[102]

They had a platform and the attention of antislavery activists across the free states. Now all they needed was a leader.

That's when Martin Van Buren came back into the picture.

———————————

"If you wish to be immortal, take this home with you, complete it, revise it, put it into proper shape, and give it to the public," Van Buren told the young man visiting him on a wintry night in New York's Washington Square.[103] He was speaking to Samuel Tilden, a close friend of his son John (and future Democratic presidential nominee). Van Buren was joking about immortality, but he knew that his manuscript would make news. Soon dubbed "the Barnburner Manifesto," it announced that the West would be settled either by white workers or by Black slaves. "Free and slave labor," Van Buren wrote, "cannot flourish under the same laws."[104] The conclusion was unavoidable: in self-defense, the Democracy had to defeat the slave power.

The exact reasons for Van Buren's antislavery conversion remain a mystery. Principle was a factor. He had opposed annexing Texas before he lost the Democratic nomination, and his resistance to expansion had hardened under Polk. Bitterness over his defeat in 1844 and subsequent declining influence surely played a part. So did his concern that Southern Democrats were asking too much from their Northern counterparts, endangering the party and perhaps even the union. "A northern Democratic party," one supporter told him, could "bring the despots and ingrates of the South and their obsequious satellites of the North, to their senses."[105]

With the 1848 election approaching, Barnburners and Hunkers sent rival delegations to the Democratic Convention in Baltimore. John Van Buren traveled south with instructions from his father to accept a compromise. But when the party nominated the conservative favorite Lewis Cass, the Barnburners forgot about his advice, storming out of the convention—and into a new party.

Two months after their dramatic exodus, Barnburners headed to Buffalo for the first national convention of the Free Soil Party. They were joined by some twenty thousand allies—other dissident Northern Democrats, antislavery Whigs, and abolitionists stepping tentatively into electoral politics. The Barnburners brought their Jacksonian disposition into the antislavery cause. They wanted to speak for the people—meaning, of course, for white men. Democrats had defeated the money power by separating bank and state; they would crush the slave power by breaking the planter class's hold on the government. Even their slogan was Jacksonian to the core: "Free Trade," a hallowed bit of Democratic dogma; "Free Labor," another tribute to workers; "Free Soil," a promise to distribute homesteads at no cost to settlers in the West and purge the territories of slavery, just as Jackson had purged it of Indians; "Free Speech," a defiant rebuke of slaveholders trying to silence debate; and "Free Men," the free men being white people declaring their independence from the slave power.[106]

But Free Soilers had to reach beyond disgruntled Jacksonians. Their movement had bubbled up from the grass roots, forcing Barnburners to work with the material at hand. They kept demands for racial equality out of the platform, but they allowed Black abolitionists, including Frederick Douglass, to speak at the convention.[107] Crisis had forced a marriage of convenience upon white supremacists and racial egalitarians. What happened next was anybody's guess.

Van Buren accepted the presidential nomination, a sign of the Barnburners' influence over the proceedings. As his vice president, the convention selected Charles Francis Adams, child of John Quincy Adams.

FREE SOIL — FREE LABOR — FREE SPEECH —

TEMPLE OF LIBERTY

MARTIN VAN BUREN CHARLES F. ADAMS

GRAND DEMOCRATIC FREE SOIL BANNER.

From — Daguerreotypes by Plumbe.

616

Twenty years after Jackson's triumph, Old Hickory's protégé was running alongside the son of JQA, leading a movement that counted both David Wilmot and Frederick Douglass in its ranks. Abolitionists didn't love Van Buren, but they didn't have to. "I am willing to take him," said the Massachusetts radical Charles Sumner. "With him we can break the slave-power; that is our first aim."[108]

Slavery's enemies were congratulating themselves before the first votes were counted. "It is gratifying to see the old parties dissolving," wrote the abolitionist firebrand William Lloyd Garrison, "like the baseless fabric of a vision."[109]

The euphoria lasted right up until the election. The Free Soil crusade fell to earth with a thud, winning just 10 percent of the popular vote. Van Buren could take personal satisfaction in spoiling the election for the Democracy. The overwhelming majority of Democrats and Whigs stuck with their respective parties. But Van Buren was a strong candidate in New York, doing especially well in areas hit hardest by the economic downturns of the 1830s.[110] Carried along by these bastions of Jacksonian radicalism, he poached enough Democrats in New York to hand the state—and with it the election—to the Whig nominee Zachary Taylor.

It was a defeat, then, but not a painful one for Van Buren. He had taught Southern Democrats a lesson. Now he could return to his old party with dignity. The other Barnburners followed him back, bringing the Free Soil revolt to a speedy conclusion.

And that, he thought, would be the end of the story.

Except the great trilemma remained: expansion, union, democracy. So long as there was no way to satisfy all three demands, every debate over the territories would drop the country back into the slavery wars. Each time a compromise failed to put the issue to rest, the middle ground shrank a little more. Meanwhile, the economic issues that gripped Democrats and Whigs during the age of Jackson lost their potency.[111]

The Bank of the United States was dead, and commerce was thriving anyway. And so it was back to slavery, the argument that over the next decade would destroy the Whigs and shatter the Democracy—along with the country.

As the union fractured, Van Buren occupied himself with the life of a country gentleman. He renovated his Hudson Valley manse, turning a spacious Dutch colonial into a faux-Venetian villa with a piazza overlooked by a four-story tower.[112] In his spare time, he tinkered on an ever-expanding autobiography. Filled with exhaustive details on the legislative battles of his youth, it passed by his private life in almost total silence. He gave up the project after he reached 1,247 pages and had not even made it to his presidency.

Undaunted, he tried his hand at another book, a history of American political parties that chronicled an epic clash between aristocracy and democracy. Like his abandoned memoirs, it went unpublished in his lifetime.

History was a refuge. Contemporary politics brought only disappointment. He denounced the newborn Republican Party, dismissing it as the latest Hamiltonian plot to divide the Democracy. "Slavery agitation," he declared, "must be eradicated."[113] His top choice for president in 1852 was Roger Taney, who had played a key role in Jackson's bank war and been rewarded with the chief justiceship of the Supreme Court. Taney would soon author the *Dred Scott* decision, announcing that African Americans "had no rights which the white man was bound to respect."[114]

The Democracy was more a creature of the slave power than ever. Calhoun died in 1850, but his shadow loomed over a radicalizing South. Democrats rolled out the welcome mat for conservative Whigs, urging them—in the words of a Massachusetts partisan—to put "love of the Union and the white race" over "false philanthropy for the negro."[115] The party became the fullest expression of what it had been tending toward since its inception: a hybrid of Van Buren and Calhoun that used a cross-sectional coalition and mass-party politics to defend the planter class. Van Buren hadn't intended it to serve this purpose, Calhoun didn't think it could be done—and there it was, all the same.

Yet the Democratic legacy wasn't confined to the Democratic Party. "Much of the plain old democracy is with us," claimed Abraham Lincoln, the ex-Whig turned Republican, during his 1858 Senate campaign against Stephen Douglas, "while nearly all of the old exclusive silk-stocking whiggery is against us."[116] That was overstating things: plenty of the plain old democracy stuck with Douglas, and Republicans had their silk-stocking supporters. But there was enough Jacksonian DNA in the new party to give Lincoln's point credibility.

Van Buren's New York symbolized the paradoxes of antislavery politics. Lincoln easily carried the state in 1860, the same year that 63 percent of the electorate voted down a referendum extending universal suffrage to Black men.[117] The referendum's failure left the status quo intact—the same $250 property requirement for African Americans that Van Buren helped push through the state's constitutional convention almost four decades earlier. New Yorkers were barreling toward a war over slavery while jealously defending their own racial hierarchy.

And who had done more to bring the country to this point than Martin Van Buren? Americans had been arguing about slavery since before there was a United States. Its danger was already obvious at the Constitutional Convention in 1787. Only when slavery was brought to the center of the country's freewheeling democratic politics did the bullets start flying. As a young Jeffersonian, Van Buren had been a pioneering figure in the development of mass democracy. Then, as the elder statesman in the Free Soil Party, he helped weave together antislavery politics with white supremacy, pointing the way toward a platform and a coalition that Republicans later rode into the White House. In the long run, the Free Soilers won their 1848 campaign; it just took twelve years to count the ballots.

———————

Van Buren, of course, was horrified. Maybe that's why he couldn't finish his memoirs. There was too much to regret.

For most of his life he thought that American democracy was a triumph. The country had avoided the twin dangers of oligarchy and mobocracy, crushing the money power without succumbing to destructive class warfare. Signs of prosperity were everywhere: railroads and telegraphs binding the nation together, coal fueling an industrial revolution, cotton tying the nation to a global marketplace.

With the economy booming, income inequality kept rising long after Jackson slew the dreaded Bank of the United States. Jacksonians weren't responsible for the widening gap between rich and poor, but they hadn't figured out how to close it, either. Whigs and Democrats made sure that the merchants, financiers, and manufacturers who dominated the emerging economic order had deep ties in both parties—for one, August Belmont, a onetime agent of the Rothschilds who became head of the Democratic National Committee.[118] While revolutionary movements were surging across Europe, American capitalists rejoiced in the majesty of popular government.

The destruction of the money power, it turned out, did wonders for the people with money.

When Van Buren set out on his short-lived campaign against the slave power, he might have expected a similar result: a slap on the wrist that cured the planter class of its hubris without endangering its livelihood, allowing Northerners and Southerners to go back to enjoying peace and prosperity. He didn't realize that slave owners would view matters differently—that free soil would look like an existential threat, or that slavers had the political muscle to start a war.

But he learned. In April 1861, as the union was disintegrating, a letter arrived at Van Buren's home with a proposition from ex-president Franklin Pierce, who had mailed similar letters to all the other living former presidents. Pierce thought that, as onetime holders of the nation's highest office, they had a duty to find a compromise that could stitch the nation back together—a league of presidents, jumping in to save the day. Because Van Buren was the eldest of the five, Pierce requested that he call the meeting.[119]

With impeccable politeness, Van Buren declined. Beneath his

courtly rhetoric, the message was clear. No amount of eminence was going to patch the union back together. Their time had passed, just as surely as the age of Publius had so many years earlier. Better to step away now, before they embarrassed themselves.

And so, for his last trick, the Little Magician made himself disappear.

3

————————————————————

Liberators

Charles Sumner believed in America, the Republican Party, and himself—not always in that order. Broad-chested, with full lips and liquid brown eyes, he was considered one of the finest speakers in the Senate, where he courted death threats for his attacks on the slave power. In marathon orations that he memorized ahead of time for maximum dramatic effect, Sumner blended allusions to antiquity with lurid re-creations of plantation depravity, rapturous visions of a coming emancipation, and lyrical tributes to the equality of man.

He spoke with the authority that came from almost dying for his beliefs. In 1856, the South Carolina congressman Preston Brooks had attacked an unsuspecting Sumner with a cane, thrashing away while Sumner's legs were pinned under his desk.[1] Years of painful recovery followed, where Sumner battled with what would today be called post-traumatic stress disorder. He returned to the Senate in 1859, a near martyr to freedom—and, as Frederick Douglass called him, "the best embodiment of the Anti-Slavery idea now in the councils of the nation."[2] He stayed in office until his death fifteen years later, by which time he had become the longest continually serving member of the Senate and one of the last connections to the Republican Party's founding.

But Sumner never saw himself as a typical politician. "This is the tribe I eschew, and detest," he wrote in 1850, shortly before joining the Senate. "Their trade compels them to be faithless to principles. . . . A *politician* in the service of a *party* cannot be trusted."[3] The only way out of this bind was to create a new kind of party, where principles— antislavery principles—would be safe.

Just as Van Buren's career would not have been possible without the Democracy, Sumner's was unimaginable without the Republican Party. "Most of our Republican statesmen have a political history antecedent to our existing organizations," the *New-York Tribune* observed. "Mr. Sumner, nearly alone, is nowhere regarded as having Whig or Democratic predi- lections, but as purely and wholly Republican."[4] It seemed as if he had come out of the womb with a stem-winding denunciation of slavery on his lips, a pure representative of what he called "the party of freedom."[5]

Charles Sumner, circa 1850.

Sumner had a radical's moral clarity and a conservative's faith in American institutions. It was an unlikely combination, made possible by his certainty that he belonged in the governing class.[6] A natural aristocrat gone rogue, he was a descendant of Puritans with degrees from Harvard College and Harvard Law School. When Charles Dickens toured Massachusetts in 1842, he asked Sumner to be his guide. Sumner flaunted his erudition, peppering his speeches with references to Plato and Kant, Euripides and Shakespeare. But he wrote those learned addresses with a national audience in mind. "The Crime Against Kansas," the address that provoked Brooks's assault, ran to ninety-five pages in print. The *New-York Tribune* editor, Horace Greeley, estimated that three million copies were in circulation by Independence Day 1856.[7]

When abolitionists such as William Lloyd Garrison urged radicals to give up on politics, arguing that a country founded on slavery could not be redeemed, Sumner replied that only a democratic majority could break the slave power. He would use the tools of partisan politics to make Van Buren's nightmare a reality: an electoral realignment that forged a coalition of free states, powered by mass democratic politics, dedicated to abolishing slavery. Instead of denouncing the founders, Sumner insisted that he was following the nation's founding principles to their logical conclusion. *"Every man is entitled to life, liberty, and the pursuit of happiness,"* he declared, *"whether black or white."*[8]

An incongruous mixture of Thomas Jefferson, Edmund Burke, and Frederick Douglass, Sumner became a leader of the Republican faction known as Radicals. But if you had to choose a single word to describe his politics, the best option is "liberal." Although the intellectual history of liberalism reaches back centuries, the term was only coined early in the 1800s, and Sumner was part of the first generation of Americans to give the concept real political heft. Like other liberals of his time, he believed in free markets, government by the best men, and the inevitable march of progress.[9] But he carved out an exception for civil rights, maintaining that the federal government had an obligation to destroy white supremacy—an effort that he acknowledged would amount to a revolution.

An idiosyncratic liberal in his time, Sumner was, in a sense, the first liberal of ours. And the questions that dogged him would return to haunt his successors. Did he believe in democracy? In defending the rights of the oppressed, no matter how unpopular the cause? Or, as his critics said, did he just want to prove his own righteousness?

"In the consciousness of right," he said near the end of his life, "I was willing to be alone."[10] But Sumner didn't really think he was alone. He welcomed the burdens of statesmanship, casting himself as the voice of the true Republican Party, a guardian of his country's democratic tradition, and a champion for African Americans denied a representative of their own in the Senate. He had no doubt that in the ordeal of Charles Sumner, all of them were being put to the test. And he would not let them fail.

Sermonizing came naturally to Sumner. Though not inclined to theological ruminations—"I am," he said, "without religious feeling"—he shared the hunger for a sacred mission that brought his Puritan ancestors to the Massachusetts Bay Colony in the 1630s.[11] "I have never had much to do with bishops where I live," Abraham Lincoln said after meeting him. "But, do you know, Sumner is my idea of a bishop."[12]

It was obvious early on that Sumner wasn't like other boys. At ten, he taught himself Latin in secret, surprising his father one morning with a recitation delivered while the older man shaved. As a teenager, he woke before dawn to peruse tomes on Roman history. During his first year at Harvard he checked out more books from the library than anyone else in his forty-person class.

When a subject fell outside his interests, it might as well not have existed. He was hopeless at math, useless in sports, and all but humorless. Though he traveled across Europe as an adult, he never developed an ear for music or an eye for art. Women were a lifelong mystery. According to his most thorough biographer, he was probably a virgin until he entered a brief and disastrous marriage at the age of fifty-five.[13] (After the newlyweds began living together, he installed a bust of Minerva, goddess of chastity, in the entryway to his house.)[14]

Sumner was happiest—maybe he was only happy—when he lost himself in a calling. After toying with the idea of a literary life, he got a glimpse of a different future while he was at law school, where he came under the mentorship of Joseph Story.[15] One of the period's towering legal thinkers, Story served simultaneously as a professor at Harvard and as a justice on the Supreme Court. Distraught at the rise of Jacksonian democracy, Story took it upon himself to train a new generation of leaders who could restrain the excesses of the mob. Sumner was one of his prize specimens. At a time when students could glide to a degree, Sumner was a constant presence in the library. Bloodshot eyes, a sallow complexion, and a barking cough: these were tokens of his commitment, signs of his vocation.

There was one crucial respect, however, where the star pupil diverged from his teacher. While Story despaired over the fallen state of the republic, Sumner believed that Americans had a privileged position at the dawn of a glorious new era. "Indefinite improvement," he said, "is the destiny of man, of societies, of nations, and of the Human family."[16] Americans were uniquely blessed to live in a nation whose founding principles matched the spirit of the age. The Declaration of Independence and the "Law of Human Progress" fit seamlessly together in Sumner's mind, the keystones of his secular faith.

Borrowing elements from both conservatives and radicals, Sumner became known as one of Boston's "ultra liberals."[17] He embraced the fashionable causes of the time: public education, prison reform, gradual emancipation, world peace. Statesmen weren't the thin line separating civilization from anarchy. They were shepherds encouraging the flock to follow its best instincts, pointing out what was right, then waiting for the people to come around.

Still, "statesman" was an ideal, not a profession. The life of a career politician was out of the question. "Politics are my loathing," he told Story after a trip to Washington in 1834.[18] "There is so much passion,

and so little principle; so much devotion to party, and so little to country," he complained during the 1840 election.[19] "There are some (among
whom I am willing to be counted)," he noted primly, "who think success obtained by such vulgar means of very doubtful value."

With hopes of one day returning to academia, Sumner launched
his own legal practice. His expectations were never high. "I look upon
a *mere* lawyer, a reader of cases and cases alone, as one of the veriest
wretches in the world," he said before entering law school.[20] Prospec-
tive clients picked up on the indifference, verging on contempt, and
took their business elsewhere. Not for the last time, Sumner was, unknowingly, following Van Buren's example. But where the Little Magician reveled in legal practice, Sumner could not reconcile himself to a
life spent wading through the paperwork of Boston merchants.

Sumner's floundering embarrassed Story, who had already started
to question his protégé's judgment because of their political differences.
The implicit promise of a position at Harvard was quietly withdrawn.
"You cannot fathom the yawning depths of my soul," Sumner moaned
to his friend Henry Wadsworth Longfellow in 1843. "I am *alive*; that
is, continue to draw breath, and stride through the streets. But what is
this? I am becoming every day duller and duller; I have nothing to say
to any body. I am like an extinct volcano."[21]

At a personal and professional impasse, Sumner longed to join a
cause larger than himself—a movement that would change the country, give his life meaning, and rescue him from the tedium of law.

In 1844, he found it.

━━ ━ ━ ━ ━ ━ ━

Sumner had opposed slavery as far back as he could remember. His
father, an egalitarian in the tradition of Thomas Paine, visited Haiti
during its revolutionary struggle for independence and came away impressed by the nascent Black republic. Back in Boston, he had friendly
relations with members of the city's free Black community.

The younger Sumner first encountered the peculiar institution during his 1834 trip to Washington, when he saw a group of slaves while passing through Maryland. "They appear to be nothing more than moving masses of flesh, unendowed with anything of intelligence above the brutes," he wrote at the time.[22] During a tour of Europe, however, watching Black students at the Sorbonne convinced him that slavery was to blame for this lowly condition. "The distance between free blacks and the whites among us is derived from education," he wrote, "and does not exist in the nature of things."[23] In 1836 he told a friend in South Carolina, "We are becoming abolitionists at the North fast."[24] Anti-abolitionist riots, the gag rule controversy in Congress, the uncompromising rhetoric coming from the South—all of it, he reported, was driving enlightened opinion toward emancipation.

It was one thing to support abolition, quite another to make it your life's work. For Sumner, the shift began with Texas statehood. To Van Buren, the issue had been a political inconvenience; to Sumner, any case of slavery's expansion was a moral atrocity. The more he focused on slavery, the larger it loomed in his consciousness. "All the acts of our Government [are] connected, directly or indirectly, with the institution," he concluded.[25] He saw its pernicious influence wherever he looked: in Congress, where the ranks of the slave power were multiplied by the three-fifths clause; in the courts, where judges chosen by slave-owning presidents staffed the bench; even in the North, where former slaves who had escaped to freedom could be snatched back at any second. "Slavery," he announced, "stops every thing that is good."[26]

But what to do about it? Massachusetts Whigs said they opposed slavery, but party leaders dropped their resistance to annexing Texas after deciding it was a losing battle, and in 1848 the party chose slave owner Zachary Taylor as its presidential candidate. Garrisonians, meanwhile, denounced the Constitution as a "covenant with death" and called for the union to be destroyed.[27]

Opposed to both, Sumner joined with "political abolitionists" who saw a democratic path to emancipation. He depicted the slave power as an alien force that had taken over a government whose framers meant to put slavery on the road to ultimate extinction. Slavery was a malignant tumor in an otherwise healthy patient, not a congenital defect. "You already support the Constitution of the U.S. by continuing to live under its jurisdiction," he tweaked one Garrisonian. "Let us, then, continue to live under it; but . . . strive in all ways for its purification."[28]

Abolitionists would use the tools of politicians to overthrow a corrupt status quo. "If bad men conspire for Slavery, good men must combine for Freedom," he said.[29] "The moralist and philanthropist must become for this purpose politicians,—not forgetting morals or philanthropy, but seeking to apply them practically in the laws of the land."[30] These righteous leaders would preside over a democracy where "politics and morals, no longer divorced from each other, become one and inseparable in the holy wedlock of Christian sentiment."[31]

Despite the utopian rhetoric, Sumner was happy to compromise on issues that didn't touch his central convictions. "Our great object must be to encourage *union* among all who are against Slavery," he insisted.[32] "They should look upon each other with good will, and generosity," he said, "and direct their powers,—never against each other—but always against the common enemy."[33]

He was agnostic on how to bring this new party to life. At first he thought antislavery would take over the Whigs, but he soon gave up on overthrowing the "Cotton Whig" establishment. He struck up correspondences with political abolitionists outside Massachusetts looking to form a national third party. His short history in politics made him an ideal mediator for Whigs, Democrats, and recovering Garrisonians ready to plunge into party building. He strategized with Ohio's Salmon Chase and discussed the "inglorious confusion" of existing coalitions with John Van Buren.[34] An enthusiastic Free Soiler, he threw his support behind John's father in 1848. After Van Buren's defeat, he switched his focus back to Massachusetts, now convinced that fusion with the Democracy was their best option.

As Sumner rotated through potential allies, his overarching strategy remained the same. In order to build a united front across the North, political abolitionists had to fix the public's attention on slavery, which meant sidelining the issues that Whigs and Democrats preferred talking about—tariffs, banks, Indian removal, and other subjects that cut across the sectional divide. "All the ideas put forward in the controversies of party are now practically obsolete," Sumner announced. "Freedom is the only question now before the American people."[35]

He became a pariah in high society. Antislavery was welcome in Brahmin circles, but the worthies of Beacon Hill considered his fixation on the topic unseemly. Old friends avoided him on the street. Outsiders to Boston watched in disbelief as literal shudders passed through the room when his name was mentioned at fashionable soirees.[36] He was, however, welcome at meetings of the city's politically active free Black people, making regular appearances at a Black-owned barbershop known for hosting antislavery discussions, an abolitionist sequel to Abraham Van Buren's tavern.

With his social standing in free fall, Sumner discovered his inner populist. In 1848 he railed against "an unhallowed union—conspiracy let it be called—between two remote sections: between the politicians of the Southwest and the politicians of the Northeast,—between the cotton-planters and flesh-mongers of Louisiana and Mississippi and the cotton-spinners and traffickers of New England,—between the lords of the lash and the lords of the loom."[37] Drawing on a resonant piece of Jacksonian rhetoric, he announced, "The money power has joined hands with the slave power. Selfish, grasping, subtle, tyrannical, like its ally, it will not brook opposition."[38]

When Southern oligarchs locked arms with Northern capitalists, Sumner concluded, the wealthy posed a greater threat to liberty than the mob.

But he was an inconsistent democrat. Although he denounced the slave oligarchy, it wasn't clear whether he rejected oligarchy itself or merely a "vulgar . . . aristocracy of the skin."[39] He wanted to redeem the propertied class, not abolish capital. If all that was wrong in American life sprang out of the slave power, then emancipation and integration need not upset the country's underlying social structure. The United States after slavery would be its best self, only more so. And with abo-

litionists still a despised minority, simple majoritarianism wasn't an option. "Aloft on the throne of God, and not below in the footprints of a
trampling multitude, are the sacred rules of Right, which no majorities
can displace or overturn," he announced, using words that could have
been taken out of Joseph Story's mouth.[40]

Luckily, Sumner's faith in the people was looking more realistic. In
1849 he enlisted as cocounsel in *Roberts v. City of Boston*, a case arguing for integrated schools. Introducing arguments that would be picked
up in *Brown v. Board of Education* more than a century later, he argued that educational segregation was inherently unequal. Although he
lost the case, in 1855 Massachusetts abolished school segregation, an
encouraging sign that he might not stay in the minority for long.[41]

He pressed onward, supplementing high-flown theorizing with organizational grunt work—editing newspapers, planning rallies, and delivering speech after speech on behalf of the cause. Swept up in a perennial
campaign, he lost any bit of interest he had in practicing law, along with
the melancholy that hung over him when he contemplated life as "a *mere
lawyer*." His eloquence made him one of antislavery's most effective advocates, and his prestige made him one of their most valuable. John
Quincy Adams came to see him as an heir. "I see you have a mission to
perform," Adams told him. "You will enter public life; you do not want
it, but you will be drawn into the current, in spite of yourself."[42]

Sumner assured Adams that he had no interest in elected office,
and he kept on denying it even after he was chosen for the Senate. His
election was a fluke product of antebellum politics, when senators were
still selected by the state legislature, not popular vote. In 1850 Massachusetts delivered a mixed verdict. The Whigs won a plurality, but
Democrats and Free Soilers had a narrow majority. Forging an ad hoc
coalition, Democrats took the governor's chair, and Free Soilers got
the Senate. Sumner's enthusiasm for this shotgun marriage outweighed
concerns among Democrats about sending a "red-hot Abolitionist" to
the Senate, though not without months of protracted negotiations—
and, perhaps, some shady backroom dealings.[43] When victory came, it
was by the slimmest of margins: 1 vote out of 385 total.

"For myself, I do not desire public life," Sumner told his sister Julia as he set out for Washington. "I have neither taste nor ambition for it; but Providence has marked out my career, and I follow."[44]

Sumner was not impressed by his new home. "I begin to be a-weary of this life," he said after eight months in office. "The scenes of the Senate have disgusted me. No man, who cares for happiness, should consent to come here."[45] Although Southern politicians were friendly in private—much friendlier to him than was Boston high society—he traced the "inexpressibly low" tone of Washington society to slavery, calling it "the source of all meanness here from national dishonesty down to tobacco-spitting."[46] Prolonged exposure did not warm him to the city. "Truly—truly—this is a godless place," he said in 1856, the same year he won reelection to a second term.[47]

He arrived at a transitional period in Washington's history. The old generation was passing into twilight: John Calhoun was dead, Henry Clay a spectral presence, Daniel Webster ensconced at the State Department (and horrified that Sumner had inherited his seat). "You have come upon the stage too late," Sumner was told by Missouri's Thomas Hart Benton, a thirty-year veteran of Washington. "Not only have the great men passed away, but the great issues, too," Benton said. "Nothing is left you, sir, but puny sectional questions and petty strifes about slavery."[48]

Sumner hoped to make a career out of turning these "puny sectional questions" into a national cause, but as one of just a handful of Free Soilers in Congress he had few allies. Defiant, he claimed that the people were on his side. "The rising public opinion against Slavery cannot flow in the old political channels," he warned. "If not *through* the old parties, then *over* the old parties, this irresistible current *shall* find its way."[49]

Certainly there was a widespread sense that realignment was coming. In 1854, *The New York Times* reported that both parties had lost their hold on the public. "Their machinery of intrigue, their shuffling evasions, the dodges, the chicanery and the deception of their leaders have excited universal disgust, and have created a general readiness in the public mind for any new organization that shall promise to shun their vices."[50]

Politicians felt the same dissatisfaction, especially the younger ones. "Old parties, old names, old issues, and old organizations are passing away," wrote the forty-two-year-old Alexander Stephens, a Whig congressman from Georgia (and future vice president of the Confederacy). "A day of new things, new issues, new leaders, and new organizations is at hand."[51]

But if the old regime was coming apart, it wasn't at all clear what the new order would look like. In Sumner's home state, the nativist American Party, better remembered today as the Know Nothings, won the governorship, the whole congressional delegation, the entire state senate, and all but 3 of the 379 state representatives in the 1854 elections.[52] Know Nothings elected governors in seven other states the same year, along with more than fifty members of the House. Mixing animosity toward the country's rising immigrant population (mostly German and Irish) with a wide-ranging hostility to the political establishment, Know Nothings positioned themselves, in a remarkably short period of time, as a major force in American politics.

In 1856, however, the party split along the same divide over slavery that destroyed the Whigs.[53] Know Nothings received just 21.5 percent of the popular vote in the presidential election, putting them behind the newly formed Republican Party.[54] Emerging from a combination of top-down and grassroots activism—private meetings in Washington and local conventions across the free states—the Republican Party first took shape in 1854.[55] Sumner embraced the Republican label early, even as other antislavery politicians—including Abraham Lincoln—kept their distance, unsure as to whether it was a majority in embryo or another doomed crusade.[56]

Though Sumner was too radical and idiosyncratic to speak for Republicans as a whole, he was one of their most compelling preachers. The party owed a sizable number of their most popular slogans—

including "the barbarism of slavery," "freedom national," and "the backbone party"—to the senator from Massachusetts. His framing of the debate was just as influential. According to Sumner, there was no middle ground in the clash of civilizations between North and South. It was the *Mayflower* or the slave ship, Plymouth Rock or Jamestown, knowledge or ignorance, prosperity or misery, progress or reaction, civilization or barbarism, freedom or slavery—in short, "a solemn battle between Right and Wrong, between Good and Evil."[57] More than anything, he owed his success to the force of this simple story.

Sumner had learned about the power of polarization by watching the South. "It is right to be taught by the enemy," he said. "With them Slavery is the mainspring of political life, and the absorbing center of political activity."[58] Northerners would have to be just as single-minded. He urged voters in free states to put aside their former differences, making a place for recovering Democrats and former Whigs, conservatives and radicals, "the true American" and "the foreign-born."[59]

Unlike most Republicans, Sumner's coalition had a central place for African Americans. This was more a matter of principle than of politics. The United States was an overwhelmingly white nation, and the free states were whiter still—98.8 percent white in 1860.[60] Racially restrictive suffrage laws further diminished Black influence at the polls. And most antislavery voters—along with most antislavery politicians—showed no interest in turning the United States into a multiracial democracy. Abraham Lincoln underlined the point in 1854. "This government was made for the white people," he said, "and not for the negroes."[61]

With precious few allies to choose from, African Americans from around the country looked to Sumner. "All the friends of freedom, in every State, and of every color, may claim you, just now, as their representative," Frederick Douglass told Sumner in 1854, calling himself "one of your sable constituents."[62] He was the very rare white politician of his era to keep up an active correspondence not just with Black leaders such as Douglass but with ordinary African Americans. In his letters, Sumner could be prickly, imperious, and condescending—but that was just as true in his exchanges with white people.[63]

Sumner lived his principles. Henry McNeal Turner, a Black pastor visiting the capital from Georgia, described his first meeting with Sumner this way: "To my astonishment the greatest statesman the sun ever shone upon walked up between us and locked our arms, and proceeded through the streets and buildings as unconcernedly as if he had been in company with his senatorial colleagues; he thought no more of asking a black man to dine at his table than he did of the whitest man on earth."[64]

Republicans held together a coalition mixing antislavery white supremacists and racial egalitarians by focusing on a common enemy. Whether they believed that slavery was a national sin or an economic anachronism—and Sumner thought it was both—Republicans insisted that the slave power was to blame. *They* perverted the Constitution. *They* seized control of the government. *They* kept alive an institution that should have passed away long ago. *They* stood in the way of the free labor dream, where every man could climb the ladder from wage earner to independent producer. *They* stood in the way of the simple request that slavery not spread across the western territories.* *They* were splitting the country in two.

Calling for the death—even the slow death—of the wealthiest slave society in history was a revolutionary demand. But Republicans were pursuing a radical goal for conservative reasons. The South had to be transformed, they argued, so that the North could stay the same. Industrialization and urbanization were remaking the free states, and even small farmers were increasingly drawn into the marketplace. In an era of railroads, telegraphs, and ocean-crossing steamships, the yeoman farmer's days were numbered. Wage labor was becoming more common, propertied independence less so. Economic inequality had been rising for decades, and it showed no signs of abating.

---

* Perhaps reflecting the importance of western expansion to the Republican platform, Sumner's racial egalitarianism did not include Native Americans, who, he said, were not "willing to learn" the "improvements of civilization." Sumner, *Complete Works*, vol. 15, 85.

Republicans needed a way to speak to both the winners and losers of this great transformation. They found it by glorifying the virtues of free labor over slavery, conjuring visions of a society populated by small-time farmers and shopkeepers. Former Whigs might stress the harmony of interests between capital and labor, while ex-Jacksonians paid more attention to class conflict. But with the slave power as their nemesis and free soil as their goal, Republicans called for a political revolution to maintain the status quo.

The debates over the Kansas-Nebraska Act brought the stakes of the conflict over the territories into focus. Led by Stephen Douglas, sectional conciliators argued that the citizens in the territories should vote on whether to allow slavery—the doctrine of "popular sovereignty." Sumner tore into the compromise in a Senate address laced with sexual innuendo about slave owners and their defenders in Congress, including South Carolina's Andrew Butler. It was an outrageous violation of Senate norms. Michigan's Lewis Cass, one of Washington's grayest eminences, called the speech on the Kansas-Nebraska Act "the most un-American and unpatriotic that ever grated on the ears of the members of this high body."[66] "From a man of character of any party I have never seen any thing so offensive," tutted the Boston grandee Edward Everett.[67] "That damn fool will get himself killed by some other damn fool," Douglas predicted.[68]

Preston Brooks, nephew of Andrew Butler, almost vindicated Douglas's prophecy when he assaulted Sumner on May 22, 1856. The attack made Sumner into a Northern icon, turning a controversial politician into a victim of the slave power. "When the intelligence of the assault . . . reached Boston," Everett said, "it produced an excitement in the public mind deeper and more dangerous than I have ever witnessed."[69] Behind the furor was disbelief that a flower of Northern society like Charles Sumner could be treated like . . . well, like a slave.[70]

And, crucially, it happened during an election year. Republicans had their first presidential nominating convention less than a month after Sumner's caning. The scandal and the party strengthened each other: a senator's near murder gave a visceral charge to condemnations of Southern tyranny, and Republicans ensured that the incident would be front and center during the campaign. The rules of the old system, where Democrats and Whigs each had an incentive to downplay sectional controversy, had been tossed out the window. Now a major party existed for the sole purpose of uniting the free states against the South. Sumner became a kind of mascot for the Republicans, almost a sacrificial offering to the cause of political abolitionism.[71]

As a symbol, he was invaluable; as a person, less so. The real Sumner spent most of the next four years watching the rise of the Republicans from a distance while he recovered from the attack. He traveled across Europe without complaint but crumbled when he was dragged back to Washington, where he moved unsteadily, suffered from debilitating headaches, and waged a losing battle against insomnia. On those sleepless nights he wondered if he would be "doomed . . . to spend my time on earth in a living sepulcher."[72] An experimental treatment of "moxibustion"—burning his skin with a combination of fungus and wool—left him in agonizing pain. There was no medical reason for why this approach should have alleviated his symptoms, but Sumner seems to have treated the torture as a psychological permission slip that allowed him to return to the Senate. As he recovered from the flames, he vowed, "I will repay to slavery and the whole crew of its supporters every wound, burn . . . ache, pain, trouble, grief which I have suffered."[73]

Although Sumner would have preferred that Republicans pick a more radical standard-bearer than Lincoln, he had no doubt the election would be theirs in 1860.[74] The campaign played out like a fun-house version of the Harrison–Van Buren race of 1840. "In '40, all was jubilant," an Indiana congressman explained. "Now there is little effervescence— but a *solemn earnestness* that is almost painful."[75] Where 1840 confirmed the emergence of a two-party system that bound the union together, 1860 broke it all apart.

Whigs who were unable to accept Abraham Lincoln rallied behind the Constitutional Union Party. Also known as "the Old Gentlemen's Party," they implored Americans to restore sectional harmony by recognizing "no political principle other than THE CONSTITUTION OF THE COUNTRY, THE UNION OF THE STATES, AND THE

ENFORCEMENT OF THE LAWS."[76] But they were no match for the party of freedom.

Lincoln racked up a landslide Electoral College victory despite receiving just 39.9 percent of the overall popular vote.[77] (He was not even on the ballot in many Southern states.) The geographical distribution was so lopsided that Lincoln would have won the Electoral College even if his opponents had pooled all their votes in a single candidate. Overall, Republicans did best with middle-class voters in the country and in small towns. Although much of Lincoln's support came from onetime Whigs, he also drew new or infrequent voters to the polls and picked up a respectable number of former Democrats. And thanks to soaring participation rates—81.2 percent of the electorate cast a ballot, the second-highest turnout in American history—he won more votes than any earlier presidential candidate.[78]

As the secession campaign gathered momentum in the wake of Lincoln's victory, Sumner looked on the Southern ruling class with disbelief and grudging admiration. He thought disunion was "absurd on the face."[79] Slavery was too weak, freedom too strong, and the tide of history too overwhelming. But the planter class's determination offered ironic proof of his analysis: the mighty slave power could not survive without the government's support.

"Much as I desire the extinction of slavery, I do not wish to see it go down in blood," he wrote in December 1860. "And yet the existing hallucination of the slave-masters is such that I doubt if this calamity can be avoided. They seem to rush upon their destiny."[80]

Sumner was rushing alongside them.[81]

———————

Abraham Lincoln was a puzzle for Sumner. The two were a study in contrasts: the Yankee moralist who quoted Juvenal in the original Latin versus the Illinois politico who rose from a log cabin to the White House. Personality differences aside, the two were bound to clash over policy. Though Sumner considered Lincoln an "honest Anti-Slavery man," by October 1861 he was already complaining in private that Lincoln wasn't moving against slavery quickly enough.[82] In 1862 he told the British reformer John Bright that a true statesman would have already broken the Confederacy.[83] In the fall of 1864, with Lincoln's reelection just a few weeks away, Sumner glumly concluded that "he has no instinct or inspiration."[84]

Despite Sumner's frustrations, the two forged an effective partnership—and, ultimately, a real friendship. Though they differed on timing and tactics, both wanted to move in the same direction. During an early conversation about emancipation, the president told him, "The only difference between you and me on this subject is a difference of a month or six weeks in time."[85] Like Sumner, Lincoln revered the Declaration of Independence, called slavery a moral atrocity, and believed that the institution could be put on the road to extinction by constitutional means. There were practical benefits for each side, too. Sumner's backing gave Lincoln credibility with Radical Republicans, while loyalty to the president demonstrated that Sumner was a loyal party man.

The turning point in their relationship came in September 1862, as Sumner was struggling through a difficult reelection campaign. A coalition of Massachusetts Democrats, former Whigs, and conservative Republicans had formed a "People's Party" that called for a single-minded focus on restoring the union. Insisting that they were the true Lincoln loyalists—the president had won 62.9 percent of the vote in Massachusetts in 1860—the party claimed that Sumner's fixation on abolition was prolonging the war. Then Lincoln changed everything by issuing the Preliminary Emancipation Proclamation. Announcing that he accepted the president's decision "without note or comment," Sumner depicted himself as marching in lockstep with an administration that recognized that the South would be defeated only when slavery was destroyed.[86] He won easily.

As the war ground on, more people were coming to agree with Sumner. In 1862, when Sumner referred to slave owners as "slaughterer[s] of human hopes," the Ohio Republican John Sherman responded that it was not "proper or courteous to use such language . . . when Senators on this floor are with us, associating with us, who are included by the appellation 'slaveholder.'"[87] Two years later, Sherman's brother, the Union general William Tecumseh Sherman, set out to "make Georgia howl" during his march to the sea.[88]

In another sign of the changing times, the Republican Party temporarily dissolved for the 1864 campaign. Rechristening itself as the National Union Party, the former Republicans held their nominating convention in Baltimore.[89] The choice of a Southern state was no accident, nor was the selection of Tennessee's Andrew Johnson as Lincoln's new running mate. A former Democrat, Johnson was the only senator to remain in office after his state—Tennessee—seceded. The new party's rhetoric echoed the language of the failed Constitutional Union Party of 1860, with one crucial difference. Where the Constitutional Unionists had pledged to drive abolitionism out of public debate, the National Union platform called for a constitutional amendment guaranteeing slavery's "utter and complete extirpation from the soil of the republic."[90]

Democrats countered appeals for unity with a strategy that mixed calls for peace with blatant pandering to white racism, running perhaps the most crudely bigoted campaign in American history. They dwelled on the dangers of "miscegenation," a term coined by two writers at the Democratic *New York World* to describe (and condemn) "the blending of the races."[91] Lincoln, predictably, came in for heavy abuse. Anonymous pamphleteers exposed the secrets of "Abraham Africanus I" and uncovered a secret "Lincoln Catechism" whose ten commandments began "Thou shalt have no other God but the negro."[92]

The result was a resounding triumph for Abraham Africanus. Buoyed by progress on the battlefield, Lincoln improved on his 1860 performance across the North and West. Speaking to a jubilant audience outside the White House, he described the election as a victory for democracy. "It has demonstrated," he said, "that a people's government can sustain a national election, in the midst of a great civil war."[93]

Lincoln was being typically modest. Sumner was just as typically

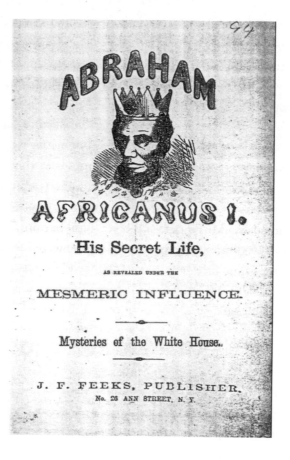

exultant. At a celebration in Boston he told the roaring crowd, "Thus do I hold up the head of the Democratic party and say, 'This is the head of a traitor!' Let it be buried out of sight, and let the people dance at its funeral."[94]

Before the votes were counted, Sumner was bracing himself for the next phase of the battle. With Union troops on the advance, victory looked certain. Now they had to win the peace. "Too much blood and treasure have been spent to allow these states to come back again until they are really changed," he wrote. "The whole social and political system must be remodeled."[95]

Sumner took the lead in outlining a Radical program for Reconstruction. He argued that seceded states had regressed to the condition of territories, allowing the federal government to set the terms of their readmission to statehood. Three principles guided his approach: former slaves must be made full members of the polity; the remnants of the slave power must be stamped out forever; and the egalitarian principles of the Declaration of Independence must be cemented in the Constitution. White people and Black people would discover their common interests, and so would the rich and the poor—but only after Reconstruction destroyed the slave oligarchy and empowered freedmen.

Reactions to Sumner's proposals split along predictable lines. The Democratic-leaning *New York Herald* said it was the first step on the road to racial Armageddon: "Alternate anarchy and despotism would characterize the history of the country, and wars of race and mutual extermination would go forward till the whites were well thinned and the blacks utterly destroyed."[96]

Moderate Republicans sprinted away from Sumner as Radicals cheered. "The friends of Freedom all over the country have looked to you, and confided in you, of all men in the United States Senate," wrote Frederick Douglass. "God grant you strength equal to your day and your duties! is my prayer and that of millions."[97]

The president saw matters differently. Where Sumner believed that African Americans were the South's only true unionists, Lincoln thought that most white people would act reasonably after the shooting stopped. As the war drew to a close, Sumner worried about what the president would do next. "The more I have seen of the Presdt. the more his character in certain respects has risen, and we must all admit that he has said some things better than any body else could have said them," he wrote in April 1865. "But I fear his policy now."[98]

Two days later, Sumner was having drinks with two other Republican senators when a servant ran into the room, shouting, "Mr. Lincoln is assassinated in the theatre!" All three hurried to the White House, where they delivered the news to Lincoln's oldest child, Robert. With Robert in tow, they went to the president's deathbed. Sumner stayed at Lincoln's side for the next eight hours, holding his hand, crying intermittently, and watching him breathe. Around seven, when the end was near, Robert broke down. Weeping, he rested his head on Sumner.[99]

At a memorial for the slain president, Sumner depicted John Wilkes Booth as the agent of an even more malevolent force. "It is Slavery that has taken the life of our beloved Chief Magistrate," he said. "On Slavery let vengeance fall."[100] The president's murder was a tragedy, and Sumner's grief was real—but he couldn't help seeing its advantages. Privately, he predicted that Lincoln's "death will do more for the cause than any human life."[101]

———————

Sumner had great hopes for Andrew Johnson. Squint a little, and he looked like the Great Emancipator. Both were born in the South—Lincoln in Kentucky, Johnson in North Carolina—to families that, as Lincoln's friend and biographer William Herndon put it, could be "significantly comprehended by the term, 'the poor whites.'"[102] Lincoln had less than a year of formal education. Johnson had none and learned to read only as an adult. They were both talented politicians who had shaky records in the battle for equal rights before ascending to the White House. Sumner thought Johnson would grow into the office, just as Lincoln had before him. He called the new president a "sincere friend of the negro" and assured the abolitionist Wendell Phillips that "there is no difference between us."[103] Familiar with Johnson's hatred of the plantation elite, Sumner looked forward to watching the new president demolish the last vestiges of the slave power.

The people who knew Johnson best would have told Sumner not to be so optimistic. Loathing the Southern elite had not made Johnson into a defender of racial equality. He was an old-line Jacksonian and a vicious racist who believed that slavers and the enslaved had formed an alliance against the common white man. "Damn the negroes," he told a friend during the war. "I am fighting these traitorous aristocrats, their masters."[104]

Dreaming of realignment, Johnson intended to put himself at the head of a majority coalition that triangulated between extremists in the North and South.[105] In Sumner's vision, Radicals remained the base of the Republican Party; in Johnson's, they were just as much of a threat as die-hard ex-Confederates.

Sumner was quickly disillusioned. "The Presdt. is a person without statesmanship and with very little real humanity," he wrote in November 1865. "What could you expect from an old slave master and an old democrat?"[106] Lapsing into a familiar snobbery, he lamented that Johnson had "all the narrowness and ignorance of a certain class of whites, who have always looked upon the colored race as out of the pale of Humanity."[107] Because of ignorance and bigotry, Sumner warned, Johnson would return the planter class to power.

Most Republicans fell somewhere between the two. They agreed that the government had an obligation to defend freedmen's civil rights, but they stopped well short of endorsing universal male suffrage. Rather than embark upon a sweeping project of social transformation, a majority would have been satisfied with swift restoration of the union, safety for freedmen, mercy for the typical white Southerner, and a touch of discipline for the rebellion's former leaders.[108]

But none of the relevant parties in the South were willing to accept the deal. African Americans insisted that Reconstruction would be a sham without civil rights and the vote, driving home the point with countless petitions, parades, and mass meetings. All-white Southern governments put in place by Johnson responded with a wave of "Black Codes" that attempted to restore slavery in all but name. At the same time, white backlash produced an unplanned but systematic campaign of racial terrorism. "The number of murders and assaults perpetrated upon negroes is very great," reported Carl Schurz, a close friend of Sumner's, after a tour of the South. "Although the freedman is no longer considered the property of the individual master, he is considered the slave of society."[109] While African Americans battled for survival, Johnson urged Republicans to accept that "white men alone must manage the South."[110] And if the existing Southern electorate got its way, those white men would include many former leaders of the Confederacy—including Alexander Stephens, whom the Georgia state legislature elected to the Senate in 1866.[111]

With the middle ground collapsing under their feet, moderate Republicans were forced toward the Radicals. Sumner and his allies never commanded a majority, not even within the party, but they alone had a plan for what to do when compromise failed. In the 1850s, Southern intransigence fueled the rise of the Republican Party. After Lincoln's election, it drove the nation to war. Now it was pushing the center ever closer to Sumner.

Over the president's opposition, congressional Republicans embarked on what Schurz called a "second founding."[112] A vastly empowered federal government undertook a campaign to guarantee equality under the law regardless of race. Legislative decrees were given life on the ground by African Americans rushing to the polls. In the fall of 1867, Black turnout ranged from a low of around 70 percent in Georgia to a high of almost 90 percent in Virginia.[113] Over the next ten years, Black votes helped put thousands of African Americans into office, including sixteen congressmen and more than six hundred state legislators.[114] "To-day we make the Declaration a reality," Sumner announced when Hiram Revels, the first Black senator, was sworn into office in February 1870. "For a long time a word only, it now becomes a deed."[115]

Sumner looked on with the satisfaction—but he couldn't do much more than look. The final wording of the legislation was always drafted by others, and he never thought it went far enough. As important as civil rights and voting rights were, he believed they would be a "barren scepter" unless former slaves had access to integrated schools and their own piece of land.[116]

There were still lines not even Sumner would cross. Earlier in the century, eliminating economic restrictions on voting had encouraged states to erect new barriers along the lines of race. Now, with racial limitations falling, sex became an object of debate. When Sumner inveighed against discriminating on the basis of race, the Maine Republican William Pitt Fessenden observed that his argument "would just as well apply to women as to men; but I noticed that the honorable Senator dodged that part of the proposition very carefully."[117] Responding with the kind of pragmatic reasoning that he elsewhere disdained, Sumner called women's suffrage "the great question of the future" but said that racial equality was too important to be "clogged, burdened, or embarrassed by anything else."[118]

Time and again, Sumner was forced back to the same question: How far did Reconstruction have to go? Before the war, he insisted that slavery was a singular evil preventing Americans from reaching their glorious destiny. But emancipation had come, and glory was still out of reach—even in the North, where *The New York Times* announced the emergence of "a system of slavery as absolute if not as degrading as that which lately prevailed at the South . . . [where] manufacturing capitalists threaten to become the masters, and it is the white laborers who are to be slaves."[119]

While the South ended the war poorer and more economically equal, the North was becoming richer and more stratified.[120] Republicans had pushed through a raft of far-reaching economic reforms that set the stage for a historic expansion after the war: protective tariffs, public universities, a national income tax and currency, a transcontinental railroad, free territory for settlers in the West, and more.[121] But industrialists and financiers ruled the new economic order, not farmers and shopkeepers, and by 1870 two-thirds of the labor force worked for wages.[122] The stirrings of an organized labor movement scrambled familiar coalitions, putting some Radicals on the side of Northern Democrats representing working-class districts and leaving others muttering about the shortcomings of universal suffrage.

Sumner was torn. Despite his jabs at the money power, he was inclined toward economic orthodoxy. A disciple of Adam Smith, he said that *The Wealth of Nations* had "contributed more towards the happiness of man than has been effected by the united abilities of all the

statesmen and legislators of whom history has preserved an authentic
account."[123] He had a moral aversion to inflation, loathed high taxes,
denounced paper currency, flip-flopped on the eight-hour day, and declared that contracts must be honored "until the laws of the universe
tumble into chaos."[124] Though he eventually grew more supportive of
labor's agenda, he was unfriendly enough in the early postwar years for
one movement leader to decide that workers could "hope of no sympathy from the class of which Mr. Sumner is a representative."[125]

But when it came to slavery, the usual rules didn't apply. Property
rights were sacred, except for the right to property in man. If Sumner
had his way, plantations would have been divided up and distributed to
loyal African Americans. When asked why loyal white men didn't deserve similar help from the government, he replied, "White men have
never been in slavery."[126]

Behind this tension over the government's role lay a more troubling
set of questions. If free and slave states belonged to fundamentally distinct civilizations, why had the lords of the loom and the lords of the
lash formed such a cozy alliance? If the slave power had forced itself on
an unwilling population, why had it been such a formidable opponent
during the Civil War? And why did so many white Southerners now
have to be compelled at the barrel of a gun into accepting civil rights?

Rather than dwelling on ambiguities in his own politics, Sumner
threw himself into the campaign to impeach Andrew Johnson. The chief
accusation was that Johnson had acted improperly in firing the secretary
of war, Edwin Stanton. But Sumner dismissed the formal charge as a
secondary element in the case against a "foul-mouthed menace" and
"impersonation of the tyrannical Slave Power."[127] ("If I have played the
Judas, who has been my Christ that I have played the Judas with?" asked
Johnson. "Was it Charles Sumner?")[128]

Sumner was shocked when seven Republicans defected during
Johnson's trial, saving the president by one vote. But a weakened Johnson, with only ten months left in his term, no longer posed a threat.
Attention turned to Ulysses Grant, the man Republicans hoped would
take Johnson's place in the White House. Grant was a national hero,

the unanimous choice of the Republican Convention, and—though neither man knew it yet—Sumner's most fearsome enemy.

It was as if they had been engineered to despise each other. Grant would always be a soldier in Sumner's eyes, not a statesman. "Put him on a horse and he'll blunder along somehow on the field. There's where his vocation ends," Sumner sniffed. "He is not a man capable of understanding principles," and therefore not a man capable of understanding politics.[129]

Grant was, however, capable of understanding condescension when he saw it. "Dogmatic, opinionated, infallible in his own estimation," he later said of Sumner. "He believed his own illusion without regard to the facts. It really amounted to a mental delusion."[130] Though Grant put on a pleasant face in private, he vented his frustration when Sumner was out of sight, shaking his fist as he passed the senator's house and fuming, "That man who lives up there has abused me in a way which I never suffered from any other man living."[131]

"Sumner did injustice to Grant; Grant did injustice to Sumner," observed the Massachusetts senator George Hoar. "The judgment of each was warped and clouded, until each looked with a blood-shotten eye at the conduct of the other."[132]

But they were the two most prominent Republicans in the country, and they had a common enemy. Racial terrorism was resurgent in the South, spearheaded by the newly formed Ku Klux Klan. "Colored men have been shot by scores for simply voting the republican ticket, heads have been smashed, throats cut, limbs broken," one of Sumner's Black correspondents told him in 1870. "United States Marshals have been chased by mobs and hunted like foxes, election managers arrested, and the ballot boxes taken possession of by the democrats, and mad rabble." With Sumner's ardent support, Grant deployed federal troops to break the Klan—and defend his voters.

Although Republicans were not yet willing to look the other way as slavery was reimposed by another name, an increasing number was searching for a way out of Reconstruction. Even after racial barriers to suffrage were abolished, most Southern states were majority white, and their votes became more attractive as frustration with Reconstruction mounted. Among younger Republicans, a group of so-called Stalwarts laid the groundwork for a return to normal politics, where party organization trumped ideological purity.[133] The Stalwarts were led by the New York senator Roscoe Conkling. A favorite of Grant's—the president called him "the greatest mind . . . that has been in public life since the beginning of the government"—Conkling was a kind of bizarro Sumner, with all of the Massachusetts senator's intellectual talent and none of his disdain for partisan hackery.[134]

As Sumner was losing ground in Congress, he fell into a vicious struggle with the White House. It began in 1870, when Sumner, chair of the influential Senate Foreign Relations Committee, came out against an administration bid to annex Santo Domingo (later called the Dominican Republic).[135] Sumner feared that the move was a step toward establishing an American empire in the Caribbean, and he successfully maneuvered to kill the initiative. Grant's allies in Congress retaliated by stripping Sumner of his chairmanship on the committee.

The relationship deteriorated from there. The White House's coziness with the Stalwarts, and early rumblings about corruption scandals that later consumed the administration, sealed Sumner's break with the president. He denounced Grant as corrupt, lazy, and nepotistic. "His rule for the second term would be the imperialism of selfishness and vindictiveness,—without moral sense, without ideas, without knowledge," he predicted in August 1871. "He is the lowest President, whether intellectually or morally, we have ever had."[136]

Convinced that Grant could not win reelection, Sumner mounted the case against him in another showstopping Senate oration, delivered in May 1872. His discontent had matured into a comprehensive indictment of what he called "Grantism," a cult of personality that covered up an orgy of corruption. "Utterly unrepublican Caesarism has mastered the Republican Party," he declared, turning the party into "the instrument of *one man and his personal will*."[137] "I stood by its cradle," he said of his party. "Let me not follow its hearse."[138] While Sumner thundered, Conkling took his seat in the chamber, picked up a newspaper, and ripped it into tiny pieces.

Sumner insisted that history was on his side. A lifetime in politics had taught him that ideals won out in the end. Progress was inevitable, and nobody—not even a Republican president—would stand in its way.

The public certitude masked a dark, depressive streak that Sumner had been battling for years. "After constant work, it seems as I can accomplish nothing," he wrote in 1864. "Life is weary and dark—full of pain and enmity. I am ready to go at once."[139] Still alive almost a decade later, he turned more often to his legacy, devoting his spare hours to editing a multivolume edition of his collected works. "If this were done, I should be ready to go," he told a friend. "These speeches are my life . . . especially as I have nothing else."[140]

Nothing except the cause, that is. However lonely he felt in private, Sumner assured his followers that he would defend human rights until he drew his last breath. Just as in his youth, the two parties were in crisis. And though it pained him to think of Republicans going the way of the Whigs, a new movement was emerging that just might revive the party of freedom.

"Many persons who have been Radicals all their lives are in doubt whether to be Radical any longer," explained E. L. Godkin, a onetime abolitionist and founding editor of *The Nation*, "but at the same time have such a traditional horror of standing still, that they shudder at the thought of bringing on themselves the name of 'Conservatives.'"[141] So they settled on a new name for the new era: liberals.

Liberal ranks were heavily populated with such veterans of antislavery politics as Godkin. They relished the demise of the slave power but recoiled at what came next. Instead of purified politics, corruption was rampant. Instead of social harmony, class conflict was surging. Instead of national unity, there was the unending battle over Reconstruction.[142] Liberals were especially popular with members of a self-conscious intelligentsia who disdained the machine politics of Roscoe Conkling's Stalwarts while agreeing on the need to move on from the war. New issues beckoned, above all the challenge of cultivating a political elite that could transcend the struggle between, in the words of one reformer, "an ignorant proletariat and a half-taught plutocracy."[143]

Neither proles nor plutocrats, the liberals came out of the country's educated, Protestant elite. They were students of the social sciences who fancied themselves honest mediators in the clash between labor and capital. Both their elder statesmen and their youthful insurgents wanted government by figures of intelligence and culture—that is, people like them—and they were willing to overturn the political system to get it.

In 1872 the reformers launched a political party with precisely this goal in mind—the Liberal Republicans. Step one in restoring principles to politics was evicting Grant from the White House. In May, they chose the *New-York Tribune* editor Horace Greeley as their presidential candidate, and in July the Democrats seconded the nomination, presenting voters with a fusion ticket that promised to restore sectional harmony and put an end to machine corruption. According to the *Chicago Tribune*, they aimed to "dissolve existing parties and enable the best men of both old parties to unite as a new political organization."[144]

Sumner looked like a natural recruit for the movement. Economic questions were not as significant for him as for most liberals, but he had inveighed passionately against loose money and high taxes, giving Boston's well-to-do a newfound appreciation for this onetime scourge of the money power.[145]

Removing slavery from the agenda made it easier for others to see Sumner as the reasonable man he always considered himself to be. Political independence, devotion to reason, faith in progress, hope for purity in government, and disdain for vulgar moneygrubbing had all been hallmarks of Sumner's career. He was an early advocate of civil service reform, arguing that if the government was going to take on new powers, it should be overseen by professionals with an eye on the bottom line. His closest friend in the Senate—Missouri's Carl Schurz—was one of the most prominent Liberal Republicans. And, like the other liberals, Sumner hated Grant. "*You* ought to be the great leader of this movement," Schurz told him. "It is the only manner in which the equal rights of all can be permanently secured in the South."[146]

But that was the catch. By 1872, Liberal Republicans were ready to turn the page on Reconstruction. Whatever Sumner's objections to Grant, he recognized that the president had acted decisively against the KKK. Liberals, on the other hand, hoped that a chastened planter class would resume its rightful leadership of the South. To African Americans, the crusade against corruption looked like a thinly veiled attack on Black participation in politics, and paeans to laissez-faire sounded like refusals to grapple with the legacy of slavery.

Liberals wanted to proclaim Reconstruction finished in 1870, after the passage of the Fifteenth Amendment, which prohibited states from denying the vote because of "race, color, or previous condition of servitude."[147] Sumner was still convinced that suffrage was useless without broader protections for African Americans. He led the charge for a civil rights bill that he considered the "crowning work" of his career. "I know nothing further to be done in the way of legislation for the security of equal rights in this Republic," he said of the bill, which would have abolished segregation in schools, juries, theaters, and even churches.[148]

No other white politician of similar prominence had ever laid out such a sweeping program. (And when Hiram Revels stepped down in March 1871—he had been elected only to fill out the remainder of a term—the Senate was once again all white.) Sumner worked tirelessly on behalf of the bill, speaking time and again in its favor from the Senate floor, a massive bouquet of flowers supplied by African American supporters resting prominently on his desk.

The bill was a test for the Liberals, and they failed it spectacularly.

Calling the measure a misguided attempt to promote social equality, they lined up in opposition. Sumner's doubts were further heightened by the nomination of Greeley, whom he considered woefully unprepared for the presidency. The Liberal rapprochement with the Democracy was another warning sign for Sumner, who had spent years lecturing fellow Republicans about the danger of fraternizing with the party of treason.

Months passed as Sumner agonized. He saw himself as a voice for African Americans, and his Black supporters were urging him to stand by the president. "The Democrats here hate us as bad as ever," a Black correspondent informed him. "It is only through the Great Republican party that we are safe."[149] "I can do nothing by which the cause of the colored people is in any way weakened or compromised," Sumner promised.[150]

Sumner announced his decision in an open letter to the nation's "colored citizens": he was supporting Greeley, and they should too.[151]

The need to justify breaking with the Republican Party spurred him to extraordinary heights of self-justification—and delusion. He called the Democratic nomination of Greeley "a peace-offering . . . of infinite value."[152] With slavery abolished, he argued that white Southerners were sincerely interested in racial reconciliation. He promised that Greeley's defense of civil rights would be just as vigorous as Grant's, minus the corruption. "Revolutions do not go backward," he declared.[153] "Slavery will never be revived, nor will you be restrained or limited in any of these rights you now enjoy." Remarkably, he asserted, "Reconstruction is now complete."[154]

The reaction was immediate, and ferocious. Denunciations from Republicans were as scathing as they were predictable. In Boston, a Republican audience hissed when a speaker mentioned Sumner's name. The Massachusetts legislature contrived a reason to censure him.[155] Letters from outraged Black supporters flooded into Sumner's office. "The alliance you have made with the haters and persecutors of our race," one New Yorker told him, "has struck the colored population of this city with astonishment."[156]

"He stands on a bridge," his friend the political scientist Francis Lieber observed, "and has set fire to both ends."[157]

The rest of the campaign went about as badly as it could have for Sumner. Republicans picked off the most popular pieces of Greeley's platform, and they spread their message with a disciplined political machine the Liberals couldn't hope to match. Grant won in a rout, confirming the return of organizational politics. To politicians with an eye on the future, there was just one lesson in the Liberal fiasco: the time of great reforms and holy wars, of Horace Greeleys and Charles Sumners, had come to an end.

Defeat looked good on Sumner. It was easy to admire his stubborn adherence to principles when those principles stood no chance of being translated into law. Though many questioned his judgment, nobody doubted his integrity. As scandals piled up during Grant's second term, he came to stand for a lost ideal of statesmanship. No longer a threat, Sumner dwindled into respectability.

He welcomed the reprieve from political skirmishing. Poor health kept him away from the Senate most days. Recurring bouts of chest pain could be relieved only with morphine, and prostate troubles woke him to urinate upward of thirty times a night. He concentrated his diminishing energies on assembling his collected works and mounting one last attempt to revive his civil rights bill. Grant's victory broke the temporary bout of political insanity that gripped him in 1872. The work of Reconstruction, Sumner once again believed, was far from over. "Much has been done," he said, "but more remains to be done."[158]

But not by him. After a prolonged decline, death came quickly. Working at the Senate in March 1874, he complained about "a toothache in my heart."[159] He collapsed at home later that night. Word spread among his friends that time was running out. To visitors coming to pay their last respects, he repeated one message: "Don't let the bill fail."[160]

After receding in life, Sumner became a national icon in death, provoking the greatest outpouring of public grief since the Lincoln assassination. His body lay in state at the Capitol—he was the fourth person to receive that honor—before a funeral train escorted him back to Massachusetts, where the task of eulogizing Sumner fell to Carl Schurz. He described Sumner as a hero who defied polite society without pandering to the multitude, a partisan who never sacrificed his principles. Schurz's Sumner was, above all, a liberal—tormentor of the slave power, father of civil service reform, and champion of "a government composed of the best and wisest of the land."[161]

A more surprising tribute came from Lucius Lamar, a Mississippi Democrat who had been elected to Congress in 1872 after serving as the Confederacy's minister to Russia. "Impossible as it would have been ten years ago to make it," Lamar told the House, "it is not the less true that to-day Mississippi regrets the death of CHARLES SUMNER."[162]

Lamar understood, as he observed in private, that his people wouldn't regain "control of their own affairs" until the Yankees were satisfied "that the results of the war were fixed beyond the power of reaction."[163] Enlisting Sumner in the campaign for reunion, Lamar commemorated a nationalist who "believed that all occasion for strife and distrust between the North and South had passed away, and that there no longer remained any cause for continued estrangement between these two sections of our common country."[164] The speech was a watershed in the reconciliation between North and South, as white people in both regions moved beyond the Civil War by repressing the memory of what they had fought over.

African Americans mourned Sumner too, and more honestly. In Boston, Frederick Douglass led a procession of some two thousand "colored citizens" commemorating Sumner. An honor guard of Black soldiers flanked the casket, and a bouquet in the shape of a heart bore the inscription "Charles Sumner, you gave us your life, we give you our [heart]." Next to a marble bust of Sumner, the words "equal Rights to all" were written in violets.[165]

THE LATE SENATOR SUMNER.—CEREMONIES IN THE CAPITOL—COLORED PEOPLE OF WASHINGTON, HEADED BY FREDERICK DOUGLASS, VIEWING THE REMAINS.—SKETCHED BY JOSEPH BECKER.—SEE PAGE XI.

But the cause of equal rights was looking shakier than at any time since the Civil War. In an 1875 speech that might have been composed on Sumner's old desk—the senator bequeathed it to him—Douglass posed a question that would determine both his old friend's legacy and the future of American politics: "If war among the whites brought peace and liberty to blacks, what will peace among the whites bring?"[166]

———

The answer was not long in coming. Congress passed a watered-down version of Sumner's civil rights bill, but it was gutted by a Supreme Court composed entirely of Republican appointees. Assisted by another wave of racial terrorism, Democratic "Redeemers"—including Andrew Johnson, who returned to the Senate in 1875—brought Reconstruction to a close. The Republican Party made its peace with the restoration of white supremacy, spurred along by former Liberal Republicans, who had been welcomed back into the party fold. And so the promise of Reconstruction gave way to Jim Crow and the Gilded Age.

What happened to Sumner's party of freedom? From one perspective, Republicans had accomplished more than he could have hoped for when he arrived in Washington in 1851. The party had broken the slave power and passed—with enthusiastic support from the North and co-erced acquiescence from the South—three constitutional amendments and a raft of civil rights legislation that gave the national government authority to institute civil and political equality, by force if necessary.

Aside from abolition itself, however, all those victories were rolled back with the collapse of Reconstruction. The biggest winner in the Republican war against the slave power was, arguably, the same as in the Jacksonian war against the money power: Northern capitalists. A generation earlier, sacrificing the Bank of the United States had given industrialists and financiers democratic legitimacy while keeping the basic structure of the economy intact. Now they had removed their chief rival for national power—the Southern planter class—and were reaping the lion's share of the benefits from the economic boom that followed the Civil War.[167]

During Reconstruction, Black cries for land reform went unheard, but vast swaths of public land were handed over to railroad companies. Republican capitalists had their crowning achievement in 1886. Three years after eviscerating Sumner's civil rights bill, the Supreme Court extended the Fourteenth Amendment's protection of the right to due process to corporations. The inspiration for the argument came from an eminent source: Roscoe Conkling, retired from politics and enjoy-ing a lucrative legal career, who assured the justices that Republicans had been just as concerned with corporations as they were with former slaves.[168]

Sumner had been right to worry that Reconstruction hadn't gone far enough, but the very coherence of his worldview blinded him to facts that didn't fit with his vision. The slave power was supposed to be tossed aside by history, not ground to death in a brutal war. Non-slaveholding white people were supposed to abandon the planter class. Resistance to integration was supposed to fade away after a few months. The right to vote was supposed to be irrevocable. Progress was supposed to be inevitable. Revolutions weren't supposed to go backward.

With distance, the forces undermining Reconstruction are easy to see: a national government constrained by the prerogatives of the states and ill-equipped to oversee a social revolution; a rapidly developing capitalist elite preoccupied with staving off challenges from its own restive workforce; racism's persistent hold on white voters across the country; and ambiguities in a Republican worldview caught between a radical commitment to erasing slavery's legacy and the humbler ambitions of free labor ideology.[169] They were the Reconstruction-era versions of perennial liberal dilemmas: the tensions between capitalism and democracy, the dream of a rational state and the reality of flawed bureaucracies, the clash between minority rights and majority rule, and the temptation to confuse the march of history with one's own dreams for the future.

Then there was Sumner. He rose to office by telling a story about a great country, founded on immortal principles, led astray by a nefarious slave power. The force of truth, the majesty of American democracy, the irresistible pull toward humanity's glorious destiny—all of it was supposed to inaugurate an age of "Hope, Progress, Justice, Humanity," in all their capitalized glory.[170]

It was a beautiful story. If only it were true.

4

Organizers

"Are we a plutocracy?"[1]

It was a disturbing question for Americans in the Gilded Age, and a new one. They hadn't talked much about plutocracy before the Civil War. By the 1890s, the term was everywhere—in novels like *Plutocracy, Or, American White Slavery* and in plays like *The Plutocrat: A Drama in Five Acts*.[2] Today, a search through the American English corpus in the Google Books archives confirms what Americans at the time already knew: by the end of the nineteenth century, "plutocracy" had arrived—at least in name, and perhaps in reality.

Plutocracy in America, 1850–1900[3]

The explosion of talk around plutocracy was the consequence of an economic revolution. After decades of breakneck development, the United States had become an industrial powerhouse that produced more manufactured goods than France, Britain, and Germany combined. Such goliath corporations as John D. Rockefeller's Standard Oil Company replaced the small family firm as the driving force in the nation's economic life. Mass production, mass consumption, mass culture—in short, mass society—were all coming into existence. It was an extraordinary set of changes, arguably the most important in the history of capitalism.[4]

It also laid the basis for an American oligarchy. Between 1870 and 1910, the wealthiest 1 percent's share of the national income almost doubled.[5] The country had more than four thousand millionaires, but real wages were falling, and per capita GDP was about the same as that of modern-day Egypt.[6] As economic growth rates were rising, Americans were literally shrinking: by 1880 the average man was shorter in height than at any time in the country's history. Americans were dying earlier, too—about five years earlier in 1900 than in 1800.[7] Factories turned into armed camps, and state militias were routinely called upon to break up labor disputes—twenty-three times in 1892 alone.[8] In streets and docks, mines and rail yards, it was a time of violent uprisings and brutal crackdowns. "Economically, we are all at war with one another," observed the novelist William Dean Howells in 1894. "We have ceased to be a democracy and have become a plutocracy."[9]

But if the United States had become a plutocracy, it had a funny way of showing it. Almost 80 percent of eligible voters regularly turned out at the polls.[10] At the state and local levels, hundreds of third parties sprang up to challenge the two-party duopoly. Just outside the realm of formal politics, a new crop of voluntary associations—the Grange for farmers, the Knights of Labor for workers, the Woman's Christian Temperance Union for prohibitionists—brought more than a million Americans together under the banner of reform.[11] It was a golden age for utopian thinking, where Edward Bellamy's *Looking Backward*— a Rip Van Winkle for the industrial era, following a narrator who wakes in the year 2000 to discover that rapacious capitalism has given way to collective ownership and perpetual abundance—sold more copies in its early years than any other American novel since *Uncle Tom's Cabin*.[12]

And yet none of this grassroots energy—not the local political revolts, not the visionary schemes—could break into national politics.[13] Even as third parties proliferated in the states, Republicans and Democrats maintained a lock on federal office. At least 96 percent of voters chose one of the two parties in every national election between 1872 and 1888. In theory, Republicans were the party of centralized government and economic nationalism, while Democrats were the defenders of local authority. In practice, debates often focused on the distribution of spoils—which industries were protected by tariffs, which party machine handed out jobs.[14]

Without stark ideological distinctions between the parties, campaigns devolved into battles between competing partisan tribes divided along lines of race, ethnicity, faith, and region. Republicans won native-born Protestants and the South's dwindling number of African American voters, while Democrats relied on Catholics, immigrants, and the Solid South. The two coalitions were evenly matched, regularly trading Congress and the White House back and forth in elections decided by slender margins.[15]

Until, suddenly, a new majority broke the partisan stalemate. It began with the formation of the People's Party, better known today as the Populists.[16] Calling themselves a "union of the labor forces of the United States," Populists sought to unite "the plain people" in a single movement, a party to end all parties, that would rescue American democracy from machine bosses and industrial tyrants. It seemed as if Populists might get their shot in 1896, after William Jennings Bryan—not technically a Populist, but a Democrat who had run on fusion tickets with Populists—won the Democratic presidential nomination. Bryan's victory dealt a stinging rebuke to the Democratic establishment, upended Republican electoral calculations, and brought the American political system closer to a full-blown crisis of legitimacy than at any time since the Civil War. Decades of simmering local discontents finally gained national expression, demolishing the bipartisan alliance that protected capitalists during long years of painful economic transition and historic income inequality.

Then, almost as quickly as it appeared, the Populist revolt was crushed. A party realignment did take place in 1896 that produced a coalition with deep roots in the working class—but it was Republicans, not Bryan's Democrats, who spoke for the new majority. Rallying behind the titanic blandness of William McKinley, the Republican Party—which had by now acquired the nickname Grand Old Party (GOP)—shattered the Gilded Age partisan stalemate and broke the last major challenge to the emerging corporate order. It was an early demonstration of what became a global pattern in the twentieth century: a party of the right defying the hopes of radicals and the fears of reactionaries by reconciling industrial capitalism with representative government. Call it democratic conservatism.[17]

Backed up by a cross-class majority, the GOP became the dominant national party for a generation.[18] Where the first Republican coalition took shape around the politics of slavery, the second put capitalism front and center. The battered remnants of Charles Sumner's party of liberty gave way to the party of business. Free labor was out. Prosperity, jobs, and rising wages were in.

And that was just the beginning. Over the next three decades, Americans took decisive early steps in the making of the modern federal bureaucracy (also known, for the most part unlovingly, as the administrative state), the U.S. emerged as the world's most powerful nation, and the Nineteenth Amendment struck down barriers to voting based on gender. Each of these transformations—the making of a government leviathan, the rise of American empire, and the largest act of enfranchisement in U.S. history—seemed like it could spur a political revolution. Combined, they rivaled anything Bellamy could have conjured. Through it all, the Republican majority endured.

Which raises the question of where that majority came from. Despite the lasting consequences of the GOP's victory in 1896, historians have tended to focus more on why Populists lost than on how Republicans won. At the time, even McKinley's opponents treated him as a sideshow. He was a familiar type: a lawyer by training who used a successful legal practice as a springboard into elected office, serving as a congressman and governor before winning the White House. McKinley, in short, was boring.[19]

Mark Hanna was not. A millionaire Cleveland industrialist, Hanna ran McKinley's 1896 campaign and then won election to the Senate in his own right. In Washington, Hanna served as a kind of prime minister for the McKinley administration while retaining control of the national Republican machine.[20]

Before 1896, Hanna was almost unknown outside of Ohio. By Election Day, he was a national icon. "McKinley is of no present or future consequence," declared William Randolph Hearst's *New York Journal*, the only major northeastern newspaper to endorse Bryan. "Hanna is casting the shadow in this campaign. The candidate is swallowed by the manager."[21]

His enemies called him Dollar Mark, depicting Hanna as the puppet master yanking poor McKinley's strings on behalf of the nation's economic overlords. To Republicans, he stood for the changing relationship between economics and politics—"a statesman in all that the modern use of the word implies," as one admirer put it, who "recognized business as the genius of the age."[22]

As Martin Van Buren was to Jacksonian Democracy, and Sumner was to the early GOP, Hanna was to the ascendant Republican majority—symbol of the new era, standard-bearer for business in politics. He embodied the democratic conservatism that defined American politics from the twilight of the Gilded Age to the dawning of the New Deal. And wherever his name appeared, it seemed like one question was never far behind: *Are we a plutocracy?*

It depended on what you thought of Mark Hanna's Republican Party.

"Children have been brought to look upon him in the same class with the bogy man of the nursery," wrote the *Denver Times* in 1902.[23] A South Dakota newspaper called him "the being who believes that the man with some money should be able to purchase everything he wants from a president down to a common voter."[24] When Hanna traveled though Nebraska in 1900, a poster nailed to a telegraph pole warned:

POPULIST FARMERS BEWARE!!!
CHAIN YOUR CHILDREN TO YOURSELVES
OR
PUT THEM UNDER THE BED
MARK HANNA IS IN TOWN[25]

Cartoonists turned him into the incarnation of plutocracy, a bloated sack of flesh bursting out of a suit covered with dollar signs, porcine jowls sagging away from his face, labor's skull at his feet, underneath the lash of his whip.

Dollar Mark in repose.

Investigators who set out looking for the real Hanna were usually surprised by what they found. At five feet nine, he wasn't nearly as imposing as the caricatures suggested. The piggish features that made him a cartoonist's dream looked, in person, like they belonged on a small-town shopkeeper. Except for marathon bouts of whist—he would play until his wife passed out from exhaustion—Hanna was usually in motion, walking in swift, almost dainty steps. What people remembered most were his eyes, liquid and brown. "X-rays," a journalist observed, "are not more penetrating than Hanna's glance."[26]

When the first major biography of Hanna appeared, in 1912, readers had good reason to expect a takedown. The author, Herbert Croly, was a leading progressive intellectual, a reformer looking to move beyond the kind of politics Hanna symbolized.[27] (He was also the son of David Goodman Croly, coauthor of the pamphlet that coined the term "miscegenation.") But as Croly sifted through dozens of interviews with people in Hanna's orbit—friends, family, political allies, political opponents, business rivals, the manager of Hanna's favorite Washington hotel—he discovered that almost to a person, their stories contradicted the public image.* If Hanna was a plutocrat, then he was, as the journalist William Allen White put it, "the best of the plutocrats."[28]

To Hanna, money was a tool for solving problems. "Politics is a business," he said, "and very serious business at that."[29] There were speakers to be paid, campaign literature to be produced, indebted candidates to be silently paid off. That was how the game was played, and Hanna was never one to challenge the rules. "I always felt that he lacked ideals, politically," said James R. Garfield, son of president James A. Garfield. "He said you had to take human nature as it came."[30]

A native midwesterner and a college dropout, Hanna never developed the cultural pretensions that often come with money. Highbrow conversation was a chore, and he had no appetite for gourmet cuisine. He didn't swear, aside from the occasional "damn," and abstained from alcohol until after turning forty. "It didn't make any difference whether it was a conductor or a motorman or a horse car driver, it made no difference to him, he was just the same," one employee said.[31]

Hanna was a genius for the practical. As a young entrepreneur, it seemed that wherever he looked, there was money to be made—factories to build, trade routes to streamline, raw materials to pull out of the earth. M. A. Hanna Company extended its scope to cover each step in the production and distribution of coal and iron. The larger the company grew, the easier it was to keep growing. Hanna funneled his profits into new territory, buying up railways, a local newspaper, even an opera house. The business was complicated in its particulars but simple in principle: everything traced back to Hanna.

For a real glimpse of things to come, Hanna turned to John D. Rockefeller. They had attended high school together in Cleveland, where Hanna was an outgoing athlete and Rockefeller a pleasant but reserved wallflower.[32] With a mixture of admiration and condescension, Hanna described Rockefeller as "a kind of economic super-clerk,

---

* Except for some bitter comments from Hanna's brother-in-law. But you can't please everyone.

the personification of ledger-keeping."[33] By the early 1870s the super-clerk had taken over the local oil industry. Soon Rockefeller was the richest person in the United States, and the Standard Oil route to growth—eliminate the competition by buying them out—was being copied throughout industrial America.

Hanna's economic ambitions were never so grand. He was good at making money, and he enjoyed spending it, but business alone couldn't satisfy him. He had always been interested in politics. After making his fortune, that interest became an obsession.

A lifelong Republican, Hanna cast his first presidential vote for Abraham Lincoln and fought in the Civil War (briefly—he already had a business to run at home). He had no patience for idealists who dreamed of exploding the two-party system. He took the structure of American politics as a given, picked his team, and stuck with them. In 1880 he founded a "Business Man's Republican Campaign Club" in Cleveland and served as one of the chief fundraisers for James Garfield's successful presidential run, marking Hanna's debut as a (minor) national figure.[34] An early supporter and longtime friend of William McKinley's, he stepped naturally into the role of campaign manager for his 1896 presidential race.

By the time Hanna entered national politics, a revolt against democracy had been building for decades. Anarchists, paupers, Native Americans, Chinese immigrants, and even lumberjacks were all excluded from voting in some parts of the country. The campaign against the ballot went furthest in the South, where poll taxes, literacy tests, disenfranchisement for ex-felons, racially restricted primaries, and a host of other measures were used to curb voting. African Americans were the primary target of these reforms, but many poor white people found themselves locked out of the electoral process, and turnout rates among Mexican Americans also plummeted. Looking down jealously from their strongholds in New York and Boston, liberal reformers—now known as Mugwumps—dreamed of a government overseen by the enlightened few. Meanwhile, industrialists and financiers spoke ominously about an impending class war.[35]

Hanna saw matters differently. His brand of democratic conservatism held that Republicans could build a new majority by promising *more*— more production, more profits, more of everything for everyone. He was certain that if labor and capital kept their demands reasonable, there would be plenty to go around. Tired of refighting the Civil War, unmoved by nativist attacks on immigrants, and wary of stirring up anti-Catholic prejudice, he wanted to turn the GOP into the party of business, building a coalition of workers and bosses united by their shared commitment to prosperity. He had watched as the modern corporation changed the scale of American life. Now he planned to carry those principles into politics, updating American democracy for the age of industrial capitalism. Historians call this period an "organizational revolution."[36] And as the Republican power broker George Cortelyou observed, "Mr. Hanna was what might be termed an organization man."[37]

Hanna was shrewd. Even better, he was lucky. In 1892, Democrats took back the White House and Congress for the first time since the Civil War. One year later, a wave of bank failures set off the sharpest economic downturn the country had yet experienced, bitter proof of the extent to which the nation was now bound together in a single marketplace. In 1894 the GOP picked up more than one hundred House seats in the midterm elections. With the depression grinding on, even the most unexceptional of Republicans would have been the odds-on favorite to take the presidency.[38]

McKinley certainly fit the model for a GOP president. Like the four other Republicans to win the White House since Lincoln—Ulysses Grant, Rutherford Hayes, James Garfield, and Benjamin Harrison—he was an Ohio native. A Civil War veteran, he had spent more than a decade in Congress, rising to become chair of the powerful House Ways and Means Committee, then served two terms as governor.

But McKinley was more than just an interchangeable cog in the Republican machine. Industrialization and immigration were altering the makeup of the electorate, and he was eager to reach beyond the GOP's shrinking base of economically comfortable, native-born Protestants. He courted workers by supporting labor arbitration and protective tariffs. In 1893 he took on the country's leading nativist organization, the American Protective Association. With his gubernatorial reelection campaign in full swing, he rejected an APA demand to fire two Catholic prison guards. (Recognizing a publicity coup when he saw it, Hanna sent a priest around Ohio lecturing on McKinley's behalf.) On Election Day, McKinley won 54.5 percent of the vote.[39]

Fresh off an impressive victory, McKinley vaulted to the top tier of the Republican presidential field. As a midwesterner, he was never going to be the favorite of the eastern GOP establishment known as "the Combine." His embryonic campaign turned the Combine's hostility into a strength by casting McKinley as the leader of a movement pitting "the people against the bosses."

A popular governor from a swing state with a reputation as a friend to the workingman, a record defending Catholics and immigrants, and a hint of the outsider taking on party elites—this was good material to work with. The campaign built on these strengths by focusing relentlessly on economics, calling McKinley "the advance agent of prosperity."[40] Working at a scale that Van Buren could not have imagined, the McKinley team sent representatives around the country to build support for the candidate. In Illinois, every delegate to the Republican convention received daily copies of newspapers supporting McKinley. Fashioning a national political infrastructure out of nothing didn't come cheap, and most of the funding came out of Hanna's pocketbook.

The South was McKinley's secret weapon. With 223 delegates, the region held almost half of the total needed for the nomination. Hanna began the courtship early, acquiring a house in Georgia so that McKinley could woo delegates in person. Southern Republicans were split between a mostly Black group committed to defending civil rights and a "lily white" faction that accepted racial exclusion. Pariahs in the Democratic South, both factions were important players in internal GOP politics. The irony was especially acute for African Americans, who could still make a president even as they were being stripped of their right to vote.[41]

The campaign navigated racial politics carefully, aware that they needed Black votes in the primary but unwilling to sacrifice an opportunity to crack open the Solid South in the general election. McKinley pressed forward in public and in private, meeting with African American delegates at Hanna's Georgia home and speaking in front of predominantly Black audiences. He opposed disenfranchisement but insisted that white Southerners would soon correct the injustice, a message designed to satisfy both sides of the issue—or, at least, to avoid antagonizing them.

Republicans trooped to St. Louis for their national convention loaded down with McKinley buttons, canes, and badges. "He had the South practically solid before some of us awakened," marveled the New York GOP boss Thomas Platt. "Then he picked off enough Western and Pacific Slope States, before the convention met, to render him and McKinley invincible."[42] The campaign won the nomination on the first ballot, carrying the South 196½ to 26½. "These McKinley fellows have almost taken our breath away," an Indiana Republican swooned.[43]

Speaking on McKinley's behalf, Hanna attributed McKinley's victory to "the people."[44] Then he was chosen as the head of the Republican National Committee. The vote was unanimous.

———————————

When Hanna discovered that Democrats had chosen William Jennings Bryan at their national convention in Chicago, he thought the party had lost its mind. But as anxious reports trickled in from the field, Hanna realized that he had miscalculated. "The Chicago convention," he said, "has changed everything."[45]

Democrats had been limping into the fall, dragged down by their association with Grover Cleveland's failed response to the economic crisis. Bryan allowed Democrats to make a clean break with politics as usual while giving the Populist message instant access to a national party infrastructure. Lifelong Democrats were thrown together with radicals like Eugene Debs, who had just been released from a six-month stint in jail after leading a strike against the Pullman Company, which manufactured railroad cars. "You are at this hour the hope of the Republic," Debs wrote to Bryan, calling him "the People's standard bearer in the great uprising of the masses against the classes."[46]

The electoral math was simple. Adding the Democratic and the Populist totals from the 1892 election would give a candidate 53.5 percent of the vote, more than any president had received since Grant. Bryan promised a new Democratic coalition rooted in support from "the plain people"—farmers in the countryside and wageworkers in the cities. For decades, national campaigns had focused on a handful of battleground states, or, as they were known at the time, "doubtful states." Nominating Bryan redrew the map, turning the country into one large doubtful state.

Bryan's strategy came at a price. When Populists stood outside the political establishment, they offered a clear alternative to the status quo. Fusing with Democrats forced Populists to make their peace with the two-party system while giving up their most ambitious reforms, including a progressive income tax, an eight-hour workday, and public ownership of railroads. Bryan plucked the most popular issue from this expansive platform, trading the broad Populist agenda for a campaign focused on free silver. Rather than overhauling American capitalism, he promised a targeted assault on the money power that would inflate away debts for cash-strapped farmers. Although most Populists accepted the deal, true believers never went along with the bargain. "The Democracy," howled a Minnesota Populist, "raped our convention while our own leaders held the struggling victim."[47]

Of course, not even the Populists aimed to unite *all* the people. They put off taking a stand on women's suffrage, not wanting to divert attention from the campaign against corporate power. Their 1892 platform dismissed the country's swelling immigrant population as "imported pauperized labor"—both European and Asian—brought in to crush workers.[48] And although some African Americans were drawn to the movement, they were dwarfed by the number of Black Republicans.[49] Populists tried to woo Black voters with appeals to economic interest. Occasionally, Southern Populists fused with the GOP. But they were first and foremost a white man's party, an article of faith confirmed by their alliance with the Democracy in 1896.

Watching the campaign unfold from their Chicago headquarters, McKinley's team saw fissures opening up in the party of the people. Free silver had an understandable appeal to farmers, but inflation wouldn't solve the problems facing wage earners. What was the country's expanding urban population supposed to make of Bryan's unapologetic agrarianism? Were Democrats who were loyal to the Cleveland administration—a sizable fraction of the party elite—going to accept their abrupt demotion? Why should immigrants back a platform that denounced "foreign pauper labor"?[50] How would Catholics react to Bryan's fervent evangelicalism? Would reformers be persuaded to give up their reservations about the Democratic machine? Could any party speak for "the plain people" if it had zero chance of winning over most African Americans?

Republicans had a powerful argument to make, and virtually unlimited funds to make it. "Everybody that had a dollar was willing to give fifty cents of it to save himself; not Republicans alone but all business men," recalled the GOP operative Cornelius Bliss.[51] Major banks were expected to contribute 0.25 percent of their capital, a kind of tax for protecting the country from Bryanism.[52] Standard Oil gave $250,000, and Rockefeller chipped in an additional $2,500, saying, "I can see nothing else for us to do, to serve the Country and our honor."[53]

There's no way to know how much Republicans raised in total, but private documents prepared for Hanna show that the party spent at least $3.5 million.[54] That alone would be ten times more than Bryan raised, and it doesn't take into account in-kind donations from corporate benefactors, such as discounted railroad tickets that brought an estimated 750,000 Americans to hear McKinley speak from his Ohio home during his celebrated front porch campaign.[55]

The money rushing into the party, the compressed calendar of the election season, and the complexity of the new electoral calculus encouraged Republicans to concentrate authority for decision-making in a few hands, chiefly those of Hanna and his immediate subordinates. The operation grew so large that Republicans split their headquarters in two—one in New York, where most of the money was raised; one in Chicago, where most of the money was spent. Hanna was becoming a new kind of power broker, not a local machine politician but a national boss with the resources of an entire party at his fingertips.

After lunch in Chicago one day, Hanna took a group of the campaign's largest donors on a tour of the offices to show what their money had bought. More than twenty departments had been tasked with mobilizing different slices of the electorate. The party had organizations for veterans, first-time voters, Germans, African Americans, traveling salesmen, and insurance agents. A women's department concentrated on the handful of states—Utah, Colorado, and Wyoming—with female suffrage. In the mail room, a hundred women were assembling packages of campaign literature to be shipped out of the city by the carload. Confederate veterans received knives bearing McKinley's portrait, the American flag, and the slogan "No East, No West, No North, No South, the Union Forever."[56]

The GOP's coffers were flush enough that Hanna decided to funnel some of his donations to gold-standard Democrats running a third-party campaign to steal votes from Bryan, hoping that four years of Republican rule would bring the Democracy back to its senses. Grover Cleveland watched approvingly from the White House, pleased that "the glorious principles of the party have found defenders who will not permit them to be polluted by impious hands."[57]

By the end of the election, Republicans had distributed a hundred million campaign documents, including some 275 different pamphlets in over twenty languages. That was about fourteen pieces of GOP propaganda for every voter, more than the party had produced in its entire history to date.[58]

The race climaxed on October 31, which Republicans christened as Flag Day. McKinley supporters took to the streets brandishing flags, more than a million in New York City alone. "I landed myself in New York just in time for the biggest political demonstration in world history," reported a journalist for the *Daily Mail*. "There was every manner of man in the procession: millionaires in shining silk hats, and working men in corduroy trousers. . . . The whole thing was prodigious, crushing, final."[59]

It was a perfect symbol for the new Republican Party. Like Bryan, McKinley cast himself as the voice of the people. But where Bryan saw a country divided between the many and the few, McKinley believed that Americans were bound together by shared patriotism and common economic interests, updating the Whig message of social harmony for an industrial age. "Every attempt to array class against class, 'the classes against the masses,' section against section, labor against capital, 'the poor against the rich,' or interest against interest in the United States is in the highest degree reprehensible," he maintained. "We are dependent upon each other, no matter what our occupations may be."[60]

Republicans were making their case at a time of economic crisis and widening inequality. And it worked. Bryan delivered on his electoral strategy, holding the South, carrying ten western states that Cleveland had lost, and winning more votes than any previous Democrat. But Republicans more than compensated for those losses by increasing their margins in the Northeast, the Midwest, and the Upper South. (Maryland, Delaware, Kentucky, and West Virginia all broke for the GOP.) McKinley turned out 7.1 million votes at the polls, giving him 51 percent of the popular vote and making him the first president to take office with a popular vote majority since Ulysses Grant. Participation rates in the fiercely disputed midwestern battlegrounds—Illinois, Michigan, Iowa, Indiana—soared to 95 percent. McKinley took them all.[61]

The new Republican Party bore a striking resemblance to the old Republican Party. State by state, McKinley's electoral map in 1896 looked almost identical to Lincoln's in 1860. But the country had changed in the intervening years, and so had the party. Moving from the Civil War to the class war, the GOP cast itself as a voice for both capital and labor, bound together—or so it claimed—by shared interests. In the industrializing states that broke for McKinley, Republicans strengthened their performance across the social spectrum. They did better in urban areas, carrying nine of the ten largest cities, but also improved with rural communities. They ate into Democratic margins with Catholics and immigrants while tightening their grip on the bourgeoisie. To an astonishing degree, Hanna achieved his coalition of labor and capital. "In spite of it all," groaned one Populist, "the bankrupt millions voted to keep the yoke on their own necks."[62]

They *voted* for it—that was the essential point. A novel kind of democracy was taking shape, fitted to the age of capital. "We have won a great victory," Hanna said, "made possible only by organization."[63]

The good news kept coming. "Our business interests are placed in a position of safety that has not been enjoyed for years," Hanna told McKinley in November 1898.[64] An economic recovery was under way, and Hanna predicted more boom times ahead. A wave of corporate mergers—nearly three thousand between 1897 and 1902—brought almost half the country's manufacturing capital under the control of just three hundred companies. The bureaucratic corporation was now the foundation of the country's economic life, just as McKinley's Republican Party was the center of its political universe.[65]

As the chief spokesman for business in politics, Hanna believed he had a special role to play in negotiating the revised terms of the relationship between capitalism and democracy. He won election to the Senate in 1898, discovering that he had an unexpected talent for campaigning. In the Senate, he conducted business from the vice president's office. At home, he met with supporters like J. P. Morgan from a suite at the Arlington Hotel, the most luxurious in Washington. Hanna was a busy spider, weaving a web whose threads reached into union halls and businessmen's associations, government agencies and state party offices.

The South remained the base of Hanna's support within the GOP.

He stayed neutral in the fight between African Americans and white Republicans who wanted to make their peace with Jim Crow—1896 was also the year of *Plessy v. Ferguson*—allowing local organizations to distribute patronage as they saw fit. The steady advance of racial disenfranchisement crushed any lingering hopes of Black politicians winning office in the South. But there were jobs to be had so long as McKinley was in power, and Hanna made sure the spigot kept flowing for Republicans.[66]

One issue consumed his attention. "There is no more engrossing question," he said in 1904, "than that of the relation between labor and capital."[67] After Bryan's defeat, the populist virus mutated into a more lethal variant—an outright socialist movement led by the former Bryan supporter Eugene Debs. In public, Hanna assured audiences that a European import like socialism would never take root in American soil. Privately, he predicted that the choice would come down to "the Republican Party or Socialism."[68]

While still in the Senate, Hanna served as the founding president of the National Civic Federation, a volunteer association meant to provide businessmen and labor leaders with a place to negotiate—"a sort of Hague tribunal," in Hanna's words.[69] (Samuel Gompers, head of the American Federation of Labor, was Hanna's vice president.) "My plan is to have organized union labor Americanized in the best sense," Hanna explained, "and in this way to make it the ally of the capitalist."[70] Unions would train employees in the obligations that came with their enhanced powers and provide employers with negotiating partners at the bargaining table. "Life is a matter of mutual interest between labor and capital," he said. "It is not possible for one to prosper permanently unless the other shares in that prosperity."[71]

If prosperity was the carrot, the threat of another depression was the stick. "The laws of industry and finance cannot be violated any more than can the laws of this or any great nation," Hanna told audiences on the campaign trail.[72] Just a whiff of trouble would send businessmen scrambling for cover, plunging the country back into depression. "Think twice," he warned, "before you cast your vote."[73]

Hanna trusted that common sense would win out. Americans, he said, "are not so much interested in the theories of economics. . . . What they want to judge from and judge by is result."[74] His confidence was borne out in 1900, when McKinley sailed to reelection in a rematch against Bryan that had none of the drama of 1896. Hanna welcomed four more years of harmonious relations between captains of industry and their labor lieutenants, supported by the Republican Party and its millions of voters. He had built an exquisite machine, refining it over years of painstaking effort. Hanna's position looked unshakable, right up until the moment an anarchist fired at point-blank range into McKinley's gut.[75]

Theodore Roosevelt's presidency was one of history's inevitable accidents. Without Leon Czolgosz's untimely assistance, McKinley would have served out his second term. If New York Republicans hadn't been desperate to get their reform governor out of Albany, Roosevelt never would have been nominated as vice president. And if McKinley's first vice president, Garret Hobart, hadn't passed away in 1899, TR wouldn't have been anywhere near the line of succession for the White House.

Chance pushed Roosevelt into a part he was born to play. A purebred scion of the American elite, he was raised in a Manhattan home of dowdy respectability on East Twentieth Street.[76] His father, Theodore Roosevelt Sr., was a wealthy businessman. His mother was a product of the Georgia planter class, and he grew up hearing sepia-toned stories of plantation life, filled with kind masters and cheerful slaves. He idolized his maternal uncles, both of whom had fought for the Confederacy. "I know what a good side there was to slavery," he later said. "But I know also what a hideous side there was to it, and this was the important side."[77] It was quintessential Roosevelt, acknowledging the opposing sides of an argument, placing himself at an ideal midpoint between the two, and somehow floating above the fray.

A childhood spent reconciling the sectional divide in his own family prepared him for a lifetime of straining to embody the nation as a whole. He was the Dakota rancher with a magna cum laude degree from Harvard, a good-government reformer and canny politician, a fervent nationalist and globe-trotting cosmopolitan, plus a respected amateur historian with a special interest in the lives of statesmen. (He wrote biographies of Oliver Cromwell, Gouverneur Morris, and the Missouri senator Thomas Hart Benton.)

In other words, Roosevelt was the kind of person who wasn't supposed to degrade himself by pleading for votes. "The men of cultivated taste and easy life," he said, "laughed at me, and told me that politics were 'low'; that the organizations were not controlled by 'gentlemen'; that I would find them run by saloon-keepers, horse-car conductors, and the like."[78]

A family friend tried to set the young Roosevelt straight during a lunch that he would remember for the rest of his life. The older man explained that there was no such thing as purely political power. Instead, there was an "inner circle" made up of businessmen, lawyers, judges, and the occasional politician—"the people who would always in the long run control others and obtain the real rewards which were worth having."[79] No matter which career he chose, Roosevelt would need to win backing from the inner circle—and, if he wanted real influence, become part of it.

Roosevelt saw the rest of his career as one long attempt to prove that he could join the governing class without surrendering to the "inner circle." He wanted to bridge the divide between ordinary voters and the elite, using each to check the other, speaking for what the people would want for themselves if they had been properly taught. Enemies surrounded him on all sides: radicals intoxicated with their own self-righteousness; cultivated gentlefolk whose "Chinese timidity" kept them out of the arena; and grasping plutocrats whose "ideals . . . in their essence are merely those of so many glorified pawnbrokers."[80]

Against all that, Roosevelt cast himself as "a thoroughly practical man of high ideals who did his best to reduce those ideals to actual

practice."[81] Though he loathed Charles Sumner—"professional abolitionists," he sniped, "were about as undesirable a class of people as the
country ever saw"—there was more than a passing resemblance between the two Harvard-trained gentlemen politicians.[82]

The two even shared a nemesis: the New York Republican boss Roscoe Conkling, last seen in this book shredding a newspaper during one
of Sumner's orations and helping extend the Fourteenth Amendment
to corporations. Conkling earned Roosevelt's enmity by torpedoing the
nomination of his father as collector of customs to the Port of New
York in 1877. As the battle dragged on, the elder Roosevelt's health
declined. Two months after the Senate voted against the appointment,
a message arrived for young Theodore, then a sophomore at Harvard,
urging him to come back to New York. By the time Roosevelt arrived
at the family brownstone, his father was dead, the victim of what was
later diagnosed as a malignant tumor in his bowels.[83]

In one of his last letters to his son, Theodore Roosevelt Sr. wrote,
"The 'Machine politicians' have shown their colors. . . . I feel sorry for
the country however as it shows the power of partisan politicians who
think of nothing higher than their own interests, and I feel for your
future. We cannot stand so corrupt a government for any great length
of time."[84]

Roosevelt kept this letter with him, describing it as one of his "tal-
ismans against evil."[85] He didn't renounce party machines, or partisan
politics—that would be impractical. Instead, he called himself "a Republican, pure and simple," with the emphasis on purity and simplic-
ity.[86] He would be in politics, but not of it, using party machines to
subvert party bosses and represent the national interest.

To a certain breed of liberal reformer, Roosevelt was irresistible.
"We hailed him as the dawn of a new era," said the deliciously named
Poultney Bigelow, another product of New York high society. "The
man of good family once more in the political arena; the college-bred
tribune superior to the temptations which beset meaner men. 'Teddy,'
as we called him, was our ideal."[87]

Then, in 1901, an assassin's bullet put this practical idealist and aristocratic democrat into the White House, giving him control of the Republican Party in the process.

Mark Hanna was not pleased.

———

Roosevelt and Hanna were just similar enough to truly loathe each other. Despite TR's later reputation as a scourge of the robber barons, the two had no major disagreements over policy while Roosevelt was in the White House. Both of them wanted to rewrite the rules of Gilded Age politics, taming party bosses while teaching the new industrial titans how to exercise power responsibly. Neither sympathized with do-gooders who refused to hustle for votes, or with businessmen who wouldn't compromise with their workers. They were both democratic conservatives working within the same broad tradition.

And still Hanna could not stand Roosevelt, doing everything in his power to stop TR from getting the vice presidential nomination, well aware of his independent streak. After the convention, Hanna told McKinley, "Your *duty* to the country is to *live* for *four* years from next March."[88]

Roosevelt was more ambivalent, charmed by Hanna's personality and impressed by his intellect but repulsed by what he symbolized. Hanna was giving the "inner circle" a human face, not leading the charge against it. He was, Roosevelt concluded, "a man with many good qualities, but who embodied in himself more than any other big man, all the forces of coarse corruption that had been so prominent in our industrial and political life"—the same forces Roosevelt thought it was his mission to purge from politics.[89]

That crusading zeal is exactly what terrified Hanna. He wanted peace and stability, not a glorious struggle. It was the difference between the bourgeois and the aristocrat, the businessman and the warrior.

The contrast between the two was clearest in foreign policy. Hanna's view on the country's role in the world was simple. "The United States," he said, "must not have any damn trouble with anybody." He had been a reluctant supporter of the Spanish-American War, afraid of its impact on business. Roosevelt, then serving as assistant secretary of the navy, was its most passionate advocate. "I hope to see the Spanish flag and the English flag gone from the map of North America before I'm sixty!" he exclaimed at a Washington reception. A bemused Hanna asked, "What's wrong with Canada?"[90]

Only when Hanna could see a clear economic advantage for the United States did he warm to the notion of flexing American muscle abroad. In 1903 he had the Senate draped with maps and illustrations of Central America, visual aids to a statistics-laden speech making the case for building the Panama Canal, which he delivered over two days.[91] Hanna turned the debate in Panama's favor—until then, Nicaragua had looked like a stronger candidate—and a bill soon landed on Roosevelt's desk, where the president happily signed it. Under McKinley, the United States had taken over most of Spain's overseas possessions—the Philippines, Puerto Rico, and Guam—along with Hawaii, Wake Island, and American Samoa. With the Panama Canal, it linked two oceans and shrank the world. Mixing Hanna's economic calculation and Roosevelt's geopolitical ambition, Republicans set the terms for an American empire, one more offshoot of the new GOP majority.

At home, the gap between the party's two leading men was widest on issues related to race. Hanna didn't spend much time talking about the subject, reluctant to stray from a tight focus on labor and capital. With Roosevelt, race was something like an obsession. It spoke to so many different sides of his personality—the foreign policy strategist who thought in continents, the historian preoccupied with the rise and fall of civilizations, the amateur naturalist eager to keep up to date with the latest racial science, and the son of an unreconstructed Southerner.[92] He warned that dwindling birth rates among white people could lead to "race suicide," a subject "infinitely more important than any other question facing this country."[93] Although willing to grant that African Americans might one day prove themselves equal, he thought that "as a race and in the mass they are altogether inferior to the whites." (He was less confident about Asians. "The latest scientific theory," he told one correspondent, "is that the Negro and the white man as shown by their skulls, are closely akin, and taken together, differ widely from the round skulled Mongolian.")[94]

After Roosevelt took office, much of the GOP establishment assumed that Hanna would be their nominee in 1904. "Men of power and influence [were] practically demanding that he should put himself in position to accept the nomination," recalled a New York Republican.[95] J. P. Morgan invited Hanna to Thanksgiving dinner at his New York home and spent the evening pestering Hanna to run. Outside, electric light bulbs flashed "HANNA FOR PRESIDENT."[96] Grassroots party activists could be just as insistent. "While we admire the presidint [sic] Theodore Roosevelt," the head of the New York Irish Republican League wrote to Hanna, "what we wan [sic] is a man of the people."[97]

There's no evidence, however, that Hanna seriously considered taking on Roosevelt. The new president moved deftly to consolidate his influence, installing loyalists in key posts, both in Washington and in state parties. Putting aside his qualms about racial equality, he gave Black Republicans an important symbolic victory when he asked Booker T. Washington to dinner at the White House. Then, to avoid alienating white people, he made sure not to issue a second invitation. Through deft use of patronage Roosevelt curried favor with both sides in the Southern GOP's internal civil war. Having built so much of the party machine, Hanna understood its power—and he knew that it was no longer his to operate.[98]

Even if Hanna wanted to challenge the president, he was in no condition to run a campaign. Arthritic joints left him in constant pain. His quick stride had given way to a limp, and he hobbled along with assistance from a cane, dragging his feet as he walked. Early in 1904 he was diagnosed with typhoid fever. A team of doctors was brought in for support, drugging him into an etherized stupor, injecting his abdomen with eight-ounce shots of brandy, ordering him to drink cocktails of whiskey, champagne, and nitroglycerine. News of Hanna's rapid decline circulated around Washington. On a cold February evening, congressmen, generals, cabinet secretaries, and other Washington notables crowded into the lobby of Hanna's hotel, waiting for news.[99]

"He held a unique position in our American life," wrote *The New York Times* in its obituary the next day. "He was not a dreamer, but a hard-headed man of business who was also engaged in large politics."[100] There was no grandeur here, only the prospect of enough today and a little more tomorrow. But when combined with the right political strategy and millions of dollars, that simple promise helped transform American politics.

And Republicans weren't done with Hanna yet. The last lingering threat to Roosevelt's renomination had been cleared from the stage, and the president spent the months before the party's national convention immersing himself in the details of the event, down to the seating arrangements.

But he forgot to ask about the decor. Delegates might have expected that the room would be festooned with images of the president, but the organizers had different plans. As Republicans made their way into the

Chicago Coliseum, they were confronted with a giant portrait—seven feet wide, twenty feet tall—of Mark Hanna.[101]

———————

Still, the party couldn't nominate a portrait, and a dead hero was no match for a living president. The GOP belonged to Roosevelt. The problem was that he didn't know what to do with it. He saw himself as a Lincoln for the Industrial Age, but there was no Rooseveltian counterpart to the Emancipation Proclamation, only a series of initiatives—establishing a Department of Commerce and Labor, a modest expansion of the federal government's regulatory authority, selective antitrust prosecutions—that nibbled away at the power of the "inner circle."[102]

As Roosevelt inched toward a bolder position on the labor question, he beat a hasty retreat on civil rights. "If you ever get the ear of the President," a Mississippi planter told one of Roosevelt's intimates, "tell him that we are with him, that we are not blind, and 'know a good thing when we see it.'"[103] Lincoln's heir, it seemed, could not afford to waste political capital fighting for racial equality.

With such an ambiguous legacy, heavy on rhetorical posturing and short on substantive achievements, the odds were good that Roosevelt would be disappointed with whoever replaced him in the White House. If anyone could have lived up to Roosevelt's expectations, it should have been his hand-picked successor. William Howard Taft had the mix of eastern establishment credentials and worldly experience that Roosevelt prized: second in his class at Yale, solicitor general of the United States, governor of the Philippines under McKinley, and secretary of war under TR.[104] Although Taft had never been elected to office, he came from a family that had extensive political connections in his home state of—you guessed it—Ohio. After leaving the presidency, however, Roosevelt quickly decided that his friend and chosen heir wasn't up to the job. (The exact mixture of political disagreement and personal pique is impossible to determine.) When a Draft Roosevelt movement emerged, pleading with him to challenge Taft for the nomination, he accepted the call to take the party back, this time with a program designed to shatter "the whole system of alliance between big business and big politics."[105]

In the White House, Roosevelt had called himself both a conservative and a man of the center-left. The new TR preferred "progressive," the catchall term for reform that emerged in the wake of Populism's collapse.[106] Latching onto the movement, he endorsed policies that were more ambitious than anything he had proposed as president, ranging from state-led industrial planning to universal health insurance. Although much of Roosevelt's agenda could have come out of a Populist manifesto, there was no mistaking his campaign for a revolt of the laboring masses. His base remained "men of good family" who had always been drawn to his cause, along with a rising professional class made up of doctors, lawyers, teachers, engineers, and administrators of all kinds.[107]

Roosevelt's vision was an incongruous blend of technocracy and direct democracy. He proposed a string of measures designed to weaken party machines, replacing smoke-filled rooms with ballot initiatives, direct primaries, and the popular election of senators. The old custom of handing out government jobs to partisan loyalists would have to go. Instead, Roosevelt foresaw an administration staffed by "an absolutely nonpartisan body of experts, with no prejudices to warp their minds."[108] At the center of this new political universe would sit the president, voice of the people and master of the federal bureaucracy.

As usual, Roosevelt was straining to find a unifying theme in contradictory influences. He worshipped at the shrine of efficiency while promising to restore a lost golden age of pure democracy. And he still wanted a politics that spoke to "the things that are elemental in civilization"—the hunger for justice, glory, and national greatness that the Mark Hannas of the world could never understand.[109]

The only sacrifice he seemed willing to accept was the continued marginalization of African Americans. Roosevelt's steroidal nationalism disappeared when he turned his gaze to the South, where he trusted "the best white men" to look after things.[110] "We have made the Progressive issue a moral, not a racial issue," he explained. "Wherever the racial issue is permitted to become dominant in our politics, it always works harm to both races."[111] Progressives couldn't allow themselves to be distracted by ancillary concerns—especially when the South might be up for grabs. "If I could carry one of the eleven ex-Confederate states," he said, "I should feel as though I could die happy."[112]

The GOP establishment was committed to denying him that opportunity. The Republican elite united against him, handing Taft a victory at the GOP convention. Convinced that the inner circle had stolen the nomination, Roosevelt decided to launch his own party.[113]

Two months later, Roosevelt accepted the first presidential nomination from the Progressive Party. He summoned his army to a crusade for social justice, transporting them into an almost religious ecstasy. "We stand at Armageddon," he thundered, "and we battle for the Lord."[114]

The audience cheered along to Roosevelt's declaration of war against his old party. You can imagine the ghost of Mark Hanna scowling as he watched the damned cowboy from East Twentieth Street confirm his worst fears. It's harder to picture what he would have done when he saw that one of the faces in the crowd shouting for Roosevelt belonged to his daughter.

———————

Ruth Hanna was her father's youngest child, and probably his favorite. She inherited his brown eyes, X-ray stare, and passion for politics (along with a massive fortune). "It was the ambition of my life," she said, "to walk in a torchlight parade. When I was finally permitted to, I walked until my legs nearly fell off. I screamed and yelled until my throat was sore. I waved the torch until it dripped on me and my face was black and burned."[115]

Like Hanna, Ruth was an indifferent student. Uninterested in college, she became her father's secretary after graduating from high school. Hanna assigned clerical chores to another (male) secretary, asking Ruth to spend her time examining legislation and studying Senate debates. Marriage to a scion of the McCormick family—inventors of the McCormick reaper, owners of the *Chicago Tribune*—brought her to Illinois, where she helped launch a women's division of the National Civic Federation.

But she wasn't just her father's daughter. Where Hanna came late to power, Ruth spoke the language of privilege without an accent. She moved easily within the East Coast aristocracy—Alice Roosevelt, daughter of Theodore, was one of her closest friends—and was carried along by the passion for social change common in elite circles during the period. Her husband, Medill McCormick, was a blue-blood reformer of the purest sort: idealistic, cerebral, born to wealth, and trained to rule at Groton and Yale. After marrying, the two moved into a settlement house run by the University of Chicago, living alongside the Poles, Russians, and Lithuanians crowded together near the slaughterhouses.

Ruth might have stayed there, too, if not for Medill. Sensitive and prone to mood swings, he would today probably be diagnosed with bipolar disorder. He used alcohol to even out his emotions, sometimes taking his first drink at nine in the morning. The search for help took the McCormicks away from the stockyards, all the way to Zurich, where Medill was psychoanalyzed by Carl Jung, who attributed his struggles to "infantile relations with the mother."[116] It was decided that Medill would curb his destructive impulses by finding a cause larger than himself, where he could channel his energy—like politics.

Back in the United States, the McCormicks threw themselves into the battle to replace Taft with a Progressive Republican. In 1911, with Roosevelt still insisting that he was not a candidate, they turned to Robert La Follette, a Wisconsin senator and hero of GOP reformers. The couple moved to Washington, where Medill (with Ruth's assistance) took over publicity for the campaign. When it became clear that Roosevelt could be talked into running, they helped push La Follette out of the race and consolidate reformers behind TR. They returned to Chicago in 1912, serving as de facto co-managers for the western branch of Roosevelt's campaign while Medill ran for the Illinois state legislature on the Progressive ticket.

The rest of the election unfolded just as Ruth's father would have predicted. With the Republican coalition divided, Woodrow Wilson's 41.8 percent popular vote plurality gave him a landslide in the Electoral College, returning Democrats to the White House for the first time in sixteen years.[117]

Overnight, Roosevelt gave up his flirtation with radical democracy, blaming his loss on "the great mass of ordinary commonplace men of dull imagination who simply vote under the party symbol and whom it is almost as difficult to stir by any appeal to the higher emotions and intelligence as it would be to stir so many cattle."[118] He was particularly bitter about the role played by African Americans at the GOP convention, where he was convinced that Black delegates had sold their votes to Taft.

If he had been less preoccupied with his own defeat, Roosevelt might have seen 1912 as a breakthrough for the progressive movement. Wilson accelerated the turn toward a more powerful central government, working through an administrative state overseen by an empowered president, reflected in the creation of such new agencies as the Federal Reserve—a technocratic fix to the problem of currency that would have been impossible to imagine coming from the party of William Jennings Bryan in 1896. Ballot initiatives, referendums, recalls, party primaries, and the direct election of senators all became accepted features of American politics. And even though Roosevelt lost, Progressive candidates won hundreds of elections down-ballot, including thirteen congressional races. Taken as a whole, it was the most impressive debut of any third party in American history, with the debatable exception of the GOP in 1856.

The problem was organization. Progressives had permanently damaged their standing within the GOP when they followed Roosevelt out of the party, tying their fortunes to the mercurial ex-president. When their hero's appetite for reform vanished, no successor emerged who could turn the promising start of 1912—millions of votes, a cadre of passionate supporters, and a foothold in elected office—into a lasting political movement. Charisma could electrify an audience, but it couldn't build a party.

Which put the McCormicks in a difficult spot. While Roosevelt narrowly lost Illinois, Medill won his seat in the state legislature, along with twenty-six other Progressives. It was an enviable position at first. Medill took charge of the Progressive caucus, which held the swing vote in a legislature where neither party had a majority. But the Progressives collapsed in the next election, reducing their numbers in the legislature to two. Medill was one of the survivors. He rejoined the GOP, winning election to the House of Representatives as a Republican in 1916, then moving up to the Senate two years later.[119]

It was a remarkable ascent. But friends of the couple weren't sure which one of them had the brighter future. Roosevelt, characteristically, didn't hesitate to share his opinion. Watching the McCormicks stroll around the grounds of his home at Sagamore Hill—they had come to New York to visit with the former president—Roosevelt pulled aside the progressive writer and activist Raymond Robins.

"Raymond," he said, clicking his teeth, "my money's on the ma-r-re."[120]

———

Ruth Hanna McCormick had the intelligence, the connections, and the money to make a career out of politics. But there was one thing she didn't have: the right to vote. So she decided to start there.

By 1912, women had won the franchise in several states, all in the West.[121] (The first woman elected to Congress was also a westerner: Jeannette Rankin of Montana.) Ruth believed that her adopted home state was ready to push this winning streak east of the Mississippi. She joined the Illinois Equal Suffrage Association, where she helped to shape the movement's political strategy. Already a seasoned operative, she played the inside game expertly, cajoling legislators, managing the press, and fending off attempts to kill the bill with amendments. After the measure passed in the state legislature—Medill was among the supporters—Governor Edward Dunne gave Ruth one of the pens he used to sign the bill.[122]

Building on her success in Illinois, Ruth agreed to serve as chief congressional strategist for the National American Woman Suffrage Association. With more than two million members, NAWSA was the largest voluntary organization in the country and the leading force in the suffrage campaign. At NAWSA, Ruth took over a position previously held by Alice Paul, a Quaker with an intellectual bent and a doctorate from the University of Pennsylvania. The twenty-seven-year-old Paul was a born agitator with a gift for orchestrating attention-grabbing publicity gambits: marches, civil disobedience, hunger strikes.

Ruth favored a less confrontational approach.[123] "I am a suffragist," she said, "not a feminist."[124] Women could gain the vote, she argued, only by "playing the game as American politicians understand it."[125] Paul condemned the system from the outside; Ruth manipulated it from within. Like Hanna and Roosevelt in their different ways, she was a democratic conservative.

Suffragists of all stripes claimed victory when the Nineteenth Amendment finally passed in 1920, just five years after a similar measure went down to an easy defeat in the House. The abrupt shift in public opinion underlined the significance of World War I. Women's importance on the home front made access to the ballot look like overdue recognition of their civic role, and horror at the costs of battle persuaded some conservatives that the gentler sex could restrain male belligerence.[126]

A revolution was under way, born out of the intersection between decades of activism and the shock of World War I. Ruth called it "the greatest political victory ever won in the history of this country."[127] After women secured their rights as citizens, Ruth wanted to turn suffragists into Republicans, fulfilling her twin ambitions simultaneously—bringing women into party politics and preserving the GOP majority for a new generation.

The two projects came together in 1920, a golden opportunity for Republicans to reclaim the presidency and the first election after the ratification of the Nineteenth Amendment. Establishment candidates won both major party nominations, and no significant third-party alternative emerged to challenge them, although Eugene Debs made a valiant effort, campaigning from a prison cell after being arrested on charges of sedition during World War I.

Republicans chose Warren Harding, and so did the country, including millions of newly enfranchised women. He earned 60 percent of the vote and carried every state outside the South. The GOP was swept along on his coattails, winning a 22-seat majority in the Senate and an extraordinary 168-seat majority in the House. The old Republican coalition had been stitched back together by a familiar type. Before entering the White House, the new president had served one term as lieutenant governor and one term as senator from the great state of Ohio.[128]

Now that women could vote, Ruth wanted to persuade them—along with a majority of men—to cast a ballot for her.

It was an unusual position. Most former suffragists were drawn toward nonpartisan organizing of a kind exemplified by the League of Women Voters—broadly in favor of good government, reluctant to enter the political scrum.[129] A smaller group, led by Alice Paul, shifted its energy to pushing for an equal rights amendment. The Republican establishment, meanwhile, adopted a policy of separate and unequal, forming distinct women's groups that kept decision-making authority in male hands. Against her better judgment, Ruth agreed to serve as head of the RNC's "Women's Division." The experience confirmed her suspicion that the party wanted women only to serve as window dressing.

Just a few years after the double triumphs of 1920, when first-time women voters helped deliver a Republican landslide, Ruth's career had stalled. It was saved by the death of her husband.

Medill's decline began in 1924, when he was defeated for renomination in the Republican primary. A statesman without a public, he was cut off from the work that was supposed to anchor him in the world. "My dreams," he told Ruth, "show a desire to escape reality."[130] On February 24, 1925, his body was found in a Washington hotel room near a locked suitcase that contained—as Ruth later discovered—empty vials of the barbiturates Medill used to kill himself.

If Medill had lived, Ruth might have spent the rest of her life acting the part of the political spouse, wielding influence behind the scenes but dependent upon her husband. Medill's death forced her into freedom. She had decades of experience on campaigns and a successful track record lobbying in Springfield and Washington. Although she resisted the ghettoization of women inside the party, her work with GOP women's clubs gave her a firm base of support, along with access to organizers whose talents were being slighted.

Ruth Hanna McCormick speaking to a Women's Republican Club.

She infuriated her old colleagues from Roosevelt's 1912 campaign by stumping on behalf of Calvin Coolidge in 1924, spurning reform icon Robert La Follette's third-party race. But she was independent-minded enough to break from Coolidge—and most nonpartisan women's organizations—by opposing U.S. entry into the World Court. She had inherited her father's aversion to entangling alliances, and she launched a six-month lecture tour depicting the World Court as a back door into Woodrow Wilson's hated League of Nations. She also had her father's easy speaking style and a gift for being effortlessly herself, offering the glamour of privilege without a hint of condescension.

The party of Calvin Coolidge and Ruth Hanna McCormick wasn't the progressive champion Theodore Roosevelt briefly dreamed of, but it wasn't a throwback to the Gilded Age, either. The culture wars that dominated politics in the 1920s—Prohibition, immigration, Jim Crow—cut across the parties, and the most reactionary voices often came from the Democratic side of the aisle. (Woodrow Wilson's administration put Eugene Debs in jail; Harding pardoned him.) On the core progressive issues—strengthening the federal bureaucracy and opening up American democracy—Republicans offered a compromise. Experts had strengthened their role in government, and voters had more direct say over picking candidates and policies, but the basic structure of the peace of 1896 remained intact: big business and party bosses—"the inner circle"—could rest easy.

As experts marched into government, politics lost some of its hold on the public. In retrospect, 1896 marked the beginning of the end for the stratospheric voter turnout that had defined American democracy since the Jacksonian period. Despite impassioned rhetoric from Progressives about the rule of the people, just under 59 percent of eligible voters came to the polls in 1912. Eight years later, participation rates fell under 50 percent, the lowest since 1824. No election for the rest of the twentieth century matched the levels that were common in the nineteenth.[131]

A number of causes worked in tandem to drive away potential

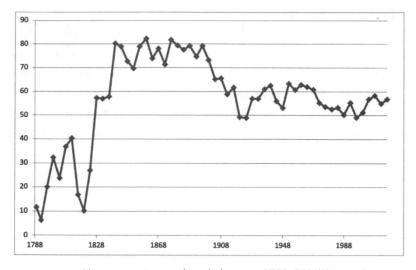

Voter turnout in presidential elections, 1788–2016[132]

voters: Jim Crow restrictions, the spread of the secret ballot, waning two-party competition in much of the country, the weakening of party machines, the rise of independent bureaucracies, a reluctance on the part of some women to exercise their new right to vote, and the arrival of better distractions—why go to a torchlight parade when you could watch a movie?—combined to bring the fevered mass politics of the nineteenth century to a close.

But if the voters who did show up offer any indication, this was a contented apathy. Beginning with Harding, Republicans held unified control of the federal government for a decade. Industrial titans, veteran progressives, cigar-chomping party bosses, and ancestral Republican loyalists all fit inside the GOP's big tent. They were the party of business, and business was booming. Instead of choosing between Roosevelt and Hanna, the next generation of Republicans blended the two influences together.

Such as, for example, Ruth Hanna McCormick. After contemplating a bid for Illinois governor—"I'm not strong for women governors but . . . I think you are the man for the job," a school principal wrote to her—she decided to run for Congress in 1928 against a Republican incumbent weakened by internal party feuds.[133] It was an at-large position, meaning that it would be voted on by the entire state. With so much ground to cover, the election would come down to organizing. And Ruth Hanna McCormick was an organization woman.

Borrowing from the 1896 playbook, she reached out to representatives from constituencies across the social spectrum—labor, business, farmers, immigrants, and African Americans. She played nice with the GOP machine while courting reformers. Money, of course, was never a problem. She navigated carefully through tricky domestic controversies: Prohibition was a misguided policy, but the law had to be enforced; immigration should be limited "along humane lines."[134] She was bolder on foreign policy, where she remained a dogged opponent of the World Court.

With Black voters, she benefited from the assistance of Roscoe Conkling Simmons.[135] A nephew of Booker T. Washington, Simmons made his start in politics when his uncle arranged for him to work under Mark Hanna—"my dearest friend and greatest benefactor," he later said. Simmons quickly rose through the ranks of the GOP, gaining a reputation as one of the party's most effective speakers. (He strode to podiums with a black walking stick as an organist played the "Battle Hymn of the Republic.") Simmons remained close to the Hanna family throughout his life, serving as a kind of all-purpose consultant on Black politics—"in many respects a family retainer," as Ruth's daughter later described him.[136]

Gender was a different problem—and an opportunity. McCormick downplayed the history-making aspect of her candidacy, depicting herself as an "old hack politician" who happened to have two X chromosomes (a recent scientific discovery).[137] "It would be just as ridiculous for me to appeal to the voters of my state on the ground that I am a woman as on the ground that I have dark eyes," she said.[138] Privately, she was taken aback by the amount of resistance to electing a woman. "I would not think of voting for a woman for Congressman-at-Large any more than to vote for one of my cows for such a responsible office," one letter announced.[139] But there were advantages to her position, the most important being the thousands of women volunteers who flocked to her candidacy. (She did, however, appoint one male supporter as head of her campaign's "men's division.")[140]

Organization trounced sexism in the primary, where she received more than eight times as many votes as her opponent. *Time* put her on its cover, making her the first female politician to receive that honor (and the last for more than thirty years). She cruised to an easy victory in the fall, carried along by the same Republican wave that brought Herbert Hoover into the White House. One of four women elected to Congress for the first time that year—weirdly, three were named Ruth—she walked into the House on her first day arm in arm with fellow freshman Ruth Bryan Owen, daughter of William Jennings Bryan.[141]

FIFTEEN CENTS   April 23, 1928

TIME
The Weekly Newsmagazine

RUTH HANNA McCORMICK

Rumors were already circulating about her next steps. "She says she knows some women who are qualified right now for Cabinet positions," *Time* reported. "Some day, she says, a woman will be President of the U.S. Whether or not she can guess who it will be is not divulged."[142]

By winning one statewide election, she had laid the groundwork for a still more ambitious race—a challenge in 1930 to the incumbent Republican senator Charles Deneen, the man who had defeated Medill six years earlier. In rural downstate Illinois she emphasized her opposition to the World Court. In Chicago, she counted on backing from women, trade unions, and African Americans. Oscar De Priest—a member of McCormick's class in the House and the first Black congressman elected outside the South—was the only representative in the Illinois congressional delegation to support her.[143] The state party, however, was more evenly divided, and she picked up endorsements from the governor and from the Chicago mayor Bill Thompson.

McCormick relied on massive campaign expenditures to make up for Deneen's advantages as an incumbent. Although definitive estimates are impossible to come by, it's likely that she outspent Deneen by at least ten to one, pouring her money into—as she put it—"literature, halls, advertising, traveling, radio, banners, canvassers, pledge cards, sample ballots, and many incidentals" (that last category being hazy enough to cover the old-fashioned graft that a self-described "hack politician" would recognize as part of the game).[144]

There was, of course, no escaping the question of sex. The idea of a woman senator repelled many voters, including Theodore Roosevelt's Progressive running mate from 1912, Hiram Johnson, who said that McCormick's victory led to the Senate's "thorough breakdown and demoralization."[145] Although she continued to wave away the issue, she acknowledged the symbolic importance of her candidacy. "I am carrying a big load," she told a reporter. "Women all over this country are watching this election. I intend to be careful for their sakes."[146]

Her tested formula—playing the game of American politics better than any man—carried the day. Buoyed by strong turnout in women and African Americans, she earned 50.7 percent of the vote to Deneen's 35.2 percent, with the rest divided among other minor candidates. *The Washington Post* called it "the most remarkable campaign ever conducted by a woman."[147] Looking ahead to the general election, *The New York Times* predicted a fiery campaign fought over the World Court and Prohibition, with a historic victory for women's equality a real possibility. It would be, they announced, "a fascinating show."[148]

———————

The Republican majority had survived the rise and fall of populism, a world war, and the enfranchisement of women, all while remaining more or less intact. Then came the Great Depression.

The severity of the downturn was difficult to gauge at first. But as the unemployment rate soared and breadlines snaked around Chicago's streets, McCormick slowly realized that the Depression would be the decisive issue in the race. She struggled to adapt to the altered landscape, minimizing the slump and tracing its origins to economic dislocations in Europe, a problem safely outside the GOP's control.

It was not a persuasive message, especially coming from an heir to both the Hanna and McCormick fortunes. (When she died, her estate was valued at just over $6 million, about $95 million today.)[149] The World Court, Prohibition, even the possibility of a woman senator—none of it outweighed the Depression. With her Democratic opponent inveighing against "a woman whose inherited riches were wrung from the poor," McCormick lost by more than a two-to-one margin.[150] The brightest spot in an otherwise miserable night was her impressive performance with African Americans. Oscar De Priest campaigned aggressively on her behalf, telling Black Chicagoans, "No sane man . . . would ask the colored people to vote for a Democrat." The argument carried three of the city's majority Black wards for McCormick. But she lost the city's 47 other wards, along with all but 13 of the state's 102 counties.

She had company in the losers' corner. Nineteen thirty was a disaster for Republicans, costing the party eight seats in the Senate and fifty-one in the House.[151] More than a simple rebuke of Hoover, the election marked the beginning of the end for the cross-class coalition that had kept Republicans in power for a generation. Not even Oscar De Priest weathered the storm. In 1934 he was replaced by Arthur Mitchell, the first African American Democrat to serve in Congress and a harbinger of the coming Black exodus from the party of Lincoln.[152] Just as Mark Hanna had been present when the depression of the 1890s created one majority, his daughter was now watching an even larger economic crisis give rise to another.

But the Democratic Party of Franklin Roosevelt was more a mirror image of Mark Hanna's GOP than a repudiation: a party committed to good jobs and decent wages that worked through political machines and maneuvered carefully around the culture wars of its time. Both were designed, from the ground up, with the interests of white male breadwinners in mind. The key difference was that Democrats shifted the balance of power from capital to labor, trading the Chamber of Commerce for the Congress of Industrial Organizations (CIO). Where Hanna turned business leaders into Republicans, Roosevelt made workers into Democrats. If the GOP had given plutocracy a human face, then New Dealers translated social democracy into the American vernacular.[153]

Recognizing that Democrats had the advantage, McCormick stepped away from politics after her defeat, taking shelter during a Republican winter. She married a former House colleague, Albert Simms, another victim of the 1930 Democratic wave. The newlyweds settled at a sprawling ranch outside Albuquerque. Ruth dabbled in politics, seconding Alf Landon's successful nomination at the 1936 Republican National Convention and speaking on his behalf in seven midwestern states. Most of the time, she enjoyed the life of the idle rich.

It took another presidential election to draw her back into politics. In 1940 Thomas Dewey was a thirty-seven-year-old Republican wunderkind, the crusading New York district attorney who had taken on the Mob, Wall Street, and Tammany Hall. He became a folk hero and inspiration for several films. (In one, the Dewey stand-in was played by Humphrey Bogart.) Dewey parlayed his celebrity into a near upset of the popular New York Democratic governor Herbert Lehman in 1938, a shock to the political system that established him as a possible contender for the next GOP presidential nomination.[154]

Full of promise but lacking experience, Dewey turned to McCormick for guidance. Although he could be remote and vain, Dewey was a gifted performer with a star power that outshone his rivals in the GOP. A storm was gathering in Europe, and McCormick—a substantial donor to the America First Committee—was desperate for a candidate who would keep the United States out of war.[155] She agreed to serve as manager of his campaign, adding another historic first to her catalogue.

In an interview with *The New York Times*, "Dewey's right-hand woman" reflected on how much politics had changed since her father's day. Party bosses were losing their grip on power in the age of television and radio. "No amount of talk, literature and strategy can vie with the impression that a man makes over the air and on the screen," she said. Candidates had become "the neighbors of people everywhere," bringing front porch campaigns into living rooms across the country.[156]

McCormick spent most of the race in New York, wooing delegates, overseeing the staff, and composing detailed memoranda educating her candidate in the nuances of electioneering. "Everywhere you go around Dewey headquarters in New York you hear them saying, 'I'll have to ask Ruth,'" reported the *Washington Daily News*.[157] Dewey came up short at the convention, but he left the race with a burnished national reputation. He was elected governor of New York two years later, certifying his front-runner status for 1944.

As Dewey moved closer to the nomination, he drifted away from McCormick. Their relationship began unraveling after Pearl Harbor. She remained stubbornly opposed to the war, while he became a convert to internationalism. Dewey's evolution triggered deep-rooted suspicions among his midwestern supporters, where distrust of the northeastern establishment ran deep. "He has bought and been bought by the prospect of millions for his campaign fund from New York bankers," fumed the editorial page of the *Chicago Tribune*, a Republican bastion whose controversial publisher happened to be Medill McCormick's younger brother.[158] Although Ruth continued writing to Dewey, his responses became shorter and more erratic, until eventually they stopped coming altogether.

Dewey won the nomination in 1944 without McCormick's assistance. She spent Election Day in a hospital bed, watching Roosevelt win his fourth term while she recovered after a nasty fall from a horse. Later that month she was diagnosed with pancreatitis. By the time doctors operated, her pancreas had already ruptured. She died on the last day of 1944.

———————

What had the Republican majority accomplished during its thirty-odd years in power? At the most basic level, it had elected an enormous number of GOP politicians, sidelining Democrats and burying populism, socialism, and the Progressive Party. The structure of American politics was transformed many times over between McKinley and Hoover, first by the ascent of the modern corporation, then by the turn toward a bureaucratic centralized state, and then by the enfranchisement of women. The Republican Party—the party of Mark Hanna, Theodore Roosevelt, and Ruth McCormick—survived it all, animated by a flexible conservatism keenly aware that no status quo could survive for long without a baseline of public support. Yes, the field was always tilted in favor of the powers that be. But after decades when radicals felt that power was within their grasp, and at a time when revolutionary movements were toppling governments across the Atlantic, the stability of American politics was no small achievement.

If anything, Republicans did their jobs too well. Economic inequality soared during the 1920s as union membership plummeted. The decade's roaring economic boom drowned out grumbles over the widening gap between the rich and the poor. But social peace—and the GOP majority—were tied to prosperity. When the Depression arrived, the party of business went into retreat.

Already in 1944, however, there were signs in Dewey's defeat of a Republican comeback, a party built of the Midwest, the Plains states, and an increasingly restive South. Mixing pieces of the old Republican and Democratic coalitions, it would unite the business-oriented voters Hanna brought into the GOP and Southern conservatives wary of the federal government's expanding reach. In his campaign, Dewey had hinted at the outlines of a coalition united against "the ill-assorted, power-hungry conglomeration of city bosses, communists and career bureaucrats which now compose the New Deal."[159]

Snooty pencil pushers, crooked urban machines, and the Red Menace—toss in a resurgent civil rights movement, and you had the enemies list for a potential new majority. Democrats were still confident in their hold on the public. But when the time was right, Mark Hanna's party would get its revenge.

Interlude: The Party of Everyone

With the 1948 election approaching, Harry Truman looked over a guide to his ungainly party. Republicans had won control of Congress in the midterms, and they were counting on taking back the presidency soon. According to the memo Truman was now reading—written by the Democratic operative James Rowe, with light revisions from White House counsel Clark Clifford—his only hope was to reassemble the New Deal coalition.[1]

Which would not be easy. At its core, Rowe and Clifford explained, FDR's majority was an uneasy partnership of Southern conservatives, western progressives, urban machines, and organized labor. (They included a separate discussion for liberals, describing them as a small but formidable group that punched above its weight because of their influence in the media.) Cultural identity loomed large in their analysis, which featured sections on the "The Negro," "The Jew," "The Catholic," "The Italian," and "The Alien Group" (for immigration supporters). Labor belonged in the Democratic tent, but Democrats were not a labor party, or a Southern party, or a western party.[2] Four years later, straining to hold this fracturing alliance together, Adlai Stevenson called it "the party of everyone."

The strongest and strangest coalition in American history, the New

Deal majority was a brittle colossus, able to push through historic reforms but always in danger of cracking open. FDR's Democratic Party
would become a model and a cautionary tale for future realigners of the
left and right. To tell *their* story, it's worth stepping back to look more
broadly at the making and breaking of the party of everyone.

———————

Nobody could have dreamed up an unlikelier coalition—and before it
appeared, nobody did. It's easy to pick out prophets of other realignments. Van Buren sketched the Jacksonian majority in the 1820s.
Sumner envisioned a Northern party of freedom in the 1840s. Hanna
anticipated the next Republican Party in the 1890s. By the 1960s, conservatives were forecasting a coming age of GOP dominance. Not long
after, liberals began predicting the arrival of what in the Obama years
would be called the "coalition of the ascendant"—young, diverse, and
solidly Democratic.

Franklin Roosevelt's party was an accidental empire. There were
plenty of calls for realignment early in the Depression, but they tended to
come from left-wing thinkers predicting the emergence of a third party
that would push aside both Democrats and Republicans.[3] Instead, New
Dealers stitched together a crazy-quilt coalition by delivering tangible
rewards to their constituents: a big step toward social democracy for the
North and Midwest; industrialization for the South and West. Unions
for Michigan, electricity for rural Texas. West Virginia, home to the
United Mine Workers, got both.

Just consider the numbers. In 1928, Hoover won 58.2 percent of
the vote while carrying forty states, and Republicans had a firm grip
on Congress (a majority of 106 seats in the House and 14 in the
Senate). Then Democrats picked up seats in the next *four* elections, one
of the longest winning streaks in American political history. In 1936,
the party won 334 seats in the House to 88 for the GOP. The margins
were even more lopsided in the Senate, where 76 Democrats faced off

against just 16 Republicans. Add up all the Republicans in national office, and the party just barely made it to triple digits.

But no majority lasts forever, and by the 1950s, long-term structural shifts were undermining the New Deal order, from declining union membership to the growing importance of television advertising (and therefore of raising money from wealthy donors to compete on the airwaves). Crucially, the kind of person who wielded political power was also changing. Machine politicians were giving way to activists who cared more about principle than about patronage. In 1962, the political scientist James Q. Wilson called these largely college-educated reformers "amateurs."[4] With their numbers increasing, thanks to the rapid expansion of higher education, amateurs were moving up the ranks of both parties—and looking to shake up the status quo.

The GOP's motives are easy to understand. Unless there's a countervailing force, parties bend toward majorities like sunflowers to the light. The outlines of an alternative Republican coalition were already coming together in the 1930s. Southern Democrats in Congress moved toward the right as the decade advanced, creating an informal conservative alliance in the legislature. Republicans won the popular vote for the House in 1942 before reclaiming Congress in 1946. The onset of McCarthyism gave the GOP a populist makeover, strengthening the party with midwesterners and Catholics.[5] Bolstered by Dwight Eisenhower's popularity, Republicans won unified control of the government in 1952 by breaking open the Solid South, eating into Democratic margins with the white working class, and dominating in prosperous suburbs. When Kevin Phillips announced the dawning of a conservative realignment in *The Emerging Republican Majority*, published in 1969, he was heralding the arrival of a coalition that had been decades in the making.[6]

As Republicans were piecing together their new party, an emboldened conservative movement was preparing to launch a hostile takeover of the GOP. An uneasy partnership from the start, the modern American right brought together businessmen looking to unwind the New Deal, hard-line anti-Communists bracing for World War III,

religious conservatives who feared for Christianity's survival in a secular age, white supremacists concerned that Washington bureaucrats
could bring an end to Jim Crow, and a looser collection of marginalized
figures who felt out of place in the modern world.[7]

Democrats were just as eager for a great re-sorting. "We've run out
of poor people," one New Dealer was said to have exclaimed after seeing the 1952 election returns.[8] The problem, supposedly, was that Roosevelt's policies had worked too well. The welfare state was lifting more
Americans into middle-class contentment, and ungrateful voters repaid
Democrats by casting their ballots for Eisenhower. Led by Stevenson,
influential liberals concluded that it was time to move beyond the New
Deal coalition. Without giving up on the party's identity as the champion of the little guy, they wanted to draw in comfortable suburbanites
who rolled their eyes when Democrats tried to run against the ghost of
Herbert Hoover.

And when liberals won, they wanted to govern. Tired of catering to
Southern conservatives, a broad array of mainstream party operatives,
labor leaders, civil rights activists, and outspoken liberals joined forces
to make Democrats an authentically progressive party. Radicals on the
left agreed. "American socialism must concentrate its efforts on the battle for political realignment," argued Michael Harrington, a member
of the Socialist Party's "Realignment Caucus." Instead of turning the
Socialists into a viable third party, Harrington urged his comrades to
burrow into the Democrats from within, making "a real second party
that will unite labor, liberals, [and] Negroes."[9]

Eventually, amateurs on the left and right got their wish. The parties traded the core of their old coalitions, with Democrats picking up
the Northeast and Republicans gaining the South and West. At the
same time, the connection between income and partisan affiliation
broke down, pushing working-class white people into the GOP and
drawing educated professionals toward the Democrats.

This shift was already evident by the middle of the 1960s, thanks
to the growing significance of a loosely connected collection of subjects that the political analysts Richard Scammon and Ben Wattenberg

dubbed "the Social Issue": civil rights, drugs, crime, busing, welfare, the draft, protests in cities and on campuses.[10] A vocal contingent of left-leaning observers quickly realized that their side might come out on the losing side of this realignment. In 1970, the political scientist Walter Dean Burnham predicted that dividing the parties around "a polarized cultural conflict" would pit a Democratic alliance of elites and the marginalized against a threatened Republican majority, turning "peripheral regions against the center, 'parochials' against 'cosmopolitans,' blue-collar whites against both blacks and affluent liberals . . . a top-bottom coalition against a 'great middle.'"[11]

Burnham doubted that anything good would come out of this change. If the country avoided a crisis, he believed it would probably descend into a soft authoritarianism, where responsibility for governing was handed over to a technocratic executive branch walled off from the public.

But what if there *was* a crisis, some catalytic event that forced a reckoning? Burnham warned that a political system divided between incompatible worldviews "would have as large a civil-war potential, would place as great a strain on political consensus—including, perhaps, the willingness of the losers in the electoral-politics arena to accept the outcome of an election" as any previous alignment in American history.[12] An endangered center could turn into a breeding ground for reactionary politics—perhaps even fascism.

Americans had put together a combustible mixture. "What would happen should it be ignited would," Burnham wrote, "be anyone's guess."[13]

———

It doesn't take nearly as much guessing today, when Burnham's prophecy has become our reality. Polarization has remade the parties, turning Democrats into the home for liberals and Republicans the home for conservatives. But it also changed the meaning of liberalism and conservatism, establishing a bond between technocracy and social justice at the same time it fortified the populist strain in the American right.

As the partisan divide has widened, the walls separating Washington from the rest of the country grew higher. Economic inequality and concentrated political power fed off each other, giving rise to an interlocking network of politicians, well-heeled donors, policymakers, political consultants, contractors and lobbyists, and media operatives.[14] They are winners in a society where the costs of losing are brutal and the game is rigged—in the first instance toward the superwealthy and then more broadly to an affluent, college-educated overclass.[15]

A combination of partisan polarization around identity, the withering of political machines, ascent of the amateurs, and mounting discontent with the state of the country now prevents either party from establishing a stable governing coalition—no sequel to the Age of Roosevelt for Democrats, no return to the dominance of Mark Hanna's GOP for Republicans. And so, instead of just asking how majorities were made, the pages ahead will also look at why they became so difficult to sustain.

The sudden rise and prolonged fall of the New Deal coalition is the essential backdrop for this story. To explain how the party of everyone was broken by the politics of principle, it helps to cheat a little bit. The New Deal order was born out of alliances too bizarre for anyone to see coming, and it can't be told through a single observer. So the next two chapters will bring a pair of contrasting witnesses to the stand.

W.E.B. Du Bois and Walter Lippmann both straddled the divide between the worlds of ideas and politics, mixing admiration for noble crusaders with a frank elitism and a keen sense of the constraints that reformers faced. If not separated by race, they might have had virtually identical careers. Instead, they tell the story of the New Deal era in Black and white. Although neither was a politician, Du Bois and Lippmann each pointed the way toward the new kind of liberalism created by polarization. The civil rights revolution and the liberal establishment matured alongside each other during the New Deal years. They were joined together by force in the 1960s, partly out of mutual affinity and partly as targets of a shared backlash.

Republicans now had an enemy to polarize against. Or, to be more accurate, two enemies—the coalition of top and bottom, Ivy League aristocrats and a racialized underclass. If liberals were going to play the part of Charles Sumner, conservatives would reach out to the heirs of Andrew Johnson. Brimming with enthusiasm, Kevin Phillips wrote that populists on the right "could hardly ask for a better target than a national Democratic Party aligned with Harvard, Boston, Manhattan's East Side, Harlem, the *New York Times*, and the liberal Supreme Court."[16] The Democratic Party, in other words, of Lippmann and Du Bois.

At the end of this road lies the politics of our time, with its eerie resemblance to the future that Burnham conjured half a century ago. But even if the journey was predictable, it wasn't inevitable. Although class-based voting declined across much of the world after the 1960s, fueled by the same structural factors at work in the United States, there has been enough variation—from country to country, and even campaign to campaign—to demonstrate the importance of choices made by political elites.[17]

So let's go back to the turn of the twentieth century, when the future looked bright—and W.E.B. Du Bois and Walter Lippmann knew that history was on their side.

5

Prophets

The year 1912 was a test for American democracy, and for W.E.B. Du Bois. He had quit academia two years earlier, leaving Atlanta University and heading to New York City, where he served as founding editor of *The Crisis*, the monthly journal of the recently founded NAACP.[1] *The Crisis* became mandatory reading in the group Du Bois named the Talented Tenth: lawyers, teachers, doctors, and other members of an emerging Black professional class. As the leading representative of a new phase in the civil rights movement, Du Bois was becoming, in his words, "a person whom every Negro in the nation knew by name at least and hastened always to entertain or praise."[2]

Now, in the early days of his eminence, Du Bois had to pick a candidate in the most crowded presidential field since 1860. In a close race where African Americans might hold the balance of power in battleground midwestern and Northern states, Black men couldn't afford to waste their votes.

Taft was the safe choice. For African Americans, the Republican was always the safe choice. On the other hand, Roosevelt was beloved by some of the NAACP's most important white supporters. And Du Bois's heart was with Eugene Debs. He had voted for the perennial socialist candidate in 1904, and he had joined the Socialist Party after moving to New York.

With his reputation on the line, Du Bois weighed the options carefully. Then he resigned his membership in the Socialist Party and endorsed Woodrow Wilson.

It was a surprising decision, but not a ridiculous one. Writing in *The Crisis*, Du Bois acknowledged that Wilson probably preferred a world of "flaxen haired wax dolls with or without brains" to one of "Chinese, Jews or Negroes."[3] But he thought that Roosevelt and Taft were just as flawed, and as much as he admired Debs—"if it lay in our power to make him President of the United States we would do so," he wrote—a socialist had no chance of winning.[4]

That left Wilson. Despite the Democratic nominee's troubling record, Du Bois thought the Johns Hopkins–trained political scientist was "too honest and cultured a gentleman to yield to the clamors of ignorance and prejudice and hatred."[5] Du Bois assigned Wilson's scholarship to his students, and in 1901 the two men published articles in the same issue of the *Atlantic Monthly*.[6] Wilson contributed a grand survey on the state of democracy, Du Bois wrote an essay that became a chapter in *The Souls of Black Folk*—a book he wrote in part to recruit white liberals such as Wilson to the cause of racial justice. At minimum, he thought, supporting Wilson enabled African Americans to punish Republicans for acquiescing to Jim Crow. At best, it could begin the process of integrating the Democrats, allowing enlightened reformers of both races—the Wilsons and Du Boises—to clasp hands across the color line.

Du Bois soon realized that he had miscalculated. Instead of racial progress, he later wrote, the Wilson years delivered "cruelty, discrimination, and wholesale murder," culminating in the mass slaughter of African Americans during the race riots of 1919.[7] But Du Bois held on to his self-appointed role as chief political strategist for Black America. In more than eighty years of writing—history, sociology, and journalism, along with plays, two autobiographies, five novels, and a steady stream of poetry—he returned time and again to the question of how African Americans might turn themselves into an electoral force.[8]

Though Du Bois was a global thinker and an early Pan-Africanist, he was also a student of American democracy who weighed in regularly with what he called "heart-to-heart talks with the Negro American voter."[9] The peak of his public career coincided almost exactly with the period—1901 to 1929—when African Americans were locked out of national office. Du Bois considered himself the closest thing his people had to a public voice, the statesman for a race denied representation in the government.

Luckily for him, the position was never submitted to a vote. "I never was, nor ever will be, personally popular," he acknowledged. "My leadership was a leadership solely of ideas."[10] The first African American to receive a doctorate from Harvard—which, he explained, was a consolation prize for having been unfairly denied a PhD from the University of Berlin—Du Bois was an elitist to the core. He wanted to lead a movement without sacrificing his independence, always a tricky balancing act and sometimes an impossible one. Stubborn and imperious, he made enemies easily. Nor could he honestly claim to speak for African Americans as a whole. Though beloved within the Talented Tenth, he struggled to connect with the group that Martin Luther King Jr. archly referred to as "the 'untalented' 90 per cent."[11]

Left to his own devices, Du Bois might have blissfully toiled in academic obscurity. White supremacy forced him into solidarity. "In my life," he observed at the age of seventy-two, "the chief fact has been race."

> Had it not been for the race problem early thrust upon me and enveloping me, I should have probably been an unquestioning worshiper at the shrine of the social order and economic development into which I was born. But just that part of that order which seemed to most of my fellows nearest perfection, seemed to me most inequitable and wrong; and starting from that critique, I gradually, as the years went by, found other things to question in my environment.[12]

From 1619 to the present, Du Bois later wrote, "the Negro in the United States has been the central thread of American history."[13] Once he started pulling, the whole tapestry unraveled.

With a confidence that looks astonishing in retrospect, Du Bois sought to use politics to make a social order that deserved his worship— mobilizing Black voters to trigger an electoral realignment, gain political power, and compel Americans to live up to their supposed ideals. He became the intellectual architect of the civil rights movement, with high schools named after him in Illinois and West Virginia. Then he turned into a pariah in his own country, eventually fleeing to Ghana, where he spent his final years waiting for a communist revolution to bring authentic democracy to the United States. He was, in turn, a pioneering liberal reformer, a pragmatic political operator, an heir to the Radical Republicans, and a revolutionary waiting for capitalism to self-destruct.

Three strategies vied for Du Bois's support over his very long life: liberal, socialist, and separatist. The liberal approach, on display in the Wilson endorsement, involved seeking integration from the top down. It assumed that rational arguments would convince educated white people to abandon racial prejudice, forging an alliance between elites in both races. The socialist alternative—the one he gave up by not endorsing Debs—involved seeking change from the bottom up, with a coalition of workers, white and Black, pursuing their collective emancipation. The separatist approach repudiated the faith in multiracial organizing shared by the socialist and liberal strategies. Treating white racism as an unmovable fact, it concentrated on building a Black community that could survive, and perhaps even thrive, in a hostile country.

Du Bois was drawn toward each of these strategies at different stages in his career, often mixing elements of all three. Ultimately, none could solve what he called, in the language of his time, "the Negro Problem."[14] But in combination, and supplemented with additional weapons—for instance, a Christian moralism that did little for an unrepentant agnostic like Du Bois—they spurred a political revolution.

"I am either a genius or a fool. O I wonder what I am," Du Bois wrote the night before his twenty-fifth birthday, when he was still an anonymous graduate student in Berlin.[15] He already knew one thing for certain: if "the Negro Problem" had a solution, W.E.B. Du Bois would find it.

"The political contest is near at hand, and the colored men of the town should prepare themselves accordingly," announced the *New York Globe* in the fall of 1883. "If they will only act in concert they may become a power not to be despised."[16]

The town in question was Great Barrington, Massachusetts, situated across the border from New York and home to just a few thousand people.[17] Local elections were often close enough that the town's small Black population could sway the outcome. "It would be a good plan if they should meet and decide which way would be most advantageous for them to cast their votes," concluded the author, "W.E.D.," better known to his family and friends as Great Barrington's teenage prodigy, Willie Du Bois.[18]

Growing up in New England left Du Bois with an image of democracy that Tocqueville would have recognized and Norman Rockwell could have painted. "There was little of what could be called politics in the local situation," he later wrote, describing a pure democracy run out of a little redbrick town hall.[19] Instead, the townsfolk debated roads and bridges, schools and budgets. Far-off capitals were sites of corruption, and politics was even more distressing when it slithered close to home. "I remember going downtown and staring fascinated at the marks of bullets in the door of a public building where a politician had been shot to death the day before," he said.[20] For a slight and slender boy who never grew above five feet six inches, it was better to stick with more refined pursuits. Although local democracy was noble, national politics was an unworthy—and perhaps deadly—pursuit for a young Black man with grand ambitions.*

* Disdain for politicians, especially African American politicians, was a running theme in Du Bois's work. His first two novels both feature rising-star Black politicos acting as puppets for the ruling class. "We can't touch political conditions in the South; perhaps this sop will do," a Republican senator explains in the first novel: W.E.B. Du Bois, *The Quest of the Silver Fleece: A Novel* (Chicago, 1911), 277. The hero

Armchair political consultant, therefore, was only one of the young Du Bois's occupations. In addition to writing occasional articles for the *Globe*, he picked up odd jobs, devoured the five volumes of Thomas Macaulay's *History of England*, and served as secretary of his church's sewing circle. Raised by a single mother after being abandoned by his father, Du Bois decided early that education was the path toward a better future, for himself and for his race. Reconstruction's failure struck him as a temporary setback. African Americans were marching out of slavery, and the logic of democracy dictated that they would one day rule the South—so long as they had the right guidance. "They needed trained leadership," he remembered. "I was sent to help furnish it."[21]

In 1885, the journey took him to Nashville's Fisk University, where he received a rigorous liberal arts education alongside the children of former slaves (many of whom were also the children of former slave owners). Like most of his classmates and teachers, Du Bois dismissed the initial signs of Jim Crow as a temporary inconvenience. Fisk students were trained to take their place alongside the future leaders of the white South as part of an interracial governing class, where access to the ballot would be determined by education rather than skin color.

Extending his analysis of Great Barrington politics to the nation as a whole, Du Bois predicted in 1887 that "the South will not always be solid, and in every division the Negro will hold the balance of power."[22] At his graduation a year later, he delivered a commencement address on Otto von Bismarck, the German chancellor whose leadership had made a nation "out of bickering peoples"—an alluring model for the young Du Bois.[23]

Next he moved on to Harvard for a second undergraduate degree.

---

of the second eventually renounces electoral politics, declaring, "I'd rather go to hell than to Congress": W.E.B. Du Bois, *Dark Princess: A Romance* (Jackson, MS, 1995), 210 (orig. pub. 1928). It doesn't take much effort to see these two as stand-ins for a life that Du Bois thought he could have chosen for himself.

"It was the greatest and oldest college," he said, "and I therefore quite naturally thought it was the one I must attend."[24] Only the sixth African American student in the university's history, Du Bois always felt as if he were in but not of Harvard. He sampled classes across the humanities and social sciences. For his favorite professor, the philosopher William James, he produced a fifty-two-page essay diving into metaphysics, from medieval Scholasticism to Kant. But when Du Bois told his instructor that he intended to become a philosopher, James urged him to consider a safer career path. His highest grade, an A+, came in a course titled "Constitutional and Political History of the United States," taught by the meticulous scholar and thoroughgoing racist Albert Hart, who viewed Du Bois's success as proof "that a mulatto may have as much power and passion as any white man."[25]

Preoccupied with the life of the mind, Du Bois looked on politics from a distance. Presidential elections passed without catching his attention, and the rise of the Populists looked to him like a case study in vulgar democracy. He even shrugged off racial disenfranchisement. "We must remember that a good many of our people south of Mason and Dixon's line are not fit for the responsibilities of republican government," he told a Black audience in 1891. "When you have the right sort of black voters, you will need no election laws. The battle of my people in the South must be a moral one, not a legal or a physical one."[26]

He wanted to lead this battle on his own terms. After graduating from Harvard with honors, he won a scholarship to pursue a doctorate at the University of Berlin, inspiration for the new American research universities. As he explained at the time, he intended to specialize in social science, with an eye "to the ultimate application of its principles to the social and economic rise of the Negro people."[27]

Academic training would allow him to seek political change without being tainted by politics. He set sail for Europe with dreams of turning American democracy into a grand New England town hall meeting, where university-trained experts played the role of city elders and racial prejudice had melted away under the harsh glare of reason.

"The Negro race, like all races, is going to be saved by its exceptional men," he believed.[28] W.E.B. Du Bois was going to make himself one of them.

———————

Reflecting on his life, a ninety-two-year-old Du Bois claimed that his goals were simple. "I very early got the idea," he said, "that what I was going to do was to prove to the world that Negroes were just like other people."[29] But it felt so much larger at the time. "Is it the silent call of the world spirit that makes me feel that I am royal and that beneath my scepter a world of kings shall bow?" he asked himself after living in Berlin a few months. "These are my plans: to make a name in science, to make a name in literature and thus to raise my race. Or perhaps to raise a visible empire in Africa thro' England, France or Germany. I wonder what will be the outcome? Who knows? I will go unto the king . . . and if I perish—I PERISH."[30]

In Germany, Du Bois's instructors confirmed his belief that the path to power ran through the social sciences. Studying economics in a faculty that included a young Max Weber, he was taught that laissez-faire was dead. The future belonged neither to capitalists nor to revolutionaries but to experts wielding the power of the state.[31]

Du Bois was intrigued by the country's thriving socialist movement, but he was not going to be enlisting in a war against the bourgeoisie anytime soon. Although he sat in on a few meetings of the German Social Democratic Party—the largest socialist party in the world—he was repulsed by what he called "that anarchistic, semi-criminal proletariat which always, in all countries, attaches itself to the most radical party."[32] The world he dreamed of would come about through reforms instituted from above, not a revolution from below.

But it wasn't at all clear how a graduate student scribbling notes to himself in Berlin would put himself at the vanguard of a new world order—or whether he would even have a job when he came back home.

After finishing all the academic obligations for his doctorate in three semesters rather than the mandatory four, Du Bois was informed that without the extra semester, he did not meet the requirements for a degree. Unable to secure funding for additional time in Berlin, he returned to the United States in 1894 without his PhD, only later earning his doctorate from Harvard with a dissertation on the history of the slave trade.

After a brief stint teaching Greek and Latin at Wilberforce University—a small, historically Black campus in rural Ohio—Du Bois found temporary harbor at the University of Pennsylvania with a one-year assignment to study Black life in Philadelphia. The city was home to the North's largest African American population, and local politics were controlled by a Republican machine elected with Black votes. Reformers looking to break the GOP's stranglehold on government hoped that Du Bois's research would give them weapons in the fight.[33]

Du Bois tried to satisfy their aims and his own with *The Philadelphia Negro*. Drawing on 835 hours of interviews conducted with twenty-five hundred households, he argued that the African American community had split into four distinct groups: an underworld of "criminals, prostitutes, and loafers," followed by the working poor, then one notch up a "respectable working class," and at the top an emerging "aristocracy of the Negroes"—the group he would soon dub the Talented Tenth.[34] African Americans had already created their own leadership class. Give this homegrown aristocracy the power to lead, Du Bois argued, and the entire country would benefit.

The Philadelphia Negro set the template for the next phase of Du Bois's career: an attack on the intellectual foundations of white supremacy, one monograph at a time. From Atlanta University, where he was offered a professorship after his year in Philadelphia, he presided over the release of studies ranging from "The Negro in Business" to "The Health and Physique of the American Negro." The Bureau of Labor Statistics recruited him to produce a series of reports on "the economic progress of the colored people" in the South.[35] For the 1900 Paris World's Fair, he worked with a team of assistants to produce dozens of

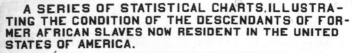

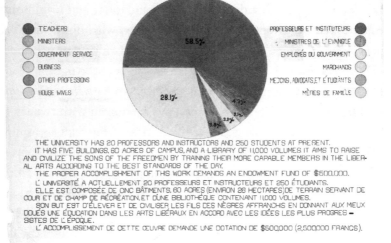

charts on the condition of African Americans, along with tributes to Black achievements in education and literature.[36]

Du Bois paired empirical research with psychological explorations of life on his side of the racial divide. "Between me and the other world there is ever an unasked question," he wrote in his debut article for *The Atlantic Monthly*, published in the summer of 1897.[37] "How does it feel to be a problem?" (The problem being "the Negro Problem.") A breakthrough for Du Bois, the essay established his national reputation and in adapted form became the opening chapter of his next major work, *The Souls of Black Folk.*

Though *Souls* is remembered today for its proto-existentialist musings on the African American experience, the book also offered the fullest expression of Du Bois's idiosyncratic synthesis of New England democracy and progressive reform. Written by an author with the soul of a poet and the mind of a technocrat, it sought to rouse Black consciousness while building an alliance of elites that transcended the color line. According to Du Bois, Jim Crow was damaging because it kept apart "the best element" in both races while allowing for intermingling "at the bottom of social group, in the saloon, the gambling-hell [*sic*], and the brothel."[38] Still a defender of suffrage restrictions, he insisted, "I am not saying a word against all legitimate efforts to purge the ballot of ignorance, pauperism, and crime," but only against discrimination based on race.[39] "The ignorant Southerner hates the Negro, the workingmen fear his competition," he wrote. "Others—usually the sons of the masters—wish to help him to rise."[40] Your fathers sinned, he told the children of the planter class, but you can be redeemed.

As Du Bois called on the South's governing class to live up to its own standards, he was also challenging the country's Black leadership—especially, and inevitably, Booker T. Washington.[41] A former slave, Washington had built an empire that Du Bois called the "Tuskegee Machine," as if Washington were the party boss of Black America.[42] It was an ironic label for a leader who urged his people to give up on electoral politics and focus on economic gains. "He was a man who believed that we should get what we could get," Du Bois later said. "Washington was a politician."[43]

Precisely because Du Bois didn't consider himself a "politician," he had more faith in democracy, properly understood—that is, a democracy guided by the "talented." Rather than working through a machine handing out graft, he wanted to pursue integration by cultivating the best in African American culture: "Negro colleges, Negro newspapers, Negro business organizations, a Negro school of literature and art, and an intellectual clearing house, for all these products of the

Negro mind, which we may call a Negro Academy."[44] That was the crux of the debate with Washington, as Du Bois saw it: segregation versus integration, the hacks versus the reformers, the Tuskegee Machine versus the Negro Academy, Booker T. Washington vs. W.E.B. Du Bois (PhD).

Souls changed Du Bois's life, catapulting him to a level of fame within the Black community exceeded only by that of Washington. He fashioned a coherent philosophy out of town halls in Great Barrington, seminars in Berlin, and the Jim Crow Car. There was still much work to be done, but it looked like a solution to the race problem might just be within his grasp.

Then it all fell apart.

———————

"I began to realize that I had overworked a theory," Du Bois remembered.[45] The realization came in fits and starts.

There was the spring day in 1899 when he saw a store window displaying the burnt knuckles of Sam Hose, a Black laborer who had been lynched after killing his white employer in self-defense.[46]

Then there was the day, just a month later, when he walked through the same streets with the coffin of his only son. Burghardt Du Bois died of diphtheria a few months shy of his second birthday. As Du Bois and his wife, Nina, escorted their son's body to a train carrying them north for the funeral, white onlookers turned their heads to watch. "They did not say much, those pale-faced hurrying men and women," he remembered. "They only glanced and said, 'Niggers!'"[47]

And there was the day in September 1906 when some ten thousand white Atlantans, whipped up by reports of Black men assaulting white women, went looking for revenge. "In some portions of the streets," *The Atlanta Constitution* reported, "the sidewalks ran red with the blood of dead and dying negroes."[48]

His studies were filling up shelves of libraries in the United States and Europe. Careful measurement, astute analysis, interpretive rigor—none of it changed a thing, at least not anything that mattered.

"The cure wasn't simply telling people the truth, it was inducing them to act on the truth," he decided.[49] "One could not be a calm, cool, and detached scientist while Negroes were lynched, murdered, and starved."[50]

Du Bois set out to build a counter-Tuskegee, institutional backup for his skirmishes with Washington. In 1905 he started a short-lived magazine, *The Moon Illustrated Weekly*. That same year he joined twenty-nine exemplary members of the Talented Tenth for a meeting in Niagara Falls that culminated with a declaration of principles calling for an end to racial segregation and disenfranchisement. The Niagara Movement soon had chapters in twenty-one states. Then, in 1907, Du Bois returned to magazine publishing, overseeing production of the monthly *Horizon: A Journal of the Color Line*. But he lacked Washington's talent for organization, and by 1910 the Niagara Movement and *Horizon* were both defunct.[51]

The more Du Bois pushed into the world, the further his politics drifted to the left. "While I would scarcely describe myself as a socialist still I have much sympathy with the movement and I have many socialistic beliefs," he wrote in 1904, the same year he backed Eugene Debs's presidential run.[52] Du Bois hadn't given up on bringing liberal-minded white Southerners to his side, but he was more hopeful about building interracial, working-class coalitions. In 1907 he described himself as a "socialist-of-the-path" and urged African Americans to seek alliances with "not the rich but the poor, not the great but the masses, not the employers but the employees."[53] He had no residual affection for the GOP, writing in 1908 that the party had "forfeited its claim to the Negro vote."[54] That same year, he endorsed William Jennings Bryan over Taft, a striking departure from his earlier disgust with populism.

As Du Bois built his public reputation, his academic career was crumbling. Funding for his studies on African American life dried up, and his relationship with the Bureau of Labor Statistics soured. Booker T. Washington, still the Black leader who white donors most wanted to hear from, made no secret of his belief that "it is too bad that an institution like Atlanta University has permitted Dr. Du Bois to go on from year to year stirring up racial strife in the heart of the South."[55]

Except Du Bois wasn't interested in stirring up racial strife, or staying in the South. "I had realized that a purely racial organization couldn't fight for Negro rights," he later said. "You have to have not only Negroes united but whites united too."[56]

That's where the NAACP entered the picture. The product of an alliance between white reformers and African Americans, the NAACP was a monument to the integrationist ideal.[57] They set up offices in New York in 1910 and offered Du Bois the position of director of publicity and research. The NAACP wasn't the "Negro Academy" Du Bois had dreamed of, but it was as close as he was going to get. "Stepping . . . out of my ivory tower of statistics and investigation," he recalled, "I sought with bare hands to lift the earth and put it in the path in which I conceived it ought to go."[58]

It began soberly enough. "The object of this publication is to set forth those facts and arguments which show the danger of race prejudice," Du Bois wrote in the debut issue of *The Crisis*, voice of the NAACP. "Its editorial page will stand for the rights of men, irrespective of color or race, for the highest ideals of American democracy, and for reasonable but earnest and persistent attempts to gain these rights and realize these ideals."[59]

Then came a caveat that would make Tuskegee cringe. "Agitation is a necessary evil," Du Bois wrote. "It is Pain; Pain is not good but Pain is necessary."[60]

Du Bois spent more than two decades as editor of *The Crisis*, struggling to maintain this precarious balance between assurance and agitation, comfort and pain. The magazine reflected his capacious interests and evolving politics. Depending on the issue, readers could find a tribute to the Soviet Union or a celebration of Black small business owners.

And there were many readers. At its height, *The Crisis* had more than a hundred thousand subscribers, trumping the venerable *Nation* and the upstart *New Republic*.[61]

Critics dismissed him as erratic, but Du Bois considered himself a pragmatist. With the NAACP as a vehicle and *The Crisis* as his platform, he planned to nurture a Black elite and teach novice leaders how to look out for their race, with the ultimate goal of achieving recognition as equal citizens of an integrated United States. He would build alliances with anyone who could help their cause—including, he acknowledged, "the rich, the white, and the powerful."[62]

Attacks came from all directions. He infuriated Black radicals during World War I by urging Africans Americans to "forget our special grievances and close our ranks shoulder to shoulder with our own white fellow citizens."[63] To the flamboyant Jamaican Marcus Garvey, leader of the Back-to-Africa movement, Du Bois was an "unfortunate mulatto who bewails every day the drop of Negro blood in his veins."[64] The white supremacist Lothrop Stoddard, like Du Bois a Harvard history PhD, echoed Garvey.[65] Stoddard called Du Bois a textbook instance of miscegenation's tragic results, condemned to an "unhappy and uncertain existence . . . literally suspended in a vacuum, allied to both races yet really belonging to neither."[66]

But Du Bois outlasted Garvey, who was convicted of mail fraud in 1923 and deported four years later. And he made quick work of Stoddard when the two met in the Chicago Coliseum (the same building that hosted the Republican National Convention's tribute to Mark Hanna in 1904). With Stoddard visibly uncomfortable in front of a mostly Black audience, the crowd roared when Du Bois asked, when confronting the familiar specter of interracial marriage, "Who in Hell asked to marry your daughters?"[67]

Du Bois reveled in the luxuries that he believed his position earned him, including the respect of his peers, a tidy income, and serial adultery. "I was not, on the whole, what one would describe as a good husband," he later admitted.[68] Insiders referred knowingly to the "casting couch" at *The Crisis*. In the case of Marvel Jackson, his assistant at the

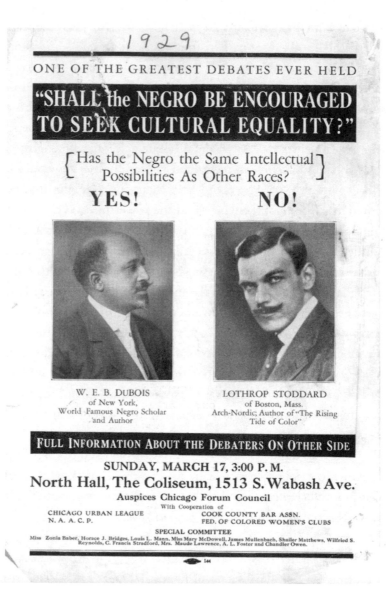

ONE OF THE GREATEST DEBATES EVER HELD

"SHALL the NEGRO BE ENCOURAGED TO SEEK CULTURAL EQUALITY?"

⎡ Has the Negro the Same Intellectual ⎤
⎣   Possibilities As Other Races?   ⎦

YES!   NO!

W. E. B. DUBOIS
of New York,
World Famous Negro Scholar
and Author

LOTHROP STODDARD
of Boston, Mass.
Arch-Nordic; Author of "The Rising
Tide of Color".

FULL INFORMATION ABOUT THE DEBATERS ON OTHER SIDE

SUNDAY, MARCH 17, 3:00 P. M.
North Hall, The Coliseum, 1513 S. Wabash Ave.
Auspices Chicago Forum Council
With Cooperation of
CHICAGO URBAN LEAGUE   COOK COUNTY BAR ASSN.
N. A. A. C. P.   FED. OF COLORED WOMEN'S CLUBS
SPECIAL COMMITTEE
Miss Zonia Baber, Horace J. Bridges, Louis L. Mann, Miss Mary McDowell, James Mullenbach, Shailer Matthews, Wilfried S. Reynolds, C. Francis Stradford, Mrs. Maude Lawrence, A. L. Foster and Chandler Owen.

144

magazine, philandering edged into what would today be considered sexual harassment. "You know, when we were working up at the magazine," Jackson later said, "he'd put his hand on my leg, and I was so in awe of him—his intellect—that I really didn't know [what to do]." According to David Levering Lewis, author of a comprehensive two-volume biography of Du Bois, "Jackson's experience was not unusual."[69]

Male colleagues at the NAACP had their own troubles with their organization's presiding genius. Du Bois was committed to making *The Crisis* one of the world's great journals, and he did not mind stepping over those he considered his intellectual inferiors—a large group indeed—to get it done. "Many people whose devotion to this cause is as deep as yours or mine . . . think you are the chief if not the only source of the disorder and lack of unity in our organization," warned Joel Spingarn, chairman of the NAACP.[70] Du Bois acknowledged the problem, telling Spingarn, "I do not doubt in the least but that my temperament is a difficult one to endure. In my peculiar education and experiences it would be miraculous if I came through normal and unwarped."[71]

Such were the wages of genius, he told himself. In a now forgotten novel—John Vandercook's *Black Majesty*—Du Bois underlined this passage: "To be great, Duncan, is to be lonely. To be magnificent is to have men hate you."[72] And not just men.

―――――――――

However far he ranged, Du Bois never let his attention stray for long from American politics. Burned by his gamble on Woodrow Wilson, he was guided by one overarching principle: *"Vote for friends of our race and defeat our enemies."*[73]

But how to tell the difference? Despite giving up his membership in the Socialist Party when he endorsed Wilson, Du Bois still planted himself firmly on the left. "The editor of *The Crisis* considers himself a socialist," he wrote in 1921.[74] With images of victory in a global class struggle dancing before his eyes, he announced during a 1926 trip to the Soviet Union, "If what I have seen with my eyes and heard with my ears in Russia is Bolshevism, I am a Bolshevik."[75]

At home, Du Bois sharpened his attacks on the status quo. "We must realize that this country is not a democracy; that it is an oligarchy

ruled by the Rich and Powerful," he thundered.[76] He gave up on converting the sons of the planter class to racial justice. "The real deep and
the basic race hatred in the United States," he now argued, "is a matter
of the educated and the distinguished leaders of white civilization."[77]

But he couldn't rely on the white working class, either. The more
convinced Du Bois became of socialism's necessity, the more he despaired of winning over the proletariat. "Throughout the history of the
Negro in America, white labor has been the black man's enemy," he
told readers in *The Crisis*. "It is white labor that deprives the Negro
of his right to vote, denies him education, denies him affiliation with
trade unions, expels him from decent houses and neighborhoods, and
heaps upon him the public insults of open color discrimination."[78]

He wasn't completely unsympathetic to the socialists' dilemma. African Americans were about 10 percent of the total population. Thanks
to Jim Crow, Black people were an even smaller proportion of the overall electorate. Although the moral case for civil rights was impeccable,
the politics were treacherous at best.

Du Bois knew the socialist future he wanted, and he knew his obligations to African Americans in the present, but he couldn't figure
out how to reconcile the two. What to do about party machines that
stymied reformers but put Black cops on the street? What about a judicial system that struck down legislation regulating corporations but
also had the power to defend civil rights? And what about big business
itself, which might be the ultimate enemy to true emancipation, but
which right now was responsible for jobs that kept Black families from
starving? Part of him longed to join the revolution; the other part was
convinced that when the fighting started, people who looked like him
would be the first to die.

The obstacles looked insurmountable, and that didn't even take into
account the challenge of navigating the two-party system. Returning
to the strategy he first suggested to Great Barrington's Black voters
in 1883, he toyed with the idea of setting up an independent "Negro
Party" (modeled on Alice Paul's National Woman's Party) that would
endorse whichever candidate was strongest on civil rights. Despite his

best efforts, however, ordinary African Americans showed little interest in breaking from the GOP. It was a confounding experience for Du Bois. Black voters were sticking together, as he wanted, but instead of using their power to jolt American democracy back to life, they lined up behind a Republican Party that promised "neglect, indifference, and misunderstanding."[79]

With the Negro Party dead on arrival, Du Bois turned his attention to building a multiracial third party. But he was reminded time and again that white reformers who cared about civil rights typically viewed the subject as another item on a checklist, and often not a terribly important one. After reading a pamphlet making the case for a progressive party, Du Bois dashed off a note reprimanding the author—the University of Chicago economist Paul Douglas—for omitting any discussion of Black disenfranchisement. Douglas's reply brought home why building interracial coalitions was so difficult. "I had not realized that we had omitted the Negro from our program," he apologized, jauntily adding, "It is not necessary to stress every issue all the time!"[80]

The more Du Bois thought about American politics, the more Black voting seemed like the only issue—or, at least, the indispensable one. No left-wing party could gain traction, he argued, while disenfranchisement ensured that reactionaries controlled the South. "On account of the 'Negro problem,'" he concluded, "we are making democratic government increasingly impossible in the United States."[81]

African Americans were left with no good options. "If we keep out of politics, we give the whip hand to our enemies," he wrote in 1928. "When we vote, we do not have a chance to vote on the real merits of the questions presented. We cannot consider the tariff, farm relief, war, peace, municipal ownership, superpower, and a dozen other pressing political questions. No, we have got to ask: Does Herbert Hoover believe that Negroes are men or sub-men?"[82] They could support party machines in the hopes of eking out small gains, and, in doing so, lose the respect of white reformers—but what good were white reformers if they couldn't stand against Jim Crow?

The tensions were agonizing, and that was before the Great Depression convinced Du Bois that capitalism had entered its final crisis. Torn between conflicting impulses, he complained in private about the "group of elderly reactionaries" running the NAACP, while in public he insisted that progress would come about only through incremental change.[83] He was caught in an impossible position, denouncing American democracy as an irredeemable oligarchy at one moment and at the next urging radicals to come up with piecemeal reforms to win over white capitalists.

And he was doing it all while losing his confidence that reason could triumph over white supremacy. In a string of essays for *The Crisis*, written in 1933 and 1934, he renounced the founding vision of the NAACP.[84] Racism had beaten facts and logic time after time, and he couldn't see when that would change. The only realistic option left to African Americans was to make the best of segregation. Sounding like a radicalized version of Booker T. Washington—as if the Wizard of Tuskegee had just emerged from a Marxist reading group—Du Bois called on African Americans to create a separate, pseudo-socialist economy within a disintegrating capitalist system.

Du Bois's turn against integration marked a decisive break with the NAACP. He resigned from *The Crisis* and arranged a face-saving appointment at Atlanta University. (His replacement at the magazine, a young journalist named Roy Wilkins, had been briefly engaged to his former assistant Marvel Jackson.) After a lifetime spent thinking about the race problem, he didn't feel any closer to a solution. Everything he tried had failed. Now he wanted to find out why.

———————

He started with a crash course in Marxism. Rather than dwelling on the intricacies of the labor theory of value or commodity fetishism, he focused on a few simple lessons: exploitation was real, class struggle drove history, and a society's economic foundations determined the outlines of its politics and culture. Freshly converted, Du Bois announced in 1935, "I believe in Karl Marx."[85]

But like other Marxists at the time—Antonio Gramsci in Italy, the Frankfurt School in Germany—Du Bois wanted to push beyond a narrow focus on economics.[86] He was reading Freud, too, and using psychology to analyze what economics alone couldn't explain—above all, racism. Even if racial prejudice was a by-product of capitalism, Du Bois thought that racism had long ago taken on a life of its own. "We were not facing simply the rational, conscious determination of white folk to oppress us," he realized. "We were facing age-long complexes sunk now largely to unconscious habit and irrational urge, which demanded on our part not only the patience to wait, but the power to entrench ourselves for a long siege against the strongholds of color caste."[87]

Du Bois's shotgun marriage of Marx and Freud wasn't an immaculate piece of social theory. Ultimately, either class conflict determines the course of history, or racism can spin off from its economic foundations and follow a path of its own. But theoretical niceties were less important to him than the practical value of holding race and class together in the same analysis, and here the payoff was substantial.

Although he didn't believe in revolution, Du Bois could now explain why he had so little to show after so many years of attempted reform. Capitalists reaped material benefits from keeping the working class at war with itself, and white labor received a "psychological wage" from membership in the master race.[88] He thought that neither liberals nor Marxists recognized both sides of the problem. The NAACP refused to confront the power of capital, while socialists downplayed the racial fault line running through the American proletariat.[89]

Which raised the question of what to do next. "I see but one path of salvation for American Negroes," he declared. "Get a growing group of young, trained, fearless and unselfish Negroes to guide the American Negro in this crisis, and guide him toward the coming of socialism throughout the world."[90]

But young Black radicals refused to act out the part he scripted for them. Even as Du Bois moved left, his intellectual children were staging a full-blown Oedipal revolt, dismissing him as a closeted liberal who couldn't see that class solidarity was already trumping racial division.[91]

The most cutting assessment came from George Streator, a Du Bois protégé who later became the first Black correspondent for *The New York Times*.[92] Writing to Du Bois in 1935, Streator reprimanded the older man for being too soft on Black capitalists ("a lousy minority bourgeoisie") and too harsh on the white working class.[93] "Your information on the present-day labor problem, its possible trends, your information on Southern white labor are on the whole poor," Streator told him. "And there is no place for you to learn these things except from the 'youngsters' you are tending to bawl out, these days."[94] Then he gave the knife one last twist. "You want security, prestige, and the good life, and socialism without a sacrifice. And you are easily fooled by flatterers."[95]

Du Bois was unbowed. "Radical reform in the United States is letting itself be hypnotized into extreme communism," he warned Streator.[96] No matter how much leftists wanted to dream a united proletariat into existence, the real working class was divided by race and, for the most part, wedded to the status quo. "The great majority of them are thoroughly capitalistic in their ideals," he wrote. "The last thing that they would want to do would be to unite in any movement whose object was the uplift of the mass of Negroes to essential equality with them."[97]

Du Bois still believed that socialism would come to the United States, but joining with a revolutionary movement to overthrow capital would be suicidal for African Americans (and potentially undercut white radicals, too: expropriating the bourgeoisie would be hard enough without also taking on white supremacy).

"I am, therefore, absolutely and bitterly opposed to the American brand of communism, which simply aims to stir up trouble and to make Negroes shock troops in a fight whose triumph may easily involve the utter annihilation of the American Negro," he told Streator. "What I want is a realistic and practical approach to a democratic state in which the exploitation of labor is stopped, and the political power is in the hands of the workers."[98]

And that brought him back to the case for a radicalized version of the Talented Tenth. With the right guidance, African Americans could build a cooperative economy that would link up with the broader socialist movement when the time came. "Either we get such a group leadership of the Negro race or we are lost."[99]

———

As he argued with Streator, Du Bois was bracing for the release of his fullest exploration yet of his case for despair. Even with more than six hundred densely packed pages to work with, *Black Reconstruction in America* strained to accomplish all the tasks he set out for it: overturning a historical consensus that viewed Reconstruction as a tyrannical period of misgovernment; putting the Black experience at the center of American history; tracing the development of a system of racial exploitation that turned white labor against the colored people of the world; and providing an obituary for American democracy.[100]

Politically, it's a book at war with itself. The heroes of the narrative are the champions of what Du Bois called "abolition democracy": Southern Black precursors to the Talented Tenth and their Radical Republican allies in the North.[101] Like all tragic heroes, abolition democracy had a fatal flaw. It did not understand that guaranteeing the civil rights of former slaves required a wholesale transformation of American life, North and South. "Charles Sumner," Du Bois lamented, "did not realize, and that other Charles—Karl Marx—had not yet published *Das Kapital* to prove to men that economic power underlies politics."[102] Liberals did not grasp the unpleasant fact that democracy in America could be achieved only through undemocratic means, "a vast single-eyed dictatorship" that could shepherd a "provincial and bigoted" electorate to the promised land.[103] When Republicans pulled back from imposing a "dictatorship of labor," they midwifed a "dictatorship of capital" born out of an alliance between Northern capitalists and Southern planters.[104] And this marriage produced an American oligarchy that "murdered democracy in the United States so completely that the world does not recognize its corpse."[105]

Du Bois was generous with his newly acquired radical vocabulary, describing Reconstruction as "one of the most extraordinary experiments of Marxism that the world, before the Russian revolution, had seen."[106] Yet his account of the demands made by the "dark proletariat" was surprisingly modest.[107] According to Du Bois, all the planter class had to do was acknowledge that freed people had won the right to a few basic goods—land, a decent education—and they would have been invited to retake their old place at the top of the social hierarchy. It took a colossal failure from the old ruling class to crack open the door for a radical alternative. And still, Du Bois's tone was bleak enough that, in an otherwise favorable review, *The New York Times* fretted, "There runs through the book a note of challenge which seems to point, in the author's mind at least, to the imminence of an inescapable and deadly racial struggle."[108]

All of Du Bois's former political personalities were on display. There were vestiges of the liberal reformer, certain that there would be enough for everyone in a rationally ordered world. But he was also the last Radical Republican, trying to push the American creed to its limits. And he was a Marxist, writing against the backdrop of the Great Depression, certain that he could hear capitalism's death rattles. Through it all, he was the veteran of a lifelong war against white supremacy—a war that broke his liberalism, his radicalism, and his Marxism, a war that part of him doubted could ever be won.

This same ambivalence runs through the book he almost wrote next, a novel of ideas he planned on calling "A Search for Democracy." After diving into American history for *Black Reconstruction*, he embarked in 1936 on a tour around the world that took him across Europe, the Soviet Union, China, and Japan. He returned to the United States six months later with the rough draft of a novel chronicling the adventures of "Abraham Lincoln Jones," a Black college professor who enters the political equivalent of a midlife crisis when a student asked him to define "democracy." Shocked to realize that he doesn't have an answer, Jones sets out on "a voyage of democracy" modeled on the journey Du Bois had just undertaken.[109]

At the end of his travels, Jones decides that "the fundamental differences between governments today are not differences between Democracy, Fascism, and Communism, but differences as to how far and in what way governments are going to attack the problem of work and wages and the distribution of wealth." He prefers a humanistic socialism that combines communist efficiency with a respect for democracy, but he gives up on seeing any progress against American oligarchy in his lifetime. Instead, he finds love with a woman who shares his belief that "Poverty is sin; Profit is Theft; Sex is Joy." The two give up on changing the world and find anonymous work in Alabama, where "they lived happily and in the shadow of the fear of starvation all their lives"—not exactly a rousing conclusion, which is perhaps why Du Bois's publisher passed on the manuscript.[110]

Du Bois was just as skeptical about the prospects for American democracy as his fictional alter ego. With memories of the last time he endorsed a Democrat for president still fresh, Du Bois voted for the Socialist candidate Norman Thomas in 1932. After Roosevelt's victory, Du Bois prepared himself for the Democrats to waste four years trying to resuscitate a dying capitalist system.

His views softened as the New Deal took shape. By the end of Roosevelt's first term, Du Bois saw FDR as part of a broad left-wing coalition—which is why he endorsed the president for reelection in 1936, and why he assumed that Roosevelt would lose. Early in the campaign he predicted that conservative and liberal Democrats would turn their fire on each other, and Republicans would use the Mark Hanna playbook to buy their way back into the White House, where they would overturn the New Deal.[111] A lifetime of studying American democracy had taught him not to ask for more.

But history is a slippery thing. After Roosevelt waltzed back into office with one of the largest victories in U.S. history, Du Bois began to suspect that his obituary for American democracy had been premature.

The key player in this story was the Democratic Party. FDR's base was still in the Jim Crow South. He swept through the former Confederacy in 1936 with margins normally reserved for dictators: 86 percent of the vote in Alabama, 89 percent in Louisiana, and—almost unbelievably—99 percent in South Carolina.[112] But a different kind of party was taking shape in the rest of the country. As unions were moving to the center of the Democratic coalition, John Lewis's CIO was actively recruiting across the color line. And in states where African Americans still had the franchise, they were casting ballots for Democrats. In a sample of majority-Black districts across the North and Midwest, Roosevelt carried just 31 percent of the vote in 1932. Four years later, his total soared to 66 percent.[113]

Those are the kind of numbers that make politicians take notice. Roosevelt appointed more African Americans to high-level government posts than any president in history. The Fair Employment Practices Committee, established in 1941, gave institutional heft to the battle against discrimination in the federal workforce. FDR wasn't a champion of racial equality. Fearful of alienating the South, he wouldn't even support a federal anti-lynching law, a top priority for the NAACP. But for all his flaws, Roosevelt was a distinct improvement on the low standard set by his predecessors, and ambitious Democrats in the next generation paid attention to his example.[114] Driven by activist pressure and raw political calculation, Democrats were inching toward becoming the party of civil rights.

The racial economics of the New Deal were a trickier matter for Du Bois. He was well aware that compromises with the South blocked African Americans from receiving much of the New Deal's benefits, further widening the divide between white people and Black people. But the disparities weren't as severe in the rest of the country, and he thought that even modest victories were worth appreciating. "It is not the part of wisdom to sneer at the hand that feeds you," he warned activists.[115]

And he meant "feeds" literally. According to Du Bois's calculations, the Works Progress Administration alone saved a million African Americans from starvation. By 1940, he was optimistic enough to call FDR "the only living man who can lead the United States further on the path which will eventually abolish poverty"—an economic revolution that would transform Black America.[116] The victories were partial, and no substitute for socialism. But until capitalism buckled under its own weight, Du Bois would settle for a New Deal.

His optimism had limits. Despite the gains made under FDR, the twinned forces of oligarchy and white supremacy held sway over most of the country, and liberals had not figured out a way around the Solid South. Black disenfranchisement, a Congress that overrepresented rural America, and a seniority system that gave power to the long-serving defenders of Jim Crow—put it all together, and votes in the South were simply worth more than in the rest of the country. He illustrated the point with this diagram.[117]

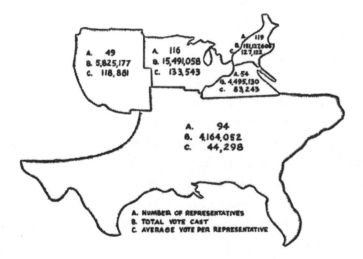

But Du Bois once again thought that history was moving in his direction. "Reason can and will prevail," he announced in a 1946 speech predicting an alliance between African Americans and the "white slaves of modern capitalistic monopoly."[118] Putting aside the fears about intractable racism that haunted him just a few years earlier, he summoned his audience to "a great and holy crusade, the emancipation of mankind black and white."[119]

Flush with enthusiasm about the prospects for interracial working-class politics, Du Bois abandoned his faith in the Talented Tenth. Instead of counting on racial patriotism, he laid out stringent prerequisites for the Black elite. They would, of course, have to be committed socialists, displaying a "willingness to sacrifice and plan for . . . economic revolution in industry and just distribution of wealth."[120] On top of this, he added cultural requirements that mixed Victorian values and soft eugenics: "deliberate planning of marriages, with mates selected for heredity, physique, health and brains, with less insistence on color, comeliness or romantic sex lure, miscalled love."[121]

That sounds . . . creepy. But it fit with Du Bois's hard-edged vision of self-government. "Democracy does not and cannot mean freedom," he said. "On the contrary it means coercion. It means submission of the individual will to the general will."[122] To Du Bois, a certain measure of elitism was an inevitable part of politics, including radical democratic politics. "The mass in its ignorance, and through no fault of its own," he maintained, "can never raise itself save through that saving nucleus of a conscious dictatorship of intelligence."[123]

Du Bois's own place in the American elite was firmer than ever. As U.S. bombs fell over Germany, more and more white liberals started taking a guilty look at their country's racial politics. Du Bois became a favorite explainer for Black America, a coveted speaker at academic conferences that would not have invited him before the war.

The rapturous reception of Gunnar Myrdal's *An American Dilemma* illustrated the shifting climate. Lavishly funded by the Carnegie Corporation, the fifteen-hundred-page survey of American race relations centered on the tension between what its subtitle called "The Negro Problem and American Democracy."[124] The book's success was a bittersweet experience for Du Bois. The Carnegie Corporation had declined to fund his own proposal for an "Encyclopedia Africana" at the same time it directed $300,000 (about $5 million today) to a Swedish economist with no previous experience studying Black life. With Myrdal scooping up the best researchers, Du Bois abandoned the encyclopedia. Myrdal sought out Du Bois's counsel and cited him dozens of times in the book. Du Bois was generous in a review, calling Myrdal's achievement "monumental."[125] The book's reception confirmed the young Du Bois's belief in the political power of social science. He just hadn't realized how much easier it would be for white audiences to listen when the author wasn't Black.

Du Bois's rehabilitation was confirmed in 1944, when he was brought out of semi-voluntary exile at Atlanta University to rejoin the NAACP. He was astonished to discover that the organization's staff had grown threefold and its income quadrupled in the last ten years, leaving room in the budget for a sinecure that was meant to provide him with a cushy retirement. Despite some minor irritations—he fell into a low-grade civil war over internal NAACP politics with his office neighbor, Thurgood Marshall—Du Bois expected to round out his career as a voice for respectable radicalism.[126]

"To what future can the Negro look forward?" Du Bois asked in a 1948 essay for *The New York Times*. His answer was more optimistic than he could have imagined just a decade earlier. "If the progress in race relations and Negro advancement which has marked the last thirty years can be maintained for another generation," he announced, "the goal of democracy in America will be in sight."[127]

———

Du Bois's love affair with American democracy was short-lived. Although he could still put on a happy face in public, the postwar years had been a trying experience. As onetime New Dealers evolved into Cold War liberals, Du Bois turned himself into a steadfast critic of the global crusade against communism, opposing the Marshall Plan, NATO, and the Korean War. Harry Truman struck him as a party hack elevated beyond his talents by an accident of history, a fomenter of anticommunist hysteria who talked a good game on civil rights but couldn't bring his party along with him.

With Democrats still chained to the Solid South, Du Bois endorsed Henry Wallace's Progressive campaign in 1948, insisting that it was "infinitely better for us to throw our votes away upon a great man who stands for real democracy than to shame ourselves, our people, our country."[128] He finished his 1948 tribute to democracy for the *Times* just weeks before the election.[129] Even if Wallace came up short this time, Du Bois was confident that his principles would triumph in the long run.

Then the votes came in: 2.4 percent of the electorate sided with Du Bois, putting Wallace and the Progressives just behind Strom Thurmond's Dixiecrats.[130]* Earlier defeats at the polls had led Du Bois, temporarily, to turn away from politics. This time he pushed deeper. He called Stalin "a great man" and said that Truman ranked alongside Hitler as "one of the greatest killers of our time."[131] When the Cold War was at its frostiest, he testified to Congress, "I am a fellow traveler with Communists."[132] Then he traveled to Moscow, speaking as the only American at a Soviet peace conference.

Partisan activism violated NAACP policy, and flirting with communism was toxic for an organization that needed to maintain its respectability. Just a few years after his triumphant return, Du Bois resigned from the NAACP. Taking advantage of his independence, he decided to run for the Senate in 1950 on the American Labor Party ticket.

Du Bois was proud of what he accomplished with the limited resources at his disposal, including a climactic address at Madison Square Garden that drew an audience of seventeen thousand. He spoke

---

* Also in 1948, Illinois elected a new senator: Paul Douglas, the University of Chicago economist whom Du Bois had chastised in 1930 for excluding racial disenfranchisement from his case for a radical third party. Eighteen years later, Douglas was a partisan Democrat and an ardent Cold Warrior—and now senator-elect. With a thriving civil rights movement to focus his attention, Senator Douglas became a staunch advocate for racial equality during his three terms in office.

deliberately, reading from a prepared text. "There are no two parties," he declared. "All of them listen to their master's voice . . . the more than 200 giant corporations which wield the power that owns the press and the magazines, and determines what news the news agencies will print, and what the movies will screen." The brief moment when Democrats and Republicans stood for distinct visions of the future had passed. Now they formed "one combine, with one aim and one policy, one kettle of graft and one pool of grafters; one set of lies and one bunch of liars."[133]

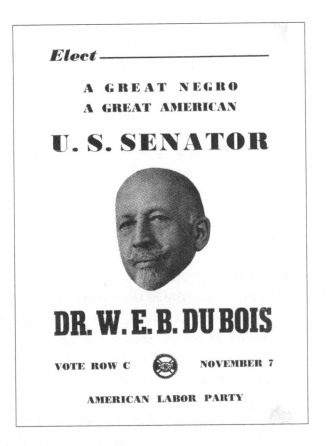

New Yorkers gave Du Bois 4 percent of the total vote on Election Day, which he treated as a moral victory.[134] Under no illusions that he could win, he had wanted to drive up the vote for other left-wing candidates. He took a simple lesson from the experience: "Anyone who thinks that money does not buy American elections is a fool."[135]

Then, in February 1951, two weeks before turning eighty-three, Du Bois was indicted by a grand jury on charges of acting as an unregistered agent of the Soviet government. The accusation stemmed from his work as a peace activist and carried the possibility of five years in prison.[136]

Even at the height of the Red Scare, the case against Du Bois collapsed when subjected to mild scrutiny. A judge dismissed it before a verdict could be reached (and before Du Bois could call his star character witness, Albert Einstein).

But the damage was already done. Du Bois was stripped of his passport and rendered politically untouchable. Hinting at a larger conspiracy, he warned, "The attack on me for socialism is but the cloaked effort of Southern whites to deprive Negroes of leadership in my and other cases."[137] In response, the Talented Tenth—the group that he had named, that he had spoken for, that he had done more than any other person to bring into being—performed the collective equivalent of slowly backing away from a person muttering wildly to himself on the street.

"Churches and Negro conferences refused to mention my past or present existence," he said. "I lost my leadership of my race."[138]

But he gained something, too. Du Bois always wanted to hold on to the particular without losing sight of the universal—to be the student of double consciousness and the humanist walking alongside Shakespeare; the voice of his people and the cosmopolitan floating beyond the nation-state. "Provincialism" was one of his favorite ways of describing what he tried to avoid; it was a cage that white supremacy built for his mind.

Deprived of his place in Black America, he joined an interracial community of marginalized radicals—trade unionists and peace activists, socialists and communists. "I found new friends and lived in a wider world than ever before," he said, "a world with no color line."[139]

A world with no color line—and no real hope for American democracy. By 1956 he was calling for an electoral boycott. "The result of the election I cannot change, but I can at least refuse to condone it," he wrote. "I can stay home and let fools traipse to the polls."[140]

While Du Bois exhorted Americans of all races to give up on partisan politics, civil rights activists were discovering that new possibilities had opened up for their cause. The movement broke through for multiple reasons. Longtime activists were joined by newer recruits, including organized labor and a rising cohort of baby boomers. With Black voters up for grabs, both Republicans and Democrats had an incentive to make progress on civil rights. Continuing the pattern set by World War II, the Cold War pressured self-described champions of the free world to address racial authoritarianism at home—partly to confront their own hypocrisy and partly to win over the dozens of newly decolonized nations that emerged in the aftermath of World War II.[141]

Brown v. Board of Education was an early indicator of the coming shift. Du Bois was stunned by the decision, saying, "I have seen the impossible happen."[142] He might have been just as surprised that the verdict was the result of a legal strategy orchestrated by his old NAACP nemesis, Thurgood Marshall, and that the majority opinion cited *An American Dilemma*.[143]

Next came the Montgomery bus boycott and its charismatic leader, Martin Luther King Jr., the preacher who took over Du Bois's role as unofficial representative for Black America. Du Bois had a conflicted view of King, and of the new stage of the civil rights movement that he embodied, but he grasped the genius of protests that shifted attention to the personal toll of white supremacy. "They have put their finger on the one thing that most people don't think about," he said, "the dozens and hundreds of petty insults that you get every day, and that are unnecessary."[144]

He shared King's admiration of Gandhi, too. Back in 1929, Du Bois tried to persuade Gandhi to write an article for *The Crisis*, telling him that "the race and color problems are world-wide, and we need your help here."[145] Gandhi replied with a "little love message" that Du Bois published alongside a profile calling him "the greatest colored man in the world, and perhaps the greatest man in the world."[146]

But Gandhi had an economic program that Du Bois thought conspicuously absent in the agenda promoted by the "young colored man of good family" commanding the nation's attention.[147]* That was just one difference between Du Bois and his successor. King was a native Southerner, not a Northern transplant; a Baptist minister, not an unrepentant agnostic; a movement leader to his core, not a scholar dragged into activism. And there was the delicate issue of age. Du Bois turned eighty-seven in 1955, the year that King became a national figure at the age of twenty-six.[148]

Then there was the question of race itself. Du Bois now regretted that his focus on Black equality had prevented him from building the same emotional identification with the white working class. "I was bitter at lynching, but not moved by the treatment of white miners in Colorado or Montana," he wrote. "It was hard for me to outgrow this mental isolation, and to see that the plight of the white workers was fundamentally the same as that of the black, even if the white worker helped enslave the black."[149]

Even as Du Bois chastised himself for racial provincialism, he once again concluded that in much of the country the battle against racism could not be won. "We have today in the South millions of persons who are pathological cases," he wrote in 1957. "They cannot be reasoned with in matters of race. They are not normal and cannot be treated as normal."[150]

---

* The private King was more radical than his public image led Du Bois to believe. "On my first date with Martin I was surprised because I had never met a black socialist before," Coretta Scott King later recalled: quoted in Cornel West, ed., *The Radical King: Martin Luther King, Jr.* (Boston, 2015), 221.

Why was Du Bois resurrecting Freud at the same time that he rushed toward orthodox Marxism? His loss of faith in the American political system was one factor; fear that a new generation would repeat his earlier mistakes was another. But a lifetime of abuse must also have taken a toll. Du Bois kept the most virulently racist letters he received in a special file labeled "sick." One correspondent, referring to him as "Dubious," wrote:

> The great civilization[s] of the past were all white, but they fell when their pure white blood became polluted by black blood. It's tragic, Dubious, your being mulatto. . . . Don't you wish you could change into a white man? But you are doomed to remain a coon—just a cocoanut . . . be happy in the thought that you have some white blood—hence your degree of intelligence. . . . You are a very amusing WOOLY.[151]

Nothing here was new, and that was the point. He had been fighting against racism for almost a century. And still the letters kept coming.

When Du Bois wanted inspiration, he looked abroad. He regained his passport in 1958 and set out on a tour of the Soviet Bloc and China. Wherever he went, he proved adept at seeing what he wanted to see. Politics in the USSR looked like a scaled-up version of a Great Barrington town hall. "Nowhere are public questions so thoroughly and exhaustively discussed," he rhapsodized. "They sit and sit and talk and talk, and vote and vote; if this is all a mirage, it is a perfect one."[152]

China was the true revelation. Here, finally, was proof that socialism could transform a "land of colored people" emerging from oppression that "no depths of Negro slavery in America have plumbed."[153] Arriving at the start of the Great Leap Forward, Du Bois announced that the beneficiaries of communist rule "will not starve as thousands of Chinese did only a generation ago."[154] (Millions had already died, and millions more would be lost in the coming years from the worst famine in history.)[155] He was awed, enchanted, overwhelmed. "I have seen most of the civilized world," he said.[156] "But I have never seen a nation which so amazed and touched me."[157]

None had tried so hard to win him over, either. Du Bois celebrated his ninety-first birthday while he was passing through the country. Mao Zedong declared it a national holiday, and an audience of more than a thousand students and professors attended a birthday extravaganza at Peking University.[158] Chinese officials arranged for him to deliver a radio address broadcast across Africa. "Once I thought of you Africans as children, whom we educated Afro-Americans would lead to liberty," he confessed. "I was wrong. We could not even lead ourselves, much less you." How could they? "In my own country for near a century, I have been nothing but a 'nigger.'"[159]

Du Bois meets with Mao Zedong.

Yet he still considered himself a patriot. "I know the United States," he wrote in his final autobiography. "It is my country and the land of my fathers. It is still a land of magnificent possibilities. It is still the home of noble souls and generous people. But it is selling its birthright. It is betraying its mighty destiny."[160]

It was the cry of a dissident nationalist, a spurned lover plagued by visions of what might have been. But Americans wouldn't have the chance to read *The Autobiography of W.E.B. Du Bois* until 1968, when the book was finally published in the United States—six years after the first edition appeared in the Soviet Union and seven years after Du Bois left the land of his fathers.

Kwame Nkrumah, the prime minister of Ghana and a longtime admirer of Du Bois, had been pressing him for years to come to the newly independent country. Du Bois relented in 1961, departing the United States for the last time.

Before embarking on his self-imposed exile, Du Bois sent a farewell gift to his native country: a short political memoir that he included with his successful application for membership in the Communist Party. He wrote about hearing of Karl Marx at college and attending meetings of the German Social Democratic Party in Berlin. He mentioned his tenure at the NAACP, a "capitalist orientated" group with "a strong Socialist element."[161] He described joining the Socialist Party in 1911 and then dropping out when he foolishly endorsed Wilson.

"For the next twenty years I tried to develop a political way of life for myself and my people," he said. "Today I have reached a firm conclusion: Capitalism cannot reform itself; it is doomed to self-destruction. . . . In the end communism will triumph. I want to help bring that day. The path of the American Communist Party is clear: It will provide the United States with a real third party and thus restore democracy to this land."[162]

Which was all he had ever wanted.

Du Bois became a citizen of Ghana on February 23, 1963, his ninety-fifth birthday. Complications from a prostate infection the previous year were slowly killing him, but he couldn't resist an opportunity to get in one last jab at the United States.

Six months later, Martin Luther King Jr. stood in front of the Lincoln Memorial and told an audience of more than two hundred thousand people that he had a dream. "When the architects of our republic wrote the magnificent words of the Constitution and the Declaration of Independence, they were signing a promissory note to which every American was to fall heir," King announced. "We've come to cash this check."[163] He was using a strategy Du Bois would have recognized, marking a new chapter in the history of "abolition democracy," the radical effort to apply the principles of the American founding across the color line.

Du Bois had kept track of the limited reports about the preparations for the march that appeared in Ghana. He spent the day before the event resting at home.

That night, he died in his sleep.

————————

Word of Du Bois's passing arrived in the United States as the March on Washington was under way. The task of announcing the news fell to Roy Wilkins, Du Bois's replacement at *The Crisis*, Marvel Jackson's ex-fiancé, and now the executive secretary of the NAACP. Wilkins's first instinct was to say nothing. "I'm not going to get involved with that Communist at this meeting," he is rumored to have snapped at Bayard Rustin, the march's chief organizer, relenting only after Rustin explained that if the head of the NAACP didn't pay tribute to Du Bois, a more radical speaker would do the job for him.[164]

Rustin was one of those radicals, and his career was its own kind of tribute to Du Bois. Born in 1912, he was raised by his grandparents in a household of NAACP supporters just outside Philadelphia, where

Du Bois himself stayed on his travels. Rustin enrolled at Wilberforce University in 1932, arriving on campus almost forty years after Du Bois's departure. Also like Du Bois, Rustin clashed with university administrators. After either being expelled or deciding to leave—accounts differ—he made his way to Harlem, where he joined the Young Communist League.[165]

A committed pacifist, he cut ties with the party over World War II and served two years in prison for refusing to be drafted. But he stayed on the left, working with various causes at the intersection of socialism and civil rights. One of the shrewdest thinkers in either movement, he was also uniquely vulnerable: a Black ex-Communist and former convict who was dragged out of the closet by Strom Thurmond in the run-up to the march. Working from information provided by the FBI, Thurmond announced in the Senate that Rustin had been convicted of "sex perversion" a decade earlier after police officers discovered him performing oral sex on two men in the back of a car.[166]

Though Rustin's career was held back by the stigma around his sexuality, he remained a bridge between worlds, advising Martin Luther King Jr. by day and going out for drinks with Michael Harrington at night. Despite Thurmond's attempted sabotage, the march, whose full title was "The March on Washington for Jobs and Freedom," provided the culmination to the first phase of Rustin's career—an effort, he explained, to "mobiliz[e] all workers behind demands for a broad and fundamental program of economic justice."[167]

Already, though, Rustin was preparing for the movement's next steps. Again like Du Bois, Rustin believed that African Americans could not achieve meaningful equality without a fundamental overhauling of the American economy that would lift up workers of all races. But the structural reforms he envisioned—full employment, abolishing slums, revamping public education, redefining work itself—would be enacted only if a majority demanded them. And so he turned to politics.

"We need allies," Rustin wrote in a 1965 essay outlining his strategy. "The future of the Negro struggle depends on whether . . . a coalition of progressive forces . . . becomes the *effective* political majority."[168] According to Rustin, Lyndon Johnson's reelection signaled the emergence of a "March on Washington coalition" made up of African Americans, labor, and liberals. Without denying the importance of racism, he insisted that shared economic interests could bind working-class white people and African Americans together in the short term, allowing Democrats to push through structural economic reforms that would, over the long run, destroy the material underpinning for white supremacy. The trick, he argued, was to make "the program for racial equality . . . so intertwined with progressive economic and social policies as to make it impossible to choose one without the other."[169] It was an updated version of the interracial working-class politics that Du Bois embraced in the heady aftermath of World War II, tailored by Rustin to fit the requirements of the contemporary Democratic Party.

As Rustin was trumpeting its arrival, the March on Washington coalition was breaking apart. Even before Johnson was driven out of office, the twenty-eight-year-old GOP operative Kevin Phillips was hard at work exploring the countermovement in his guidebook to the new era, *The Emerging Republican Majority*.

If Rustin spoke to hopes that had pulled Du Bois forward, Phillips struck at the doubts that were never far behind. "The whole secret of politics," he said, is "knowing who hates who."[170] Where Rustin emphasized the importance of shared material interests, Phillips observed that American parties had never been neatly divided by class— especially, he noted, in "states with the largest Negro populations and the most Negrophobe politics."[171] The New Deal reversed that pattern, splitting voters along economic lines and giving Democrats a lopsided majority. But now the party of Franklin Roosevelt was coming apart, and Republicans were poised to reap the rewards.

Du Bois might have welcomed Phillips's candor about the origins of this political revolution. "The principal cause of the breakup of the New Deal coalition," Phillips explained, was "the Negro problem."[172]

Rustin's dreams and Phillips's prophecies, the March on Washington coalition and the emerging Republican majority—those two sides of American democracy, what Du Bois loved about his country and what he feared—all lay in the future that summer day in 1963 when Roy Wilkins had to figure out how to commemorate the NAACP's most troublesome founder. The event came out of the confluence of liberal and radical traditions Du Bois had vacillated between throughout his life, a marriage of elites working inside the system, outsiders striving to change it, and intermediaries like Rustin laboring to hold the two together. It was a triumph for interracial organizing that combined appeals to moral outrage and material self-interest. And it contained the elements of its own undoing, forging a partnership between liberalism and civil rights that Republicans would unite against.

Putting questions about the march's larger significance to the side, Wilkins focused on Du Bois. He proceeded with the caution of a nuclear technician handling radioactive material glowing an ominous shade of green. "Regardless of the fact that in his later years Dr. Du Bois chose another path, it is incontrovertible that at the dawn of the twentieth century his was the voice that was calling to you to gather here today in this cause," he said. Then he shifted to safe ground. "If you want to read something that applies to 1963 go back and get a volume of *The Souls of Black Folk* by Du Bois, published in 1903."[173] Having spoken longer than he wanted to, Wilkins asked for a moment of silence.

The younger members of the audience looked at one another curiously. It had been twelve years since the Justice Department charged Du Bois with acting as a foreign agent. Since then, he had all but disappeared from public consciousness. In the last decade, *The New York Times* had mentioned his name just four times, in articles totaling a little over one thousand words.

Dr. Du Bois? Leaders of the movement knew him, and students of civil rights history recognized the name. The rest had no idea what Wilkins was talking about.[174]

6

Insiders

It was a scene Americans were used to seeing on television: a white man, handsome in an unobtrusive way, explaining how the world worked. But his subject was unusual for the small screen, and potentially dangerous—politics. Broadcast news was still in its infancy, and fear of stirring up controversy kept networks away from political analysis. But CBS found a way around the problem in 1960 by turning to an authority of unquestioned eminence, the wisest of Washington's wise men. His name was Walter Lippmann.[1]

If the political establishment in the golden years of the American Century had taken human shape, it would have carried itself as Walter Lippmann did—supremely self-confident, serious but not charmless, always ready with a lecture on the responsibilities of power.

Here was the pundit—Henry Luce's *Time* borrowed the word from Sanskrit to capture the essence of "Pundit Lippmann"—who in his twenties had been deemed by Theodore Roosevelt "the most brilliant young man of his age in all the United States"; who told Franklin Roosevelt in 1933, "You may have no alternative but to assume dictatorial powers"; who helped launch Dwight Eisenhower's 1952 campaign; and whom Lyndon Johnson called "the greatest journalist in the world."[2]

"Saw the King, the prime minister, etc.," Lippmann wrote during a trip to Greece. "The usual people."[3]

The only child in a wealthy Republican family, Lippmann had been raised to be a gentleman, and he did not disappoint. The boy who dressed for trips to Central Park in outfits like this:

grew into the man who strolled on the beach dressed like this:

It helps to think of Lippmann as the person W.E.B. Du Bois could have become if he had been white.[4] Where Du Bois saw himself as the voice of an oppressed people, Lippmann spent a lifetime trying to strip away any bits of his identity that could interfere with his ability to divine the public interest. Though of German-Jewish descent, he was a religious skeptic, and the subject of his Judaism was awkward enough that friends weren't sure if they could use the word "Jew" when they played against him in Scrabble.[5] When Du Bois was most despairing about American politics—the consensus years of the 1920s and 1950s—Lippmann was most hopeful. Only once did they support the same candidate for president (FDR in 1944).

Lippmann divided the world between insiders and outsiders and then made a career out of bridging the divide between the two. Once the pride of Harvard's Philosophy Department, he became an intellectual for a town where nobody had time for Kant, a dispenser of timeless wisdom for book-of-the-month clubs. His syndicated column, "Today and Tomorrow," served as a one-man Washington and foreign affairs bureau for newspapers that couldn't afford offices in D.C. or abroad. Typing away in his Georgetown mansion, he instructed politicians on the arts of statecraft while offering readers a glimpse of "what informed and responsible men say when they do not have to keep up appearances in public."[6] The model of a new kind of democratic elite, he wielded more influence than most politicians, without subjecting himself to the indignities of an election.

He was also, indisputably, a liberal. When he launched "Today and Tomorrow," he was advertised as "the Spokesman of American Liberalism."[7] He held the title for the rest of his career, into the golden years of the postwar consensus. If "plutocracy" was the key word of Gilded Age politics, then "liberal democracy" was its midcentury successor. You can see the arrival of the concept in this measurement of how often the phrase was used between 1900 and 1950.[8]

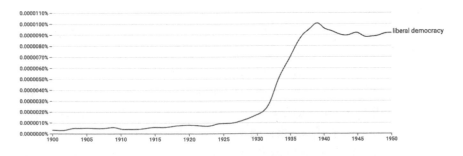

The invention of liberal democracy, 1900–1950

Part juristocracy, part technocracy, part national-security state, liberal democracy was supposed to represent self-government's coming of age. It was the doctrine of a liberal elite presiding over a liberal establishment. And it had no better exponent than Lippmann, whose selected works, published in 1963, were titled *A Political Philosophy for Liberal Democracy.*[9]

Rhetorical success masked liberalism's political retreat. If returning to laissez-faire was out of the question, so was a campaign against economic royalists. Working-class revolts of the 1930s—labor militants leading factory occupations, tenant farmers organizing against evictions, unemployed leagues demanding public jobs—fueled the New Deal's revolution in political economy, helping narrow the gap between rich and poor while raising living standards for ordinary Americans. But this same shift also concentrated authority in the hands of a governing class where, by the 1950s, the difference between a Republican and Democrat was about as significant as the distinction between a Princeton man and a Yalie. An insurrection from below had culminated in Lippmann's telling Walter Cronkite that a booming economy rendered class struggle obsolete.[10]

Except the liberal consensus was never as solid as it looked on TV. Take away the good times, and the national tone could change in an instant, especially if the parties divided around the kinds of culturally charged subjects that both Republicans and Democrats had an incentive to downplay in the 1950s—for instance sex, race, and religion, where American life remained decidedly illiberal. Consider all the exceptions, and the joke writes itself: the liberal consensus was neither liberal nor a consensus.[11]

But it didn't feel that way in Lippmann's world. In the rarefied circles in which he traveled, it was taken for granted that politicians challenged the American consensus at their peril. Both parties were ideologically messy, with liberal Republicans and conservative Democrats regularly bolting to the other side of the aisle. GOP leaders feared the consequences of waging an outright assault on the welfare state. Aging New Dealers had lost the reforming zeal of the Roosevelt years, and Democrats of all stripes were keenly aware that the second Red Scare had given big government a subversive tinge. Cold War anxieties fostered a culture of conformism at home, assisted by the outsize influence wielded by a handful of national media outlets—above all the big three television networks, which until 1960 were concerned that *Walter Lippmann* was too spicy for the airwaves. The liberal consensus might have existed mostly in the heads of the American elite, but fictions have power when they become articles of faith.

Lippmann certainly sounded confident on television. In 1960, he waved off a question about whether democracy was out of date and spoke optimistically about the coming election, when either John Kennedy or Richard Nixon would replace a tired Eisenhower. A satisfied tone ran through the conversation. After being asked whether the White House had acquired too much power, Lippmann replied, "That's the kind of government we have, and none of us wants to change it too radically."[12]

The interview was a surprise ratings hit. *The New York Times* announced that Lippmann's deigning to appear on television marked "a turning point in the video medium." Soon the appearances became an annual ritual, as if Lippmann were a doctor tasked with giving the body politic its yearly physical.

Off camera, however, Lippmann wasn't nearly so upbeat. For a writer who made a career divining the will of the people, he had a strange habit of putting himself on the wrong side of public opinion. He spent decades producing caustic assessments of democracy's limitations. After initially supporting the New Deal, he turned against it midway through FDR's first term. A decade later, he was an early critic of the Cold War—a term that he popularized—warning of anticommunist hysteria at home, incipient totalitarianism on the McCarthyite right, and potentially world-ending nuclear brinkmanship. In his last major book, published in 1955, he wrote darkly about a spiritual sickness at the heart of modern civilization. And by 1960 he was becoming more and more worried about mounting tensions over civil rights, an issue whose explosive potential he recognized even as he struggled to understand the passions it unleashed. In his maturity, Lippmann viewed radicalism of all kinds as a sign of bad taste. "Every truly civilized and enlightened man is conservative and liberal and progressive," he said, "because he must work and live, he must govern and debate in the world as it is"—a bit of word salad that reflected his scorn for the limits that mere ideology sought to impose on the realities of power.[13]

In his superficial confidence and quiet doubts, Lippmann truly was a fitting spokesman for American liberalism, a creed that by midcentury was both ubiquitous and uncomfortable going by its own name. Which made it all the more surprising that his journey to national eminence started at the age of twenty-two, when he left a gilded Manhattan youth behind to bring socialism to Schenectady.

—————

Before he turned into the granite-faced incarnation of the American establishment, Walter Lippmann was one of the country's brightest young radicals. A founding member of the Harvard Socialist Club, he was a fixture on the university lecture circuit, where he delivered speeches on behalf of the Intercollegiate Socialist Society. "Our object," he remembered, "was to make reactionaries stand-patters; stand-patters, conservative liberals; conservatives, liberals; liberals, radicals; and radicals, Socialists."[14]

Always an outstanding student, Lippmann came to Harvard in 1906 with a trunkful of books, six tailored suits, and plans of becoming an art historian. He switched to philosophy after studying under the same teachers who inspired Du Bois. William James invited him to weekly teas, and George Santayana treated him to regular dinners in Boston. Where Du Bois had been subtly nudged away from academia, Lippmann was groomed to lead the next generation of Harvard philosophers. When graduation neared, Santayana arranged for his prize student to spend an extra year in Cambridge pursuing a master's degree. The rest of his life, it seemed, was secure.

Except Lippmann didn't want security. He wanted to change the world.

It was a new dream for him. As a teenager, he was a Roosevelt Republican. Lippmann caught his first glimpse of TR at the age of nine, when the Rough Rider was campaigning for governor in the resort town of Saratoga Springs. Watching from the sprawling veranda of the Grand Union Hotel, Lippmann was overwhelmed. "From that day," he remembered, "I was his unqualified hero-worshipper."[15]

Roosevelt Republicanism was perfectly compatible with a gentlemanly disdain for commerce. Over the course of Lippmann's first year at Harvard, this contempt flowered into an inchoate longing for social justice that blended dreams of universal brotherhood, disgust for a culturally bankrupt ruling class, and faith that order could be imposed on a chaotic economic system. Lippmann's transformation was complete by the spring of his sophomore year. "I have come around to socialism as a creed," he declared with all the gravitas of a young man accustomed to taking himself very seriously indeed.[16]

Lippmann's politics were both utopian and cynical, egalitarian and aristocratic. Like Du Bois, he was drawn to the Fabian Society, a group of elite British reformers, including H. G. Wells and George Bernard Shaw, committed to finding a technocratic road to socialism. A seminar with Graham Wallas—a onetime Fabian visiting at Harvard—left Lippmann with an abiding skepticism of direct democracy. Justifying his conversion, Lippmann told his father that socialism was "a hardheaded, sound, scientific business proposition . . . which is the next, logical, and practically inevitable phase of industrial society."[17]

However tempting philosophy might have been, it couldn't compete with the thrill of building socialism. With just a few weeks left in his master's program, Lippmann dropped out of Harvard and joined the staff of a struggling left-wing newspaper in Boston. The job was disappointing—"the work is so mechanical that I am learning nothing," he complained—but he loved the idea of journalism and landed a position as assistant to the renowned muckraker Lincoln Steffens.[18]

Lippmann's silk-stocking socialism was an extreme instance of a common trend. "In the United States probably more than anywhere else, socialism is recruiting heavily from the better classes of society," observed the Socialist Party leader Morris Hillquit.[19] The vision of a society governed by reason and overseen by a public-minded elite was tailor-made for the ballooning class of young professionals who saw a country ripe for remaking.

It wasn't crazy to think the revolution might start in Schenectady. Hillquit put Lippmann in touch with the city's incoming socialist mayor, George Lunn, late in 1911. Lunn was a political neophyte, and Lippmann saw an opportunity to shape a distinctly socialist agenda.

Lunn was sworn into office on January 1, 1912. His new assistant was already at his desk, ready to work.

———

Disillusionment set in quickly. Lunn started lowering expectations with his inaugural address, where he confessed, "We cannot abolish the capitalist system in Schenectady."[20] The new mayor simply wanted to prove that socialists could run a city, from building skating rinks to inspecting milk. Lippmann's office, where he prepared legislation, drafted speeches, and met with party bosses, was located just outside Lunn's in City Hall. ("I wasn't a stenographer," he later assured an interviewer. "We had girl secretaries for that.")[21]

Lippmann kept up a brave face in public, writing in the left-wing journal *The Masses* that Schenectady had become a "laboratory" for socialism.[22] He was more honest in private. "Being in Schenectady isn't as inspiring as it sounds," Lippmann wrote at the end of his first week on the job. "What appalls me is the smallness of our power and our knowledge and our ability in the face of the problems we are supposed to solve," he explained. "It's really pathetic to see as I do every day twenty-five to fifty men out of work, hungry, cold, come here with shining eyes to participate in this new heaven on earth which socialism promised them. Many of them lost their jobs because they worked for the victory. And we can't do anything essential for them."[23]

Orthodox Marxists had a simple explanation for the problem. Schenectady's capitalists were not about to accept state ownership of the means of production, meaning that any socialist revolution would be stillborn. But Lippmann thought the challenge went deeper. Voters had elected a socialist because they were frustrated with the political establishment, not because they wanted to abolish private property. Even if the people were on Lunn's side, nobody in the mayor's office had a clear sense of where to start. "I'm becoming more and more sure," Lippmann concluded, "that the obstacles are not the greed or bad will of capitalists one half so much as the unimaginative, dry, timid, mechanical boxes of wood which go by the name of brains."[24]

He had another, less high-minded reason for his dissatisfaction. The quotidian work of managing a small city might be valuable, but he also found it boring. "There are plenty of people in this country bothering about playgrounds and dental clinics," he wrote. "Why not let the 'progressives' do them?"[25]

Socialists had a grander calling, and Lippmann had better things to do with his time. He quit after just four months on the job. Back in New York City, he kick-started a debate over the causes of Lunn's failures and their implications for socialists.

According to Lippmann, the root of the trouble was that Lunn had muddied the distinction between socialism and progressivism. "The keystone of our principal difficulties is that large and decisive group of progressive voters which holds the balance of power in America today," he wrote.[26] The socialist movement was expanding rapidly, but it was still tiny. Progressives had a larger presence in politics and ideals that were similar enough to be a threat. "If Socialists are to make anything of political action," Lippmann insisted, "they have got to keep themselves clearly distinguished from the progressives."[27]

It was easy for socialists to explain what separated them from progressives in theory. Everything came down to class struggle. Progressives claimed to speak for the people, socialists for the proletariat. But socialists wanted to seize power from capital, a process that required the support of a mobilized working class.

The problem in Schenectady was that this theoretical distinction crumbled after Lunn took office. "We try to do the things that reform-

ers can do at least as well as we, and we try to represent at the same
time a profoundly revolutionary movement," Lippmann wrote. "Super-
men might do it. We can't."[28]

Lippmann wasn't simply explaining why he left Schenectady. He
was urging socialists to step away from electoral politics. "If we cannot learn to play politics with a long vision and ability to distinguish
between Socialist power and the external clap-trap of victory, then we
haven't learned the first steps in revolution," he wrote.[29] "Elections are
the last goal of political action, and not the first. They should come only
when the social forces are organized and ready."[30] Without the support
of a united working class, socialist victories at the polls would result
only in more failed socialist governments—and, eventually, the end of
American socialism.

He kept up the attack in his first book, written in a rush during
the months after he left Schenectady. *A Preface to Politics* was the live-
liest book he would ever write, moving across topics in short, punchy
chapters delighted with their own iconoclasm. "We live in a revolutionary period," he declared, "and nothing is so important as to be
aware of it."[31]

There was plenty in his argument for leftists to cheer. After nodding
to the "prophetic genius of Marx," Lippmann said that "class interests
are the driving forces which keep public life centered upon essentials."[32]
He credited the Socialist Party with giving voice to the American proletariat, and he denounced the "unimaginative greed and endless stu-
pidity of the dominant classes."[33]

But there were already signs that Lippmann was straying from the
socialist path. There was something flirtatious about his jabs at the
elite, like a boy pulling on his crush's pigtails. "Business and political
leaders don't mean badly," he wrote. "The trouble with them is that
most of the time they don't mean anything."[34] The ruling class wasn't
evil, just misguided—and perhaps it could be pointed in the right
direction. Citing Nietzsche, Lippmann paid tribute to "the political
creator" who could transform the inchoate mass of public opinion
into a transformative governing agenda.[35] The boy straining to catch

sight of Teddy Roosevelt from the veranda of the Grand Union Hotel was now a pundit-in-training working on a statesman's guide to
modern life.

Was this socialism? Lippmann claimed that he hadn't lost his faith,
but the evidence was ambiguous. After the doldrums of Schenectady,
he was searching for an ecstatic vision of politics—and sounding suspi-
ciously progressive. "We shall feel free to choose among alternatives," he
announced, "to take this much of socialism, insert so much syndicalism,
leave standing what of capitalism seems worth conserving. We shall be
making our own house for our own needs."[36]

Whatever their ideology, nobody else in American politics seemed
to be having so much fun. "The world was never so young as it is today,"
he wrote, "so impatient of old and crusty things."[37]

Then, on September 23, 1913, Walter Lippmann turned twenty-four.

Life moved swiftly now. He became a star attraction at Greenwich
Village salons where anarchists mingled with the tuxedoed scions of
the American aristocracy. His shots at the ruling class won him the
admiration of Theodore Roosevelt, who confided to Lippmann over
breakfast at the Harvard Club that he was contemplating running for
president in 1916. They also got him a job offer from Herbert Croly, recently finished with his biography of Mark Hanna and looking to start
a political magazine that would "be socialistic in direction, but not in
method, or phrase, or allegiance."[38]

Croly's description of the infant *New Republic*'s mission fit perfectly
with Lippmann's evolving politics. "I come definitely nearer to the Progressives," he confided to his diary. "At any rate I find less and less
sympathy with the revolutionists . . . and an increasing interest in administrative problems."[39] His name stopped appearing in radical journals, and he ended his affiliation with the Socialist Party. By 1916, the
onetime socialist was a leading progressive intellectual.[40]

Lippmann reveled in his independence. "I feel now as if I had never before risen above the problems of a district nurse, a middle western political reformer, and an amiable civic enthusiast," he told his former teacher Graham Wallas.[41] His shift toward the progressives was already clear in his second book, finished before he started at *The New Republic*. Like its predecessor, *Drift and Mastery* consisted of brief essays that were drunk on their own irreverence. But there was an important addition to his analysis, a concept he called the "Great Society."

Lippmann borrowed the phrase from Wallas, who had coined it in a book of the same name published in 1914.[42] (The text opened with a letter to Wallas's favorite student, Walter Lippmann.) As Lippmann explained, the ascent of the modern corporation had ushered in a "general change of social scale . . . without precedent in history."[43] It was a world-historical account of an economic revolution that Mark Hanna witnessed firsthand. Small towns, local businesses, and an anemic central government were relics of the past. In the Great Society, small was no longer an option.

With increased size came a relentless focus on rationality. Administrators concerned with maximizing production were shoving aside robber barons fixated on profits. As businessmen evolved into "industrial statesmen," the old distinctions between capitalism and socialism lost their meaning.[44] A managerial turn was also under way in government, where experts trained in the social sciences were challenging partisan operators.

In the expanding empire of reason, any theoretical loss of freedom was more than offset by the increased power that Americans had at their fingertips. Lippmann dismissed his former comrades on the left as "old-fashioned, fatalistic Marxian socialists . . . the interested pedants of destiny."[45] Leftists put their faith in the proletariat. Capitalists lionized entrepreneurs. Lippmann turned to the emerging managerial elite, "the new type of administrator, the specialist, the professionally trained business man."[46]

Lippmann believed that science and democracy went together, just like mastery and freedom. Statesmanship in the twentieth century was the art of shuttling between these poles, recognizing the value of expertise without forgetting that public opinion must ultimately rule. Wise leadership could give Americans the best of both worlds—a government that used the extraordinary productive capacity of the Great Society to promote the general welfare. Lippman presented himself as a Machiavelli for the managerial class, offering political guidance for a new elite raised to power by its influence over the bureaucracies—private and public—that dominated modern life.

He dismissed examples of persisting irrationality as unworthy of his attention. "There is no mention of the fearful obstacles of race prejudice in the South," he breezily acknowledged, "no mention of the threat that recent immigration brings with it, the threat of an alien and defenseless class or servile labor."[47]

World War I accelerated Lippmann's turn away from the left. A crash course on geopolitics left him with a newfound respect for grand strategists who had the vision to put their stamp on world affairs. (Alexander Hamilton was a particular favorite.) Spotting a potential ally, the Wilson administration began courting Lippmann. A meeting with the president—"So you've come to look me over," Wilson said as the journalist walked into the Oval Office—won over the previously skeptical Lippmann.[48] He wrote speeches for Wilson during the 1916 campaign and was talked into making a few of his own at Democratic rallies across upstate New York. After the United States joined the war, Lippmann quit *The New Republic* and used his connections to secure a position inside the government. A healthy twenty-seven-year old man, he was eminently eligible for the draft. But he was convinced that he could do more good with a typewriter than with a bayonet, and his latest employer—Secretary of War Newton Baker—agreed.

"We are living and shall live all our lives now in a revolutionary world," Lippmann declared, celebrating Wilson's marshaling of "the largest assembly of force for an entirely disinterested purpose ever known to history."[49] Progressives were going to war.

The results were catastrophic. After a short-lived burst of euphoria following the armistice of 1918, when it seemed as if Wilson's promise of a peace without victory was in reach, old-fashioned power politics returned during peace negotiations at Versailles. "I can't see anything in this treaty but endless trouble for Europe," Lippmann wrote. He recruited a new friend, John Maynard Keynes, to make a case in *The New Republic* against Wilson's peace plan. The Senate voted against ratifying the treaty, dealing the last blow to Wilson's dream of remaking the global order. By then, Bolsheviks had seized power in Russia, and governments across Europe were trembling.

Matters at home were almost as dire. Wartime mobilization had turned the nation into an ideal breeding ground for disease, leading to more than half a million deaths from the Spanish flu in the United States alone.[50] Draconian sedition laws put many of Lippmann's former comrades on the left behind bars; *The Masses*, where he once debated the future of democratic socialism, was banned. Angry mobs were more than willing to work outside the law, with a smile from the authorities. (A shop clerk in Ohio was bound up in an American flag, hauled through the street, then compelled to purchase a Liberty Bond. "A thoroughly unexceptional episode," writes the historian Christopher Capozzola, "repeated hundreds of times across the country.")[51] Conditions deteriorated further when peacetime brought a steep economic downturn. With unemployment soaring, a fifth of the country's workforce went on strike—an unprecedented display of militancy for the American labor movement.[52] Anarchist bombings provoked another crackdown on dissent. In unruly times, violence easily spilled outside prescribed channels: the Red Scare coincided with the deaths of hundreds of African Americans during the race riots of the Red Summer.

Lippmann beat a hasty retreat from the ruins of the Wilson administration. Shedding the now discredited label of progressive, he rebranded himself as a liberal. Already in 1919 he identified "liberal" as the new term of art for reformers who "wished to distinguish their own general aspirations in politics from those of the chronic partisans and the social revolutionists." But liberalism was a label, not yet an ideology. "American liberalism is a phase of the transition away from the old party system," he noted. "But it is an early phase and there is no agreement as to ends or methods."[53]

He set out to give liberalism substance, and he did not lack for platforms. He took up a position on the editorial page of the *New York World*, the city's most influential Democratic newspaper. Lippmann's walking stick and bowler hat set him apart in the newsroom, but he could turn out copy as quickly as any ink-stained wretch. Chastened by the disasters of the Wilson years, he turned into a skeptic of state power. "The Washington vampire sucks the life out of the states and local communities," he wrote in 1924, a shift that put him in line with Democrats seeking to revive the party's traditional hostility to centralized government.[54]

In the cultural conflicts that dominated headlines during the twenties—a reborn Ku Klux Klan, Prohibition, the Scopes monkey trial—Lippmann reliably played the part of urban cosmopolitan. "My own mind has been getting steadily anti-democratic," he confided to a friend in 1925. "The size of the electorate, the impossibility of educating it sufficiently, the fierce ignorance of these millions of semi-literate priestridden and parsonridden people have got me to the point where I want to confine the action of majorities."[55]

He channeled that frustration into three books—*Public Opinion* (1922), *The Phantom Public* (1925), and *A Preface to Morals* (1929)—that amounted to a sustained investigation of democracy in the Great Society. The critique was ruthless in its rigor—an exercise, as Lippmann described it, in putting "the public . . . in its place, so that it may exercise its powers."[56] His favorite targets were romantic descriptions of democracy as a system where all-knowing citizens expressed their collective wisdom at the polls and politicians executed the wishes of their masters.

In reality, he said, all organizations were hierarchical, and in the Great Society hierarchy was more important than ever. Citing the Italian sociologist Robert Michels on the iron law of oligarchy, he argued that democrats should give up the dream of abolishing elites and focus on making a ruling class that served the general welfare. "Men do not long desire self-government for its own sake," he wrote. "They desire it for the sake of the results."[57]

This was the hinge of the argument: the will of the people was a delusion, but the public interest was real, and voters could be trusted to decide whether they were better off today than they were four years earlier. "To support the Ins when things are going well; to support the Outs when they seem to be going badly, this, in spite of all that has been said about tweedledum and tweedledee, is the essence of popular government," he explained.[58]

It took statesmen to translate between the ignorant many and the expert few. "In the crystallizing of a common will," Lippmann wrote, "there is always an Alexander Hamilton at work."[59] The public could feel, and experts could analyze, but it took politicians to *act*—to pick the symbols, tell the stories, and write the laws that turned the inchoate mass of public sentiment into a program that technocrats could implement. They were the creators and inventors who found greatness in the messy facts of democratic life.

Despite his exasperation with the priestridden and parsonridden public, Lippmann was quite happy with the American political system. Reformers had spent decades condemning the ideological incoherence of the GOP and the Democrats. Not that long ago, so had Lippmann. But he had changed his mind. If elections were meant to keep the ruling class on its toes by replacing tired incumbents with fresh voices, then campaigns couldn't be allowed to turn into ideological missions. "One might say," he concluded, "that a nation is politically stable when nothing of radical consequence is determined by its elections."[60]

The 1928 presidential race fit Lippmann's model of American politics to perfection. "If Mr. Hoover and Mr. Smith met in a room to discuss any concrete national question purely on its merits," he speculated, "they would be so close together at the end you could not tell the difference between them"—or between their views and his own.[61] All three were liberals in Lippmann's sense of the term, responsible men of affairs balancing a desire for reform with a wariness of concentrated federal power.

Not even the Great Depression shook Lippmann's confidence in the status quo. After the slump forced the *New York World* out of business, a bidding war broke out for its star pundit. Harvard wanted him as a professor. *The New York Times* asked him to run its Washington bureau. William Randolph Hearst offered him a position as a columnist. So did the *New York Herald Tribune*, a surprising move for the favorite newspaper of Republican industrialists and financiers.

As Lippmann weighed his options, a cover story in *Time* dubbed him the "prophet of liberalism."[62] The magazine quoted at length from a speech he had delivered at a banquet in his honor organized by Thomas Lamont, a partner at J.P. Morgan, where Lippmann systematically dismantled the case for radical change.

He started with politics. "Who but a political hack can believe today, as our forefathers once sincerely believed, that the fate of the nation hangs upon the victory of either political party?" he asked.[63] The parties were, thankfully, too similar for elections to change the direction of the country.

Next he moved on to economics. "The simple opposition between the people and big business has disappeared because the people themselves have become so deeply involved in big business," he announced.[64] There was no winding the clock back to the time before the corporation's triumph, no socialist utopia waiting to be realized, no alternative to making the system work. Sounding like another Mark Hanna, he urged reformers to trade sweeping critiques of capitalism for the "subtler and greater" work of attempting "to civilize and rationalize these corporate organizations in which we are now almost all of us inextricably involved."[65]

He closed with an austere assessment of democracy. "It is vain to suppose that our problems can be dealt with by rallying the people to some crusade that can be expressed in a symbol, a phrase, a set of principles or a program," he said.[66] Experience had taught him that the costs of uniting the country were too high: "The objectives to which a nation like this could be aroused in something like unanimity are limited to a war or to some kind of futile or destructive fanaticism."[67]

The parties were interchangeable. Capitalism was here to stay. Democracy slid all too easily into brutal repression. The only humane option was to move carefully, learning from experience, advancing one step at a time.

"This, perhaps," Lippmann said, "is the testament of liberalism."[68]

Two days later, he set off for a three-month sojourn in Europe, traveling across the Atlantic in a first-class cabin, keeping his days free for contemplation, and setting aside his nights for black-tie dinners. He decided that he would accept the *Herald Tribune*'s offer, bringing the prophet of liberalism to the paper of Wall Street.

Meanwhile, back in Albany, Franklin Roosevelt was thinking about the White House.

—————

Lippmann knew what to look for in a statesman. Americans needed discipline, and they would reward politicians who demanded it. "When they are troubled," he explained, "the thing that voters most want is to be told what to want."[69]

Lippmann knew Franklin Roosevelt, too. They'd met in Washington during the Great War, and Lippmann had kept an eye on Roosevelt as he climbed to the top of New York politics, winning election as governor in 1928.

Lippmann knew statesmen, he knew Roosevelt—and he knew that Roosevelt was no statesman. "He just doesn't happen to have a very good mind," he told Newton Baker in the autumn of 1931, as he was trying to coax the former war secretary into a presidential bid. "I consider it extremely important that he shouldn't be the Democratic candidate for president."[70]

He took the Baker campaign public in 1932, enlisting with a desperate stop-Roosevelt effort at the Democratic National Convention. When Roosevelt struggled to win the necessary two-thirds of delegates, Lippmann urged the party to coalesce around Baker, "the real first choice of more respectable Democrats."[71]

But there weren't enough respectable Democrats to keep Roosevelt from winning, and the spokesman of American liberalism couldn't attack the Democratic presidential nominee forever. In October, after months of agonizing, Lippmann endorsed Roosevelt. Though he continued to snipe against FDR in private—Roosevelt's vaunted Brain Trust, he clucked, "would rate, even in the academic world, as not much better than B plus"—after the election he defended both the New Deal and the new president.[72]

This wasn't just a conversion of convenience. Although Lippmann did not believe that the frenetic experimentation and aggressive state interventions of the early New Deal were sustainable, he was willing to set aside his concerns during an economic emergency. It helped that readers looking for a guide to Roosevelt's Washington flocked to him. At the end of his first year as a columnist, "Today and Tomorrow" appeared in a hundred newspapers, with a total readership of ten million.[73]

When the country began to claw its way out of the Depression, Lippmann quickly moved to charting a new path for liberalism. He got a glimpse of the road forward during a leisurely lunch with his friend John Maynard Keynes at the Cambridge don's London club. Though Lippmann never managed to wade through Keynes's masterpiece, *The General Theory of Employment, Interest, and Money*, the book's underlying thesis struck him with the force of revelation. Rather than intervening directly in particular industries, policymakers could manipulate the economy as a whole with well-timed changes to tax rates and the money supply. If governments struck the right balance, they could conquer the business cycle, wrenching the economy out of the Depression and ushering in a new era of sustained prosperity.[74]

Even before *The General Theory* appeared in print, Lippmann finished a book trumpeting Keynes's discoveries. Based on lectures he delivered at Harvard in the spring of 1934, *The Method of Freedom* announced the coming of "an epoch-making invention" that would bring about a "new species of government."[75] Lippmann called Keynes's synthesis "free collectivism," drawing a contrast between both dogmatic laissez-faire and the "absolute collectivism" of communism and fascism.[76] He believed that government had an essential role to play, not by dictating prices and wages, but by keeping the economy growing.

More than a clever piece of economic reasoning, Keynesianism allowed Lippmann to reconcile his youthful aversion to the aimless drift of Gilded Age politics with his mature fear of a tyrannical state. It urged policymakers to act, but only within prescribed limits. It called for a mandarin elite, but not an endless proliferation of planners. And it restored an aura of greatness to the work of governing. Here was an authentic third way between laissez-faire and socialism. Here was the future of liberalism.

New Dealers had other plans. "This isn't a do-gooder tea club, patching things up here and there," one explained. "This is a real people's movement."[77] The emerging Democratic Party had a strong family resemblance to the working-class coalition that Lippmann had envisioned back in his socialist days—and the mature Lippmann was horrified. Even as he commended Roosevelt's policy achievements, he privately urged the administration to tamp down class conflict. "The President could have had the collaboration of able influential conservatives from both parties," Lippmann protested.[78] Instead the New Deal split the country in two, creating "unreal and unnecessary divisions in the nation at a time when solidarity and union are of the highest importance."

By 1936 Lippmann had given up hope for a gentle transition away from the emergency measures of the New Deal. Washington bureaucrats were cooking up new programs every day, and Roosevelt was telling voters that economic royalists were modern-day heirs to King George. Proletarian politics and a metastasizing bureaucracy were advancing together. Whatever this was, it wasn't liberalism, at least not according to Lippmann.

To grasp what drove Lippmann away from the New Deal, it helps to contrast him with other politically minded intellectuals who were drawn toward FDR, a group that bore a striking resemblance to the young Walter Lippmann.

For instance, Leon Keyserling and Mary Dublin Keyserling. A husband-and-wife duo brought together by the New Deal, the Keyserlings were children of prosperous Jewish immigrants who shared a keen intelligence and a commitment to politics. Leon graduated from Columbia in 1928, Mary from Barnard in 1930, each with a BA in economics. Mary then moved on to graduate research, first at the Geneva School of International Studies, then to the London School of Economics, finally returning to Columbia. Leon, too, left Columbia—in his case, earning a law degree at Harvard—then came back to pursue a PhD in economics. Both quit before finishing their doctorates, he to join the government in Washington, she to teach at Sarah Lawrence. Despite traveling in the same narrow circles, they did not meet until 1934 and did not begin dating until 1939. By the time they married, in 1940, Mary and Leon had independently established themselves as figures to be reckoned with in the small world of up-and-coming New Dealers.[79]

And they did it while espousing an unabashed leftist politics more radical than anything Lippmann had ever flirted with. A classmate of Mary's called her the Eugene Debs of their high school. She sang "The Internationale" in Geneva, bristled under Friedrich Hayek's instruction at the LSE, and sparred with fellow graduate student Milton Friedman at Columbia. "Many of us have come round to an acceptance of the major elements of Communism," she told her parents in the summer of 1932. "Altho I think we or I shall work thru the Socialist Party for a while until we can build up a better party on the further left. Even the young militants, as the more active bunch in the S.P. so romantically call themselves, are not beginning to be thoroughgoing enough to please me."[80]

Leon was just as militant. He supported Norman Thomas in 1932, predicting that the campaign would "mark in the future the definite turn toward socialism in this country."[81] Although he played a key role in drafting landmark New Deal legislation—and the Democratic Party platform—he believed that Roosevelt's reforms were incremental steps toward lasting change. "Without revolution which transfers power to the workers and sets up a socialized state, little will be gained," he wrote to his father in 1933.[82] He doubled down in a subsequent letter home, writing, "There is no chance for lasting gains to either farmer or laborer save by revolution."[83] Leon warmed to FDR with time, but it's not clear whether he voted for Roosevelt's reelection in 1936. "The amazing thing," he wrote to a friend during the campaign, "is that, with the Democrats having done so little that is real, the class divisions with respect to the election are becoming so pronounced."[84]

What wasn't amazing, to their contemporaries, was the ease with which the Keyserlings blended radical politics and high-level policy-making. In Washington, the line separating left-liberals from either socialists or communists was fuzzy, often coming down more to temperament than to ideology. Mary could visit with the Marxist economist Paul Sweezy one night, dine with the labor lawyer (and Communist) Lee Pressman and his wife another, then spend an evening with un-abashed liberals Abe and Carol Fortas the next.[85] The CP member Nathan Weyl, son of the *New Republic* founder Walter Weyl, asked Leon to join an underground cell of Washington Communists.[86] Leon declined, then went back to advancing his cause from inside the upper echelons of the New Deal state, joined by Mary, who in 1942 became a personal assistant to Eleanor Roosevelt.

As the Keyserlings rose up the bureaucratic ladder, they developed a greater appreciation for reformers who worked within the system. Like Lippmann, they recognized that the significance of the New Deal couldn't be reduced to a debate over the size of government. In 1932, federal spending was 7.83 percent of GDP; in 1938, five years into the Roosevelt revolution, federal spending was . . . 7.83 percent of GDP.[87]

Far more important was a transformation in the character of the state, and of the Democratic Party. A political coalition rooted in the working class, spurred forward by an authentically left-wing labor movement, supported by pragmatic leftists in Washington—here, the

Keyserlings thought, lay the seeds of a peaceful revolution. Although class lay at the center of their politics, they believed that social change—including racial and gender equality—went hand in hand with economic reform. They complained less about the limits of the New Deal and spent more time celebrating its achievements, while insisting that the best was yet to come. The future, along with liberalism, belonged to them.

———————

Which is exactly what Lippmann was afraid of. Deeply disturbed by the New Deal's evolution, he laid out an alternative vision for liberalism in a book that became his most influential and most misunderstood work. *The Good Society*'s mixture of history, economics, and philosophy reflected both Lippmann's continued debt to Keynes and his sympathy with some of Keynes's sharpest critics, above all Hayek. But the roots of his argument stretched back further, all the way to Adam Smith.

The young Lippmann had dismissed *The Wealth of Nations* as a piece of eighteenth-century dogma. A quarter century later, he saw it as the founding text of liberalism, which he now defined as the only ideology that had come to grips with capitalism—"not the rationalization of the status quo, but the logic of the social readjustment required by the industrial revolution."[88]

According to Lippmann, even central planners with the best of intentions were doomed to fail—and there was no guarantee of good intentions. "It is beyond the power of the Lenins, Stalins, Hitlers, and Mussolinis to revolutionize the mode of production," Lippmann wrote. "They can merely attack it, and impair it."[89] Complex societies functioned best when governments kept the rules simple: clear laws set out ahead of time, not shifting mandates from all-too-human government administrators. Nobody could make sense of the countless individual transactions that took place in a modern economy, least of all the poor Washington bureaucrats who would be saddled with the task, "men studying papers at desks . . . [who] would often rather go fishing, or make love, or do anything, than shuffle their papers."[90]

Rapturously received by critics of economic planning, *The Good Society* became a landmark in the development of what a few people were already calling neoliberalism.[91] The term itself appears to have been coined at "The Colloque Walter Lippmann," a conference held in Paris in 1938 to celebrate the French translation of the book. Lippmann had generously acknowledged Hayek's influence, and Hayek would be just as complimentary in the future. Writing in 1959, shortly before the publication of his masterwork, *The Constitution of Liberty*, Hayek called his book "the final outcome" of a "trend of thought which may be said to have started twenty-two years ago when I read *The Good Society*."[92]

Yet Lippmann did almost nothing to encourage the movement that he helped to found. When Hayek toured the United States in 1944, he said he had "the impression that [Lippmann] deliberately avoided meeting me."[93] Lippmann also ducked a request to write a preface for *The Road to Serfdom*, though he found time to dash out an introduction for a dog-training manual. ("For dogs, as well as for others," he observed, "education and discipline are not the prerogatives of tyranny but are necessary to the pursuit of happiness.")[94]

Signs that Lippmann would be an unreliable ally were already present in *The Good Society*. His heroes were figures like John Stuart Mill, "a sensitive man in touch with practical affairs," not righteous ideologues challenging all comers in the name of Truth.[95] Despite his warnings about the collectivist path to dictatorship, Lippmann carved out a long list of acceptable state interventions. The catalogue included Keynesian economic management, public works, "large social expenditure on eugenics," "drastic inheritance and steeply graduated income taxes," and "many other things."[96] Much more concerned about corporate power than the typical market defender, he viewed monopolies as privatized collectivism and called for vigorous antitrust regulations.

Despite the ominous warnings about tyranny, Lippmann had quietly moved away from the thoroughgoing skepticism of concentrated government power that characterized his pre–New Deal years. He

didn't want unity imposed by bureaucrats, and he feared that demagogues could rally the outsiders against the insiders. But he had regained his faith in statesmanship. "As the progress of the industrial
revolution destroys legitimacy, prescription, and habitual obedience
to established authority," he wrote, "the fundamental question is how
the formless power of the masses shall be organized, represented, and
led."[97]

Here was the key difference between Lippmann and Hayek. The
prophet of liberalism once again yearned for a leader who could summon the people to a cause worth fighting for. And with another war
looming in Europe, he was about to get his wish.

It was astonishing how quickly the world changed. Lippmann decided
early that Germany could be restrained only by military force. After
Pearl Harbor, he became a vigorous defender of Roosevelt's foreign
policy. With the president saying that "Dr. New Deal" was stepping
aside for "Dr. Win-the-War," a path back to power was cleared for administration critics of all sorts—precisely the "able influential conservatives from both parties" whose absence Lippmann had bemoaned.[98]
"I am convinced that with the new prestige which industrialists have
gained since Pearl Harbor," Lippmann wrote in June 1942, "they can
save themselves and the order which they belong to."[99] Under cover of
war, he also saved himself.

Putting his flirtation with heterodoxy behind him, Lippmann
slipped comfortably into the role of Washington wise man. Parties at
his home opened the city's social season in the spring and closed it in
the fall. At annual New Year's Eve soirees, carefully chosen guests—
artists, journalists, the inevitable statesmen—formed a circle at mid-
night, clasped hands, and sang "Auld Lang Syne."[100]

Between the celebrations, presidents came and went, all of them
disappointing to Lippmann in some degree. But the stakes of holding

the White House never felt as high as they did in the 1930s. Both parties had coalitions that reached across the left and the right. In the governing class, early exemplars of meritocracy—the term was coined in 1958—mingled alongside surviving remnants of the WASP elite, with products of New York City public schools taking their place in the governing class alongside alumni from Groton and Choate.[101] And they all read Lippmann.

To an extraordinary degree, Democratic and Republican elites converged on the program that Lippmann sketched during the Depression, a third way between laissez-faire and collectivism. Memories of the Great Depression pushed the GOP to the center on economics, while the Cold War turned socialism into a byword for treason. Republicans lived in fear of being tagged as the party of Hoover, and Democrats scrambled to avoid being cast as useful idiots for Stalin. Both sides accepted that the government's chief task was to ensure steady economic growth while maintaining a welfare state that guaranteed a baseline quality of life. Industries would be regulated without being nationalized. Otherwise, the market could usually be left to its own devices.

Although Lippmann shifted easily between parties, Democrats were especially drawn to the cult of Lippmann. Arthur M. Schlesinger Jr., the party's foremost intellectual, was particularly fond of *The Method of Freedom*, calling it Lippmann's "most brilliant and prophetic work."[102] Schlesinger was a leading historian of the New Deal, but he was eager for Democrats to move beyond the Age of Roosevelt. According to Schlesinger, the world that FDR made—with its growing economy, enlightened businessmen, and empowered unions—rendered the New Deal irrelevant.[103] Liberals had reformed themselves out of a job by turning blue-collar Democrats into Eisenhower-voting suburbanites.

"If the economic problem at home seems to be fixed up for the moment," Schlesinger announced in a 1957 essay bidding farewell to the Roosevelt era, then "liberalism must for the moment shift its focus from economics and politics to the general style and quality of our civilization."[104] Concretely, this meant a liberalism not just of decent wages and shorter hours but of parks, libraries, museums, clean air, and a more beautiful public life—a politics of moral uplift that would "fight spiritual unemployment as it once fought economic unemployment."[105] Schlesinger called his program "qualitative liberalism."[106] From this perspective, Lippmann's earlier tangles with FDR were less a sin to be forgiven than a sign of his prescience.[107]

Lippmann shared the underlying sense of moral unease and dissatisfaction with material prosperity that drove Schlesinger's flight from the New Deal. He labored for years over a slender volume, *Essays in the Public Philosophy*, lamenting "the sickness of the Western liberal democracies."[108] But after the book received lackluster reviews and disappointing sales, Lippmann pivoted away from apocalyptic musings. In columns and television appearances he echoed Schlesinger's calls for a more active federal government, with not a hint of his earlier concern about overweening bureaucrats paving a road to serfdom.

The vogue for qualitative liberalism in elite circles marked an important shift in postwar politics, and it was responded to, vigorously, within the Democratic policymaking class by defenders of the New Deal faith—including Mary and Leon Keyserling.

Both of them were members in good standing of the Democratic establishment. Harry Truman appointed Leon as chairman of the Council of Economic Advisers. Mary became a high-ranking economist at the Department of Commerce, where she helped design the Marshall Plan. They each joined Americans for Democratic Action (ADA), the command center for liberal Democrats. Mary rose quickly through the ranks of the Women's National Democratic Club, eventually becoming its president. In 1960 she was the only woman to serve as a member of the national party's platform committee.

In their radical days, the Keyserlings denounced capitalists and demanded revolution. Now they focused their ire on Republicans at home and Communists abroad while celebrating the virtues of piecemeal reform. Rather than depicting capitalism as torn apart by its own contradictions, the Keyserlings turned into champions of regulated markets. Because the economy was booming, Americans could pay for a sweeping program of domestic reforms—and a global war against communism—without pitting classes against one another. Instead of cutting into the wealthy's slice of the pie, they would just get more for everyone. "Our concepts of our capacity to work within the status quo for economic expansion in the benefits of which all can share is still a very strange one to those steeped in the Social Democratic tradition of Europe," Mary wrote to a friend in 1957, dismissing not just social democrats but the radical flank of the New Deal.[109]

Most of the time, the Keyserlings' politics were almost indistinguishable from qualitative liberalism. But there was a crucial difference. Although the Keyserlings renounced socialism, they held on to their belief in the reality of class conflict—and in the importance of working-class voters to the Democratic coalition. It was a reprise, in moderated tones, of the distinction that a young Walter Lippmann had drawn between socialism and progressivism.

As the Keyserlings saw matters, technocratic institutions like the Council of Economic Advisers were worthwhile only if they fit into a larger political vision. And their politics still came back to class. The vogue for qualitative liberalism, they feared, would distract from the more important work of raising living standards for ordinary Americans. "I would let each citizen decide for himself," Leon wrote, "whether he would rather listen to the Fifth Symphony than Elvis Presley."[110] Liberals had accomplished the most, he argued, when they focused on lifting "the relative and absolute economic and social status of the common man; they were not interested in what he read." Anything else should stay in the faculty lounge.

There was one other major respect in which the Keyserlings' version of liberalism differed from that of Lippmann or Schlesinger. The columnist glided back into the mainstream in the postwar years, and Schlesinger never left it. To the outside world, it looked as if the Keyserlings were just as secure. Away from the camera, however, they had been dragged into a battle for their political lives.

McCarthyism was the opening salvo in the revolt against the liberal establishment, an attack not just on Communists in government but on the New Deal order itself.

Lippmann was beyond purging. He had abandoned socialism when Joseph McCarthy was barely out of diapers, and his jeremiads against planning during the Depression had demonstrated his respect for capitalism. An early critic of Stalinism, he also cautioned against taking the Cold War to extremes. He opposed the creation of NATO, called the speech where Winston Churchill coined the phrase "iron curtain" an "almost catastrophic blunder," and urged Truman against putting troops on the ground in the run-up to the Korean War.[111]

For Lippmann, anticommunism was all about proportion. A moderate dose encouraged Americans to accept their country's role as a superpower with great influence on the world stage. But too much of it fostered unrealistic expectations about a final triumph against evil. Minor setbacks would seem like existential threats, and realistic policymakers would look like appeasers—or traitors.

McCarthyism vindicated all his fears. He detected "seeds of totalitarianism" in the movement, led by "an ambitious and ruthless demagogue" who was, for a time, capable of bending the government to his will.[112] Lippmann blamed liberal Cold Warriors for turning the clash with the USSR into an existential battle, sharpening blades that the right later turned against them.

Lippmann's anti-anticommunism weathered the revelation that one of his former secretaries had spied on him for the Soviets. In the summer of 1948, the former Communist agent Elizabeth Bentley—dubbed the "Red Spy Queen" by tabloids—told the House Un-American Activities Committee that Mary Price, Lippmann's secretary from 1939 to 1943, had been one of her sources. Although Price denied the charges, declassified records from the National Security Agency later confirmed the allegations. After Price quit, in 1943, Moscow kept tabs on Lippmann (code-named "Imperialist") through regular meetings the columnist had with his friend Vladimir Pravdin, a correspondent for the Soviet news agency TASS and an undercover KGB operative.[113]

The Keyserlings weren't so lucky. A federal investigation of their past radical ties began in 1940. It eventually covered hundreds of interviews with acquaintances from every stage of their lives, along with multiple grueling interrogations for both Keyserlings. Mary and Leon denied under oath that they had ever belonged to either the Communist Party or a CP front. But a witness told the FBI that in the 1930s Leon had disagreed only with "minor points" of Communist orthodoxy—specifically, on the need for violent revolution—and suggested that Mary could "still be [a] top leader in CP underground."[114] Hauled before a confidential Senate committee in 1951, the Keyserlings offered implausibly moderate summaries of their political biographies. Mary insisted she had been "very conservative in college," and Leon claimed that he "might even have been a Republican in 1933"—that is, a few months after voting for Norman Thomas, following months of toying with supporting the Communists.[115]

McCarthy publicized the accusations in 1952, eliciting vehement denials from the Keyserlings and yawns from the mainstream press. ("Ho Hum," wrote *The Washington Post*.)[116] The investigation continued, given new life by discrepancies between the Keyserlings' testimony and easily verifiable facts—for instance, Mary having once been a registered member of the Socialist Party. Leon's weight ballooned, and the two bickered ferociously in private. Mary contemplated divorce. Although both were eventually found innocent of disloyalty, Mary lost her security clearance in January 1953, forcing her and Leon to step down early from their positions at the Commerce Department and the Council of Economic Advisers.[117]

Still adamant in their denials, the Keyserlings emphasized their loyalty and danced around Mary's denied security clearance. They also redoubled their commitment to the Cold War. "The Communist danger is the central, overwhelming danger which our economy faces," Leon maintained.[118] "If that danger is not met, our economy and way of life may be destroyed." Their anticommunism was zealous, even by the standards of the time, and far more extreme than Lippmann's—but Lippmann didn't have anything to prove.

McCarthyism was just one part of the revitalized conservative movement. Lippmann was a favorite target for activists on the right. (Sometimes literally: college Republicans used pictures of him for dart
practice.)[119] "The most alarming single danger to the American system,"
William F. Buckley Jr. declared in the first issue of *National Review*,
bible for the nascent movement, "lies in the fact that an identifiable
team of Fabian operators is bent on controlling both our major political
parties—under the sanction of such fatuous and unreasoned slogans
as 'national unity,' 'middle-of-the-road,' 'progressivism,' and 'bipartisanship.'"[120] They couldn't have conjured up a more fitting antagonist
than Lippmann, a former card-carrying member of the Fabian Society
turned arbiter of the American consensus. He stood for a politics that
was simultaneously radical and devoid of principle.

Backlash to the civil rights movement gave the resurgent right its
next major boost. Lippmann was a late-arriving supporter of the campaign for integration, and he was taken aback by the passions it elicited.
"It is only the parvenu, the snob, the coward who is forever proclaiming
his superiority," he sniffed, as if white supremacy were just a marker
of ill-breeding.[121] Racial equality rarely figured in his books and appeared in only a handful of the hundreds of columns he wrote between
1931 and 1957. One of those columns sided with Southern senators
who were filibustering an anti-lynching law, arguing that "a minority
must never be coerced unless the reasons for coercing it are decisive and
overwhelming"—the minority in question being white senators, not
African Americans.[122] When the push for equal rights gained momentum in the 1950s, Lippmann assured his readers that Southern politicians would preside over a peaceful transition to equality. "We need not
doubt," he predicted after the Supreme Court ruled in *Brown v. Board*,
"that the states will accept loyally the principle of the law."[123]

When the decision was instead met with a coordinated campaign
of massive resistance spearheaded by the Southern elite, Lippmann be-

gan to suspect that he had miscalculated. His anxieties heightened as incidences of violent retaliation against African Americans multiplied. "The whole civil rights affair," he fretted in 1964, was "an explosive thing under our society."[124]

But Lippmann had faith that the center would hold. In the run-up to the 1964 campaign, he all but dared the GOP to nominate the conservative icon Barry Goldwater. "We have been hearing for a generation that the Republican candidate is never a real Republican, and that's why he doesn't get elected," he grumbled. "They might as well get something out of their system which they need to get out of their system."[125] He was less sanguine during the campaign, calling Goldwater a "radical reactionary who would . . . dismantle the modern state" while turning "the party of Lincoln into the party of white supremacists."[126] But after Lyndon Johnson trounced Goldwater, Lippmann said that it offered "indisputable proof that the voters are in the center," leaving Republicans "with virtually nothing more than a handful of states, won by racist votes"—a striking bit of moralizing from a columnist who once defended filibusters of anti-lynching laws.[127]

Goldwater's defeat was all the sweeter for Lippmann because it doubled as a vindication for Lyndon Johnson, a self-described "consensus man."[128] LBJ's version of consensus did not mean inertia. Although the Great Society is today remembered as a high-water mark for postwar liberalism, anchored in the Democratic Party, almost all of its landmark measures passed with significant Republican support, including Medicare, the Civil Rights Act, and the Voting Rights Act.[129]

Walter Lippmann approved. Drawing a sharp distinction between the Great Society and the New Deal, he praised Johnson for pushing through a liberal agenda without exacerbating class divisions. A booming economy made it possible to expand the welfare state without soaking the rich. The War on Poverty didn't require a war on capitalists, just a willingness to share the fruits of abundance.[130] It was qualitative liberalism at a grand scale, both more technocratic and more expansive than its New Deal predecessor—but also more vulnerable to attack.

Hints of an impending Democratic crack-up were already evident in 1964. Although Johnson's popular vote margin was larger than any of Roosevelt's, this was no longer FDR's party. LBJ outpaced Roosevelt throughout the Northeast, winning two states—Maine and Vermont—that eluded Roosevelt over four elections. But he did worse in former Democratic strongholds, including much of the South, the Great Plains, and the Mountain West. The only historically Democratic region where Johnson posted comparable numbers with Roosevelt was in the old Jacksonian territory of Greater Appalachia, including Kentucky, Missouri, Ohio, and West Virginia.[131] With the economy roaring and the nation still grieving over the death of its slain president, that was more than enough to win. But shift the environment slightly—a recession, maybe, or a flare-up of racial tensions—and the results could take a nasty turn for the Democrats.

Lippmann's solution, as usual, was statesmanship. "The only real way to solve a problem like, for instance, the racial problem," he said, "is by having an overwhelming majority in favor of enforcement of civil rights."[132] The more divisive the subject, the more important it was to build a majority coalition. "This man's genius in politics," he explained in his first CBS interview after Johnson took office, "has been finding the point at which a consensus—an agreement—is possible."[133]

"Did you see Walter Lippmann last night?" Johnson asked the Georgia senator Richard Russell the next day. "I thought he was wonderful."[134]

Lippmann's support for Johnson was sincere, the result of one consensus man recognizing another. But it was helped along by the years that LBJ had spent wooing the columnist, reaching back to Johnson's time as Senate majority leader. The courtship reached new levels of intensity after Johnson became president, beginning with a visit to Lippmann's home the week after the Kennedy assassination.

Johnson's instinct for the deal was just as attractive to the Keyserlings. With the spiky pragmatism of former radicals who grew to detest their own youthful idealism, the couple had molded themselves to fit the constraints of the American political system. They were rewarded for their loyalty by Johnson, who restored both Keyserlings to a level of influence they hadn't enjoyed since Truman.

This time, Mary had the more prominent official role. In 1964, Johnson selected her as director of the Women's Bureau, an agency within the Department of Labor. Established in 1920, the Women's Bureau took on new significance in the Great Society. Mary's position required Senate confirmation, giving congressional conservatives an opportunity to raise questions about her past radical associations. Senate liberals mocked the charges, and she sailed through.[135]

Although the bureau lacked either the funding or the staff to exert major influence within the administration, Mary used her position to wage an aggressive publicity campaign, producing a steady stream of reports, delivering speeches around the country, and organizing high-profile conferences in Washington. With her customary attention to economics, she concentrated the bureau's attention on discrimination against women in low-wage jobs, calling for better pay and publicly funded day care.

Leon was just as busy playing the outside game. Bayard Rustin brought him onto a team of economists affiliated with the AFL-CIO who were tasked with drawing up a "Freedom Budget" explaining how the civil rights movement would make the transition from protest to politics—the place where Martin Luther King Jr.'s poetry would turn into a legislative framework and Cold War liberalism would give way to multiracial social democracy.[136] "We must see to it," Rustin said, "that the reorganization of the 'consensus party' proceeds along lines which will make it an effective vehicle for social reconstruction."[137] Leon quickly emerged as the leading voice among the economists and a kindred spirit to Rustin. Though Leon had not previously devoted much attention to civil rights, he and Rustin came out of the same left-wing tradition: focused on economics, committed to organized labor, and scornful of political romantics.

Rustin included Leon among the handful of speakers at the press conference debuting the Freedom Budget in 1966. The heart of the program was a federal jobs guarantee combined with a universal basic income—ostensibly race-neutral policies that, in practice, would disproportionately benefit African Americans. According to Keyserling, the budget's $100 billion price tag (about $850 billion today) could be paid for entirely by increasing economic growth.

Lippmann and the Keyserlings reflected the two sides of Johnson's political mind, yet another reprisal of the split between progressivism and socialism that Lippmann had identified a lifetime ago. With its desire to tamp down conflict while making a more beautiful country, Lippmann's consensus-minded liberalism reached back to the softer side of progressivism. The Keyserlings' flintier approach assumed that class conflict was a given, then sought to bend the outcome in the favor of workers at the same time that they tried to harness the energy unleashed by the social movements of the 1960s.

Lippmann's neo-progressivism and the Keyserlings' hard-nosed liberalism were products of two different wings of the American establishment. Lippmann nestled within the confines of the elite, a private club where money, power, and prestige mingled together. The Keyserlings were partisans in a bipartisan age, devoted not just to the Democrats but to the unglamorous world of ward-heeling politicians and organized labor.

Lyndon Johnson held both sides together for a time, bringing all three liberals closer to the inner workings of government than they had been in decades. From those privileged seats, Lippmann and the Keyserlings watched the postwar consensus explode.

———————

If the New Deal order was made by an economic crisis, it was undone by a social one. Cities in flames, campuses under siege, a failing war in Vietnam—all of it contributed to a sense that the country was falling apart. Meanwhile, a rising generation of left-wing activists set its sights on the liberal establishment. And Lyndon Johnson, self-proclaimed consensus man, could do nothing to stop it.

Inside the Johnson administration, the lines of conflict were especially sharp at the Women's Bureau. Mary picked her battles carefully, not wanting to offend the president by pushing too hard, or to risk muddying her economic message with broadsides against the patriarchy. Like many feminists of her generation, she opposed the Equal Rights Amendment because she worried that it would invalidate protective labor legislation for women: minimum wages, maximum hours, guaranteed breaks during shifts, restrictions on night work— measures that provided security against exploitation at the cost, potentially, of putting a ceiling on how far women could advance in their careers. With the ascent of the ERA, she feared that the interests of high-achieving professionals were taking priority over the needs of working-class women.[138]

Mary's politics were increasingly out of step with the broader feminist movement. Battle lines were drawn in the summer of 1966 during a national conference on the status of women. At a meeting in Betty Friedan's hotel room—Friedan had been invited to the conference over Mary's objections—dissident feminists agreed to call for a formal resolution denouncing the Johnson administration over lax enforcement of antidiscrimination laws. Mary helped kill the proposal, worried about antagonizing the White House. Later that day, Friedan and her supporters began outlining plans for an independent group, describing it as an NAACP for women. On a paper napkin, Friedan scribbled three letters: N O W, the National Organization for Women.[139]

The Freedom Budget, meanwhile, was going nowhere. Rustin won over much of the Democratic establishment, picking up support from major unions and such liberal bastions as the ADA, but the mass movement he hoped to spark never materialized. Younger Black activists rallying behind the call for Black Power had no time for Rustin's accommodations with the Democratic machine.[140] Arguments over Vietnam were consuming the white left, from student radicals up to gray-haired liberals. And conservatives were making headway at the polls. In the 1966 midterm elections Republicans picked up three seats in the Senate and forty-seven in the House. Two years after making his national debut as Barry Goldwater's most effective spokesperson, Ronald Reagan drummed the California governor Pat Brown out of office, demonstrating the national promise of the new right.[141]

With the left divided and conservatives on the march, the Freedom Budget's fate was sealed. It died quietly, becoming a turning point where American politics failed to turn.

But the schism on the left kept widening. The Keyserlings, both supporters of the war, stood by Johnson. After Johnson announced that he would not seek reelection, they lined up behind Hubert Humphrey, confirming their allegiance to an establishment that young leftists were intent on overthrowing.

Mary's scuffles with feminists, Leon's difficulties with the Freedom Budget, and the left's resistance to Humphrey were all part of a reckoning over the meaning of liberalism. Almost sixty years earlier, the young Walter Lippmann had drawn a bright line between socialists and progressives: a politics rooted in economic interests on one side and a broader moral vision on the other. The New Deal scrambled the debate by adopting a tempered version of the socialist strategy, bringing veterans of the Old Left like the Keyserlings into the Democratic fold. But the drift away from class-based politics started early, setting up a recurring battle inside the party. Now, as the Keyserlings saw it, on one side were pragmatists like themselves, focused on pocketbook issues at home and defending freedom abroad. (The question of how they could reconcile kitchen-table politics with a willingness to torch the Democratic coalition over Vietnam went unaddressed.) On the other side were the unknowing heirs of the quantitative liberals, romantics who confused moral crusading with good campaigning, including NOW, the Black Power movement, and the New Left.

Plus Walter Lippmann. He split with Johnson over Vietnam, convinced that it was a doomed enterprise. Watching the United States spend years in a failed effort to bomb its way to peace triggered a crisis of faith. "There is a growing belief that Johnson's America is no longer the historic America," he wrote in 1967, "that it is a bastard empire which relies on superior force to achieve its purposes, and is no longer an example of the wisdom and humanity of a free society."[142]

It was shocking language coming from Lippmann, and he was just getting started. "I'm more worried about the state of the country than I think I've ever been before," he said.[143] "The taking of drugs to forget it all, the idea that only violence and sabotage and irreconcilability have any effect, the great movement of withdrawal, the movement to nihilism, separatism and alienation, the hopelessness, the despair, the cynicism—all these are the symptoms of the disintegration of the central hope of American society."[144]

As the 1968 election approached, Lippmann announced that a political revolution was coming. "The Roosevelt coalition is worn out," he declared. "The New Deal has become obsolete."[145] He welcomed the emerging Republican majority. To most electorally minded observers, the central issue of the election was whether Republicans could break into the South while reclaiming the industrial Midwest. But Lippmann believed that the real opportunity for the GOP lay with the old Progressive coalition—intellectuals, enlightened business leaders, and the young. George Wallace's third-party bid struck him as a sideshow. "Wallace does not offer the country a choice," he sniffed, "only an expression of part of the people's discontents."[146] To focus on a populist tantrum was to miss the historic opportunity for a Progressive revival.

Lippmann lowered his sights after Nixon clinched the Republican nomination. He had always considered Nixon a cut-rate demagogue. ("That must be the most demeaning experience my country has ever had to bear," he said in 1952, after the Checkers speech, where Nixon diverted attention from a campaign finance scandal with syrupy references to his family dog.) By 1968, however, Lippmann had reconciled himself to Nixon, arguing that it was better for a conservative to wield power in the years ahead.[147] "There will probably remain a considerable body of irreconcilable revolutionary dissent," he predicted. "It is better that Nixon should have the full authority if the repression should become necessary in order to restore peace and tranquility in the land."[148]

Point by point, Lippmann and the Keyserlings had sketched alternative paths for liberalism—on Vietnam, the politics of 1968, and the New Deal order. But none of them ever again came close to wielding the influence they held under Johnson. Mary drew headlines for campaigning against the Equal Rights Amendment, denouncing the "romantic folly" of a "women's lib solution" and testifying against it on

Capitol Hill.[149] Leon was just as vigorous in attacking his two favorite targets, liberal technocrats and "the so-called 'far left.'"[150] Although both Keyserlings remained loyal Democrats to the end, they shrank into the role of party elders—admired by their old friends, humored by a rising generation of Democrats looking to move beyond the New Deal.

Lippmann's fall was even more precipitous. Approaching his ninth decade, he quit his column and moved back to New York. He quickly discovered that it was much harder to get his calls returned without a massive public platform. At the height of his influence, Lippmann had forced Nikita Khrushchev to rearrange his schedule in order to keep a meeting. Now he took to eating meals at the common table of his favorite dining club because he couldn't reliably find a lunch date.[151]

He tinkered with the idea for a new book called "The Ungovernability of Man," but gave up on the project.[152] "You can be certain that anybody who thinks he has a solution doesn't know what he's talking about," he said.[153] Gazing into his crystal ball once again, the prophet of liberalism declared in 1969, "It's going to be a minor Dark Age."[154]

———————

Which was overstating things. Yes, American politics was about to remake itself. Instead of becoming the vehicle for a reborn progressivism, the GOP built a new coalition by tapping into racial animus, religious fundamentalism, and fury at liberal elites. As Republicans underwent a populist makeover, they raked in donations from business leaders, who were much more concerned with driving up short-term profits—and much less concerned with industrial statesmanship—than Lippmann realized.

Time and again, however, Republicans who railed against big government wound up strengthening the state. In 1968, Lyndon Johnson's last year in the White House, federal spending was 18.9 percent of GDP; when George H. W. Bush left office a quarter century later, it

was 20.5 percent.[155] More than half a century after the breakdown of
the New Deal coalition, the federal government remained a leviathan.
Despite periodic revolts at the ballot box, the American establishment
was just as firmly entrenched.

Liberalism proved equally adaptable. Safe inside the Democratic
Party, it still bears an unmistakable resemblance to Lippmann's creed:
technocratic, meritocratic, hungry for bold leadership, devoted to an
expansive notion of the public good, and reluctant to speak the language of class conflict. The most notable change was the infusion of
moral energy derived from the movements of the 1960s, including feminism, gay rights, and—above all—the Black freedom struggle. And
those gains have not been reversed, leaving behind a country that is far
more liberal in practice than in the glory days of the liberal consensus.

Along the way, however, the liberalism of the Keyserlings—social-
democratic in its orientation, grounded in a working-class coalition—
lost its purchase. As a question of political theory, there was no inherent
conflict between the Old Left and the New. As a practical matter,
though, partisan polarization around the social issues went hand in
hand with the breakdown of the New Deal order, driving the parties
further apart in the culture war at the same time that they both drifted
to the right on economics.[156]

It's impossible to know whether events could have played out otherwise. Too few of the combatants in the Democratic civil wars of the
1960s were looking for a middle ground, and too many relished playing
the victim. Baby boomer radicals turned against a liberal establishment
they didn't understand, but the establishment didn't want to be understood. Certainly not the Keyserlings, who never acknowledged their
own political evolution—neither the radical ideals that drew them into
politics nor the toll that McCarthyism exacted. Possessed of unwav-
ering confidence in their beliefs, they had no desire to apologize for
compromises they wouldn't admit to making.

The flattening of Lippmann's history was just as revealing. He had
been a socialist who dreamed of empowering the proletariat, a progressive intoxicated with the promise of mastery, a disillusioned lib-

eral preaching self-denial to the masses, an early champion of both the postwar consensus and its neoliberal critique, a defender of the status quo as it crumbled under his feet, and an exile predicting another dark age. Through it all, part of him was still that nine-year-old boy on the veranda of the Grand Union Hotel, straining to catch a glimpse of greatness.

And, by 1973, he was an old man in rapid decline. His wife, overwhelmed by the demands of caring for an aging husband, put him up in a nursing home on Park Avenue. There, on September 23, 1974, Lippmann celebrated his eighty-fifth birthday with thirty-odd friends and a telegram from the new president, Gerald Ford. He died two months later.

But how to remember Walter Lippmann? Religious services were out of the question, and a search commenced among his friends for alternative funeral arrangements. The organizers eventually settled on the Manhattan office of the Ford Foundation, a temple of sorts for the American liberal.[157]

Nobody knew what to say. So they didn't say anything at all. Instead, they crowded into a small auditorium and watched a collection of clips from Lippmann's interviews on CBS.

It was simpler that way.

7

Insurgents

The stars were waiting for the show to start, chairs pulled close enough that their knees could touch. As a snippet from a Brandenburg Concerto played, the camera panned to William F. Buckley Jr. The *National Review* editor was affecting his usual shabby gentility, as if he had rushed to the studio after a three-martini lunch at Le Cirque. Viewers tuning in to *Firing Line* would have recognized the woman with the upswept blond hair sitting to Buckley's left as Phyllis Schlafly—leader of the campaign against the Equal Rights Amendment, Buckley's ally in the conservative movement, and one of the most polarizing figures in American life.[1]

Decades before the term was coined, Schlafly perfected the art of trolling. Wielding domestic bliss like a machete, she depicted herself as a happily married wife and mother. Obliging journalists reported that she breastfed all six of her children and taught them to read before they started school. The problem with feminism, she insisted, was that it deprived women of the joy she had found. "I don't see that my opponents succeed in making themselves or the people around them happy," she said. "I don't see that they have fulfillment, happy marriages, or the wonderfully successful children that I have."[2] During her fight against the ERA, Schlafly took to opening rallies by thanking her husband for letting her come and speak. "I always like to say that," she explained, "because it makes the libs so mad."[3]

Except she hadn't come on *Firing Line* to talk about the ERA. Schlafly was taking a break from the campaign against feminism to speak about the cause that first brought her into politics: foreign policy. Buckley had invited her to discuss Jimmy Carter's push to hand over the Panama Canal to its home government. Like most other conservatives, Schlafly opposed the president. Buckley, in a rare deviation from movement orthodoxy, sided with Carter.

Schlafly saw the debate over the Panama Canal as the latest skirmish in a longer war. Whether she was describing sex-education classes as "in-home sales parties for abortions" or calling Democrats the party of treason, she had one overarching goal: defending the "grass roots" from the "kingmakers."[4]

According to Schlafly, the Panama Canal treaty was a smoke screen for a Wall Street bailout orchestrated by David Rockefeller—CEO of Chase Manhattan Bank, head of the Council on Foreign Relations, and grandson of the Standard Oil founder. Major banks had loaned billions of dollars to Panama, and, she argued, they would get that money back only if the local government took control of the canal.

Mixing shock with amusement, Buckley tried to brush off "this crazy motivation which really comes out of the fever swamp." When Schlafly kept up the assault, Buckley lost his composure, barking about "this bank crap." Then she moved the conversation to national security, pressing Buckley on the details of the Strategic Arms Limitation Treaty, negotiated by his friend Henry Kissinger. (Five of her books focused on nuclear weapons, and she had recently finished an 846-page polemical biography of Kissinger.) Buckley stumbled over his response, stammering, "That doesn't—it means—look."

Schlafly leaned back in her chair and smiled.[5] Their argument was fraught because it wasn't really about Panama, or about nukes. It was a clash over how the world worked, and what conservatives should do about it.

Consider how Buckley and Schlafly dealt with the John Birch

Society.[6] Buckley took pride in his role as a gatekeeper for the right. After years of dancing around JBS founder Robert Welch's conspiracy theorizing—Welch believed that Dwight Eisenhower was a Communist double agent—Buckley expelled him from respectable conservatism with a scathing five-thousand-word essay in *National Review*. Schlafly took a different path. In public, she always denied having been part of the group. But in December 1959, Schlafly wrote in a letter that she and her husband were both members and praised the JBS for its "wonderful work."[7] According to Welch, Schlafly resigned in 1964 after her national profile rose, worried about undermining her credibility with mainstream audiences. It was an amicable split, and she never denounced the society, but she was still respectable enough for Buckley to invite on his show in 1977.

A Bircher and a Bonesman: the divide was clear, even if the two sides had come to a rapprochement. Buckley had been a member of the American elite since he edited the *Yale Daily News*. His politics were diametrically opposed to Walter Lippmann's, but he was in every other respect an heir to the prophet of liberalism: two pundits with national platforms and gold-plated establishment credentials who moved easily in the highest circles.

Schlafly didn't belong to the right clubs, and not just because they didn't admit women (a point she never liked to dwell upon). A native of St. Louis, she didn't seem to care if *The New York Times* declined to review her books. When Schlafly visited Manhattan, she did it knowing that she had a flight home to catch. She aimed to win, and fraternizing with the enemy would only slow her down.

Where Buckley told conservatives they could build their own elite, Schlafly promised to break the kingmakers. Buckley flirted with populism; Schlafly embraced it.[8] She wrote in 1967, "There are really only three classes of people in the world: a very small elite group which *makes* things happen, a somewhat larger group which *watches* things happen, and a great multitude which *never knows* what happened." The categories were fixed, but Americans could decide where they belonged, if they were smart about it. "The *only* way you can join the elite group," she said, "is to plunge into political action."[9]

She was picking up where Ruth Hanna McCormick left off, looking for a way to break the New Deal order and build the next Republican coalition—a majority for a polarizing age where party bosses were giving way to ideological crusaders, smoke-filled rooms were replaced by television studios, and an influx of college-educated voters demanded more from politics than a chicken in every pot.[10]

Like both Hannas, Schlafly was a consummate organizer. But where the Hannas worked through the GOP machine, Schlafly tapped into the power of independent activist groups pushing the party from the outside. Through the conservative movement, she believed the grass roots could take control of the party. The right would then build a new coalition by tapping into the primal issues that made the Lippmanns of the world squirm: sex, family, religion, and—though this did not move to the center of Schlafly's politics until late in her life—race. The magic lay in combining the spirit of a movement with the strength of a political party, building a bridge from the democratic conservatism of the Hannas to a populist conservatism that could win at the polls and break the liberal elite.

This was the goal that in 1946 convinced a twenty-two-year-old to sign up as campaign manager for a long-shot congressional race against an entrenched Democratic incumbent. In 1964, it inspired Schlafly to write her first book, a self-published Goldwaterite manifesto that she called *A Choice Not an Echo*. It kept her working in the trenches of the conservative movement for decades, making her First Lady of the American right. And in 2016 it led a ninety-one-year-old woman diagnosed with terminal cancer to spend the last months of her life on a campaign that she thought was as important as anything she had done in her career: putting Donald Trump into the White House.

Almost forty years after her debate with Buckley, cracks that were already present in their argument over the Panama Canal were now splitting the conservative establishment in two. Buckley's successors at *National Review* tried to cast Trump out of the movement, declaring him "a menace to American conservatism."[11] One of Schlafly's own children claimed that her elderly mother had been duped into supporting a con man.

A still-lucid Schlafly thought otherwise. She had spent her life battling against the kingmakers, following the conservative movement as it marched down a road that led from Robert Taft to Donald Trump, Birchism to birtherism. Now she believed that victory was finally within her grasp. And she was going to savor every moment.[12]

———————

If demographics were destiny, she would have been a Democrat. Midwestern Catholics were supposed to revere Franklin Roosevelt, especially if they grew up in a family like hers, bouncing from home to home as her parents struggled to keep up with the rent. But even though John Stewart spent most of the Great Depression out of work, relying on his wife, Dadie, to pay the bills, the two were Republicans, and their children—Phyllis and her younger sister—inherited their parents' loyalty to the GOP.[13]

A gifted student, Phyllis Stewart graduated at the top of her high school class. After turning down a four-year scholarship at a local

Catholic college, she enrolled at Washington University in St. Louis, where she worked the night shift at an ordnance plant during World War II to pay tuition. (She remained a night owl when she had children of her own, doing much of her writing after she put the kids to bed.) She graduated in 1944 with honors in political science and moved on to a one-year master's program at Harvard. With her eyes set on a career in politics, she then made her way to Washington, D.C., arriving a few weeks after celebrating her twenty-first birthday.

Though Stewart was a Republican, she didn't yet think of herself as a conservative. In high school, she swooned over Wendell Willkie. ("His mussed hair and his gallant sincerity won everyone's heart," she wrote at the time.)[14] She came to Washington hoping for a government job, and after moving to the city, she joined a club for supporters of the United Nations. But with the war effort winding down, bureaucracies were being trimmed, and the flood of returning veterans meant more competitions for fewer posts. A single woman like the young Phyllis Stewart would have been at the back of any line, even with her glowing recommendations from Harvard.

Forced to improvise, she landed a position as a researcher at a new think tank called the American Enterprise Association. Later renamed the American Enterprise Institute, it was part of an effort to forge a united conservative movement out of the New Deal's scattered opposition: disgruntled capitalists, hard-line anticommunists, Southern white supremacists, and a litany of marginal figures consumed with other pet causes.[15] Stewart immersed herself in this new milieu, reading Friedrich Hayek's dire warnings about the global drift toward socialism and producing reports attacking what the AEA president Lewis Brown called "the sinister menace of the Welfare State."[16]

Schlafly returned to St. Louis in 1946. She soon talked her way into running a congressional campaign for Claude Bakewell, a navy veteran, St. Louis attorney, and—for her purposes most important of all—a Republican. "I was impressed by her incredible knowledge of the most nitty-gritty details of St. Louis ward politics," remembered Bakewell. "I had to keep looking at her to remind myself I was not talking to a fat, old cigar-chomping ward heeler."[17] The district leaned Democratic, but a war-weary electorate voted in droves for Republicans that year, and Bakewell eked out a victory with fewer than fifteen hundred votes to spare.

Six years later, Phyllis Schlafly's name was on the ballot. Now a housewife and mother, she had married Fred Schlafly, a Harvard-trained attorney from a prominent local family. The couple moved to an elegant house just outside St. Louis in the Illinois suburbs, complete with a white picket fence. A handful of local Republicans asked Fred if he would make a protest run against the popular Democratic incumbent, Melvin Price. The Schlaflys were part of a budding faction within the party that wanted to run a different type of campaign: a forthright challenge to what they saw as a bipartisan consensus leading toward a socialist, one-world government. All they needed was a candidate, and Fred looked like an ideal prospect—except that he didn't want to run.

An awkward silence hung over the room until someone asked, "How about Phyllis?" Before the night was over, planning for her campaign had begun.

Price was a quintessential machine politician, a Democratic loyalist who won five elections by promising to deliver voters their fair share of government pork. Schlafly was part of the growing number of college-educated reformers—James Q. Wilson's "amateurs"—who cared more about principle. Journalists covering the campaign marveled at the housewife who believed "there is a provable equation between communism, socialism, and the so-called liberalism."[18]

That Schlafly was taking on the overwhelmingly male world of machine politics underlined the contrast with politics as usual. She navigated carefully around her gender, insisting that her husband approved of the campaign, never acknowledging that sexism might cost her votes, and then turning the conversation back to policy.

Her platform mixed elements drawn from the emerging conservative movement with midwestern Republican orthodoxy, updating Ruth Hanna McCormick's agenda for the Cold War. It was, by the low standards of a political campaign, a coherent progam—a rough draft for a blue-collar conservatism that took aim at liberal elites and bureaucratic overreach while reconciling itself to the most popular elements of the welfare state. She thought Truman made a mistake entering the Korean War, but now Americans had an obligation to win it, even if that meant expanding the conflict to China. Warning against the militarization of society, she called for the abolition of the draft. The Soviet Union would be defeated by pouring money into the nuclear arms race, not by sending working-class boys off to die in foreign wars while college kids took deferments. At home, she said that the budget had to be balanced, but maintained that fiscal integrity shouldn't come at the cost of high taxes, good roads, and generous Social Security payments.

Most of all, the kingmakers had to be checked. "The New Deal has given us government by rich men who never had to wait for a paycheck," she said. "As long as the New Deal continues to be led by men like Averell Harriman, heir to forty million dollars, who believe that 'we can stand higher taxes,' labor will be taxed and taxed, drafted and drafted, expended and expended."[19] Republicans loved this populist scourge with a Harvard degree, and she coasted to victory in the primary.

The general election was a different matter. "It was really a most intellectual campaign—a nationally oriented issues campaign," Price remembered. "She was clearly knowledgeable about the national scene. Trouble was, the voters weren't."[20]

Schlafly counted on red-baiting to make up for the enthusiasm gap. Conjuring up fears of the enemy within gave the New Deal an ominously pink hue while burnishing her own anticommunist credentials. If Schlafly hadn't been accusing Democrats of enabling treason, it's easy to imagine her being portrayed as an isolationist who didn't have the guts to take on Stalin, just as Ruth Hanna McCormick had been made toxic for her opposition to World War II. A dash of McCarthyism allowed Schlafly to present herself as the true Cold Warrior, not just Robert Taft in pearls.

Plus it drove Price crazy. Here was the great irony of the campaign: Schlafly was both the most intellectually substantial challenger he ever faced and the one with the most casual relationship to the truth. She was a thinking woman's demagogue. A local paper dubbed her "the best twister of facts who has appeared on the local political scene . . . during the last thirty-five years."[21] Price was so frustrated by Schlafly's unrelenting stream of allegations that by the end of the race he refused to shake her hand.

Schlafly's bruising tactics didn't win her the election, but they made her a star inside the Illinois GOP. Her margin of defeat in the district was the same as Eisenhower's, who had the distinct advantage of running as a beloved war hero, not a twenty-seven-year-old home-maker. By the end of the campaign, she was one of the state party's most popular speakers. Over the next decade she acted as a bridge between the GOP and the grassroots right. She attended her first Republican National Convention in 1952, and she became a favorite for her lavish parties. Membership in the Illinois Federation of Republican Women almost doubled during her three terms as president. In 1964 she was chosen as vice president of the National Federation of Republican Women without a single dissenting vote.

At the same time, she spearheaded an effort to build up a conservative infrastructure outside the party, organizing seminars where guest speakers held forth on the dangers of socialism, keeping up a regular presence on the lecture circuit, and producing a popular guide to approved literature on the Cold War. (Recommended titles included *Seeds of Treason*, *Masters of Deceit*, and *No Wonder We Are Losing*.) She helped found the Cardinal Mindszenty Foundation, a home for anticommunist Catholics who felt excluded from a cause dominated by Protestants. She interviewed prominent conservatives for her syndicated radio program, *Dangers of Apathy*. Her expertise was taken seriously enough that in 1963 she was invited to testify at the Senate Foreign Relations Committee on nuclear weapons policy.

Many of the most ardent anticommunists were, like Schlafly, members of the John Birch Society. Even if she wanted to turn on the group—and there's no evidence to suggest that she did—she couldn't afford to. Birchers kept organizations like the Mindszenty Foundation alive. Schlafly wasn't going to let the kingmakers divide the grass roots, especially not when the people were about to get a champion they deserved.

———————

"This will not be an engagement of personalities. It will be an engagement of principles," Barry Goldwater promised while announcing his presidential candidacy in January 1964. "I will offer a choice, not an echo."[22]

Schlafly had been waiting for this moment. A longtime supporter of the Arizona senator, she had already set up a Volunteers for Goldwater Committee. After learning the news, she decided to write a book. Goldwater had given her the perfect title.

A Choice Not an Echo was a mystery novel disguised as a political tract. The mystery was simple: Who stole American democracy? The solution: "a small group of secret kingmakers who are the most

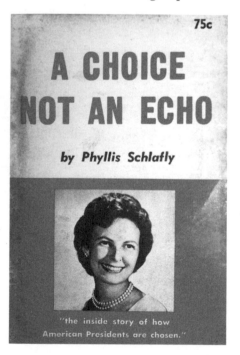

powerful opinion makers in the world."[23] Americans were locked in a battle for control over their country, and most of them didn't even know it. "The strategy of politics, like an iceberg, is eight-ninths under the surface," she wrote.[24] Her book promised to take readers below the surface, revealing the truth about American politics—a truth the kingmakers didn't want them to know.

The idea that elites wielded disproportionate influence over politics was nothing new; it was the implicit premise of every

Walter Lippmann column. Schlafly's interpretation stood out because of its specificity, its anger, and her plan for what to do next. Keep the argument vague, and it becomes a cliché. Say that on February 14, 1957, a secret cabal brought together by the Bilderberg Group met on St. Simons Island, Georgia, to plot "brainwashing and propaganda blitzes" while dining on meals flown in from New York's Pierre Hotel, and it sounded like a revelation—or unhinged conspiracy theorizing, depending on your point of view.[25]

But that was the trick: Schlafly believed that conspiracies were real. "There do in fact exist secret groups of persons high in finance, government and the press who meet secretly to make important plans they do not reveal to the public," she wrote.[26] They were the kingmakers.

The kingmakers were corporatists at home and internationalists abroad. They controlled both parties and had dictated the outcome of every Republican convention since Herbert Hoover left the White House. Elites would, of course, prefer not to see their candidates lose on Election Day, but, with both parties under their thumb, the stakes were low. Bipartisanship was their creed, and they had a morbid aversion to addressing the issues that voters cared about. What had FDR known about the attack on Pearl Harbor? How deep into the government had communists penetrated? Why did the nation's rulers go to such great lengths to keep their intentions secret from the public?

Schlafly thought the answer to the last question was obvious: if the people found out how politics worked, they wouldn't stand for it. That's why the kingmakers feared Goldwater. Forcing a manufactured consensus on the country kept the status quo intact. By offering voters a real alternative, Goldwater could blow up the entire system.

A Choice Not an Echo was the cry of a frustrated activist. "I have given thousands and thousands of hours of dedicated work to the cause of good government through the medium of the Republican Party," Schlafly wrote. "I have done this at my own expense and at great sacrifice on my part and on the part of my family—for one purpose, because I believe in working for good government, and I believe this can be best achieved through the Republican Party."[27] The GOP belonged to the grass roots, not the kingmakers. Take back their party, and they could take back their country.

Her argument tapped into veins that ran deep in the American right. A generation earlier, Henry Ford popularized the notion of a treasonous elite, depicting bankers and Bolsheviks as joint partners in a global conspiracy. The same tropes pervaded the language of the Ku Klux Klan. The enemy took a new form in the aftermath of World War II, when ivory tower eggheads, bow-tied bureaucrats, shadowy corporate executives, and sinister Russian agents blended together into a single ominous mass. Joseph McCarthy demonstrated what a semi-competent demagogue could do with this recipe. Even Robert Taft—Senate GOP leader, son of William Howard Taft, top of his class at Yale College and Harvard Law School—groused, "Every Republican candidate for president since 1936 has been nominated by Chase Bank."[28]

Then came Schlafly. She kept the story clean, steering away from anti-Semitism, overt racism, and dark mutterings about Eisenhower's Soviet loyalties. But there was plenty of red meat for conservatives, and it turned out there were lots of conservatives. She started with an order of 25,000 books. Within a month, 600,000 copies were in circulation. By November, the total had reached 3.5 million, more than twice as many as the first paperback printing of *The Feminine Mystique*.[29] A network of right-wing donors and media groups purchased copies in bulk and distributed them for free. Most of the delegates at the Republican National Convention claimed to have read it. Schlafly, who attended the convention as part of the Illinois delegation, was now an icon to the right.

Which is not to say that she was a perfect representative for Goldwater voters. Reflecting her longtime interest in foreign policy, Schlafly's case against the kingmakers focused on the Cold War. (She published a second book later in 1964, a slender volume on nuclear weapons coauthored with the retired rear admiral Chester Ward. Two million copies were soon in circulation.) In private, she urged Goldwater to downplay states' rights. Aside from a few brief passages—for instance, an attack on "gangs of savages terrorizing and killing missionaries and other white people" in the Congo—*A Choice Not an Echo* dodged race.[30] Nor was she terribly concerned with curbing government spending. Unlike Ronald Reagan, whose nationally televised speech on Goldwater's behalf made him the other breakout star on the right that year, the book didn't describe Medicare as a step on the road to serfdom. In fact, it didn't refer to the Great Society at all.

Although Schlafly didn't save Goldwater from a rout at the polls, she did wonders for her own career. At the start of the year, she had been the darling of grassroots Illinois Republicans. Eleven months, two books, and five million copies later, she had become the most prominent woman in the conservative movement. Then, shortly after the election, she gave birth to her sixth child, Anne. To her growing legion of supporters, one thing was clear. As the *St. Louis Globe-Democrat* put it, "Phyllis Schlafly stands for everything that has made America great."[31]

———————

But how were conservatives supposed to keep America great? Moderate Republicans wanted to stampede back to the center, and they looked forward to running over Schlafly along the way. As vice president of the National Federation of Republican Women, she was next in line to run one of the most important organizations in the GOP. Schlafly's newfound prominence made the contest for the federation presidency into a proxy war for control of the party.[32]

The campaign dragged on for more than a year, culminating at a rancorous convention in May 1967, where the rival camps traded accusations of ballot manipulation and fraudulent delegate selection. Schlafly's supporters marked themselves off by wearing eagle pins, a reference to Isaiah 40:31, "They shall mount up with wings as eagles; they shall run, and not be weary; and they shall walk and not faint." After a narrow defeat, her backers streamed out of the convention hall, an army of followers ready to follow their leader into battle.

Three months later, a few thousand of her devoted fans received the first issue of *The Phyllis Schlafly Report*, a four-page monthly newsletter that she would publish continually for the rest of her life. If Republicans wouldn't hand the party to her, she would build a machine of her own. "The nut fringe," sighed a Republican operative, "is beautifully organized."[33]

With the 1968 election approaching, Schlafly saw the elements of a new majority in the backlash to the era's social upheavals. She had an intuitive sense that Republicans should polarize against "demagogic politicians," "wild Negro extremists," "New Left groups saturated with Communists," "publicity-hunters who think violence is the quickest way to glory," and "assorted do-gooders who think the only way to solve the problems of the 'ghetto' is to burn it down."[34] Some were sincere radicals, others were looking for money or power, and still others were driven by fear. "Perverts are easy targets for blackmail," she explained, tapping into Cold War anxieties about a "homosexual invasion of government."[35] According to Schlafly, all these nefarious actors were part of a corrupt system ruled by an elite whose overriding goal was maintaining its hold on power.

The kingmakers were still in her sights, and her plan of attack was unchanged. "Politics is the *cause* of the major problems that confront us, and political action is their *solution*," she wrote.[36] "The urgent need today is to develop and support leaders on every level of government who are independent of the bossism of every political machine."[37] Conservatives had to outorganize the Republican establishment while keeping one central truth in mind: "Politics is too important to be left to the politicians."[38]

Except conservatives weren't nearly strong enough to dispense with the politicians just yet. Thinking pragmatically, Schlafly endorsed Richard Nixon in 1968, spurning the grassroots hero Ronald Reagan. She worked with a delegation of conservatives headed by Strom Thurmond to persuade the Nixon team not to select a high-profile moderate like Nelson Rockefeller as vice president and secured a pledge that a Nixon administration wouldn't move ahead on federally mandated busing.

Inspired by Nixon's victory, she made another bid for Congress in 1970. Her 1952 race had been a one-woman operation run on a shoe-string budget. This time she spent $250,000—about $1.8 million today—and had the full backing of the Republican machine, which had identified her opponent, the seven-term incumbent George Ship-ley, as one of the most vulnerable Democrats in the House.[39]

The GOP arranged for her to attend a weeklong training session where party officials instructed her to run as the candidate of law and order. She hired the Chicago-based firm Campaign Group, Inc., to de-sign a media blitz, taking on "campus rioters and police killers" along with "the politicians who do nothing about the criminals who stalk our streets but harass the law-abiding with 'gun control.'" John Wayne recorded an ad on her behalf, saying, "The reason I like Phyllis is that she talks straight." Gerald Ford borrowed from the *St. Louis Globe-Democrat*, telling radio listeners, "I know Phyllis stands for everything that makes America great."[40]

Republicans across the country were running similar campaigns, if they had the money. Schlafly supplemented the usual effort by drawing on devoted volunteers who had been following her for the better part of a decade, or longer. Most were women whom male candidates might have asked to fetch coffee or lick envelopes. Schlafly put them in charge of running field operations.

By August, however, the campaign was in crisis. Inflation and un-employment were both ticking upward, and Schlafly discovered that voters were more concerned with plant closings than with campus un-rest. She fired the high-priced consultants and pivoted toward an eco-nomic message focused on cutting taxes and boosting Social Security benefits.

Shipley responded by doubling down on his initial strategy of por-traying Schlafly as an elitist outsider who should stick to homemak-ing. "Who here thinks my Harvard-educated opponent ought to quit attacking my foreign-aid votes and stay home with her husband and six kids?" he asked. "I don't tell her how to take care of her family. And she shouldn't tell me how to take care of my constituents."[41]

In a tough year for Republicans, Schlafly lost by eight percentage points—a respectable margin, but still a defeat. She learned an important lesson from the setback. Economically strapped voters in Illinois might not want her in Congress, and the Republican old guard still wouldn't trust her with real power, but she had a national constituency that trusted her to lead the war against the kingmakers. There were more ways to build up power than by winning an election.

"I've got a nice home in Alton," Schlafly told a journalist. "Why in the world would I want to move to Washington?"[42]

But she needed a hook. Subscriptions to *The Phyllis Schlafly Report* were on the rise, providing readers with musings on subjects ranging from U.S. policy in Latin America to liberal propaganda in children's textbooks. Yet the diversity of coverage prevented Schlafly from channeling her energy into any single issue—until one of her supporters asked her to take another look at the Equal Rights Amendment.

Like almost everyone else in the 1970s, Schlafly favored the ERA at first. Both parties endorsed it in their platforms, and it flew through Congress. By 1977, thirty-five states had approved the ERA, just three short of the three-fourths majority needed for adoption. In Kansas, the debate took about ten minutes.

But what was everyone supporting? The text of the amendment was straightforward. Section one said that equality under the law should not be abridged on account of sex, and section two gave Congress the right to enforce the amendment. Not long ago, most states had prohibited married women from applying for credit cards without their husbands' approval. By the 1970s, however, the notion that women were entitled to equal treatment under the law seemed like unobjectionable stuff—"something between innocuous and mildly helpful," as Schlafly described her initial reaction.[43]

As she researched the amendment, however, she found a lot to disagree with. She fired the opening shot in her campaign in the February 1972 edition of *The Phyllis Schlafly Report*, devoting the entire issue to lambasting the ERA.[44] The problem, she argued, was that supporters of the ERA assumed that women were treated as second-class citizens. This was precisely backward. "Of all the classes of people who ever lived," she wrote, "the American woman is the most privileged."[45] Equal pay for equal work was fine, but Schlafly insisted that most women with young children would rather devote their full attention to raising a family. Although capitalism was a great institution, it needed to be kept in its place—and that place was outside the home.

Over time, Schlafly added features to her indictment of the ERA. It could, she eventually warned, force women to be drafted; eliminate alimony payments; guarantee abortion rights; legalize gay marriage; eliminate legislation protecting women in the workplace; and abolish gender segregation in sports, schools, prisons, and even bathrooms. These were all variations on a theme established in her first attacks on the ERA: legislators who thought they had voted for a toothless affirmation of equality had unknowingly joined an assault on the family.

Although ERA backers rightly maintained that many of Schlafly's charges had a tenuous relationship with the facts, she brought out a real difficulty for their cause. The best-case scenario for feminists was that an activist judiciary would use the ERA to launch the kind of aggressive campaign against sexism that the Warren Court had undertaken against racism. But this was a gamble, not a guarantee. As the political scientist (and ERA supporter) Jane Mansbridge later concluded, "The short-term benefits of the ERA for working women were almost exclusively symbolic, and the long-term benefits were both hypothetical and uncertain."[46] Schlafly, by contrast, could highlight specific examples of what equal treatment would cost, such as draft exemption, and she could do it while delivering a pointed political argument that feminists who needed supermajorities in state legislatures couldn't afford to make.

Schlafly gave her cause a name—"the pro-family movement"—and appointed herself its leader. In her telling, feminists and gays plotting against the family were just as much of a threat to the heartland as Black militants in the streets and hippies burning draft cards. Less than a year after her initial broadside against the amendment, Schlaflyites had set up chapters of STOP ERA (for "Stop Taking Our Privileges") in twenty-six states.

She set the tone for the campaign with frequent television appearances, monthly updates in *The Phyllis Schlafly Report*, and regular training conferences where she taught her volunteers the art of organizing: do host brunches, don't serve alcohol; do appear on TV, don't forget to wear a scarf. State directors were charged with fundraising and figuring out the specifics of their campaigns, but even here she stepped in to provide guidance. "Get Maud Rogers and that pretty young girl who had the baby and the nice looking redhead," she instructed her team in Arkansas, "to commit themselves to talk personally with ten legislators."[47]

Organizing made up for a severe financial disadvantage. STOP ERA's budget peaked at around $110,000 in 1978, less than half of what Schlafly spent in her failed 1970 race and a fraction of the multimillion-dollar budget for ERAmerica, the umbrella group for ERA backers. "While the ERA-ers were prancing around in front of the TV cameras, we were working quietly in Committee," Schlafly boasted.[48] "The pro-ERA forces are only visible when there's actually going to be a vote," one legislator observed. "The STOP ERA, Phyllis Schlafly, group is there all the time. They're always there."[49]

———————

Schlafly had been an activist for decades. Now she was a star, hopping from channel to channel on television as she made the case against the ERA. The *Phyllis Schlafly Report*'s 3,000 subscribers grew into 50,000 members of the Eagle Forum. (A successor to STOP ERA, the Eagle Forum took its name from the eagle pins Schlafly's delegates wore during her 1967 race for the presidency of the National Federation of Republican Women.) Her supporters were usually married women with good educations who belonged to households with above-average incomes. In this respect, they bore a striking resemblance to many of the feminists they attacked; most of the troops on both sides in the war over the ERA came from the college-educated middle and upper-middle classes.[50]

Unlike their opponents, Schlafly's supporters were almost always members of a church. Eager to avoid religious conflicts that had divided the anticommunist movement, Schlafly cultivated an ecumenical spirit within her ranks. "I didn't let them talk about religion," she said. "I combined the Catholics, the Protestants, all the denominations, the evangelicals, the Jews, the Mormons. I had them all."[51]

Most of them were white, too. At a time when illegitimacy rates among African Americans were about seven times higher than for white people, defenses of the nuclear family could easily take on a racial cast.[52] Ronald Reagan played on the same resentments when he denounced "welfare queens" on the campaign trail.[53] One of the leaders of Mississippi's anti-ERA movement was Dallas Higgins, wife of the state's Grand Dragon of the Ku Klux Klan.[54] Outside a Schlafly event in Houston, a woman compared the ERA to busing, saying that both used the power of the government to override the will of local communities. "That's why I support Phyllis Schlafly and that's why I oppose ERA," she explained.[55] But the story wasn't simple: one of the featured speakers at this same Houston event was Mildred Jefferson, the first African American woman to receive a medical degree from Harvard and president of the National Right to Life Committee.[56]

Schlafly had always enjoyed provoking her enemies, and her struggle with feminism was fiercer than the battle with the kingmakers had ever been. "ERA supporters aren't seeking a more just society," she said. "They're seeking a constitutional cure for their laziness and personal problems."[57] After being told that an ERA backer was going on a hunger strike, she replied, "Most of them ought to go on a diet."[58] She had special disdain for mothers she thought were trying to shirk obligations to their children, saying, "A woman who is unwilling to take care of her own baby is a pathetic sight."[59]

Feminists called Schlafly an apologist for the patriarchy who wanted to trap women in the home—and accused her of being a member of the KKK, as a popular rumor suggested. They pointed to research showing that most American families had never fit the supposedly traditional model of a male breadwinner and female homemaker. By the time STOP ERA got under way, a majority of adult women under the age of sixty-four had entered the workforce.[60] According to her critics, Schlafly was fighting a battle she had already lost.

But Schlafly's case against the ERA, and against feminism more broadly, was shrewder than her opponents let on. Left-wing feminists like Mary Dublin Keyserling had long dismissed the amendment as a pet project for the wealthy. (Like two ships in the night, Keyserling dropped her opposition to the amendment around the time Schlafly joined the movement against it.) The former Phyllis Stewart—the little girl with an underemployed father and a mother who juggled multiple jobs to support her family, the teenager who worked nights to pay her way through college—pushed the same line of attack. Playing the part of class warrior, she described the ERA as "an elitist upper-middle class cause that has no relevance to the big majority of working women," an accusation that stung, because even some feminists recognized it contained an element of truth.[61]

She understood that her campaign was doomed if it looked like she was providing cover for male chauvinists. "It was first of all a battle that had to be fought and led by women," she said.[62] She used the breadth of the pro-ERA coalition to her advantage. Instead of defending the most oppressive aspects of Eisenhower-era domesticity, she focused on radical protesters wielding such signs as SOCIALIST REVOLUTION CAN SMASH LESBIAN OPPRESSION.[63] Then she linked the fringes of the movement to its establishment center, turning the anti-ERA campaign into another case of the grass roots taking on the kingmakers, with Christian moms lined up against a feminist elite that stretched from Betty Ford to Gloria Steinem.

Schlafly was at her most effective when she put herself outside of politics, acting as more of a self-help guru than a partisan activist.

Rather than insisting that a woman's place was in the home, she argued that women should have the option to be homemakers. When feminists claimed that the male-breadwinner model was obsolete, she replied that there were millions of housewives in the country.

"The women's liberation movement literature is the greatest put-down of women that anything could possibly be," she wrote in her 1977 book *The Power of the Positive Woman*, a revealingly New Agey title.[64] Her supporters didn't want to hear about how women could free themselves from domestic serfdom; they wanted someone to say that raising a family mattered just as much as holding down an office job.

She modified her approach over the years, keeping what resonated and ditching the rest. The draft was always a favorite, but warning about unisex bathrooms fell out of the repertoire. In 1975, after growing tired of being told that she couldn't understand the nuances of constitutional interpretation, the fifty-one-year-old Schlafly enrolled at Washington University School of Law, graduating three years later in the top 15 percent of her class. "I heard her in her first arguments, which were sloppy at times—incendiary, you know, not very, very good," an Illinois legislator said. "She is so smooth now, I mean, she's got it down to an art form. I think she is totally unbeatable."[65]

"Unbeatable" was an exaggeration. Voters rejected Schlafly during her two races for Congress, and the GOP establishment sank her bid for the presidency of the National Federation of Republican Women. By the ordinary rules of politics, she was a loser.

But the rules were changing, and Schlafly was one of the first to adapt—not because she was uniquely perceptive, but because years of failing in the old system pushed her to innovate. If she had won either of her congressional races, she would have been a backbencher in the perennial House minority. If she had become head of the NFRW, she might be as forgotten today as the woman who beat her for the job. (Gladys O'Donnell, in case you were wondering.) In both cases, she would have been compelled to subordinate her personal ambitions to the demands of her party. Because the Republican establishment rejected her, Schlafly was forced to build a machine of her own, just at the moment when independent activist groups were gaining ground at the expense of the old party elites.

And now she was reaping the rewards. Thirty states had ratified the ERA by the time Schlafly got to work in earnest. By 1977, however, only three more states had approved it. When the initial ratification deadline passed in 1979, Congress voted to give the amendment three more years to pass. In 1982, the ERA still had only thirty-five states in its column, and a handful of them had tried to withdraw their support. Schlafly had done something that was quite unusual, for her and for conservatives.

She won.

As the ERA stalled, Schlafly set to work converting a setback for feminism into a victory for the right. "We saw an attack on marriage, the family, the homemaker, the role of motherhood, the whole concept of different roles for men and women," she said. "What we did was take these cultural issues and bring into the conservative movement people who had been stuck in the pews. We taught 'em politics."[66]

At first, politics meant working with both Democrats and Republicans. Support for the ERA was bipartisan, and so was the opposition. Schlafly saw the opportunity to make a new majority by luring disaffected Democrats to her side. "We always had to win with a changing mix of conservative and liberal representatives," she remembered.[67] Over multiple close votes in Illinois, one of the key states that had not yet ratified, she counted on the backing of the Chicago Democrat Tommy Hanahan, a favorite of organized labor, who referred to ERA backers as "brainless, braless broads."[68] One of her most consistent antagonists was the Illinois Republican senator Charles Percy, who won reelection in 1978 without her endorsement; one of her most effective supporters was Sam Ervin, the Democratic senator from North Carolina.

While she fought the ERA, Schlafly toyed with giving up on the GOP. At the height of the post-Watergate reaction against Republicans in 1975, she joined an effort spearheaded by the North Carolina senator Jesse Helms and the *National Review* publisher William Rusher to found a new party that, in Rusher's words, would bring together "conservative Republicans (broadly represented by Reagan) and conservative Democrats (most of whom have in the past supported [George] Wallace)."[69]

The plan hinged on persuading Reagan to run as their presidential candidate in 1976, and it died when he decided to challenge Ford for the Republican nomination. What the country needed, Reagan said, was "a new and revitalized second party, raising a banner of no pale pastels but bold colors."[70] In other words, a choice, not an echo.

Reagan paired this political strategy with an ideological vision. "Because ours is a consistent philosophy of government, we can be very clear," he said. "We do not have a separate social agenda, a separate economic agenda, and a separate foreign policy agenda. We have one agenda."[71]

Schlafly agreed. "Social issues and fiscal issues are intertwined," she wrote. "You cannot remove the beating heart and soul of conservatism and hope to save the philosophy or the movement."[72] The most important social issue was ensuring that a man could earn enough to support a family, and that wasn't going to happen unless the economy was booming, which meant cutting taxes and slashing the federal bureaucracy.

Reagan made sure that social conservatives received their due. Republicans had backed the ERA in every platform since 1940—until 1980, when delegates removed the endorsement and introduced a plank calling for a constitutional amendment banning abortion. The ERA, a classic instance of the postwar consensus, was now a fault line in a more polarized politics.

With this new kind of politics came a new kind of political actor, a more rambunctious variation on the reform-minded party amateur. "The activists, the people they [the leaders] bring with them—and this goes for both sides, the pro and the con—are pretty much wild-eyed crazies. You know, they are not professional," an anti-ERA legislator said. "These people pull at you, yank you, yell, scream, threaten; they all look wild-eyed to me."[73]

A calmer, altogether more pleasant group was also doing its part to shift the country rightward. Corporations had been relatively quiescent in Washington throughout the postwar years. That changed in the 1970s. With profits falling and regulations increasing, the business community made a massive investment in lobbying the government. Lobbyists didn't have to pull, yank, or scream. They hired seasoned Washington hands to make their case, directed money to sympathetic think tanks, gave expert advice to overworked congressional staffers, funded public relations departments, even drafted legislation. And, of course, they wrote checks.

Schlafly's bête noire David Rockefeller was adapting to the new order, too. ("Most people," Schlafly told Buckley during her appearance on *Firing Line*, "think that the presidency would be a step down for David Rockefeller.")[74] He consulted regularly with the Reagan campaign; at the same time, he bore unwitting responsibility for the Iran hostage crisis dragging Jimmy Carter down in the polls.

The story began in the fall of 1979 when Rockefeller called upon a team of wise men affiliated with Chase Manhattan—including Schlafly's other bugbear, Henry Kissinger—to pressure Carter into admitting the deposed shah of Iran to the United States. Rockefeller had been friendly with the shah for years. More important, the former dictator was one of Chase's most valuable clients. Over meetings at private New York clubs, Rockefeller's team came up with the strategy that helped persuade Carter to allow the cancer-ridden shah into the country for medical treatment. Rockefeller personally asked the president to give the shah safe passage from Mexico. Carter agreed, provoking Iranian radicals to seize the American embassy in Tehran. Which didn't stop Rockefeller from turning around in 1980 and using the same group of wise men to launch a whisper campaign that the White House was planning to bribe their way out of the crisis. The Chase CEO was, after all, a lifelong Republican.[75]

With some dramatic embellishment, the incident could have been dropped into an updated edition of *A Choice Not an Echo*—except for the part about Rockefeller plotting to elect Reagan, an early sign that the kingmakers would get much more from the Reagan revolution than Schlafly cared to admit.

Full details of Rockefeller's part in the Iran crisis only came out after the 1980 election. Along with Reagan's victory, Republicans won back the Senate, and conservatives gained a working majority in the House. But Republicans were losing voters, too, most of them women. The 1980 election marked the first major instance of a gender gap between the parties, with men voting for the GOP in significantly greater numbers than women. Schlafly's core demographic, however, stuck with the party: white married women.[76]

Schlafly didn't worry much about the gender gap. She cared about winning, and it seemed like the right would be doing a lot more of it. "Liberals should brace themselves for some news they will regard not merely as bad but as incredible," predicted the conservative pundit Joseph Sobran. "The wave of the future is rolling in, and its name is Schlafly."[77]

Reagan's victory gave a retrospective shine to the entire conservative movement. In the 1950s, it seemed as if right-wing activists were

stumbling from defeat to defeat. Now it looked like they had been creating institutions, developing ideas, and finding candidates who would
remake American politics.

Schlafly rose with the rest of the right. Her syndicated column, radio commentaries, and frequent television appearances brought her a
national audience. *The Phyllis Schlafly Report* continued to blend forays
into the more esoteric realms of domestic and foreign policy with a
steady diet of red meat for her base. She could highlight the importance
of a strategic minerals policy in one column ("Chromium is essential
to metallurgical, refractory, and chemical industries") and in another
warn about childhood obesity ("Fat Kids: Who's Responsible?").[78]

Out of the public eye, Schlafly was welcomed into the upper ranks
of the right-wing counter-establishment. At off-the-record meetings of
the Council for National Policy—a kind of Bilderberg Group for
conservatives—she hobnobbed with such movement leaders as the
Heritage Foundation cofounder Paul Weyrich and major donors like
the billionaire Texas oilman (and John Birch Society member) Nelson
Bunker Hunt.[79] The Eagle Forum thrived, and its annual leadership
conferences drew some of the biggest names on the right. Ronald Reagan didn't attend in person, but he recorded special video addresses for
the event, and he regularly invited Schlafly to meet with him at the
White House.

By the end of the century, Schlafly's place in the conservative firma-
ment was set. Leaders in the next generation of right-wing firebrands,
including Laura Ingraham and Ann Coulter, cited her as a model.[80] In
retrospect, Schlafly looked like the first example of the so-called Fox
blonde, a type around which Roger Ailes built a cable empire.[81] Three
thousand activists toasted her at a 2003 banquet hosted by the Conservative Political Action Conference.[82] In 2010 the Clare Boothe Luce
Policy Institute placed her in a calendar of "Great American Conservative Women" alongside figures such as Coulter, Michele Bachmann,
and the political strategist Kellyanne Conway.[83]

But it was a bitter victory. Despite all the tributes, Schlafly didn't
fit into the billion-dollar industry that the conservative movement was

becoming. While she stayed in Alton, the leadership of the activist right headed to Washington and New York. The children of yester-day's amateurs became the new professionals, overseeing a sprawling political infotainment complex. *The Phyllis Schlafly Report* remained proudly old-fashioned—four pages, lots of text, maybe a few pictures—as the right shifted into television, slick magazines, and, eventually, the internet.

Her enthusiasm for the GOP leadership plummeted when Reagan left office. She fell in line behind George H. W. Bush and Bob Dole after they won the party's presidential nomination, but neither of them had been her first choice. (She also helped spread news about Michael Dukakis's furlough of Willie Horton in 1988, spending $44,000 to produce a twenty-eight-minute video—*Justice on Furlough*—that circu-lated widely among Republican organizers.)[84]

Schlafly's own family was drawn into the culture wars after *Queer Week* magazine outed her oldest son, John, in 1992.[85] Forty years ear-lier, the one-year-old John had been a campaign prop in his mother's race for Congress. Since then, he had earned a law degree and joined his mother as a staffer at the Eagle Forum. After the news broke, Schlafly told reporters that she stood by her son. John remained at the Eagle Forum, where he helped Schlafly mount a vigorous campaign against gay marriage. The family stayed quiet on the details of John's private life, except for in a 2011 interview, where Schlafly said she was "not completely convinced that he is a homosexual."[86]

She was much more voluble on the moral shortcomings of pub-lic officials, above all Bill Clinton—"a national embarrassment" who used "women as things to grab, grope, and discard" and "converted the once-serious offense of lying to the American public into a daily rite."[87] She called for his impeachment in 1998, warning that if Clinton was allowed to remain in office after perjuring himself over his affair with Monica Lewinsky, "Americans can look forward to a succession of TV charlatans and professional liars occupying the White House."[88]

Her attacks on the Republican establishment were just as cutting. She now saw the Republican coalition as an alliance of three groups, none of which had been treated with the respect they deserved: traditional conservatives of the kind who had flocked to Barry Goldwater in 1964, the pro-family activists she helped draw into the party during the 1970s, and working-class voters who drifted between parties from election to election. According to Schlafly, none of these core groups was well served by the GOP.

She had always been a libertarian of convenience, opposing government programs when they promoted causes she didn't like, such as the National Endowment for the Arts, but urging Republicans to keep their hands off Social Security. In the Clinton years, she lost her faith in the marriage of free markets and family values. *Roe v. Wade* remained settled law, women were joining the labor market in record numbers, illegitimacy and divorce rates were high above their mid-century levels, gay rights activists were gaining traction in their campaign for marriage equality, and religious conservatives still felt as if they were under assault.

Pat Buchanan's surprise victory in the 1996 New Hampshire primary pointed the way toward a coalition she believed could bring authentic conservatives back into office. "It may be that the guy who didn't rise any higher than middle management, or who is a blue-collar worker, had less smarts or opportunity or energy or perseverance, but he is an American, too," she wrote. "His real wages haven't risen in ten years, and now he lives in fear and dread of losing his job altogether if his manufacturing plant is relocated overseas. There are tens of thousands more of these guys than there are of the bosses. The *Wall Street Journal* doesn't speak for them, but Pat Buchanan does."[89]

Although Buchanan's primary campaign fizzled, each presidential election gave Schlafly an opportunity to search for a leader who would push the GOP in a more populist direction. John McCain's comfort with the mainstream media and hostility to the religious right ensured that she wouldn't support him in his 2000 race against George W. Bush, but she warned that McCain's strong performance demonstrated the strength of "an anti-establishment constituency of those who think that corporate money has given us one-party government."[90]

After reluctantly backing George W. Bush in 2000, she became an early critic from the right.[91] During the run-up to the second Gulf War, she warned, "Anybody who thinks we're going to have democracy in Iraq is dreaming." When asked her thoughts about the Patriot Act, she replied with a long "hmmm," then said that government officials should spend more time policing the border and less time snooping on American citizens.[92] Although she supported the administration's signature piece of domestic legislation, a $1.35 trillion tax cut that disproportionately benefited the wealthy, she lambasted Bush for compromising with Democrats on education policy.

Schlafly's commitment to the two-party system left her with nowhere to go when Republicans disappointed her. Stifling her disappointments, she attended the 2004 Republican National Convention as a Bush delegate and contributed an essay to a campaign book titled *Thank You, President Bush*—only to decide after hearing Bush's sweeping call for global democracy promotion in his second inaugural that the newly reelected president was a traitor to the right.[93]

If this was victory, then Schlafly was tired of winning. She thought big business and big government had once again joined forces, and this time they had co-opted much of the conservative movement. The Republican establishment looked down on ordinary Americans, refused to put their candidates up for a real vote, and intended to bring about a new world order where power was concentrated in the hands of multinational corporations and international regulatory agencies. And they were in charge.

But she had faith in the grass roots—and a plan for what to do next.

———

Schlafly started by identifying the root of the problem. She still believed the kingmakers were to blame, but the word itself had grown a little musty. In the Clinton years, a new description for the ruling class entered her vocabulary: globalists. "It's beginning to look as though we are in a major realignment of the parties," she announced in 1997. "The decisive political battles are no longer between Democrats and Republicans, but between those who have adopted a global world view against those who hold fast to a national world view."[94]

This new division between globalists and nationalists ran along the lines that used to separate the kingmakers from the grass roots. Just like the kingmakers, globalists were a bipartisan ruling class. Bill Clinton and Newt Gingrich were prime examples of the species, and so were Robert Rubin and Henry Kissinger, along with the donors who kept Democrats and Republicans in office. She had spent decades warning about world government, a fear that on the right stretched all the way back to the League of Nations. But the enemy had taken a new, more dangerous form: not power-mad bureaucrats, but the unstoppable expansion of the market.

Globalists had a simple story to tell: the shift to a world economy was inevitable, and it could usher in a new era of unprecedented prosperity if Americans didn't muck it up by clinging to obsolete notions like borders. Progress would be measured in corporate profits, galloping stock markets, and steady economic growth. Globalists paired their faith in universal markets with a cultural cosmopolitanism that prized diversity, tolerance, and—a term of special opprobrium for Schlafly—"political correctness."

Schlafly's nationalists adhered to an older set of principles: "sovereignty, patriotism, American jobs, and national security."[95] They were both the truest of Americans and outsiders in their own land: the Wallace voters of 1968, the silent majority of the Nixon years, the Reagan Democrats of the 1980s, and supporters of the Texas billionaire H. Ross Perot's quixotic campaign for the presidency in 1992. They were also the biggest casualties of the new world order. "Globalism," she said, "is the enemy of the middle class."[96] A flat world with no barriers to the flow of labor and capital would be a bonanza for a few and a disaster for everyone else. The basic dynamics were already expressing themselves in the American economy: stagnant wages, manufacturing jobs shipped overseas, and the rise of a subservient class of immigrant laborers catering to the domestic needs of the elite—an elite whose vaunted tolerance didn't extend to the nationalists whose lives they were overturning.

The nuclear family was another piece of collateral damage in the transition to a global economy. Well into the 1990s, Schlafly believed that the breakdown of marriage had been quarantined to a "pathetic underclass that will never achieve what we call the American Dream."[97] But as illegitimacy rates climbed, she stopped seeing the crisis of the family as a problem for Black and brown people. In her telling, globalists and feminists had joined forces to destroy the American household. Foreign competition pushed down incomes, dragging women into the workforce, just as feminists were telling homemakers that they couldn't be full citizens unless they had jobs.

Globalists, therefore, couldn't be defeated on economic grounds alone. They had a cultural agenda too, and taking it on required a frontal assault on cosmopolitanism. "All cultures are not compatible with American values," declared the first issue of *The Phyllis Schlafly Report* after the September 11 terrorist attacks.[98] One month later, she urged readers to "ask our Mexican immigrant friends . . . are you assimilating or invading?"[99] She had already called for English to be made the national language, and she soon took to warning that "anchor babies"—American-born children of undocumented immigrants—were draining money from taxpayers.[100] And her anxieties weren't limited to Muslims and Hispanics. After a scare erupted over infant formula produced in China, she told her audience, "It's dangerous to buy products from a nation whose economy is not based on Judeo-Christian morality."[101]

Schlafly's nationalism was part of a broader repudiation of elite culture. Her hostility toward activist judges fit with her opposition to education reforms that centralized decision-making in Washington. In the 1990s she added mandatory vaccination to the list of elite power grabs. Calling the vaccine industry a "racket," she said that Big Pharma and Washington bureaucrats had joined up to force unsuspecting citizens to undertake potentially dangerous medical treatments, and then she urged her readers to consult the National Vaccine Information Center, one of the most influential distributors of anti-vaccine propaganda.[102]

Racially tinged nationalism, denunciations of globalists, and disdain for coastal elites put Schlafly in line with a marginalized cohort on the right known as paleoconservatives. Closely associated with Pat Buchanan, they denounced "Conservatism Inc." and depicted themselves as defenders of heartland values threatened by an alliance between a cosmopolitan overclass and a surging population of nonwhite immigrants. Paleocons admired Reagan—Buchanan served as his White House communications director—but shared Schlafly's disappointment with subsequent Republicans.[103]

Until Sarah Palin. The vice presidential nominee's breakout speech at the 2008 Republican National Convention persuaded Schlafly that the GOP was ready to break from the "Big Government, Big Spending, New World Order, Globalist" policies of the post-Reagan years.[104] (It didn't hurt that the Alaska governor credited her "political awakening" to Schlafly.)[105] "Sarah Palin and the 2008 Platform have given Republicans a new lease on life," she announced on September 5, 2008, when McCain had leaped ahead of Barack Obama in polls for the first time in months.[106]

Ten days later, Lehman Brothers filed for bankruptcy. The next two months played out like a script drawn from Schlafly's nightmares. A $700 billion Wall Street bailout passed Congress with bipartisan support and was signed into law by a Republican president, acting on the advice of a treasury secretary who made his fortune as CEO of Goldman Sachs. Palin's favorability ratings sank, helped along by hostile coverage in the national media and anonymous criticism from McCain's own campaign. And at the end of it all, Barack Obama was elected to the White House.

Schlafly saw the incoming president as the embodiment of the globalist elite—a radical ideologue, possible Muslim, and tool of the kingmakers—who was driving the country toward socialism with the help of public schools where children were being "secretly indoctrinated in the cult of Obama-worship."[107] (She did not mention that her son Andrew had graduated in Obama's class at Harvard Law School.) "Obama's massive makeover of American government and society amounts to a second 9/11," she declared two months after his inauguration.[108] She kept up the drumbeat of criticism, cheering the rise of the Tea Party and despairing after Mitt Romney's loss in 2012.[109]

Though Obama's margin of victory was smaller than four years earlier, his reelection was an even bigger blow to Schlafly. She attributed the result to Obama's harnessing of popular hostility toward "core Americans—those people whose great-great grandparents built our country, who largely keep it running today, who own their homes, and who have successfully kept their families together." More specifically, this meant "white married people."[110]

To break the Democratic hold on the electorate, the grassroots right needed to declare war on the political establishment in both parties. She urged conservatives to reacquaint themselves with the country one town hall meeting at a time, creating a new majority rooted in the informed consent of the electorate rather than shallow celebrity worship.

But Schlafly couldn't take her own advice. As much as she celebrated the grass roots, she longed for a leader who could take on the globalists. The ideal candidate, would, of course, have a nationalist platform: tough on immigration, economically protectionist, pro-military but anti-interventionist, unconcerned with deficits, and socially conservative (which, in practice, mostly meant appointing judges in the mode of Antonin Scalia or Clarence Thomas). Style mattered, too. "Civility gave voters the impression that there wasn't any particular difference between the candidates," Schlafly explained.[111] Conservatives shouldn't sound like ordinary politicians. They should be blunt, maybe even rude. Liberals would howl, and so would media gatekeepers, but that was all part of the fun.

Schlafly could see everything about her candidate, except who could play the part in real life. And time was running out.

———

She was cautious about Donald Trump at first. The 2016 Republican primary set off a civil war within the right, and much of the old guard in the conservative movement was anyone-but-Trump. Though she regarded the other mainstream candidates as the usual crop of king-maker lackeys—the front-runner Jeb Bush was "another Establishment loser"—she had admired Ted Cruz for years, and he had courted her endorsement.[112] ("Phyllis, I have to tell you, you inspire me," Cruz told her in 2015, trying too hard.)[113] Cruz also had supporters within the Eagle Forum, including her youngest child, Anne Schlafly Cori.

But there was something special about Trump. He combined Bu-chanan's politics and an intuitive grasp of media psychology with a unique talent for infuriating the right kind of people. "Voters don't need more happy-talk," Schlafly wrote in October 2015. "They're look-ing for a candidate who's willing and able to turn the country around and 'make America great again.'"[114] After Trump called for a ban on Muslim immigration, she told an interviewer that he might be the country's "last hope."[115]

Schlafly removed all doubt the week before the Missouri Repub-lican primary. At a St. Louis rally, two men escorted her to a podium with a sign blaring TRUMP. The audience did not know that she had already been diagnosed with terminal cancer. Looking frail in a bulky pink pantsuit, she stumbled over her words at first, her voice quavering. But the crowd was with her, and her speech was clear and steady by the time she ripped into the president. ("Obama's trying to fundamentally transform our country, and we don't want him to do it.") Then Trump entered stage right, and the crowd roared. He walked to Schlafly, tow-ered over her for a moment, then swooped in for a kiss. One week later, he scratched out a victory in the Missouri primary, beating Cruz by 1,965 votes out of more than 900,000.[116]

The battle over the nomination was far from settled, however, and the war within the right continued to play out inside the Eagle Forum. News of the internal strife leaked to the media, and one of the Cruz backers claimed that the elderly Schlafly had been manipulated into endorsing Trump. Schlafly replied by sending out a robocall to more than 123,000 activists. "Please help me stop these people from going after me and the organization that I have devoted my life to building," she said, listing Cori as the leader of the pro-Cruz faction. Then she gave out Cori's phone number and asked listeners to give her daughter a call.[117]

Schlafly turned to Trump in desperation. Her writings depicted a country that was eroding from within: too many college students were from China, too many baseball players were from Mexico, and too many refugees were coming across the border. Half a century after encouraging Barry Goldwater to downplay opposition to federal civil rights legislation, she fumed that liberals were waging a "hysterical, iconoclastic war against the Confederate battle flag" while coddling Muslims devoted to "a radicalized global ideology that wants to destroy us."[118]

Trumpists on the right used Schlafly as a human shield. "Tell somebody like Phyllis Schlafly," Sarah Palin said while announcing her Trump endorsement. "Tell her she's not conservative."[119] Schlafly became a recurring figure on the Trump-favorite *Breitbart News*, which breathlessly reported on her broadsides against the Trump resistance, even resurrecting her debate with William F. Buckley Jr. over the Panama Canal. NATIONAL REVIEW IS NOT THE AUTHORITY ON CONSERVATISM, read the headline of the piece, written by Julia Hahn, a twenty-four-year-old protégé of the *Breitbart* chairman Steve Bannon (and a millionaire heiress) who had taken over the Schlafly beat for the site after interning for Laura Ingraham.[120]

With two coauthors, Schlafly finished a book, *The Conservative Case for Trump*, aimed at bringing nervous Republicans on board the Trump train. In addition to defending her candidate on policy, it called him "an old-fashioned man grounded in his two great priorities—hard work and family" and expressed particular admiration for "his simple personal faith."[121] Schlafly said that the book marked "the culmination, for me, of more than seventy years of active involvement in Republican politics."[122]

She was on the floor of the Republican National Convention that summer to watch Trump receive the GOP nomination. This was her sixteenth RNC, and maybe the sweetest. "Donald Trump's thrilling acceptance speech proved that his vision, not Ted Cruz's, is the future of the conservative movement and the Republican Party," declared the August 2016 edition of *The Phyllis Schlafly Report*.[123]

Schlafly died the next month, on September 5. *The Conservative Case for Trump* was published the next day. It debuted at number 16 on the *New York Times* bestseller list.[124]

"She never wavered, never apologized, and never backed down in taking on the kingmakers," Trump said while delivering Schlafly's eulogy in the Cathedral Basilica of St. Louis. "What a great lady."[125]

———————

The night before his presidential inauguration, Trump took a moment to recognize the people who made his election possible. At a black-tie dinner, the tuxedoed president-elect thanked his family and his major donors, paying special attention to the campaign manager Kellyanne Conway. Then, near the close of his speech, he brought up Phyllis Schlafly. "She came out against all of her fellow conservatives," he said. "She went through hell. I'm telling you. Phyllis went through hell in that last one-third of the year and she turned out to be right."[126] When he entered the White House the next day, Trump took Conway and Steve Bannon with him, along with a new special assistant to the president, Julia Hahn.

Back in St. Louis, Schlafly's children were trading lawsuits, and the Eagle Forum had broken in two, with the Trumpists—including John and Andrew Schlafly—splitting off to form a rival group, "Phyllis Schlafly Eagles."[127] Though divided over the new president, both organizations remained committed to the cause that made Schlafly a celebrity: family values.

After a few months it was difficult to remember why the right's battle over Trump had been so rancorous. Every element of the Republican coalition had something to like: GOP donors thrilled over the administration's $1.5 trillion tax-cut package; social conservatives cheered at a wave of judicial appointments that promised to remake the federal bench; and anyone who loved triggering the libs had the president's Twitter feed. With Trump's approval rating among Republicans hovering around 90 percent, former critics on the right underwent a change of heart—including the Eagle Forum, which warned Republican congressmen in a September 2017 press release, "Back Trump or Face Defeat."[128]

The same logic of polarization that consolidated support for Trump among Republicans also strengthened opposition to him with Democrats. Feminists mounted the first major demonstration against the new administration with the 2017 post-inauguration Women's March, drawing millions of protesters in hundreds of cities and towns across the United States.[129] The 2018 midterm elections witnessed the largest gender gap in the history of American politics, with women voting for Democrats by a margin of almost twenty percentage points. The same year, Illinois became the second state of the Trump era (after Nevada) to vote in favor of the Equal Rights Amendment. Virginia followed in 2020, setting up a contentious legal battle over the ERA's future.[130]

College-educated suburban white women provided the backbone for anti-Trump resistance organizations sprouting up around the country. Sociologically speaking, these women looked a lot like the ones who had supplied the ground troops for Schlafly's war against the establishment decades earlier. Now they rallied behind such figures as the Massachusetts senator Elizabeth Warren, whom Schlafly dismissed in 2014 as another anti-family liberal. If she had paid closer attention, Schlafly might have found something to admire in Warren. "Today the game is rigged—rigged to work for those who have money and power," Warren wrote in her ninth book, a memoir, also published in 2014. "Big corporations hire armies of lobbyists to get billion-dollar loopholes into the tax system and persuade their friends in Congress to support laws that keep the playing field tilted in their favor."[131]

The parallels between Warren and Schlafly didn't end there. Both grew up in the middle of the country with mothers working full-time to keep household budgets in the black. They were also both gifted students with a talent for debating who pursued law degrees while raising a family. Warren first came to public attention in 2003 as the coauthor (with her daughter) of a book making the Schlafly-friendly argument that the flood of women into the labor market had launched a bidding war for the standard items of middle-class life, like a home and college tuition, while imposing new financial burdens, like paying for day care and a second car. It was a politically heterodox thesis, in keeping with Warren's suggestion in a law review article published a year earlier that "stylized left-right political paradigms . . . offer much heat but little light." "Are all women's issues exclusively issues of the political left?" she asked. "Does 'feminist' mean both social liberal and fiscal liberal?"[132]

NOW came in for especially harsh treatment. According to Warren, the organization gave the then senator Joe Biden a pass for championing a bankruptcy bill that would disproportionately harm women because of his earlier support for the Violence Against Women Act. NOW's defense of Biden stood in for a larger feminist establishment that, in Warren's telling, gave Democrats license to retreat on economics because the party stood with them on divisive social issues.

It should have sounded familiar to Schlafly. But by the time Schlafly turned her attention to Warren in 2014, the Massachusetts senator had rebranded herself as a consistent progressive, following the logic of polarization to the left just as Schlafly had been taken to the right. And even if Schlafly bridled against conservative orthodoxy, there was no chance she would reach out to the other side in the civil war between red and blue. After all, she had built a career around polarization. It hadn't delivered the enduring Republican majority that she promised, but it had remade American democracy. Just as Mark Hanna's party and Franklin Roosevelt's mirrored each other—two coalitions roughly split over economics, working within the framework established by the organizational revolution, backed by ideologically muddled but institutionally strong political machines—Donald Trump's party was now the inverse of Obama's: two national brands, divided over supercharged partisan identities, keenly attuned to the demands of the donor class and their activist base.

Here was the politics that polarization—and Schlafly—made. But at the end of her life, the policies advanced by Republicans (with more than occasional assistance from Democrats) had pushed the income gap between ordinary Americans and the kingmakers higher than at any period since the Great Depression. All the while, conservatives were losing ground in the culture war, convincing many on the right that they were one election away from total defeat in the battle for the American soul. The slashing political tactics that Schlafly pioneered could draw voters to the polls, but they were much less effective at changing minds—the kind of work that turns political victories into a durable cultural consensus.

She couldn't win the battle for her version of family values, and her candidates always seemed to end up doing the work of the kingmakers. But she could help put Donald Trump—the thrice-married reality TV star with a gift for making the right enemies—in the White House.

Phyllis Schlafly was one of the most talented political organizers in American history. What did she get for her work? Everything she wanted, and nothing at all.

Politicians

In the spring of 1991, not many people knew who Barack Obama was, but those who did expected great things. He had just wrapped up a term as the first Black president of the *Harvard Law Review*, the equivalent of gold medaling in the meritocratic Olympics. Journalists who interviewed Obama for the flurry of profiles that appeared after his election discovered a young man brimming with confidence. "I really hope to be part of a transformation of this country," he told Allison Pugh of the Associated Press, who came away struck by his "oddly self-conscious sense of destiny."[1]

Obama wasn't going to leave his future up to chance. He graduated from law school with a plan, elaborated at length in a manuscript of almost 250 pages that he wrote with his closest friend at Harvard, a former economist named Robert Fisher. Part policy manifesto and part historical inquiry, their manuscript offered a blueprint for escaping from stale ideological debates, restoring the New Deal coalition, and saving American democracy. The coauthors hoped to turn it into a book. They were going to call it "Transformative Politics."[2]

To Obama, the need for change was obvious. Economic inequality was soaring. The gains of the civil rights revolution were being rolled back. Cynicism about politicians was corroding faith in democracy, especially among the poor and working class. Deindustrialization had ravaged the country's manufacturing base and gutted organized labor, with particularly devastating consequences for African Americans. Polarization had fractured the New Deal order, allowing Republican culture warriors to charge into power while Democrats fumbled for a response.

Confronted with a failing status quo, Obama and Fisher proposed a sweeping agenda for structural reform. On economics, they advised liberals to harness the power of markets for progressive ends. On politics, they followed Bayard Rustin's example, endorsing universal programs whose benefits would, in practice, tilt toward African Americans—in short, "use class as a proxy for race."[3] By reversing their losses with blue-collar white people, Democrats could achieve a "political realignment" capable of delivering "long-term, structural change, change that might break the zero-sum equation that pits powerless blacks [against] only slightly less powerless whites." It was a rescue plan for a democracy caught in a dead end, where partisan polarization around a racialized culture gave rise to a politics that left the poor and working class behind.

The authors luxuriated in their realism, depicting themselves as pragmatists stripped of all illusions. "The first step to radical consciousness is to realize that the world could be different and that we have the power to make it so," they wrote.[4] "The danger to this leftist vision of collective freedom is that we will become utopian in the worst sense of that word. . . . We will forego the art of the possible and therefore be very bad politicians." And Barack Obama had no intention of being a bad politician.

Although Obama and Fisher eventually dropped their plan to convert "Transformative Politics" into a book, its vision guided Obama in the years ahead as he turned himself into the model of a twenty-first-century statesman. He made himself a scholar of the Constitution, teaching Publius's handiwork to students at the University of Chicago. He operated the Democratic machine with a skill that Martin Van Buren would have envied, and he played the part of the idealist in politics like a latter-day Charles Sumner, bringing audiences to tears by urging Americans to live up to their founding creed. He reckoned with the power of the corporate order that Mark Hanna embodied in his day and the administrative state that Theodore Roosevelt envisioned in his. He was as perceptive an interpreter of race and American democracy as W.E.B. Du Bois and as skilled a navigator of the American establishment as Walter Lippmann—all for the purpose of undoing Phyllis Schlafly's life's work by depolarizing the electorate and creating a new Democratic majority.

"We are five days away from fundamentally transforming the United States of America," he declared on October 30, 2008, at the end of a campaign that cast him as a mash-up of JFK and MLK.[5] A week later, he won the largest victory of any Democrat since Lyndon Johnson. He had channeled the energy of a movement into a political campaign. Now he could start on the next steps of the plan: convert electoral success into concrete legislation, establish a lasting Democratic majority, and—most important—build institutions that would carry on the fight long after one charismatic leader exited the stage.

But the arc of history veered off course after Election Day. Obama departed the White House eight years later with a record of policy victories and high approval ratings, but the policies didn't result in structural change. The gap between the rich and the poor was still cavernous, the distance between the two parties wider than ever, and dissatisfaction with government at historic highs.[6] There was an "Obama coalition," but its champions described it as an alliance of racial minorities, college-educated professionals, and young people—more a multicultural updating of the majority that Lippmann envisioned in 1968 than a sequel to Rustin's March on Washington coalition. Meanwhile, working-class voters—mostly but not exclusively white—continued a protracted migration into the GOP, fueling the growth of a right-wing populism that blended racial grievance, economic frustration, and a pointed critique of the elite. Disillusionment with the establishment also spurred a revival on the left, earning Bernie Sanders more votes in the 2016 Democratic primary than any socialist had received in American history.

More than any single policy, this redrawn political landscape was Obama's legacy. True, it was the opposite of what he set out to achieve.

Instead of changing the country's direction, he pushed Americans far-
ther down a path they were already traveling. But there was one thing
nobody could deny: Barack Obama had transformed politics.

———————

Obama's road to the White House started outside the remains of the
Wisconsin Steel plant. At its height, the plant employed more than
three thousand workers. By the summer of 1985, it stood like an abandoned cathedral, sprawling across 265 acres in Southeast Chicago
while rust ate into metal beams and weeds sprouted through concrete.
Standing on the other side of a chain-link fence, a twenty-three-year-
old Barack Obama glimpsed a stray cat making its way through the
dirt.[7]

It was Obama's first week in Chicago, and he was touring the
neighborhoods where he would soon be working. Next he drove south,
to Altgeld Gardens. Also called "the Toxic Donut," the public housing
complex was located alongside a fetid river, a garbage dump, and a sew-
age treatment facility. Factories like the Wisconsin Steel plant had used
the area as a storage site for tons of industrial pollution. The chemicals
outlasted the mills, giving the area Chicago's highest cancer rates.[8]

Obama saw Wisconsin Steel and Altgeld Gardens as two sides of
the same broken promise. Martin Luther King Jr.'s dream and Lyndon
Johnson's Great Society both dead-ended in the Toxic Donut, where
people of all races suffered and African Americans were hardest hit.

It all could not have seemed further from the world Obama was
born into. Hawaii in 1961 was the only U.S. state without a white majority. The island's diversity supported a fluid racial culture that turned
Hawaii into the closest thing the United States had to a true melting
pot. On Obama's fifth birthday, there were three nonwhite members of
the U.S. Senate. Two came from Hawaii.[9]

What the young Obama knew of African American life on the
mainland came to him chiefly through a hodgepodge of secondary ma-

terial. His mother supplied him with a steady diet of books and records meant to instruct him in the Black experience: histories of the civil rights movement, songs from Mahalia Jackson, speeches from Martin Luther King Jr. Her own politics, in the skeptical words of her son, leaned toward a "New Deal, Peace Corps, position-paper liberalism." Though Obama was an indifferent student at the elite Punahou School—a Groton by the sea for children of the Honolulu elite that his family stretched to afford—he worked through the canon of major Black (male) authors: James Baldwin, Ralph Ellison, Langston Hughes, W.E.B. Du Bois, Malcolm X. A minor figure in this canon, the poet and former Communist Frank Marshall Davis, was also a friend of his grandfather's.[10] (Davis moved to Honolulu from Chicago in 1948.) It was Davis who told Obama before he left Hawaii for Occidental College, "You're not going to college to get educated. You're going there to get *trained*. . . . Stay awake."[11]

Obama's grandparents, who raised him from the age of nine, offered a view of life on the other side of the racial divide. As president, Obama described Stanley and Madelyn Dunham as repositories of homespun values such as humility and responsibility. But to a teenager straining to escape their two-bedroom apartment, the Dunhams were a cautionary tale: an old man stuck in a low-paying job selling life insurance; an old woman who earned a good salary but gave it all up to be a homemaker. There was an anger simmering under the surface, especially with his grandfather.[12] Looking back in 1995, Obama called him "poor white trash."[13]

The teenage Obama was a product of this idiosyncratic blend of influences: polyglot Hawaii, the cosmopolitan liberalism of his mother, a strong but mediated relationship to Black America, and prolonged exposure to the mixed results of the American dream. Add in a healthy dose of youthful machismo, and you had the recipe for the young man his classmates met in college, first at Occidental, then at Columbia. "Some species of *GQ* Marxist," one called him.[14] "People would invite me to parties, and I'd say, 'What are you talking about? We've got a revolution that has to take place,'" Obama remembered.[15]

Community organizing was supposed to provide him with a way to turn radical ideals into real change. Working in the tradition of Saul Alinsky, organizers started from the premise that poverty was just as much about the lack of power as it was the lack of money. Alinsky was a Chicago native, and experience navigating the city's tribal divisions convinced him that electoral politics was a lost cause. Politicians were captive to their donors, and good-government reformers would always wind up pursuing their own self-interest. The poor would have to save themselves, with a little prodding from their friendly neighborhood organizer.[16]

But as Obama settled into Chicago, his attention was drawn to another model for achieving change—this time through politics. The city had recently elected its first African American mayor, Harold Washington, after a vicious campaign where much of the white Democratic establishment, and a majority of the city's white voters, turned against him.[17]

The battle kept going after the election. "Every single day it was about race. I mean, every day it was black folks and white folks going at each other. Every day, in the newspapers, on TV, in meetings. You couldn't get away from it," Obama recalled.[18]

With politics split along racial lines, gridlock ensued, which was fine with the Democratic machine. "A polarized city isn't necessarily a bad thing for a politician," Obama realized.[19] But it was a disaster for the people he was trying to help.

Still, he couldn't think of Harold Washington's Chicago as just a study in political dysfunction. He kept noticing pictures of Harold—and it was always "Harold"—in the homes he visited. The mayor was a source of pride for Black Chicago, and for Obama. Harold created his own kind of community, partly around himself and partly around the ideals he represented. This, too, was a type of power.

The longer Obama stayed in Chicago, the more frustrated he became with both organizers and politicians. He was supposed to spend his time on practical initiatives, like setting up a center to distribute news about job opportunities, but there were no jobs in the first place.

As Obama floundered in Altgeld Gardens, Harold Washington was having just as difficult a time at City Hall. After grinding through his first term, he won a comfortable reelection in 1987, only to die suddenly of a heart attack that November. Without an organization to carry on the mayor's work, the old Democratic machine was soon back in power.

Chicago gave Obama two failed examples of how to bring about change. So he decided not to choose between them. Instead, he came up with his own synthesis of Saul Alinsky and Harold Washington. Community organizers were right to emphasize the importance of material interests, and they were justified in avoiding movements built around a single charismatic figurehead. But if the only way to beat organized money was with organized people, then reformers couldn't withdraw from electoral politics. With institutional support, Harold Washington could have turned an electric candidacy into lasting change, the kind that used state power to make a meaningful difference in Altgeld Gardens. The trick was to channel the energy from an inspiring campaign into a broader movement—to be a politician but think like an organizer. "Movements dissipate," Obama said. "Organizations don't."[20] And a movement that took over an organization could get the best of both worlds.

Around this time his peripatetic mother gave him a piece of advice: "You can spend a lifetime working outside institutions. But you might get more done trying to change those institutions from the inside."[21]

Obama's institution of choice was the Democratic Party. Settling on electoral politics meant thinking seriously about how to piece together an interracial majority for the kind of transformative program he envisioned. He was drawn toward an approach laid out by the University of Chicago sociologist William Julius Wilson, the author of a recently published study of deindustrialization's effects on African Americans that concluded with a "hidden agenda for liberal policymakers."[22] Citing Bayard Rustin, Wilson argued that a program built on "race-neutral" reforms—including universal health care, full employment, and a system of national economic planning—could draw support from a multiracial coalition while addressing the problems of the ghetto underclass.

It might not have been a coincidence, then, that Obama told his boss he was quitting on the same day the two of them attended a conference featuring a lecture from Wilson.[23] He wanted to try politics, but only after getting a law degree. "I had things to learn in law school, things that would help me bring about real change," he later wrote. "I would learn about interest rates, corporate mergers, the legislative process; about the way businesses and banks were put together; how real estate ventures succeeded or failed. I would learn power's currency in all its intricacy and detail."[24] And he couldn't think of a better place to learn about power than Harvard Law School.

———————

Almost two centuries after Charles Sumner set up camp in its libraries, Harvard Law School was still a training ground for the American elite. But students who arrived looking to change the world usually graduated three years later convinced that making a difference started with a six-figure salary. Conservatives had an easy time fitting their principles to their job prospects. Liberals required more coaxing. "The thing that sold me was that they weren't all conservative Republicans," one Democrat explained after working at a corporate law firm. "They were concerned about the same things that I was."[25]

Summarizing the dominant viewpoint on campus, Obama later wrote about progressives who "believed in the free market and an educational meritocracy. . . . They had no patience with protectionism, found unions troublesome, and were not particularly sympathetic to those whose lives were upended by the movements of global capital. Most were adamantly prochoice and antigun and were vaguely suspicious of deep religious sentiment."[26]

With the skepticism of a former community organizer who still believed in the importance of appealing to self-interest, Obama registered a qualified dissent from the law school's pro-bono liberalism, a blue-state noblesse oblige.

That wasn't the only way Obama stood out. At twenty-seven, he was four or five years older than his peers, at an age when four or five years count for a lot. A classmate recalled that Obama had a gift for "projecting this image of being the adult in the room."[27] More intellectually inclined than the typical law student, he blended forays into subjects like postmodern epistemology with practical training in the craft of law. And on a campus divided along both racial and political lines, he had a knack for making all sides feel as if he was giving them a fair hearing.[28]

Obama's skill at navigating controversy was on display in his handling of a high-profile controversy kicked up by Derrick Bell, the first Black professor to receive tenure at HLS and one of the inspirations behind a then-obscure legal doctrine known as critical race theory. According to Bell, racial inequality was an "integral, permanent, and indestructible component" of American society.[29] (His 1992 book, *Faces at the Bottom of the Well*, was subtitled *The Permanence of Racism*.) Although Bell conceded that interracial coalitions might form around shared interests, his approach to politics was more existentialist than reformist. Drawing inspiration from Camus, he described the struggle against white supremacy as literally Sisyphean: a doomed effort that was justified by the nobility of fighting against inevitable defeat.

By the time Obama arrived at Harvard, Bell was years into a campaign to diversify the law school's overwhelmingly white and male faculty. Obama met Bell at an orientation meeting held by the Black Law Students Association, and he later told Bell, "It was your presence here that in large part brought me to Harvard."[30] But he never took a class with Bell and for the most part stayed aloof from the protests around faculty diversity, keeping a warm but distant relationship with the controversial professor.

The entire hothouse atmosphere of legal academia held little attraction for Obama. Three years at Harvard taught him that lawyers were more like assistant managers for the ruling class than full-fledged members of the power elite. "The study of law can be disappointing at times," he later wrote, "a sort of glorified accounting that serves to regulate the affairs of those who have power."[31] After being selected as editor of the *Law Review*, he turned down an all-but-guaranteed path to clerking on the Supreme Court. "If you're going to make change," he told his shocked girlfriend, Michelle Robinson, "you're not going to do it as a Supreme Court clerk."[32]

He wanted to leverage his micro-celebrity to make a name for himself as an author, and eventually a politician. He signed a contract for a memoir, tentatively titled "Journeys in Black and White," that combined autobiographical narrative with a larger argument about policy. Then he moved on to writing "Transformative Politics," a policy manifesto with an autobiographical core.

Obama and Fisher planned to split their book into three parts: a chapter on plant closings would lead to a broader consideration of the market; next, a discussion of the civil rights movement would examine race in American politics; then they would close with an overview of public education that focused on how the federal government could use its authority to bolster local communities. In other words, one chapter for the Wisconsin Steel plant, another for Altgeld Gardens, and a third for the schools that might save the next generation.

"The left generally and blacks in particular," announced the young authors, "stand at a cross-road."[33] When they were writing in the spring of 1991, it seemed as if a reckoning was taking place at three levels: global, national, and racial. In the wake of the Soviet Union's collapse, parties of the left and center-left across the world were struggling to adapt to an environment where it seemed as if free markets and liberal democracy were joining hands in what Francis Fukuyama labeled "the end of history." Democrats less concerned with the unfolding logic of the zeitgeist faced a more prosaic dilemma: the party hadn't won a presidential election in fifteen years, and George H. W. Bush's approval rating, buoyed by victory in the Gulf War, was hovering around 80 percent.[34]

At the same time, African Americans were confronting the mixed track record of Black politics since the 1960s. A generation of Black candidates had been elected to office—winning dozens of congressional seats and mayoral elections from Seattle to New York City, even the governorship of Virginia—only to become the public faces of urban decline. As Obama explained in an article published shortly before he arrived at Harvard, despite the "important symbolic effect" of electoral victories, "much-needed black achievement in prominent city positions has put us in the awkward position of administering underfunded systems neither equipped nor eager to address the needs of the urban poor."[35] And these depressing results pointed to an even more disquieting conclusion: a generation after the civil rights revolution, African Americans were arguably worse off than they were before Rosa Parks refused to move to the back of the bus.

The global left, the Democratic Party, and African Americans had all reached a pivotal juncture. Poised between Francis Fukuyama and Derrick Bell, the end of history and the permanence of racism, two of Harvard's brightest young minds took it upon themselves to point the way forward.

According to Obama and Fisher, the road to political wisdom began with accepting what you could not change. "Within American society exists a set of core institutional arrangements and practices—most prominently a regulated market economy and a constitutional, representative democracy rooted in the principles of classical liberalism," they wrote. "These interests mark the rough limits of viable politics at any given time."[36] The task of the realistic reformer was to bend this consensus toward progressive ends, finding the radical promise buried inside American liberalism.

On economics, they sounded like the second coming of Walter Lippmann. Joking that this section of the book could also be called "Everything the Left Ever Wanted to Know about Markets, but was Afraid to Ask," they announced, "There is nothing intrinsically conservative about recognizing the powers of the market and putting them to use to better serve the community. In fact, nothing could be more radical." Progressive taxation, national health insurance, government regulation of natural monopolies, and state ownership of banks were all consistent with their overall approach. But, ultimately, there were no loopholes in the law of supply and demand. Only an economy of nimble firms and skilled workers could survive whatever globalization had in store. "If the Left could understand and embrace this harsh economic constraint on our collective freedom," they concluded, "it would be able to properly focus its energy on the real social battleground which would redound to the benefit of all."[37]

A preoccupation with facing up to difficult truths also animated their discussion of race. "It has become increasingly apparent that the strategies rooted in the Sixties have not led blacks to the promised land of genuine political, economic, and social equality," Obama and Fisher wrote. Against radicals who argued that tackling racism required a wholesale transformation of American life, they insisted that African Americans couldn't wait for revolution. "For some on the Left, such an approach may smack of expediency," they acknowledged. "But it is precisely such expediency that must take place if we aren't to sacrifice more generations of black youth."[38]

Judges weren't going to save them, and neither were the good intentions of white liberals. Which left electoral politics—and the difficult work of cobbling together a winning coalition. "Within an admittedly racist culture, we can design and pursue strategies that either align the interests of the white majority in ways that blunt the influence of racism," they wrote, "or instead isolate blacks from potential allies and make blacks more vulnerable to racist sentiments."[39]

Despite the continuing reality of racism, Obama and Fisher argued that white racial attitudes had improved since the 1960s—and that, with the right mix of politics and policy, this progress would continue. "We believe," they wrote,

> that the majority (though by no means all) of whites would today be willing to assist in workable programs for bringing blacks into the mainstream, but feel overwhelmed by the scale of the problems in the inner city, cynical about existing efforts

to address these problems, and burdened by the real contraction of their own opportunities over the past two decades, a contraction that makes any redistributionist program that would take money from their pockets seem increasingly threatening.[40]

Drawing on the tenets of community organizing, they dismissed "the implausible idea that if blacks point their fingers long enough at whites and accuse them of racism, that whites will one day wake up, realize the error of their ways, and provide blacks with wholesale reparations in order to expiate white demons." Instead, they had to build a majority out of shared values and common interests.

Blue-collar white people were the key swing vote. Perhaps thinking of Stanley Dunham, Obama and Fisher urged progressives to recognize "the bitterness and frustration that the white working and middle classes feel toward their own constricted opportunities to find fulfilling work, buy their first house, or send their children to college." Like African Americans, they "understood in concrete ways the fact that America's individualist mythology covers up a game that is fixed against them." But that shared experience is what made them receptive to appeals based on racial identity. "If it has been working class whites who have been most vociferous in their opposition to affirmative action," Obama and Fisher wrote, "this at least in part arises out of an accurate assessment [that] they are the most likely to lose in any redistributionist game."[41]

Although Obama and Fisher's gesture to the market set them apart from William Julius Wilson's "hidden agenda for liberal policymakers," the underlying political strategy was a natural extension of Wilson's "race-neutral" universalism. Economic anxiety and racial resentment had broken apart the New Deal order, but a bold political vision might be able to bring Roosevelt's majority back together by forging an interracial coalition of the working class. With blue-collar families losing ground and inner-city communities in precipitous decline, realism became a moral obligation: reformers were obligated "to work with what we have and present the most effective platform possible for change, rather than bemoan the intractability of the racism in America." "We presume the best in white America," they wrote, "precisely to root out the worst in America."[42]

It was the kind of paradox Obama loved, a dance between despair and hope. There was no escaping the invisible hand, *but* the left could use markets to achieve progressive goals. Racism suffused American life, *but* a political movement could achieve structural change. Democracy was failing, caught between a demagogic conservatism and an ideologically unmoored liberalism, *but* a better politics was possible— a genuine democracy where the public was brought into serious debates over the common good, not distracted by empty symbolic warfare.

Graduation was looming when the coauthors finished drafts of the first two chapters of "Transformative Politics." Obama returned to Chicago soon after. He fell behind his deadline for "Journeys in Black and White," and never found time to revisit his other book project. But the manuscript had done its work. He had a handbook for remaking the country. Now he could put it into action.

———————

"Politicians are not held to highest esteem these days," Obama noted in October 1995.[43] It was a common sentiment to hear, though not in the middle of a campaign announcement. But the latest entrant in the race to represent District 13 in the Illinois State Senate didn't see himself as a typical politician.

True, he had the résumé for one: an appointment as a lecturer at the University of Chicago Law School; a position at a law firm specializing in civil and voting rights litigation; spots on the boards of prestigious and well-funded philanthropic foundations; marriage to the eminently eligible Michelle Robinson. An exemplary member of Chicago's young elite, he built a social network that reached from major campaign donors like Tony Rezko to star academics like Cass Sunstein.

Obama told the story of how he came to politics in *Dreams from*

My Father, the book that "Journeys in Black and White" evolved into. Released in the summer of 1995 to favorable reviews and modest sales, it told the story of a life made possible by the unlikely union between a white woman from Kansas and a Black man from Kenya, backed up by "a spirit that would grip the nation for that fleeting period between Kennedy's election and the passage of the Voting Rights Act."[44] The young Obama watched as tribalism broke his father in Kenya while Americans turned against the idealistic liberalism he associated with his mother. He explained how he had been drawn toward community organizing's hardheaded focus on power and self-interest. Then he described his return, as an adult, to a chastened version of his mother's liberalism. Through politics, he could escape from the binaries that trapped his parents, rooting himself in a community without losing himself in a tribe and tempering power through democratic deliberation.

Running for office allowed Obama to bring his message to an even larger audience. "I am surprised at how many elected officials—even the good ones—spend so much time talking about the mechanics of politics and not matters of substance," he told a reporter. Even Harold Washington, "the best of the classic politicians," wasn't immune to the hazards of his trade. "Like all politicians," Obama lamented, Washington "was primarily interested in maintaining his power."[45]

Like all politicians *until now*, he should have said. "What if a politician were to see his job as that of an organizer," Obama asked, "as part teacher and part advocate, one who does not sell voters short but who educates them about the real choices before them?"[46] Top-down versus bottom-up, grass roots versus elite: viewed correctly, these were more false choices. With the backing of an independent movement and a precise sense of where power lay, politicians could forge a multiracial majority that confronted the problems ravaging inner-city communities: stagnant wages, mounting economic inequality, and catastrophic unemployment rates.

Obama admitted that the odds were against him. Movements needed money, and Democratic donors showed little interest in structural economic reform. Maybe no grassroots campaign could break through when the media was obsessed with celebrity and scandal. Most depressing of all, it might be true that "the country is too racially polarized to build the kind of multiracial coalitions necessary to bring about massive economic change."[47]

Yes, his grand plan for transforming politics might be another doomed crusade, as naïve as his mother's sixties-vintage liberalism. But there was only one way to find out.

Voters in Illinois's 13th Senate District were persuaded, though they didn't have much of a choice. The Obama campaign knocked all four of his primary opponents off the ballot after proving that they had failed to produce the requisite number of legitimate signatures on the petitions that would have qualified them for a spot. With no serious opposition, Obama carried 100 percent of the vote.[48]

Not everyone was impressed. In an essay for *The Village Voice*, published in January 1996, the Northwestern political scientist Adolph Reed Jr., author of a dissertation on W.E.B. Du Bois's political thought that he was converting into a book, described Obama as "a smooth Harvard lawyer with impeccable do-good credentials and vacuous-to-repressive neoliberal politics."[49]

According to Reed, Obama's talk about remaking politics was cover for the same old surrender to capital. It was fairer to say that Obama's economic views were muddled, with the possibility to cut left or right depending on circumstances. Even though Reed loathed Obama, the Democratic Socialists of America endorsed him. Speaking at a February 1996 event co-organized by the DSA, Obama reminded the audience, "Martin Luther King's March on Washington in the 1960s wasn't simply about civil rights but demanded jobs as well."[50] With Pat Buchanan in the middle of his surprisingly successful bid for the Republican presidential nomination, Obama urged Democrats to make sure that economic insecurity "was on the Democratic agenda not just on Buchanan's."*

---

* The point was seconded by the conference's top-billed speaker, William Julius Wilson, who called for a universal jobs program that, the DSA reported, "would

Who was the real Obama? A neoliberal shill? A pragmatic radical searching for the left wing of the possible? Did even he know for sure?

The answer was still unclear, but one thing was certain. After years of preparation, Barack Obama was a politician.

"He thought he was getting into the AP class," an acquaintance of Obama's said after his election to the Illinois Senate. "And he'd really been admitted to the Special Ed class."[51] It was a disillusioning experience. Lobbyists had an effective veto over most of the legislating that was done in Springfield, which usually concerned technical matters crucial to a company's balance sheet. Reelection was all but guaranteed so long as politicians stayed on the right side of the charged social issues that riled up their base. "You don't have the court of public opinion to appeal to because nobody's listening to you," Obama said.[52] Complacent legislators, sovereign lobbyists, and a catatonic electorate—that's what Springfield's version of democracy looked like.

He tried to escape by running for Congress, announcing in the summer of 1999 that he would challenge the Democratic incumbent, Bobby Rush. Obama cast the race as a choice between a young reformer and a sclerotic political machine. Voters opted for the machine, sending Rush back to Washington by a margin of two to one.

Obama took an important lesson from the defeat. "The kind of bridge-building politics I imagined wasn't suited to a congressional race," he said. "In an overwhelmingly Black district . . . the test for politicians would more often than not be defined in racial terms."[53] That was a test that a biracial Hawaii native would have a hard time passing.

---

be available to everyone, 'including Donald Trump' if he chose to do some useful work for a change." Bob Roman, "A Town Meeting on Economic Insecurity," *New Ground*, March–April 1996, available at https://www.slideshare.net/tradeequity/new -ground-45-chicago-dsa.

If his goal was to forge a multiracial coalition, he needed to run statewide. Obama decided to gamble on a Senate campaign in 2004, obtaining Michelle's consent only after he promised her that he would give up politics for good if he lost. He shifted tactics, too. His opposition to the Iraq War burnished his reputation with the left, but he retreated from his earlier support of gay marriage and universal health insurance. At the same time, he launched a charm offensive with Democratic donors, winning support from Chicago's real estate developers, white-shoe attorneys, and corporate executives.

And, always, there was the question of race. In the Democratic primary, his strategy depended on locking down support among African Americans without raising suspicions among white voters. His biracial heritage, exotic name, and sterling meritocratic credentials ensured that suburbanites wouldn't see him as the next Jesse Jackson. But he could still count on votes—and donations—from the Black community, especially the twenty-first-century version of Du Bois's Talented Tenth. "One of the first times I needed a corporate jet for the campaign," Obama remembered, "it was a black friend who lent me his."[54]

Obama jumped to the front of a crowded field when his first television ads went on the air. The advertisements promised "hope and change," told skeptics "yes we can," and urged voters to "join the movement."[55] Campaigns were politics as usual, but movements were something special, and the Obama movement trounced the mere campaigns. He pulled in 52.8 percent of the vote in the primary, beating the runner-up by almost thirty points.[56]

Already there was an important difference between the nascent Obama coalition and the majority he sketched in "Transformative Politics." Although he did well in suburbia and won crushing victories with Black voters, his numbers were least impressive in rural counties, a troubling sign for a candidate who once hoped to unite the multiracial working class.[57]

But that was a problem for another day. Reporters were churning out stories about the Obama phenomenon, and John Kerry's presidential campaign team was looking for a keynote speaker who would bring some magic to the forthcoming Democratic National Convention. After receiving the invitation, Obama told his staff, "I know exactly what I want to say. I really want to talk about my story as part of the larger American story."[58]

It was a story about a politician who thought that his unlikely journey proved that Americans could move beyond the divide between red and blue. It was a story about the coalition he saw taking shape in Illinois, reaching from union workers in Galesburg (population 84 percent white) to young people in East St. Louis (population 98 percent Black).[59] And it was a story that led NBC's Chris Matthews to blurt out, "I've just seen the first Black president."[60]

After languishing in Springfield for almost a decade, Obama pulled off the most impressive debut at a Democratic National Convention since William Jennings Bryan. He breezed through the rest of his Senate campaign, and a reissued edition of *Dreams from My Father* topped the *New York Times* bestseller list.[61] A cover story for *Newsweek* quoted Michelle Obama saying that her husband was "not a politician first and foremost. He's a community activist exploring the viability of politics to make change."[62] It was the same argument Obama had been making since he first ran for state senate, now delivered to a national audience.

Obama was just as effective at playing the inside game. He asked Joe Lieberman—longtime Connecticut senator, 2000 Democratic vice presidential nominee, and punching bag for progressive activists—to serve as his mentor in a program for incoming legislators.[63] Conversations with such pundits as the *New York Times* columnists Tom Friedman and David Brooks kept him in touch with the arbiters of Washington's conventional wisdom.[64] He became one of the Democrats' most effective rainmakers, bringing in $800,000 for the West

Virginia senator Robert Byrd with just one email.[65] At old-fashioned fundraisers he raked in donations from celebrities (including Oprah Winfrey, David Geffen, and Steven Spielberg), the financial community (George Soros, Goldman Sachs, and J.P. Morgan), and major lobbying firms.

He had everything a freshman senator could ask for, and it was making him miserable. "Barack hated being a senator," remembered his chief strategist David Axelrod. "He was punching the clock during the day and then coming alive at night to write the book," a staffer recalled.[66]

"The book" was *The Audacity of Hope*, Obama's chance to bring together ideas he'd been working through since "Transformative Politics," updated to reflect his experience from a decade in elected office—and written with an eye on his now stratospheric potential.[67]

He started by diagnosing what ailed American democracy. The country's most pressing challenges, he argued, either stemmed from or were exacerbated by a political system that had polarized around divisive social issues, pushing aside the pocketbook questions at the heart of the New Deal in favor of cable-ready controversies. "Liberalism and conservatism," he lamented, "were now defined in the popular imagination less by class than by attitude—the position you took toward the traditional culture and counterculture."[68]

With organized labor in slow-motion collapse, Democrats had become dependent upon a donor class whose politics were updated versions of the pro bono liberalism Obama had encountered at Harvard. "My own worldview and theirs corresponded in many ways," he wrote. But he distinguished himself, gently, from "the top 1 percent or so of the income scale," siding instead with "the other 99 percent of the population . . . that I'd entered public life to serve."[69]

The question, as usual, was how to get middle- and working-class white voters to focus on economic interests that cut across cultural—and, especially, racial—divides. He told a story about a time in Springfield when a white senator had leaned over to him while another African American senator (Obama called him "John Doe") gave a speech denouncing racism. "You know what the problem is with John?" Obama recalled his colleague asking. "Whenever I hear him, he makes me feel more white."[70]

Here was the Democratic dilemma. However justified complaints about discrimination were, making voters "feel more white" was the quickest way to destroy a progressive majority. Obama thought the moral of his story was clear: "Proposals that solely benefit minorities . . . may generate a few short-term concessions when the costs to whites aren't too high, but they can't serve as the basis for the kinds of sustained, broad-based political coalitions needed to transform America."[71]

It was a delicate balancing act. By pinning the blame on a dysfunctional political system—rather than, for instance, capitalism—he opened his argument up to contradictory interpretations. He was, depending on your perspective, advocating either strategic depolarization or blanket depoliticization. Liberals heard a call for structural change, moderates (and some conservatives) a story about an otherwise healthy country dragged down by its broken politics. One group could see Obama as a second FDR, building a new Democratic majority by calling a truce in the culture wars while pushing for sweeping economic reforms. The other could picture him as a technocratic successor to Eisenhower, working to resurrect the postwar consensus, now purged of its compromises with Jim Crow.

Obama squared this circle by arguing that incremental reforms could yield radical change. He turned once again to a modified version of the playbook he'd drawn up in "Transformative Politics," urging Democrats to scramble the left-right binary by downplaying hot-button social issues while using market-friendly policies to achieve traditional liberal goals on issues like health care and poverty. The agenda was less ambitious than he once envisioned—more on tax credits, less on rethinking the corporate form—but he thought their consequences could still be transformational.

So far, much of Obama's argument could have been lifted from any number of works published around the time making the case for radical centrism. But where the typical third-way manifesto took it as a given that the major questions about democracy and capitalism had been resolved, Obama painted a much darker portrait of what the future could bring. "Shortly after 2050, experts project, America will no longer be a majority white country—with consequences for our economics, our politics, and our culture that we cannot fully anticipate," he wrote.[72] As the nation was becoming more racially diverse, it was also becoming more economically divided. If present trends continued, then economic frustration and racial hostility would feed off each other, further exacerbating partisan polarization. "Neither our democracy nor our economy can long withstand," Obama predicted, "if we stand idly by as America continues to become increasingly unequal, an inequality that tracks racial lines and therefore feeds racial strife."[73]

Luckily, there was still time to change, if progressives could figure out the politics. "Eking out a bare Democratic majority isn't good enough," he wrote. "What's needed is a broad majority of Americans—Democrats, Republicans, and independents of goodwill—who are re-engaged in the project of national renewal."[74] Out beyond left and right, a new coalition was waiting to be born.

The Audacity of Hope certified that Obama was a force to be reckoned with. Readers snatched up 182,000 copies in the first three weeks after the book was published in October 2006.[75] A *Time* magazine cover story dubbed him "the political equivalent of a rainbow—a sudden preternatural event inspiring both awe and ecstasy."[76] NBC's popular drama *The West Wing* ended its seven-season run with a character based on Obama winning the White House.[77] "Whether you're liberal or conservative, you should hope Barack Obama runs for president," wrote David Brooks in *The New York Times*.[78]

Obama played coy with journalists as he weighed his options. "My attitude about something like the presidency is that you don't want to just be the president," he told a reporter. "You want to change the country. You want to make a unique contribution. You want to be a great president."[79] Just holding the office wouldn't be enough. He wanted to transform politics.

"Save it for 2050," sniffed Mark Penn, chief strategist for Hillary Clinton's presidential campaign, in a 2007 memo for his candidate.[80] Penn told his boss that Obamamania was a bubble waiting to be popped, a passing fad driven by college students and their professional-class parents. Without the advantage of running as an outsider against a tarnished establishment, Obama wouldn't even be in the race.

But what an advantage it was. Obama was beloved by donors in Wall Street, Hollywood, and Silicon Valley, but he was also a grassroots sensation who received contributions from three million people by the end of the campaign.[81] All of them were drawn by the promise of a candidate who transcended politics—not just a politician, but the leader of a movement to remake the country.

In other words, the opposite of a political class symbolized by Bill and Hillary Clinton. The former first couple, Obama acknowledged, had run on their own version of hope and change in 1992. But in office they had been chewed up by the polarization machine. Obama jabbed the Clintons from the left for supporting the Iraq War, from the right for demonizing Republicans, and from all angles at once for embodying a dysfunctional status quo.

The biggest risk for Obama was losing his image of transcendence, turning an agent of change into just another politician—or, still more damaging, just another Black politician. That was the great threat posed by the release of incendiary excerpts from Jeremiah Wright's sermons in March 2008.[82] With cable news stations playing clips of the man he had called a spiritual mentor saying "God damn America" in heavy rotation, Obama saved his candidacy with a speech on race that brilliantly executed a by-now-familiar routine. He cast himself as a spokesman for both sides of a "racial stalemate," where each side had legitimate grievances but too often succumbed to counterproductive anger. Then he pivoted to class, arguing that racial grievance "distracted attention from . . . economic policies that favor the few over the many."[83]

Obama stumbled into a different trap one month later. Speaking at a San Francisco fundraiser—and thereby playing perfectly to the stereotype of the condescending liberal—he reflected on a recent article reporting on skepticism around his candidacy among white voters in Levittown, Pennsylvania. "The jobs have been gone now for 25 years and nothing's replaced them," he noted. "It's not surprising then that they get bitter, they cling to guns or religion or antipathy toward people who aren't like them, or anti-immigrant sentiment or anti-trade sentiment as a way to explain their frustrations."[84] Though Obama apologized for the comments, the reference to bitter working-class white people clinging to guns and religion was quoted more often than any single line in his speech on race.

Clinton jumped on the gaffe, calling it "elitist and out of touch" while her campaign gave out stickers saying "I'm not bitter."[85] "I have a much broader base to build a winning coalition on," she insisted, citing her strength with "hard-working Americans, white Americans."[86] When reporters pushed back, a defensive Clinton replied, "These are the people you have to win, if you're a Democrat. . . . Everybody knows that."

And she wasn't entirely wrong about the electoral math. The same weaknesses with rural and blue-collar white people that dogged Obama in the 2004 Illinois primary turned the presidential race into a grueling slog. Even after Obama's nomination was all but certain, Clinton thrashed him by 35 points in Kentucky and 41 points in West Virginia. The awkward fact for both campaigns was that a repudiation at this scale—like a body violently rejecting a transplant—had to be explained, at least in part, by racism.[87]

Clinton and Obama split the Democratic coalition in half, finishing the campaign with a virtual tie in the popular vote. He held on to African Americans, young people, liberals, and the college educated— all groups that were either firmly Democratic or trending that way. Clinton trounced him with the working-class white people whose ties to the party were already fraying. Here was the great paradox of the race: Obama won the nomination because of the polarization he campaigned against.

On the right, the shape of the Obama opposition was coming into focus. While the GOP base seethed over rumors that he was a secret Muslim, the editorial page of *The Wall Street Journal* issued a dire forecast of what Democratic control of the government would bring.[88] The bill of particulars included "Medicare for all," skyrocketing taxes on the rich, union supremacy in workplaces, expanded voting rights, a green revolution, and a crackdown on the financial sector—in other words, a second New Deal that would entrench the Democratic Party in power for decades to come.

Sarah Palin offered a folksier version of the case against Obama in her star-making turn at the Republican National Convention, presenting herself as a small-town hockey mom representing the kind of folks who "prefer candidates who don't talk about us one way in Scranton and another in San Francisco."[89] The McCain campaign vaulted ahead of Obama after the convention, carried along by massive gains among white voters without college degrees.[90]

The financial crisis allowed Obama to reset his relationship with the white working class. Although the campaign publicly dismissed worries about losing ground with the demographic—David Plouffe, Obama's resolutely dull campaign manager, called it "hand-wringing and bedwetting"—they carefully studied racial prejudice in the electorate, hoping to separate intransigent racists from the persuadable.[91] To the latter, they sent mailings that emphasized jobs and economic security rather than a more nebulous promise of change. And as the economy sank deeper into recession, Obama reclaimed his lead in the polls.

On Election Day, the result was historic. Obama won record-breaking totals with African Americans and young people, and improved on earlier Democratic margins with working women, Latinos, and Asian Americans. He made inroads with white-collar professionals, too, becoming the first Democrat to carry the nation's wealthiest county—Virginia's Loudoun County—since Lyndon Johnson. But aggregate measurements of class-based voting showed him doing about as well with blue-collar voters—and about as poorly with the affluent—as a typical Democrat in the glory days of the New Deal order. Almost 40 percent of working-class white people with high degrees of racial

resentment cast a ballot for the first Black president. He even carried
Levittown, inspiration for the bitter clingers gaffe.[92]

But warning signs were already flashing. Despite the resounding
popular vote total, Obama won a smaller proportion of counties than
any president since John Quincy Adams, just 28 percent. A long-term
decline in support for Democrats among Southern white people, temporarily reversed by Bill Clinton, reached new lows. As late as 1988,
Michael Dukakis handily carried West Virginia while getting thrashed
by George H. W. Bush nationally.[93] Twenty years later, Obama lost the
state by thirteen points.[94]

Not quite the coalition Obama had envisioned, then, but enough
to win the White House—and, with it, the opportunity to convert a
rejection of the GOP into a lasting majority. On Inauguration Day,
some two million people showed up to celebrate, looking not unlike a
twenty-first-century version of Bayard Rustin's March on Washington
coalition.

"What the cynics fail to understand is that the ground has shifted
beneath them, that the stale political arguments that have consumed us
for so long no longer apply," Obama declared.[95]

Nobody was quite sure what that meant yet, including the new president. But as the Republican congressman Patrick McHenry watched the crowd roar its approval, he was certain of one thing: "I thought we were completely, permanently screwed."[96]

———————

Presidencies, like life, are lived forward and understood backward. In the moment, the onrush of events has all the logic of a loose fire hose shooting at full blast. In retrospect, however, it's possible to divide the Obama era into three distinct chapters.

The first opened on election night 2008. Obama played a dual role during the campaign, presenting himself as both the leader of a people's movement against the status quo and as a consensus builder who could be the nation's designated adult in the room. After the polls closed, the insider took over. His campaign handed responsibility for its massive online operation—thirteen million email addresses, three million donors, and two million members of the social-networking platform My.BarackObama—to the Democratic National Committee, where it quickly atrophied.[97] Instead of governing as community organizer in chief, Obama would build a consensus among policymakers and let the results speak for themselves.

Unity was the watchword as the president moved to consolidate his support within the Democratic Party while reaching out to the GOP. But he was swimming against a powerful current. Ideological polarization within Congress had reached its highest levels since the Gilded Age, and the GOP leadership showed no interest in handing the new president a string of policy victories.[98] "We're not going to compromise with you on anything," a Republican operative told Jim Messina, incoming deputy chief of staff. "We're going to fight Obama on everything."[99]

Forced to choose between passing bills and restoring bipartisanship, Obama decided to go for the legislative win. "Elections have consequences," he told Eric Cantor, House Republican whip. "And at the end

of the day, I won."[100] His chief of staff Rahm Emmanuel had a more col-
orful way of making the same point: "We have the votes. Fuck 'em."[101]

And so it went for Obama's first year in the White House. Backed
up by majorities in the House and Senate, he passed a $787 billion
stimulus, a total that was both massive by historic standards and still
far below what the White House's own economists believed was necessary to restore full employment. Over the next two years his administration pushed through the most ambitious reforms of any Democrat
since the Great Society, from aggressive new financial regulations to
Obamacare. But it was hard to say what distinguished these policies
from what would have come out of a hypothetical Hillary Clinton administration. Any notion of building up institutions that would shift
power to ordinary citizens gave way to the more modest goal of making existing institutions—with their existing elites—run more effi-
ciently: a Wall Street that could better withstand the next financial
crisis while keeping its executive class intact; a health-care system that
would insure more people at a lower cost while still bringing in record
profits. Meanwhile, the reign of pro-labor terror that conservatives had
predicted was nowhere to be seen, guaranteeing organized labor's continued stagnation.

It didn't take long for disillusionment to set in. Consensus remained
out of reach, frustrating moderates. Structural change was just as elusive, disappointing progressives. The complexity of the Obama agenda
made it a difficult sell for the broader public. "The goal wasn't to have
people understand," the economic adviser Jason Furman said about the
stimulus. "The goal was to have it actually happen."[102] But technocrats
couldn't deliver the goods: the recovery was slow in coming, and even
after growth rates finally ticked back up, wages for most of the country remained stagnant, resulting in a deeply unequal quasi-boom.[103] If
the ins and outs of policymaking were difficult to fathom, there was
always the chance that a stray presidential remark could set off another
skirmish in the culture war—for instance, saying that a white Massachusetts policeman "acted stupidly" in arresting Henry Louis Gates Jr.
when the Black Harvard professor was trying to enter his own home.[104]

All of which gave the Tea Party an opening to sell its own version

of transformative politics: a clean break with a corrupt Washington establishment, restoring the country to its founding principles (and rebranding the GOP after the debacles of the Bush years). The outburst
of patriotic nostalgia among the Tea Party's mostly older, mostly white
membership was directly linked to the new president. Sometimes, the
reactions were explicitly racialized, like a protester waving a sign of
Obama dressed as a witch doctor, complete with a bone through his
nose.[105] But they were also muted, like the Tea Partier who said of
Obama, almost sadly, "I just can't relate to him."[106]

Republican outrage, Democratic dissatisfaction, and widespread
frustration with the recovery all found an outlet in the midterms, the
largest wave election against an incumbent party since 1938.[107] With
Republicans in control of the House and the Democratic majority
down to fifty-one votes in the Senate, Obama shifted his approach. His
overall goal—building a new majority out of a new consensus—stayed
the same, but the consensus shifted rightward.

Months of negotiations with Republicans in search of a "grand bargain" to reduce the long-term deficit produced budget cuts that were
significant enough to dampen the recovery but nowhere close to the
belt-tightening that deficit hawks called for.[108] Obama tried to turn
the failure to his advantage, casting himself as the voice of sanity in a
town gone mad. "We're going to have to make a series of very difficult
decisions about how we invest in our future but also get a hold of our
deficit and our debt," he said at a press conference. "We're not going
to be able to solve our problems if we get distracted by sideshows and
carnival barkers."[109]

The president had a specific carnival barker in mind—Donald
Trump, who had been making the rounds on television demanding
that he release his birth certificate. Obama complied with the request
at the press conference, using it to link Trump's conspiracy-mongering
with the GOP's stubbornness on taxes. "The president went out in the
briefing room to present his long-form birth certificate, [but] really to
continue the dance with Trump," recalled David Plouffe, now senior
adviser to the president. "Lifting Trump up as the identity of the Republican Party was super helpful to us. . . . There was a strategy behind

the material and the amount of time we spent on Trump. *Let's really lean into Trump here. That'll be good for us."*[110]

———

With his approval ratings spiraling downward and his reelection campaign looming, Obama entered the second chapter of his presidency. Putting aside the post-partisan ambitions of his first two years in office, he rebranded himself as an old-fashioned Democrat, the champion of a beleaguered middle class taking on Republican plutocrats.

He debuted the new approach in a December 2011 speech in Osawatomie, Kansas, where Theodore Roosevelt had called for a "New Nationalism" a century earlier. Obama's message owed less to TR than it did to protesters who had taken up residence in Zuccotti Park that September, turning Occupy Wall Street into a global phenomenon. "It's about class," one occupier told a journalist. "People can't unify around party or religion, but we can unify around class."[111]

Dubious sociology, but decent politics. Although Occupy's drum circles weren't designed with midwestern swing voters in mind, its attacks on "the 1 percent" tracked with the emerging consensus in Obama's campaign team that the president could weather 2012 only by keeping the focus on economics. At Osawatomie, Obama called the struggle for equitable growth "the defining issue of our time" and denounced "the breathtaking greed" of a financial elite that left the rest of the country "rightly suspicious that the system in Washington is rigged against them."[112] Obama's policies didn't quite live up to the rhetoric: strengthening penalties for financial fraud, more spending on education, vague references to a fairer tax code. But the search for a grand bargain had come to an end.

Obama had taken an ambivalent line toward Wall Street in his first two years as president, mixing swipes at "fat-cat bankers" with tributes to Wall Street's "very savvy businessmen."[113] Neither the compliments nor the administration's other outreach efforts—lunches with major executives, appearances in front of important business groups, invitations to a private Super Bowl party—assuaged the nation's executive class.[114] "With all due respect, we will be here when you're gone," the Verizon CEO Ivan Seidenberg told Obama. "Guys like me can hunker down and wait you out."[115] They could take their money elsewhere, too. After narrowly favoring Obama in 2008, Wall Street donations went to Republicans by a landslide in 2012.[116]

Despite his warnings about the dangers of economic inequality, Obama was not entirely sold on his own reelection pitch. A few weeks before the Osawatomie speech, he stayed up late into the night filling a yellow legal pad—his favorite way to write—with pages of notes detailing the subjects he wanted to tackle in a second term: gay marriage, poverty, climate change, peace in the Middle East, and closing the detention camp at Guantánamo Bay. It was a striking collection, far closer to the pro bono liberalism of the Democratic donor class than to the Obama of *The Audacity of Hope*.[117]

He ran through the catalogue in a meeting with his political team; then he listened to all the reasons why those issues had to take a back seat in the election. "As weighty as they were," David Axelrod later observed, "none of them rose to the top of the list of concerns in a country where the economy was still weak and the middle class was under siege."[118]

Obama spent the rest of the election season hewing to the Occupy-lite strategy that he'd unveiled at Osawatomie. The topics he scrawled on his yellow pad in the fall of 2011 were virtually absent from his 2012 DNC speech, which kept a tight focus on pocketbook politics and ensuring that "everyone plays by the same rules—from Main Street to Wall Street to Washington D.C."[119] His campaign backed up the message with an advertising blitz depicting Mitt Romney as a vulture capitalist circling the American dream with a hungry glint in his eyes. "This is the guy . . . who had a Swiss bank account and millions in tax havens like Bermuda and the Caymans," ran a typical ad. It closed with the tagline "Mitt Romney: Not One of Us."[120]

Discussion in the aftermath of Obama's victory emphasized his strength with what the journalist Ronald Brownstein dubbed "the co-alition of the ascendant": racial minorities, millennials, and college-educated white people.[121] In its election postmortem, *The Washington Post* attributed Romney's loss to "the inexorable power of demographic change in a country growing more diverse by the day."[122] Even Republicans agreed. "There just are not enough middle-aged white guys that we can scrape together to win," said one former GOP congressman.[123]

Only later did analysis reveal how much Obama owed to the older Democratic majority.[124] Although the electorate was more polarized by education than in 2008, just over a third of his vote came from white people without college degrees. In absolute numbers, that was more than the total for African Americans, Hispanics, or highly educated white people. Obama's performance with blue-collar voters of all races was especially strong in key battleground states, including Wisconsin, Ohio, and Pennsylvania. But the coalition of the ascendant was a better fit with the story Democrats wanted to tell. Obama was their Reagan. And it was time to declare morning in America.[125]

————

As he mapped out his next term, Obama entered the third chapter of his presidency. Although the legislative results did not compare with his first two years in office, its political legacy was more lasting. No longer the post-partisan unifier of his early presidency or the reluctant populist of his reelection campaign, he recast himself as an unapologetically progressive Democrat, tacking leftward on both economic and cultural issues. But as his agenda grew more ambitious, his rhetoric turned more conservative. Instead of promising to transform politics, he urged his followers to accept that existing institutions were for the most part working as they should (except for when Republicans took them over).

Obama kept up the focus on income inequality that drove his 2012 campaign. He drew attention in speeches to the interweaving of economic decline, spiking drug use, and social isolation—a phenomenon he'd witnessed firsthand as a community organizer in Chicago that was now spreading into rural America, changing the face of poverty from Black to white. He dismissed concerns about the national debt as "a stale debate from two years ago" while calling for stronger unions, a minimum wage hike, and increased spending on entitlements.[126] If there was no mistaking Obama for a bright blue icon like Elizabeth Warren, let alone a socialist like Bernie Sanders, it still marked a clear departure from the quest for a grand bargain.

The problem was that none of it had a chance of passing Congress, at first because Republicans controlled the House and then, after 2014, because they also had the Senate. During his reelection campaign, Obama had predicted that a Democratic victory would "break the fever" on the right.[127] Instead, Republicans plunged the government into a shutdown in October 2013 as part of a doomed attempt to repeal Obamacare, a fiasco that confirmed his low opinion of the congressional GOP. His assessment of the conservative base was just as grim. "A sizable portion of the American right," he later wrote of his time in office, "had become so frightened and insecure that they'd completely lost their minds."[128]

If Republican elites were feckless and their voters unhinged, then bipartisanship was no longer an option. Summarizing the administration's new perspective, the White House staffer Dan Pfeiffer recalled, "Compromise was dead and we pursued it at our own peril."[129]

Working through executive actions at home and diplomacy abroad, Obama entered the most productive phase of his presidency since 2010. But his achievements were only glancingly connected to the core of his reelection message. Instead, he focused on the items he'd written on his legal pad in 2011, the issues he wished he could have addressed in the first term but had kept at the margins of his reelection campaign—immigration, gun control, same-sex marriage, climate change, and investigating racial bias in the criminal justice system. Not coincidentally, these were also the kinds of subjects that most excited Democratic donors and activists.[130]

With Republicans blocking legislative action and little appetite within the administration for a crusade against concentrated economic power, the door was opened for a rapprochement with the business community. Profits were soaring, the stock market was booming, and a wave of corporate mergers promised more good times to come, even as critics outside the administration warned about resurgent monopolies. Meanwhile, a crop of "Obama millionaires" left Washington to make their fortunes in corporate America. Silicon Valley was a popular destination for White House alums, second only to Hollywood. "You can go work for Harvey Weinstein and make all this money," marveled one former administration official.[131]

Obama himself was spending more time with what *The New York Times* described as "eclectic, often extraordinarily rich groups of people."[132] During one leisurely dinner that stretched late into the evening, he sipped from an extra-dry Grey Goose martini while holding forth in front of guests who represented a cross section of the cultural and economic elite—Toni Morrison, Eva Longoria, and Malcolm Gladwell for one side, the hedge fund manager Marc Lasry, the venture capitalist John Doerr, and the LinkedIn cofounder Reid Hoffman for the other.

The candidate of hope and change had become a symbol for an American establishment that had grown comfortable with a housebroken progressivism. Obama kept calling economic inequality "the defining challenge of our time," but aside from allowing the partial expiration of tax cuts passed under George W. Bush, he couldn't do much about it.

The other side noticed. "95 percent of income gains have gone to the top 1 percent," bristled the *Fox News* host Elisabeth Hasselbeck. "So this system that he's talking about, he is the system. It's his system!"[133]

———————

Seven years to the day after Obama was sworn into the White House, a musical debuted off-Broadway.[134] "It sounds initially like it would not work at all," Obama explained of Lin-Manuel Miranda's retelling of the life of Alexander Hamilton with a cast of African American and Hispanic actors, rebranding the onetime symbol of the money power as Horatio Alger for an anti-racist era. "And it is brilliant, and so much so that I'm pretty sure this is the only thing that Dick Cheney and I have agreed on."[135] In June 2016 *Hamilton*'s producers raised the price for premium tickets to $849, the most expensive in Broadway history.[136] At a performance to raise money for Hillary Clinton's campaign, seats went from a low of $2,700 to a high of $100,000.[137]

While theatergoers snapped up tickets for *Hamilton*, readers were devouring the year's surprise bestseller, *Hillbilly Elegy*, J. D. Vance's memoir of growing up in a deteriorating Ohio steel town. The book was treated as a decoder ring for Donald Trump's America, providing a personal counterpoint to reports on an explosion of deaths caused by depression, drug abuse, and suicide among middle-aged working-class white people.

Hamilton and *Hillbilly Elegy* formed two sides of a pincer movement tearing apart the coalition that twice elected Obama. An economic elite that was still overwhelmingly white and male was becoming more diverse as it pulled further away from the rest of the country. At the same time, more white people were falling into a still disproportionately nonwhite underclass. The top and the bottom of the social hierarchy were each becoming more diverse, and the middle ground was shrinking. There were grounds for dissatisfaction on all sides, if you cared to look.[138]

Just as Obama predicted in *The Audacity of Hope*, these cultural and economic resentments were exacerbated by a polarized politics where partisan identity increasingly tracked racial lines. As his tenure in the White House drew to a close, he took to wondering with his staff if he had been "elected about a decade too soon."[139] Stagnant incomes, demographic change, technological disruption—adding a Black president on top of all this, he thought, might have been too much for the system to bear.

To young activists on the left, however, a Black president wasn't nearly enough. #BlackLivesMatter debuted on Twitter in the summer of 2013. It broke into national consciousness in 2014 after the death of Michael Brown in St. Louis, becoming for Obama's second term what Occupy Wall Street had been in his first. But where occupiers said that the 99 percent could unite around class, BLM drew attention to a racial divide that seemed like it was growing wider.[140] In 2013, 72 percent of white people and 66 percent of African Americans described race relations as either "somewhat" or "very" good, about the same level both groups had reported for more than a decade. By 2015, the total had plunged to 45 percent for white people and 51 percent for African Americans.[141]

At the start of his political career, Obama had insisted that elected officials could spark social movements by merging the roles of organizer and politician. Now even setting up a discussion with representatives from Black Lives Matter was an ordeal. "Oval Office meetings usually had CEOs or members of Congress—people who were not kids that had been arrested forty-eight hours prior," a staffer explained. "We didn't want people who were going to be upset and start flipping stuff over."[142]

Obama had almost as much difficulty reaching out to supporters of Bernie Sanders's 2016 presidential run, the other major left-wing movement of the late Obama years. Like the Obama of 2008, Sanders campaigned as an outsider taking on a crooked political establishment embodied in Hillary Clinton. Once again, the message proved especially resonant with young people, who voted for Sanders in even greater numbers than they did for Obama. But where Obama targeted cynical partisans and called for market-friendly reforms, Sanders paired attacks on the 1 percent with a platform straight out of *The Wall Street Journal*'s nightmares—a combination that won him a significant following with blue-collar voters and landslide margins with the young, but couldn't beat Hillary Clinton, now Obama's chosen successor.[143]

A left-wing movement dedicated to the same broad goals that drew Obama to politics was emerging just as he was leaving the White House. Like the Obama of 1991, Sanders argued that universal programs could build a majority out of the multiracial working class. But there was a vast, empty space between the septuagenarian Bernie

Sanders and his army of millennial supporters, like the twentysomething bartender Alexandria Ocasio-Cortez.

The resurgent left needed figures to bridge the gap between Sanders and Ocasio-Cortez—ideally, candidates who understood that movements need both grassroots organizing and charismatic leadership, who could speak persuasively about the importance of both economic equality and racial justice, who could channel activist energy into majoritarian coalition building, who could work the levers of power in elite institutions while fostering a progressive counter-establishment. They needed, in short, candidates of the kind that Obama once wanted to become.

The outlines of a new March on Washington majority were also coming into sight. It would bring together elements of the Obama and Sanders campaigns: the young people who flocked to both, African Americans who made up the core of the Democratic base, alienated working-class voters who gravitated to Sanders, and sympathetic liberals higher up the income scale. The enemy was just as clear: a populist right fueled by a mix of status and material grievances made even more toxic by polarized politics—exactly the threat Obama had warned about for decades.

A politician who seized on this opportunity just might have delivered on the goals Obama set for himself when he went into politics. But it couldn't be Obama, who—as he noted, but for the wrong reasons—had been elected a decade too soon. The problem wasn't just that he took power while financial markets were cratering and racial demographics were shifting. The deeper issue reached back to his original strategy, the bridge he wanted to build between Saul Alinsky and Harold Washington. Obama made himself president by tapping into the desire for change, but he didn't have the ideas, the infrastructure, or (by 2008) the inclination to translate a radical ambition into policy. And so the middle ground he tried to claim for himself split apart, sending a new generation of activists into the streets while Obama talked retirement plans over cocktails with a rotating cast of celebrities and CEOs.

But he had decided that the old dream wasn't realistic anyway.

"Societies don't turn 50 degrees," he observed late in his second term. "Sometimes the task of government is to make incremental improvements and to steer the ocean liner two degrees north or south."[144] In private, his sense of limits was even more acute. "All any of us could expect from democracy," he later explained, was to maintain the basic elements of

> the post–Cold War world: upholding the constitutional order; attending to the quotidian, often technical work of boosting the GDP; and expanding the social safety net. . . . Not revolutionary leaps or major cultural overhauls; not a fix for every social pathology or lasting answers for those in search of purpose and meaning in their lives. Just the observance of rules that allowed us to sort out or at least tolerate our differences, and government policies that raised living standards and improved education enough to temper humanity's baser impulses.[145]

When an interviewer brought up his 2008 prediction that Americans were on the brink of fundamentally transforming the country, Obama didn't even recognize the language. "I don't think we have to fundamentally transform the nation," he said, just barely concealing his disbelief that anyone could suspect him of such a thing.[146]

A new goal emerged to take the place that structural economic and political reform once held for Obama, another explanation for why he would be remembered as more than just another president. The transition to a majority-minority America had been on his mind since at least *The Audacity of Hope*. Back then, it had provided a deadline: break the doom loop between partisan polarization and economic inequality soon, or the country might not survive. By 2016, the rise of the coalition of the ascendant—and, ultimately, the transition to a multiracial democracy—became the end in itself, a calling that gave moral grandeur to the dreary work of policymaking. It was a narrative that, conveniently, had a starring role for the first Black president.

With demographic tides running in their favor, Democrats celebrated their transition from the party of Jackson to the party of *Hamilton*. The change was clearest in Hillary Clinton's primary campaign. In 2008, she'd reminded journalists that "everybody knows" Democrats needed to win "hard-working Americans, white Americans." In 2016 she rebranded herself as a champion of a diversifying nation, the candidate of "stronger together."[147]

Just as Obama's 2012 race offered a watered-down version of Occupy's economic populism, Clinton now put forward a moderated version of BLM's call for racial justice, a move designed to reach out to activists on the left, Black voters in the Democratic base, and college-educated white people appalled by the Trumpified GOP. The fruits of her strategy were apparent in the primaries, where she traded much of her 2008 coalition for Barack Obama's. In Virginia, for instance, she converted a loss of twenty-nine percentage points (35 percent to Obama's 64 percent) into a victory by the exact same margin (64 percent to Sanders's 35 percent), thanks to crushing margins with older African Americans and white-collar professionals. But in neighboring West Virginia the rural white voters who embraced Clinton in 2008 turned instead to Sanders, who won the state by sixteen percentage points.[148]

Party leaders welcomed the trade. "For every blue-collar Democrat we lose in western Pennsylvania we will pick up two moderate Republicans in the suburbs in Philadelphia," Chuck Schumer explained.[149] "A campaign which is largely about Main St. vs. Wall St. economics is too narrow and divisive for the story we need to tell right now," argued Jon Favreau, former chief Obama speechwriter. Instead, he encouraged Democrats to follow Clinton's example: "Embrace our growing diversity as a strength" with a message of "love and kindness."[150]

The circle of love and kindness couldn't encompass everyone, of course, as Clinton made clear when she dismissed half of Trump's supporters as a "basket of deplorables."[151] The circumstances of the remark—a gaffe by the Democratic presidential nominee at a glitzy fundraiser in sapphire-blue America—drew instant comparisons with Obama's reference to poor white people clinging to guns and religion. But the two came out of divergent views of the underlying problem.

Where Clinton's deplorables were bigots who had to be crushed, Obama's clingers were responding in misguided but understandable ways to a broken system.

That system was still broken in 2016. The economic recovery was fueled by loose monetary policy that juiced financial markets, a kind of technocratic trickle-down ensuring that the wealthiest Americans would reap most of the gains. Governing was more than ever an exercise in crisis management, as policymakers scrambled to hold the system together while it reeled like a punch-drunk boxer from one blow to the next. Polarization had grown so extreme that Republicans had given their presidential nomination to Donald Trump, going further than Obama's White House strategists had dreamed possible when they cast the aging B-lister as the face of the GOP back in 2011.

With the end of his presidency approaching, Obama preferred to focus on the positive. At the Democratic National Convention, he portrayed Trump as a demagogue who came from outside the American political tradition. Democrats had cornered the market on optimism, on maturity, on integrity—on everything the country valued. They were the party of patriotic diversity, victors in the war over national identity, a new American majority. And America, he announced, "is already great."[152]

———

When he was a community organizer, Obama used to ask himself what the world looked like from Harold Washington's office. He heard stories about election night euphoria, and he saw how important the mayor was to Black Chicago. But he couldn't tell if any of it amounted to much. "Beneath the radiance of Harold's victory, in Altgeld and elsewhere, nothing seemed to change," he wrote in *Dreams from My Father*. "I wondered whether, away from the spotlight, Harold . . . felt as trapped as those he served, an inheritor of sad history, part of a closed system with few moving parts, a system that was losing heat every day, dropping into low-level stasis. I wondered whether he, too, felt a prisoner of fate."[153]

Obama thought he could do better. By the time he left for Harvard, he was willing to gamble on a version of a liberalism that he associated with his mother—"a faith that rational, thoughtful people could shape their own destiny," as he described it.[154] When movements and politicians worked together, they could turn inspiring rhetoric into real change. That was the formula he thought could turn him into a different kind of politician, and eventually a different kind of president—a liberal counterpart to Ronald Reagan—who would build a new Democratic majority and leave behind a fairer society. "We are not trapped by the mistakes of history," he said on the fiftieth anniversary of the March on Washington, early in his second term. "We are masters of our fate."[155]

On his last day as president, Obama returned to Chicago to declare partial victory, saying, "Because of you, by almost every measure, America is a better, stronger place than it was when we started."[156]

Which should have been enough for an ordinary president. But Obama had set higher standards for himself. He had given up community organizing because he wanted to transform politics. Instead, he looked more like a national sequel to Harold Washington: a charismatic leader who failed to convert personal popularity into structural change, another prisoner of fate.[157]

Thirteen miles south of Obama's farewell address, a chain-link fence still blocked entry to the abandoned site of the old Wisconsin Steel plant. City blocks once filled with hulking factories had turned into toxic brownfields—"a post-industrial no-man's land, heading nowhere," wrote the MIT anthropologist Christine Walley in a 2013 monograph, *Exit Zero: Family and Class in Postindustrial Chicago*.[158]

Walley, who had grown up in the neighborhood, was the daughter of a Wisconsin Steel employee who never recovered from the mill's closing, moving from job to job before dying of lung cancer in 2005. She escaped by winning a scholarship to Phillips Exeter Academy, trading Southeast Chicago for the leafy New Hampshire countryside. But she couldn't leave her old neighborhood completely behind. At twenty-seven, she was diagnosed with a rare cancer that she attributed to the industrial pollution that was part of her childhood.[159]

Elevated cancer rates were a fact of life in Altgeld Gardens, too. In January 2017, a reporter from *The Washington Post* asked community members what they thought of the president who had spent a good chunk of his twenties working on their behalf. He found pride in Obama, anger at the resistance he encountered, and frustration at how much stayed the same.

"After all these years, after all that we've been through as a race, as a country, we finally got a black man into office and what did it do? What has it really changed? Our schools? The cops? Courts? The rich getting richer and the poor getting poorer?" asked one fifty-six-year-old resident. "It doesn't feel any less rigged than before. If a black president can't change that, what will?"[160]

Cheryl Johnson, a nurse who remembered meeting Obama when he was still an organizer, was more forgiving. "I don't blame him," she said. "There's only so much one man can do."

Except Obama never thought his career was just about one man. He went into politics saying he cared about organizations—not movements, and certainly not cults of personality—because organizations endure. And there was the advice his mother gave him before he went to Harvard: "You can spend a lifetime working outside institutions. But you might get more done trying to change those institutions from the inside."

The Democratic Party had certainly changed. Obama's progressive turn in the wake of the grand bargain's failure coincided with a broader shift inside the Democratic establishment. The twin shocks of 2016—Sanders's near upset in the 2016 primaries followed by Trump's victory in the general election—pushed the party's center of gravity still further to the left. The donor class that Obama had chided earlier in his career, the high achievers who believed in markets and meritocracy, might now have copies of *Capital in the Twenty-First Century*, *Between the World and Me*, and *How Democracies Die* in the built-in bookshelves of their seven-figure homes. On cable news, whose influence over politics Obama had once decried, liberal talking heads learned how to shift seamlessly from defending the country's sacred norms against authoritarian populism to calling for an overdue reckoning for a nation with white supremacy woven into its DNA.

And the Democratic Party wasn't the only institution transformed by the one-two punch of Obama and Trump. By the time Joe Biden was sworn into office, vast swaths of the American elite had locked arms in a united front against Trumpism, a revolt of the institutions. In a study of 2020 campaign donations, the only major organizations whose employees leaned decisively toward Trump were the U.S. Marines and the NYPD. A small number—Walmart, FedEx, McDonald's—were split between the two. The overwhelming majority were various shades of blue, from the Department of Defense and General Motors at the low end to Columbia and Facebook at the extreme (97 percent of donations from the house that Mark Zuckerberg built went to Biden).[161] Obama had not followed through on his early hopes of building institutions that could pressure elites from the outside, but he had, at least temporarily, helped change the way elites thought of themselves.

Like all American majorities, the new Democratic coalition that emerged in the Obama years was an unwieldly alliance. But the party of Mike Bloomberg and Ilhan Omar still wasn't large enough to deliver the systemic change that its activist base demanded. Under Johnson, Democrats had lost their grip on the Deep South; under Obama, Appalachia slipped away; in 2016, it was the Rust Belt. With the geography of the American political system against them, Democratic victories in the popular vote translated into slender electoral majorities (at best). The party was left with the problem Obama identified in *The Audacity of Hope*: if the goal is systemic reform, "a polarized electorate isn't good enough. Eking out a bare Democratic majority isn't good enough."[162]

Obama had changed, too. Most of the time he stayed out of the political arena. He cofounded a production company with Michelle and signed a lucrative deal with Netflix, with plans ranging from documentaries to children's series to films, including a biopic of Bayard Rustin.[163] He was also a regular presence on the lecture circuit, where he could earn his annual salary as president with a single speech.[164] Fundraising for his postpresidential foundation was a constant, too— $232.6 million in 2017 alone.[165]

When he intervened in politics, it still packed a punch. The senator who in 2005 called the filibuster a vital tool for promoting consensus became the ex-president who in 2020 denounced it as a "Jim Crow relic."[166] When Elizabeth Warren's primary campaign was on the upswing, Obama softened up skeptical donors for her behind closed doors. But after Warren's campaign flamed out and Sanders turned into a credible threat for the nomination, he worked to consolidate the field around Biden.[167]

More than just his presidential legacy was at stake. In an address at the 2020 Democratic National Convention, his most high-profile appearance since leaving the White House, Obama warned that democracy itself was under siege. He spoke from Philadelphia, where, he noted, "our Constitution was drafted and signed."[168] And not just anywhere in Philadelphia, but in a museum devoted to the founding, in front of a display with the words "Writing the Constitution" in bold.

"It wasn't a perfect document," Obama admitted. "But embedded in this document was a North Star that would guide future generations; a system of representative government—a democracy—through which we could better realize our highest ideals."

Now he was carrying on this tradition—a preacher of unity loathed by much of the country; a millionaire many times over denouncing the influence of concentrated wealth; a two-term president who still hadn't figured out how to bring real change to Altgeld Gardens; a guardian of the people, selected by the people themselves. As he spoke, viewers at home could see, just over his right shoulder, a picture of the young James Madison.

Conclusion: The Road to Freedom

Four months after Barack Obama told the nation that democracy was in peril, Ashli Babbitt came to Washington, D.C., on a mission to defend her country.[1]

It wasn't the first time. Babbitt, a U.S. Air Force veteran, had served near Washington in a unit known as the Capital Guardians following deployments in Afghanistan and Iraq. She left the military in 2016 after fourteen years of duty, eventually returning to her home state of California, where she took out a high-interest loan to help buy a pool-supply company.

Readjusting to civilian life was difficult. Tangles with her husband's former girlfriend led a judge to impose a restraining order on Babbitt in 2016, then again in 2017. She soon fell behind in her small business loan payments. Meanwhile, she found herself spending more time online, posting about politics. The extensive record—more than 8,600 tweets—shows her evolving from an Obama voter ("I think he jacked some shit up . . . but I think he did do a lot of good") to a believer in a worldwide conspiracy orchestrated by pedophilic members of a "political global ring/Hollywood/elite."[2] Along the way, she became a fervent Trump supporter. In 2019 she suggested launching a GoFundMe to add the president to Mount Rushmore. The next day a judge ruled that her company owed $71,000.

"Nothing will stop us," she tweeted on January 5, 2021. "They can try and try and try but the storm is here and it is descending upon DC in less than 24 hours . . . dark to light!"[3]

On January 6, Babbitt joined thousands of other Trump supporters at the National Mall for what was billed as a "March to Save America." More than a dozen funders had paid for travel to Washington, and nine "coalition partners" were listed on the march's website, including Tea Party Patriots and Phyllis Schlafly Eagles. Much of the planning, though, had taken place online through such sites as TheDonald.win or social media platforms like Parler.[4]

The crowd reflected its motley origins. Far-right groups like the Proud Boys and the Oath Keepers supplied a militant vanguard. Republican politicians circulated alongside MAGA internet personalities. Flags with Betsy Ross's original thirteen stars waved near the Confederate battle pennant. DON'T TREAD ON ME flew next to images of Trump riding a Tyrannosaurus rex while brandishing a grenade launcher. Some of the iconography was legible only to the extremely online, including pictures of the alt-right icon Pepe the frog and symbols for the imaginary People's Republic of Kekistan. It was a fun-house version of American history refracted though memes passed around in some of the seediest—and strangest—corners of the internet.[5]

Like Babbitt, most of the audience dwelled in the space between neo-Nazis and normies.[6] "It was amazing to see the president talk," Babbitt declared on Facebook while streaming herself marching to the Capitol building. "There is a sea of nothing but red, white and blue patriots for Trump."[7] (Later estimates put the total around ten thousand.)[8]

Inside the Capitol, members of the newly sworn-in Congress were counting electoral votes over repeated objections from Trump loyalists. The breakout freshman stars in the narrowly Democratic majority were Cori Bush and Jamaal Bowman, both members of the Democratic Socialists of America, and two fresh recruits for Alexandria Ocasio-Cortez's Squad. Republicans were already ducking questions about Marjorie Taylor Greene, who won her seat in Georgia after speaking warmly of QAnon, suggesting that 9/11 was an inside job, and posting a photo of herself holding a rifle with the caption "Squad's worst nightmare."[9] According to polls, 71 percent of the country disapproved of the new Congress.[10]

The first rioters broke into the Capitol a little after 2:00 p.m. Some eight hundred people followed, including Babbitt, who was wearing a Trump flag tied around her neck. She made her way to the front of a group jammed in next to glass-paneled doors closing off the Speaker's Lobby. As the mob tried to break the glass, someone shouted, "There's a gun! There's a gun!" Babbitt climbed to the upper-right corner of the door, attempting to squeeze through an open space. She was shot instantly by a police officer.[11]

Babbitt fell to the floor, thrown backward by the force of the bullet. A crowd gathered around her, their phones out to capture the moment for history. She died later that day.

Early the next morning, Congress certified Joe Biden's victory.

More than a riot but less than a coup, January 6 is what happens when history plays out as tragedy and farce at the same time. It was the coda the Trump presidency earned, with just the right mix of shocking spectacle and minimal real-world impact. Minimal, that is, except for the body count: Babbitt and three other Trump supporters (one from a heart attack, another from a stroke, a third likely from overdosing on Adderall), a police officer who died of a stroke the next day, and two others who committed suicide in the weeks after.[12]

The hardest thing to understand about January 6 is that the day itself, with its blend of the ludicrous and the terrifying, was a logical product of the current political system. When academics warn that American democracy just might come apart—and as I write this, more than a hundred experts have just signed an open letter declaring exactly that—they usually and understandably focus on the pathologies of the right.[13] See, for instance, Marjorie Taylor Greene. More important, see the ongoing

efforts of Republicans to sow doubts about the voting process while giving state legislatures the authority to undo the results in campaigns that
don't go their way. Invading the Capitol didn't keep Joe Biden out of the
White House, but future historians might see it as a step toward a power
grab that's yet to come, a turning point in the making of a Republican
Party willing to sacrifice democracy at the altar of populism.

If that day ever comes, there will be plenty of fingerprints on the
bloody knife. More than just an indictment of the GOP, it will be
the result of a comprehensive breakdown in American politics. There's the
steady buildup of popular discontent with a status quo where elite self-
dealing and technocratic gatekeeping deny most people real influence
over government. Plus the distorting effects of an electoral system that
all too often converts a strategically placed minority of voters into an
electoral majority. Then there's the failure of self-proclaimed champions
of democracy to assemble a coalition large and durable enough to reform
this antiquated system. And don't forget the polarization machine that
turns campaigns into apocalyptic struggles between good and evil while
holding the results close enough to keep the battle going another day.

Without some kind of push from the outside, Republicans will alternate between demagoguing the latest flash point in the culture wars
and shoveling cash at their megadonors, while Democrats will keep
promising structural transformation only to crash against the limits of
what their increasingly upscale electorate is willing to sacrifice. Slow-
boiling crises will become more difficult to manage, and the requirements of a decent life will keep slipping further out of reach for all but
a dwindling overclass. The whole system will continue decaying, bit by
bit, holding together just enough to continue stumbling along.

Until, one day, it can't.

———————

Which is more or less what critics of American democracy have been
predicting for centuries. "The government will fall into the hands of

the few and the great," announced Melancton Smith, the most incisive Antifederalist. "The common people will divide, and their divisions will be promoted by the others."[14]

More than two hundred years of history have borne out Smith's argument. Race, ethnicity, region, gender, religion, and party loyalty are only a few of the barriers that have kept "the common people" divided. By the end of his fifth and final presidential run, Eugene Debs had reached his own version of Smith's dismal conclusion. "The people can have anything they want," he said. "The trouble is they do not want anything. At least they vote that way on election day."[15]

There's a good reason so many of the stories in this book end with failure: Martin Van Buren watching partisan politics split the country in half; Sumner's party of freedom slipping into oblivion; Mark Hanna, Theodore Roosevelt, and Ruth Hanna McCormick each feeling betrayed by political machines they helped build; W.E.B. Du Bois leaving the United States in disgust; Walter Lippmann tucked away in a nursing home, a relic in his lifetime; Phyllis Schlafly at war with her own family; Barack Obama turned into the polarizer in chief.

Those individual failures are bound up with larger defeats. Jacksonians couldn't stop economic inequality from rising, and they helped spark a civil war they were desperate to avoid. Abolitionists vanquished the slave power, to witness the twinned rise of Jim Crow and the robber barons. Progressives yearning to remake American politics and government instead charted a path that led straight toward bureaucratic dysfunction and toxic polarization. The New Deal order fell apart, and the Reagan revolution careened into a ditch.

If there's an abiding winner in the long history of American democracy, it's the people with money. A flexibly bipartisan group most of the time, the wealthy have a knack for playing the long game. And as the founders recognized, a victory won with the consent of the public carries a unique authority. It's the clearest expression of the tension between radicalism (necessarily a minority politics, otherwise it wouldn't be radical) and democracy (where majorities count for quite a lot).

The case for fatalism, in short, is strong.

————————

But democracy's appeal has always been more about hope than about experience. It's a machine engineered to deny permanent resolutions, to keep the peace by holding out the possibility that conditions will change—which they always do. Often enough it's change for the worse, including the kind that turned Ashli Babbitt from a Capitol Guardian into a cosplay revolutionary. But even if the abortive coup that took Babbitt's life offers a sneak preview of a terrifying future, it's not the only choice.

One could dream up scenarios where the political system heals itself. If both parties decide the working class is up for grabs, a bidding war could break out for blue-collar votes, just as the chance of winning over African Americans in the Eisenhower years pushed Democrats and Republicans to stronger positions on civil rights. Partisans could keep screaming on television while policymakers struck deals away from the cameras.

This, too, has happened before: the political history of neoliberalism is the story of two parties who both learned to love markets while dividing over identity. As politicians today make their way through the wreckage of the neoliberal order, they might run the playbook in reverse, keeping up the culture war while taking a populist turn on economics. Toss in fear of Chinese competition abroad and unrest at home, and the forecast starts to seem possible.

Except policy revolutions don't usually come about because of fuzzy electoral calculations, vague concerns about foreign threats, and the charitable inclinations of elites. Which means that the crisis of democracy requires an authentically democratic solution: a multiracial majority that's large enough to break the partisan deadlock, jolt the legislative process back to life, and mobilize ordinary Americans behind systemic reform.

This coalition would be an updated version of an electoral alliance that's been a recurring character in this book. The framers of the

Constitution worried about its arrival and designed a government to restrain its excesses. The rise of abolition democracy during the Civil War and Reconstruction briefly turned it into an electoral force. It existed at the margins of the Populist movement. Socialists tried in vain to make it the vehicle of a political revolution of the proletariat. During the New Deal years, it transformed the country before collapsing from within. Liberals thought it was within reach under Lyndon Johnson. Then Barack Obama tried to bring it to life, only to have his presidency sucked into the partisan vortex.

Not the most inspiring track record. But there are moments when glimpses of a better future have come into sight, and those moments are worth holding on to.

———————

CAPITAL IS OCCUPIED BY A GENTLE ARMY, ran the *New York Times* headline on the day after the March on Washington for Jobs and Freedom.[16] Point by point, the history of that sunny day in 1963 offered a preemptive rebuttal to the very different occupation that descended on Washington almost fifty years later. Peaceful instead of violent. Disciplined instead of chaotic. Exuberantly multiracial rather than trafficking in Confederate nostalgia.

Put images of the two days alongside each other and you probably wouldn't see anything in common. But the 1963 march succeeded because its main organizers—the Black labor leader A. Philip Randolph, with Bayard Rustin as his second-in-command—tapped into yearnings that motivate every populist revolt. They were outsiders pushing against a reluctant establishment, mixing a radical economic critique (like Rustin, Randolph was a longtime socialist) with the moral fervor awakened by the crusade against segregation. John F. Kennedy tried to persuade Randolph to abandon the idea of a march. So did the head of the NAACP, before jumping on board when he realized it would go ahead without him. The AFL-CIO withheld its endorsement, concerned about the danger of riots. The Pentagon shared that fear, and it kept four thousand troops ready to deploy on the day of the event.[17]

The generals needn't have worried. Rustin's team ensured that a spirit of nonviolent resistance pervaded the day. It was just one more item on a lengthy checklist, from preparing eighty thousand box lunches to rigging up a sound system that reached from the Lincoln Memorial to the Washington Monument. ("We cannot maintain order where people cannot hear," Rustin explained.)[18]

The work paid off with the largest demonstration in American history up to that point. Although popular memory has edited the day down to Martin Luther King Jr. telling the world about a dream, the reverend's secular sermon came near the close of a six-hour ceremony that began with Randolph—who as a young man had campaigned for Eugene Debs in Harlem—announcing that his quarter-million strong audience was "the advance guard of a massive moral revolution" dedicated to abolishing poverty for all Americans.[19]

Writing in *The New Republic*, the liberal journalist Murray Kempton said that "the moment in that afternoon which most strained belief" came after King's address, when Rustin took the podium to list the march's demands, including comprehensive civil rights legislation and guaranteed employment. "Every television camera at the disposal of the networks was upon him," marveled Kempton. "No expression one-tenth so radical has ever been seen or heard by so many Americans."[20]

Not that everyone was persuaded. The organizers refused multiple requests to include women speakers, leading Pauli Murray—a friend of Rustin's and, in 1966, a cofounder of NOW—to complain bitterly about the double burden of Jim Crow and Jane Crow.[21] Malcolm X said that the "Farce on Washington" was stage-managed by the Kennedy administration.[22] And members of Randolph's revolutionary vanguard were quickly reminded of the obstacles that lay in their path. In Baltimore, rocks were hurled at buses returning from the capital. A bullet shot through the window of another as it drove through Philadelphia. Two Black men coming home to Mississippi were set upon by a mob who beat them viciously as police officers looked on.[23]

But a change had taken place. "I haven't been for this civil rights stuff and I've never liked King," an airline stewardess told one reporter, "but I watched him on TV and . . . he made my country seem so beautiful I felt like I wanted to shake his hand."[24] The *Ebony* editor Lerone Bennett focused on a shift he detected in the crowd—"a certain surprise, as though the people had discovered suddenly what they were and what they had."[25] Although polls didn't register an immediate turn in public opinion, the event firmed up support for civil rights on Capitol Hill. After declining to back the march, the AFL-CIO president George Meaney threw himself behind the push for fair employment laws, an important victory for advocates of an alliance between organized labor, African Americans, and liberal reformers—Rustin's "March on Washington coalition."

Rustin himself drew a simple conclusion from the experience: "We cannot talk about the democratic road to freedom unless we are talking about building a majority movement."[26]

Easy to say, exceedingly hard to do, as Rustin learned through painful experience. But in a history that's long on defeat, the March on Washington offers a lesson in what makes democracies thrive. Its seismic impact demonstrates what can happen when reformers treat coalition building—that is, democracy—as both a practical necessity and a moral obligation. To anyone who believes that politics can be more than a way for the few to exploit the many, that example should be a source of comfort.

And, maybe one day, of power.

Notes

INTRODUCTION: THE GOLDEN LINE

1. Eric Lipton, Kenneth P. Vogel, and Lisa Friedman, "E.P.A. Officials Sidelined After Questioning Scott Pruitt," *New York Times*, April 5, 2018, available at https://www.nytimes.com.

2. "Additional Instructions from the Inhabitants of Albemarle," September–October 1776, available at https://founders.archives.gov.

3. "Additional Instructions."

4. Frances E. Lee, *Insecure Majorities: Congress and the Perpetual Campaign* (Chicago, 2016), 18–70.

5. Lee Drutman, *Breaking the Two-Party Doom Loop: The Case for Multiparty Democracy in America* (New York, 2020), 207–209. For more on the distinctive features of the American political system, see Steven L. Taylor, Matthew S. Shugart, Arend Lijphart, and Bernard Grofman, *A Different Democracy: American Government in a Thirty-One-Country Perspective* (New Haven, CT, 2014).

6. For a classic interpretation of realignments, see Walter Dean Burnham, *Critical Elections and the Mainsprings of American Politics* (New York, 1970). Out of many skeptical appraisals, David R. Mayhew, *Electoral Realignments: A Critique of an American Genre* (New Haven, CT, 2002), is the most comprehensive. Also see Allan J. Lichtman, "Critical Election Theory and the Reality of American Presidential Politics, 1916–40," *American Historical Review* 81.2 (1976), 317–351; Richard L. McCormick, "The Realignment Synthesis in American History," *Journal of Interdisciplinary History* 13.1 (1982), 85–105; and Larry M. Bartels, "Electoral Continuity and Change, 1868–1996," *Electoral Studies* 17 (1998), 301–26. For two partial defenses of the concept from political

scientists—who, not coincidentally, are also concerned with policy and institutions, not just electoral returns—see Stephen Skowronek, *The Politics Presidents Make: Leadership from John Adams to Bill Clinton* (Cambridge, MA, 1993), and Elizabeth Sanders, "In Defense of Realignment and Regimes: Why We Need Periodization," *Polity* 37.4 (2005), 536–540. And, for an empirical defense against the prosecution, see James E. Campbell, "Party Systems and Realignments in the United States, 1868–2004," *Social Science History* 30.3 (2006), 359–386. My own definition owes more to Skowronek (who prefers to speak about different "regimes") than to Burnham. Whatever the terminology, the key point is to think systematically about the factors that bind coalitions together, including political parties, governing institutions, ideological convictions, group identity, and perceived self-interest. Each element is a piece in a larger story, informing the others and constantly open to change, but forced together by the necessities of politics. The resulting majority is an artificial creation, but a powerful one nonetheless.

7. Although statistical research is essential for understanding the makeup of coalitions, it's less helpful for explaining why those coalitions emerge in the first place. On the significance of thinkers who produce the narratives, policies, and symbols that mobilize mass audiences, see Jan-Werner Müller, *Contesting Democracy: Political Ideas in Twentieth-Century Europe* (New Haven, CT, 2011), 2–4.

8. I've borrowed the image of a tightrope walker from Michael Harrington, *Fragments of the Century: A Social Autobiography* (New York, 1973), 225. Also see Sean Wilentz's exploration of a similar theme in *The Politicians and the Egalitarians: The Hidden History of American Politics* (New York, 2016).

9. On the development and reception of the "iron law," see David Beetham, "Michels and His Critics," *European Journal of Sociology* 22.1 (1981), 81–99; Natasha Piano, "Revisiting Democratic Elitism: The Italian School of Elitism, American Political Science, and the Problem of Plutocracy," *Journal of Politics* 81.2 (2019), 524–538; and Hugo Drochon, "Robert Michels, the Iron Law of Oligarchy, and Dynamic Democracy," *Constellations* 27.2 (2020), 185–198.

10. There is an immense literature in political science emphasizing both voter ignorance and the critical influence of elites. Christopher H. Achen and Larry M. Bartels, *Democracy for Realists: Why Elections Do Not Produce Responsive Government* (Princeton, NJ, 2016), is the most thorough recent defense of this perspective. My own interpretation puts more emphasis on campaigns, including the positions taken by politicians, on which see Lynn Vavreck, *The Message Matters: The Economy and Presidential Campaigns* (Princeton, NJ, 2009), and Gary Jacobson, "How Do Campaigns Matter?," *Annual Review of Political Science* 18.1 (2015), 31–47.

11. Alexander Hamilton writing as Publius, *Federalist* 22, December 14, 1787, available at https://guides.loc.gov/federalist-papers/full-text.

12. James Madison, *Notes of Debates in the Federal Convention of 1787 Reported by James Madison*, ed. Adrienne Koch (Athens, OH, 1966), 76.

13. This is the central thesis of Edmund S. Morgan, *Inventing the People: The Rise of Popular Sovereignty in England and America* (New York, 1989), esp. 267–288.

14. Richard Hofstadter, *The Progressive Historians: Turner, Beard, Parrington* (New York, 1968), esp. 292–304.

15. John Higham gave these "consensus historians" their name in "The Cult of the American Consensus: Homogenizing Our History," *Commentary*, February 1959, 93–100.

16. For examples of histories underlining continuity over centuries, see Ibram X. Kendi, *Stamped from the Beginning: The Definitive History of Racist Ideas in America* (New York, 2016); Carol Anderson, *White Rage: The Unspoken Truth of Our Racial Divide* (New York, 2016); Heather Cox Richardson, *How the South Won the Civil War: Oligarchy, Democracy, and the Continuing Fight for the Soul of America* (New York, 2020); and Walter Johnson, *The Broken Heart of America: St. Louis and the Violent History of the United States* (New York, 2020). For an important intellectual precursor, see Derrick Bell, *Faces at the Bottom of the Well: The Permanence of Racism* (New York, 1992). Matthew Karp offers a friendly critique in "History as End," *Harper's Magazine*, July 2021, available at https://harpers.org.

17. Which is not to minimize the importance of the various ways the principle of majority rule has been violated, including suffrage restrictions, electoral fraud, and, in some cases, overturning election results by force. Then there are the antimajoritarian features built into the Constitution, along with the Senate's bias against large states and the vagaries of the Electoral College. Given all these qualifiers, it's fair to argue that the United States did not become a truly representative democracy until the abolition of Jim Crow well into the twentieth century, or that it might not even be one today. And for a caustic assessment of whether even a system of universal suffrage qualifies as democratic in any meaningful sense of the term, see Sheldon S. Wolin, *Democracy Incorporated: Managed Democracy and the Specter of Inverted Totalitarianism* (Princeton, NJ, 2008). But after all the caveats have been duly entered, it is still the case that throughout U.S. history securing political power at the national level has required winning a significant degree of popular support at the polls—a fact that, this book argues, is of decisive importance.

18. *Congressional Quarterly's Guide to U.S. Elections*, vol. 1, 6th ed. (Washington, DC, 2010), 780.

19. In arguing that there is no single majority baked into the electorate at a given time, I am defending what political theorists might call an anti-essentialist and post-foundationalist understanding of coalition building—and, ultimately, of democracy. For more on the intellectual underpinning of this argument, see Claude Lefort, *The Political Forms of Modern Society: Bureaucracy, Democracy, Totalitarianism* (Cambridge, MA, 1986), 279–306; F. R. Ankersmit, *Political Representation* (Stanford, CA, 2002), 91–132; Chantal Mouffe, *The Democratic Paradox* (London, 2000), 17–35; Emilia Palonen, "Democracy vs. Demogra-

phy: Rethinking Politics and the People as Debate," *Thesis Eleven*, January 2021, available at https://doi.org/10.1177/0725513620983686.

20. On polarization, see Nolan McCarty, Keith T. Poole, and Howard Rosenthal, *Polarized America: The Dance of Ideology and Unequal Riches*, 2nd ed. (Cambridge, MA, 2016); Lilliana Mason, *Uncivil Agreement: How Politics Became Our Identity* (Chicago, 2018); and Alan I. Abramowitz, *The Great Alignment: Race, Party Transformation, and the Rise of Donald Trump* (New Haven, CT, 2018). Although polarization has received less attention from historians than from political scientists, for a historical perspective, see Kevin M. Kruse and Julian E. Zelizer, *Fault Lines: A History of the United States Since 1974* (New York, 2019).

21. For a prescient early analysis focused on Europe, see Peter Mair, *Ruling the Void: The Hollowing of Western Democracy* (London, 2013).

1. GUARDIANS

1. What Hamilton knew of Publius came from Plutarch, *Lives of the Noble Grecians and Romans*, trans. John Dryden (London, 1683).
2. Hamilton first used the pseudonym in "Publius Letter, I," October 16, 1778, available at https://founders.archives.gov.
3. Garry Wills, *Explaining America: The Federalist*, 2nd ed. (New York, 2001), xvi.
4. Hamilton writing as Publius, *Federalist* 68, March 14, 1788, available at https://guides.loc.gov/federalist-papers/full-text.
5. On the constitutional origins of the two-party system, see John H. Aldrich and Daniel J. Lee, "Why Two Parties? Ambition, Policy, and the Presidency," *Political Science Research and Methods* 4.2 (2016), 275–292.
6. Irving Brant, *James Madison*, 6 vols. (Indianapolis, 1941–61), remains the most comprehensive source on Madison's life. The best recent one-volume biography is Noah Feldman, *The Three Lives of James Madison: Genius, Partisan, President* (New York, 2017). On Madison's political thought, see Lance Banning, *The Sacred Fire of Liberty: James Madison and the Founding of the Federal Republic* (Ithaca, NY, 1995); Colleen A. Sheehan, *The Mind of James Madison: The Legacy of Classical Republicanism* (New York, 2015); and Jack N. Rakove, *A Politician Thinking: The Creative Mind of James Madison* (Norman, OK, 2017).
7. Douglass Adair, ed., "James Madison's Autobiography," *William and Mary Quarterly* 2.2 (1945), 199.
8. Brant, *James Madison*, vol. 2, 33.
9. On Hamilton's life, see Forrest McDonald, *Alexander Hamilton: A Biography* (New York, 1982).
10. On Madison and Hamilton's relationship, see Andrew Shankman, *Original Intents: Hamilton, Jefferson, Madison, and the American Founding* (New York, 2017).
11. Benjamin Franklin to Charles Carroll, May 25, 1789, available at https://franklinpapers.org.

12. James T. Kloppenberg, *Toward Democracy: The Struggle for Self-Rule in European and American Thought* (New York, 2016), 61–93.

13. Robert H. Wiebe, *Self-Rule: A Cultural History of American Democracy* (Chicago, 1995), 30.

14. Kloppenberg, *Toward Democracy*, 329–330.

15. Willi Paul Adams, *The First American Constitutions: Republican Ideology and the Making of the State Constitutions in the Revolution* (Lanham, MD, 1973), 174.

16. Jackson Turner Main, "Government by the People: The American Revolution and the Democratization of the Legislatures," *William and Mary Quarterly* 23.3 (1966), 391–407.

17. Peter H. Lindert and Jeffrey G. Williamson, *Unequal Gains: American Growth and Inequality Since 1700* (Princeton, NJ, 2016), 37, 85.

18. On popular unrest during the critical period and the fears it provoked within the American elite, see Woody Holton, *Unruly Americans and the Origins of the Constitution* (New York, 2008).

19. Alexander Hamilton, "The Continentalist, No. III," August 9, 1781, available at https://founders.archives.gov.

20. James Madison to Thomas Jefferson, July 3, 1784, available at https://founders.archives.gov.

21. Madison, "Vices," available at https://founders.archives.gov.

22. Alexander Hamilton to George Washington, July 3, 1787, available at https://founders.archives.gov.

23. Robert Yates, *Secret Proceedings and Debates of the Convention Assembled at Philadelphia, in the Year 1787, For the Purpose of Forming the Constitution of the United States of America* (Albany, NY, 1821), available at https://founders.archives.gov.

24. Jack N. Rakove, *Original Meanings: Politics and Ideas in the Making of the Constitution* (New York, 1997), 23–93, emphasizes Madison's importance at the convention, still the dominant view among historians. But for important counterweights, see Max M. Edling, *A Revolution in Favor of Government: Origins of the US Constitution and the Making of the American State* (New York, 2003), and Eric Nelson, *The Royalist Revolution: Monarchy and the American Founding* (Cambridge, MA, 2014), 184–228. For Madison's editing of his legacy, see Mary Sarah Bilder, *Madison's Hand: Revising the Constitutional Convention* (Cambridge, MA, 2015).

25. James Madison, "Origin of the Constitutional Convention," December 1835, available at https://founders.archives.gov.

26. Madison, *Notes of Debates in the Federal Convention of 1787*, 136.

27. Madison, *Notes*, 183.

28. Madison, *Notes*, 194.

29. Madison, *Notes*, 196. Like the other founders, however, Madison believed that extreme inequalities of wealth destabilized republics, on which see Ganesh Sitaraman, *The Crisis of the Middle-Class Constitution: Why Economic Inequality Threatens Our Republic* (New York, 2017), 67–104.

30. On the meaning of "democracy" to the founding generation, where it was often contrasted unfavorably to a balanced "republic," see Bernard Bailyn, *The Ideological Origins of the American Revolution* (Cambridge, MA, 1967), 282–301; Gordon S. Wood, *The Creation of the American Republic, 1776–1787* (Chapel Hill, NC, 1969), 222–226; and Seth Cotlar, "Languages of Democracy in America from the Revolution to the Election of 1800," in *Reimagining Democracy in the Age of Revolutions: America, France, Britain, Ireland 1750–1850*, eds. Joanna Innes and Mark Philp (Oxford, 2013), 13–27. For a contrary perspective, arguing that "democracy" and "republic" were more interchangeable than historians typically assume, see Kloppenberg, *Toward Democracy*, 314–315, 328, and 766*n43*. But on the ambiguities of "republic"—a term that could be capacious enough to include even monarchies—see Nelson, *Royalist Revolution*, 115–116 and 206–207. Robert A. Dahl, *How Democratic Is the American Constitution?* (New Haven, CT, 2002), summarizes the features of the Constitution now seen as antidemocratic. On the Constitution as a corrective to the Revolution, see Wood, *Creation of the American Republic*, 471–564; Morgan, *Inventing the People*, 263–306; Terry Bouton, *Taming Democracy: "The People," the Founders, and the Troubled Ending of the American Revolution* (New York, 2007); and Michael J. Klarman, *The Framers' Coup: The Making of the United States Constitution* (New York, 2016).
31. Madison, *Notes*, 41.
32. Sheldon S. Wolin, *Tocqueville Between Two Worlds* (Princeton, NJ, 2001), 59–75, provides a succinct account of republicanism's reconciliation with popular sovereignty. Also see Morgan, *Inventing the People*; Bernard Manin, *The Principles of Representative Government* (New York, 1997); Nadia Urbinati, *Representative Democracy: Principles and Genealogy* (Chicago, 2006); Andreas Kalyvas and Ira Katznelson, *Liberal Beginnings: Making a Republic for the Moderns* (New York, 2008), 88–117; Richard Tuck, *The Sleeping Sovereign: The Invention of Modern Democracy* (New York, 2016); and Hélène Landemore, *Open Democracy: Reinventing Popular Rule for the Twenty-First Century* (Princeton, NJ, 2020), 53–78.
33. On Athens, the classic instance of democracy, see Josiah Ober, *Mass and Elite in Democratic Athens: Rhetoric, Ideology, and the Power of the People* (Princeton, NJ, 1989); Paul Cartledge, *Democracy: A Life* (New York, 2016), 13–227; and Daniela Cammack, "Representation in Ancient Greek Democracy," *History of Political Thought* 42.4 (2021), 567–601. For our purposes, the practice of Athenian democracy is less important than how it was understood by the founders, on which see Jennifer Tolbert Roberts, *Athens on Trial: The Antidemocratic Tradition in Western Thought* (Princeton, NJ, 1994), 179–193.
34. Aristotle, *Politics: A New Translation*, trans. C.D.C. Reeve (Indianapolis, 2017), 96.
35. Madison writing as Publius, *Federalist* 55, February 15, 1788, available at https://guides.loc.gov/federalist-papers/full-text.
36. Pierre Rosanvallon, *Le Peuple Introuvable: Histoire de la Représentation*

Démocratique en France (Paris, 1998), 11*n2*. According to the young Hamilton, "a representative democracy, where the right of election is well secured and regulated & the exercise of the legislative, executive and judiciary authorities, is vested in select persons, chosen really and not nominally by the people, will in my opinion be most likely to be happy, regular and durable." Alexander Hamilton to Gouverneur Morris, May 19, 1777, available at https://founders.archives.gov.

37. Madison writing as Publius, *Federalist* 63, March 1, 1788, available at https://guides.loc.gov/federalist-papers/full-text.
38. Madison, *Notes*, 327. On the debate over the popular vote at the convention, see Alexander Keyssar, *Why Do We Still Have the Electoral College?* (Cambridge, MA, 2020), 19–22. Madison later became more skeptical of direct elections for the president, on which see Donald O. Dewey, "Madison's Views on Electoral Reform," *Western Political Quarterly* 15.1 (1962), 140–145.
39. James Madison, "Vices of the Political System of the United States," April 1787, available at https://founders.archives.gov.
40. Thomas Jefferson to John Adams, October 28, 1813, available at https://founders.archives.gov.
41. Alexander Hamilton writing as Publius, November 21, 1787, available at https://guides.loc.gov/federalist-papers/full-text.
42. Madison, *Notes*, 286.
43. Madison, *Notes*, 505.
44. U.S. Bureau of the Census, *Historical Statistics of the United States, Colonial Times to 1970* (Washington, DC, 1975), 14.
45. George M. Fredrickson, *Racism: A Short History* (Princeton, NJ, 2002), 15–95, is an accessible introduction to racism's early history. For more, see Winthrop D. Jordan, *White over Black: American Attitudes Toward the Negro* (Chapel Hill, NC, 1968); Audrey Smedley, *Race in North America: Origin and Evolution of a Worldview* (Boulder, CO, 1993); and Bruce Dain, *A Hideous Monster of the Mind* (Cambridge, MA, 2002). Which is not to say that racialized thinking and anti-Black prejudice are entirely modern inventions. On their earlier history, see Benjamin Isaac, *The Invention of Racism in Classical Antiquity* (Princeton, NJ, 2004); Miriam Eliav-Feldon, Benjamin Isaac, and Joseph Ziegler, eds., *The Origins of Racism in the West* (New York, 2009); and Denise Eileen McCoskey, *Race: Antiquity and Its Legacy* (New York, 2012).
46. The most sophisticated discussions of the relationship between slavery and American political development are still Barbara J. Fields, "Ideology and Race in American History," in *Region, Race, and Reconstruction: Essays in Honor of C. Vann Woodward*, ed. J. Morgan Kousser and James M. McPherson (New York, 1982), 143–177, and Barbara J. Fields, "Slavery, Race and Ideology in the United States of America," *New Left Review* (1990), 95–118. Also see Edmund S. Morgan, *American Slavery, American Freedom: The Ordeal of Colonial Virginia* (New York, 1975); Paul Finkelman, *Slavery and the Founders: Race*

and Liberty in the Age of Jefferson (Armonk, NY, 1996); John Wood Sweet, *Bodies Politic: Negotiating Race in the American North, 1730–1830* (Baltimore, 2003); Robert Pierce Forbes, "'The Cause of This Blackness': The Early American Republic and the Construction of Race," *American Nineteenth Century History* 13.1 (2012), 65–94; Robert G. Parkinson, *The Common Cause: Creating Race and Nation in the American Revolution* (Chapel Hill, NC, 2016); and Nicholas Guyatt, *Bind Us Apart: How Enlightened Americans Invented Racial Segregation* (New York, 2016).

47. Guyatt, *Bind Us Apart*, 7.

48. Thomas Jefferson, *Notes on the State of Virginia*, ed. William Peden (Chapel Hill, NC, 1982), 138–139, 143 (orig. pub. 1954).

49. On Smith, see Dain, *A Hideous Monster*, 40–80.

50. Samuel Stanhope Smith, *An Essay on the Causes of the Variety of Complexion and Figure in the Human Species: A New Edition, with Some Additional Notes* (Philadelphia, 1788), 23.

51. Jefferson, *Notes*, 138, 143.

52. Jefferson's objections were purely theoretical. His relationship with Sally Hemings began shortly after Smith presented his findings at the American Philosophical Society; Hemings was the child of an interracial relationship, and the half sister of Jefferson's deceased wife. Jefferson named one of their four children James Madison Hemings. There have also been suggestions that Madison fathered a son with one of his slaves, a cook named Coreen, on which see Bettye Kearse, *The Other Madisons: The Lost History of a President's Black Family* (New York, 2020). Unlike with Jefferson and Hemings, there is no DNA evidence to prove (or disprove) the connection. Rumors have also long swirled that William Hamilton, one of New York's foremost Black abolitionists, was the illegitimate son of Alexander Hamilton. On William Hamilton, see Manisha Sinha, *The Slave's Cause: A History of Abolition* (New Haven, CT, 2016), 86, 141–143.

53. Samuel Stanhope Smith, *The Lectures, Corrected and Improved, Which Have Been Delivered for a Series of Years in the College of New Jersey*, vol. 2 (Trenton, NJ, 1812), 176.

54. Smith, *The Lectures*, 178.

55. James Madison to Thomas Jefferson, February 4, 1790, available at https://founders.archives.gov.

56. Madison, *Notes*, 77.

57. James Madison, "Memorandum on an African Colony for Freed Slaves," ca. October 20, 1789, available at https://founders.archives.gov.

58. The other critics were George Mason and Gouverneur Morris.

59. Jessie Serfilippi, "'As Odious and Immoral a Thing': Alexander Hamilton's History as an Enslaver," Schuyler Mansion State Historic Site, 2020.

60. Madison, *Notes*, 224.

61. Madison, *Notes*, 532.

62. For contrasting views of slavery's role at the convention, see David Waldstrei-cher, *Slavery's Constitution: From Revolution to Ratification* (New York, 2010), and Sean Wilentz, *No Property in Man: Slavery and Antislavery at the Nation's Founding* (Cambridge, MA, 2018), 58–114.

63. James Madison to Thomas Jefferson, October 24, 1787, available at https:// founders.archives.gov.

64. Alexander Hamilton, "Conjectures About the New Constitution," September 17–30, 1787, available at https://founders.archives.gov.

65. Madison, *Notes*, 107.

66. On the battle over ratification, see Pauline Maier, *Ratification: The People Debate the Constitution, 1787–1788* (New York, 2010).

67. Hamilton, "Conjectures."

68. Gordon S. Wood, "How Democratic Is the Constitution?," *New York Review of Books*, February 23, 2006, available at https://www.nybooks.com.

69. Richard Beeman, *Plain, Honest Men: The Making of the American Constitution* (New York, 2009), 387.

70. Jonathan Elliot, ed., *The Debates in the Several State Conventions, on the Adoption of the Federal Constitution*, vol. 2 (Washington, DC, 1854), 247–248.

71. John Quincy Adams, "12th," October 12, 1787, available at https://founders .archives.gov.

72. Hamilton writing as Publius, *Federalist* 35, January 5, 1788, available at https://guides.loc.gov/federalist-papers/full-text.

73. Hamilton writing as Publius, *Federalist* 17, December 4, 1787, available at https://guides.loc.gov/federalist-papers/full-text.

74. Madison writing as Publius, *Federalist* 10, November 23, 1787, available at https://guides.loc.gov/federalist-papers/full-text.

75. Alexander Hamilton, "New York Ratifying Convention. First Speech of June 21 (Francis Childs's Version)," June 21, 1788, available at https://founders .archives.gov.

76. For a contrasting interpretation arguing that Hamilton's claim should be taken more or less at face value, see Sitaraman, *Crisis of the Middle-Class Constitution*, 89–94.

77. Stanley Elkins and Eric McKitrick, *The Age of Federalism: The Early American Republic, 1788–1900* (New York, 1993), 114.

78. James Madison to Edmund Randolph, November 23, 1788, available at https://founders.archives.gov.

79. Gaillard Hunt, *The Life of James Madison* (New York, 1902).

80. James Madison to Thomas Jefferson, October 17, 1788, available at https:// founders.archives.gov.

81. James Madison to Thomas Mann Randolph, January 13, 1789, available at https://founders.archives.gov.

82. Feldman, *Three Lives of James Madison*, 255.

83. *Works of Fisher Ames*, vol. 1, ed. Seth Ames (Boston, 1854), 35–36.

84. Gordon S. Wood, *Empire of Liberty: A History of the Early Republic, 1789–1815* (New York, 2009), 92.

85. Alexander Hamilton to ——, December–March 1779–1780, available at https://founders.archives.gov.

86. According to Hamilton, "women and Children are rendered more useful, and the latter more early useful, by manufacturing establishments, than they would otherwise be." Alexander Hamilton, "Final Version of the Report on the Subject of Manufactures," December 5, 1791, available at https://founders .archives.gov.

87. Sean Wilentz, *The Rise of American Democracy: Jefferson to Lincoln* (New York, 2005), 48.

88. Hamilton writing as Publius, *Federalist* 68, March 12, 1788, available at https://guides.loc.gov/federalist-papers/full-text.

89. "Conversation with George Beckwith," October 1789, available at https:// founders.archives.gov.

90. Alexander Hamilton to Edward Carrington, May 26, 1792, available at https://founders.archives.gov.

91. Michael Schwarz, "The Great Divergence Reconsidered: Hamilton, Madison, and U.S.-British Relations, 1783–89," *Journal of the Early Republic* 27.3 (2007), 407.

92. James Madison to Thomas Jefferson, August 8, 1791, available at https:// founders.archives.gov.

93. Alexander Hamilton to George Washington, April 8, 1783, available at https://founders.archives.gov.

94. Hunt, *Life of James Madison*, 165.

95. James Madison, "For the *National Gazette*," January 23, 1792, available at https://founders.archives.gov.

96. James Madison, "For the *National Gazette*," September 22, 1792, available at https://founders.archives.gov.

97. Madison, "*Gazette*," September 22, 1792.

98. Wilentz, *Rise of American Democracy*, 53–71.

99. For a sampling of the rhetoric, see Philip S. Foner, ed., *The Democratic-Republican Societies, 1790–1800: A Documentary Sourcebook of Constitutions, Declarations, Addresses, Resolutions, and Toasts* (Westport, CT, 1976).

100. James Roger Sharp, *American Politics in the Early Republic: The New Nation in Crisis* (New Haven, CT, 1993), 102.

101. Sharp, *Early Republic*, 138–162; Elkins and McKitrick, *Age of Federalism*, 513–528, and Joanne B. Freeman, "The Presidential Election of 1796," in *John Adams and the Founding of the Republic*, ed. Richard Alan Ryerson (Boston, 2001), 142–170.

102. For details on the campaign, see John Ferling, *Adams vs. Jefferson: The Tumultuous Election of 1800* (New York, 2004).

103. Wilentz, *Rise of American Democracy*, 90.

104. Alexander Hamilton, "The Examination Number 1," December 17, 1801, available at https://founders.archives.gov.
105. Alexander Hamilton to James Bayard, April 16–21, 1802, available at https://founders.archives.gov.
106. Alexander Hamilton to Gouverneur Morris, February 29, 1802, available at https://founders.archives.gov.
107. Alexander Hamilton to Theodore Sedgwick, July 10, 1804, available at https://founders.archives.gov.
108. *Life and Letters of Joseph Story*, vol. 1, ed. William W. Story (Boston, 1851), 254.
109. On the synthesis of Hamiltonian means with Jeffersonian ends, see Andrew Shankman, "'A New Thing on Earth': Alexander Hamilton, Pro-Manufacturing Republicans, and the Democratization of American Political Economy," *Journal of the Early Republic* 23.3 (2003), 323–352.
110. Donald Ratcliffe, "The Right to Vote and the Rise of Democracy," *Journal of the Early Republic* 33.2 (2013), 250.
111. "A New Nation Votes: American Election Returns, 1787–1825," available at https://elections.lib.tufts.edu, offers a detailed breakdown of the 1820 results.
112. Lindert and Williamson, *Unequal Gains*, 101, 106.
113. Samuel Griswold Goodrich, *Recollections of a Lifetime: Or, Men and Things I Have Seen* (New York, 1856), 121.

2. PARTISANS

1. Nathaniel Beverley Tucker, *The Partisan Leader* (New York, 1861) (orig. pub. 1836).
2. On the enshrinement of partisan politics and its consequences, see Joel H. Silbey, *The American Political Nation, 1838–1893* (Stanford, CA, 1991), 1–158; Wilentz, *Rise of American Democracy*, 181–518; Jon Grinspan, *The Virgin Vote: How Young Americans Made Democracy Social, Politics Personal, and Voting Popular in the Nineteenth Century* (Chapel Hill, NC, 2016); and Mark R. Cheathem, *The Coming of Democracy: Presidential Campaigning in the Age of Jackson* (Baltimore, 2018). Daniel Peart, *The Era of Experimentation: American Political Practice in the Early Republic* (Charlottesville, VA, 2014), and Daniel Peart and Adam I. P. Smith, eds., *Practicing Democracy: Popular Politics from the Constitution to the Civil War* (Charlottesville, VA, 2015), place Jacksonian democracy at the end of a longer story about expanding suffrage for white men while restricting it for African Americans and women. Rosemarie Zagarri, *Revolutionary Backlash: Women and Politics in the Early American Republic* (Philadelphia, 2007), brings the gendered character of this process into focus. For more on the vote, see Richard Franklin Bensel, *The American Ballot Box in the Mid-Nineteenth Century* (Cambridge, UK, 2004), and Keyssar, *The Right to Vote*, 22–60. The robust turnout rates produced by the rise of parties did not always translate into an informed (or even engaged) electorate, on which see

Glenn C. Altschuler and Stuart Blumin, *Rude Republic: Americans and Their Politics in the Nineteenth Century* (Princeton, NJ, 2000).

3. Wilentz, *Rise of American Democracy*, 425.

4. Donald B. Cole, *Martin Van Buren and the American Political System* (Princeton, NJ, 1984), is the fullest modern treatment of Van Buren's life. Also see Robert V. Remini, *Martin Van Buren and the Making of the Democratic Party* (New York, 1959); John Niven, *Martin Van Buren: The Romantic Age of American Politics* (New York, 1983); Jerome Mushkat and Joseph G. Rayback, *Martin Van Buren: Law, Politics, and the Shaping of Republican Ideology* (DeKalb, IL, 1997); Joel H. Silbey, *Martin Van Buren and the Emergence of American Popular Politics* (New York, 2003); and John L. Brooke, *Columbia Rising: Civil Life on the Upper Hudson from the Revolution to the Age of Jackson* (Chapel Hill, NC, 2013).

5. Martin Van Buren, *Inquiry into the Origin and Course of Political Parties in the United States*, eds. Abraham Van Buren and John Van Buren (New York, 1867), 166.

6. On the acceptance of political parties, see Richard Hofstadter, *The Idea of a Party System: The Rise of Legitimate Opposition in the United States, 1780–1840* (Berkeley, CA, 1969).

7. On the ideas informing "the Democracy," two classic works remain essential: Arthur M. Schlesinger Jr., *The Age of Jackson* (Boston, 1945), and Marvin Meyers, *The Jacksonian Persuasion: Politics and Belief* (Stanford, CA, 1957). David R. Roediger, *The Wages of Whiteness: Race and the Making of the American Working Class* (New York, 1991), 65–92; Harry L. Watson, *Liberty and Power: The Politics of Jacksonian America* (New York, 1990); Jean H. Baker, *Affairs of Party: The Political Culture of Northern Democrats in the Mid-Nineteenth Century* (Ithaca, NY, 1983); Wallace Hettle, *The Peculiar Democracy: Southern Democrats in Peace and Civil War* (Athens, GA, 2001); and Joshua A. Lynn, *Preserving the White Man's Republic: Jacksonian Democracy, Race, and the Transformation of American Conservatism* (Charlottesville, VA, 2019), correct for blind spots on race and gender in midcentury scholarship that look glaring today. Echoes of the bitter partisan debates of the Jacksonian era can still be heard in two major surveys of the period as a whole: Wilentz's *Rise of American Democracy*, which is more sympathetic to the Jacksonians, and Daniel Walker Howe, *What Hath God Wrought: The Transformation of America, 1815–1848* (New York, 2007), which leans toward the Whigs. Joshua A. Lynn and Harry L. Watson provide a judicious assessment of recent scholarship in "Introduction: Race, Politics, and Culture in the Age of Jacksonian 'Democracy,'" *Journal of the Early Republic* 39.1 (2019), 81–87.

8. David Crockett, *The Life of Martin Van Buren: Heir-Apparent to the 'Government' and the Appointed Successor of General Andrew Jackson* (New York, 1845), 19 (orig. pub. 1835).

9. One consequence of secession was a rebirth of interest in *The Partisan Leader*, whose plot turned on Van Buren's efforts to crush an insurrection in Virginia after the rest of the South formed an independent "Southern Confederacy."

"The Yankees," a white character explains, "want to set the negroes free, and to make me a slave": Tucker, *The Partisan Leader*, 14. Tucker's book was republished in both the North and the South during the Civil War. Both editors gave the book a new subtitle—in the North, *A Key to the Disunion Conspiracy*; in the South, *A Novel, and an Apocalypse of the Origins and Struggles of the Southern Confederacy*. For more on Tucker, see Robert Brugger, *Beverley Tucker: Heart over Head in the Old South* (Baltimore, 1978).

10. Martin Van Buren, *The Autobiography of Martin Van Buren*, ed. John C. Fitzpatrick, *Annual Report of the American Historical Association for the Year 1918*, vol. 2 (Washington, DC, 1920), 7.

11. Brooke, *Columbia Rising*, 119.

12. Gore Vidal turned the rumors about Martin Van Buren's parentage into a juicy subplot for a historical novel: *Burr* (New York, 1973).

13. John Quincy Adams, *Diaries*, vol. 2: *1821–1848*, ed. David Waldstreicher (New York, 2017), 380.

14. Van Buren, *Inquiry into the Origin*, 309.

15. Meyers, *Jacksonian Persuasion*, 144.

16. Cole, *Van Buren*, 13, 110.

17. Van Buren, *Autobiography*, 9.

18. Alexis de Tocqueville, *Democracy in America*, vol. 2, trans. Henry Reeve (London, 1835), 181.

19. Howe, *What Hath God Wrought*, 237–241.

20. Nathaniel H. Carter and William L. Stone, eds., *Reports of the Proceedings and Debates of the Convention of 1821* (Albany, NY, 1821), 319. For context, see Wilentz, *Rise of American Democracy*, 190–196.

21. On racial politics at the convention, see Leslie M. Harris, *In the Shadow of Slavery: African Americans in New York City, 1626–1863* (Chicago, 2003), 116–119.

22. Wilentz, *Rise of American Democracy*, 192, 839n29.

23. Carter and Stone, eds., *Convention of 1821*, 190.

24. Harris, *In the Shadow of Slavery*, 119.

25. James Brewer Stewart, "The Emergence of Racial Modernity and the Rise of the White North, 1790–1840," *Journal of the Early Republic* 18.2 (1998), 181–217. On the early campaigns to undo these laws, see Kate Masur, *Until Justice Be Done: America's First Civil Rights Movement, from the Revolution to Reconstruction* (New York, 2021).

26. Cole, *Van Buren*, 105, 107.

27. John Quincy Adams, "First Annual Message," December 6, 1825, available at https://millercenter.org/the-presidency/presidential-speeches.

28. John Quincy Adams, "Inaugural Address," March 4, 1825, available at https://millercenter.org/the-presidency/presidential-speeches.

29. On slavery's growth after the Revolution, see Adam Rothman, *Slave Country: American Expansion and the Origins of the Deep South* (Cambridge, MA, 2007).

30. Thomas Jefferson to John Holmes, April 22, 1820, available at https://www
.loc.gov.

31. John Quincy Adams, "The John Quincy Adams Digital Diary," February 20,
1820, available at https://www.masshist.org/publications/jqadiaries/index
.php.

32. Martin Van Buren to Thomas Ritchie, January 13, 1827, available at http://
vanburenpapers.org/.

33. Van Buren to Ritchie, January 13, 1827.

34. On Calhoun's life, see Robert Elder, *Calhoun: American Heretic* (New York,
2021). Manisha Sinha, *The Counter-Revolution of Slavery: Politics and Ideology
in Antebellum South Carolina* (Chapel Hill, NC, 2000), explores the influence
of South Carolina's distinctive politics on Calhoun.

35. Elder, *Calhoun*, 241.

36. Harriet Martineau, *Retrospect of Western Travel*, vol. 1 (London, 1838), 147.

37. Elder, *Calhoun*, 43.

38. Adams, "Diary," October 15, 1821, available at https://www.masshist.org
/publications/jqadiaries/index.php.

39. Adams, "Diary," January 31, 1826, available at https://www.masshist.org
/publications/jqadiaries/index.php.

40. Adams, "Diary," May 12, 1827, available at https://www.masshist.org
/publications/jqadiaries/index.php.

41. Adams, "Diary," August 5, 1828, available at https://www.masshist.org
/publications/jqadiaries/index.php; 1828 campaign.

42. *Congressional Quarterly's Guide to U.S. Elections*, 756.

43. M. Philip Lucas, "Martin Van Buren as Party Leader and at Andrew Jackson's Right Hand," in *A Companion to the Antebellum Presidents, 1837–1861*, ed.
Joel H. Silbey (Malden, MA, 2014), 109–129.

44. "1840 Democratic Party Platform," *The American Presidency Project*, available
at https://www.presidency.ucsb.edu.

45. On the politics of "Indian removal," see Claudio Saunt, *Unworthy Republic:
The Dispossession of Native Americans and the Road to Indian Territory* (New
York, 2020), 53–83.

46. The phrase was coined by Democratic senator Thomas Hart Benton, on which
see Wilentz, *Rise of American Democracy*, 209.

47. The Jacksonian preoccupation with individual actors, rather than social systems, was part of a larger mental universe reconstructed in Gordon S. Wood,
"Conspiracy and the Paranoid Style: Causality and Deceit in the Eighteenth
Century," *William and Mary Quarterly* 39 (1982), 401–441.

48. On Jackson as slaver, see Mark R. Cheathem, "Andrew Jackson, Slavery, and
Historians," *History Compass* 9.4 (2011), 326–338.

49. Martin Van Buren to Andrew Jackson, December 27, 1832, in *Correspondence of Andrew Jackson*, vol. 4, ed. John Spencer Bassett (Washington, DC,
1929), 507.

50. John Calhoun, *Selected Writings and Speeches*, ed. H. Lee Cheek Jr. (Washington, DC, 2003), 363.

51. Adams, *Diaries*, vol. 2, 273, 547.

52. Calhoun, *Selected Writings*, 28.

53. John C. Calhoun, *The Works of John C. Calhoun*, vol. 6 (New York, 1857), 505.

54. Calhoun, *Selected Writings*, 24.

55. John C. Calhoun, *Speeches of John C. Calhoun: Delivered in the Congress of the United States from 1811 to the Present Time* (New York, 1843), 224.

56. *Congressional Quarterly's Guide to U.S. Elections*, 757.

57. William H. Seward, *An Autobiography of William H. Seward, from 1801 to 1834, with a Memoir of His Life, and Selections from His Letters from 1831 to 1846 by Frederick W. Seward* (New York, 1891), 17.

58. Crockett, *Life of Martin Van Buren*, 13, 18.

59. Schlesinger, *Age of Jackson*, 48.

60. On the economic downturn, see Jessica M. Lepler, *The Many Panics of 1837: People, Politics, and the Creation of a Transatlantic Financial Crisis* (Cambridge, UK, 2013).

61. On the antebellum period's combination of brisk economic growth and rising inequality, see Lindert and Williamson, *Unequal Gains*, 100–101, 114–121.

62. Lindert and Williamson, *Unequal Gains*, 109–111.

63. Lindert and Williamson, *Unequal Gains*, 151.

64. On escalating sectional tension during the Van Buren presidency, see Joanne B. Freeman, *The Field of Blood: Violence in Congress and the Road to Civil War* (New York, 2018), 112–134.

65. Schlesinger, *Age of Jackson*, 265.

66. Anthony F. C. Wallace, *The Long, Bitter Trail: Andrew Jackson and the Indians* (New York, 1993), 92–94.

67. Calhoun, *Speeches*, 225; Martin Van Buren, "Inaugural Address," March 4, 1837, *The American Presidency Project*, available at https://www.presidency.ucsb.edu.

68. Paulding's career deserves more attention from historians, but see Ralph M. Aderman and Wayne R. Kime, *Advocate for America: The Life of James Kirke Paulding* (Susquehanna, PA, 2003), and Michael Black, "James Kirke Paulding: Forgotten American," *New York History* 88.2 (2007), 207–213.

69. J. K. Paulding, *Slavery in the United States* (New York, 1836), 42.

70. Paulding, *Slavery*, 73.

71. Paulding, *Slavery*, 62, 280.

72. On Johnson's private life and its complex public reception, see Guyatt, *Bind Us Apart*, 159–194.

73. Guyatt, *Bind Us Apart*, 184.

74. Eric Lott, *Love and Theft: Blackface Minstrelsy and the American Working Class* (New York, 1993), 15–91.

75. On mob violence in Jacksonian America, see Howe, *What Hath God Wrought*, 430–439.

76. Michael A. Bernstein, "Northern Labor Finds a Southern Champion: A Note on the Radical Democracy, 1839–1848," in *New York and the Rise of American Capitalism: Economic Development and Social and Political History of an American State, 1780–1870*, ed. William Pencak and Conrad Edick Wright (New York, 1989), 146–167.

77. Richard Hofstadter, *The American Political Tradition: And the Men Who Made It* (New York, 1989), 115 (orig. pub. 1948).

78. Gerald S. Henig, "The Jacksonian Attitude Toward Abolitionism in the 1830's," *Tennessee Historical Quarterly* 28.1 (1969), 54.

79. Charles Ogle, *Speech of Mr. Ogle, of Pennsylvania, on the Regal Splendor of the President's Palace* (Boston, 1840).

80. Schlesinger, *Age of Jackson*, 293–294.

81. Ogle, *Speech*.

82. For a comprehensive analysis of American Whiggery, see Michael F. Holt, *The Rise and Fall of the American Whig Party: Jacksonian Politics and the Onset of the Civil War* (New York, 1999). On the ideas that drove a party often derided as intellectually bankrupt, see Daniel Walker Howe, *The Political Culture of the American Whigs* (Chicago, 1979).

83. Crockett, *Life of Martin Van Buren*, 3.

84. Crockett, *Life of Martin Van Buren*, 184.

85. Crockett, *Life of Martin Van Buren*, 177–179.

86. Eric Foner, *The Fiery Trial: Abraham Lincoln and American Slavery* (New York, 2010), 34.

87. Elizabeth R. Varon, "Tippecanoe and the Ladies, Too: White Women and Party Politics in Antebellum Virginia," *Journal of American History* 82.2 (1995), 494–521, and Ronald J. Zboray and Mary Saracino Zboray, "Whig Women, Politics, and Culture in the Campaign of 1840: Three Perspectives from Massachusetts," *Journal of the Early Republic* 17.2 (1997), 277–315.

88. William Nisbet Chambers, "Election of 1840," in Arthur M. Schlesinger Jr. and Fred L. Israel, eds., *History of American Presidential Elections, 1789–1968*, vol. 1 (New York, 1971), 667. On the campaign, see Richard Ellis, *Old Tip vs. the Sly Fox: The 1840 Election and the Making of a Partisan Nation* (Lawrence, KS, 2020).

89. "Voter Turnout in Presidential Elections, 1828–2016," *The American Presidency Project*, available at https://www.presidency.ucsb.edu.

90. "The War of the Five Campaigns," *The United States Magazine and Democratic Review*, June 1840, 486.

91. Van Buren, *Autobiography*, 394.

92. Michael A. Morrison, "Martin Van Buren, the Democracy, and the Partisan Politics of Texas Annexation," *Journal of Southern History* 61.4 (1995), 695–724.

93. Sinha, *Slave's Cause*, 461–478, and Corey M. Brooks, *Liberty Power: Antislavery Third Parties and the Transformation of American Politics* (Chicago, 2016), 15–104.

94. On Democratic antislavery politics, see Jonathan H. Earle, *Jacksonian Antislavery and the Politics of Free Soil, 1824–1854* (Chapel Hill, NC, 2005).

95. Thomas Morris, *Speech of Hon. Thomas Morris, of Ohio, in Reply to the Speech of the Hon. Henry Clay* (New York, 1839).

96. On the population and productivity of the enslaved, see Robin Blackburn, *The American Crucible: Slavery, Emancipation, and Human Rights* (London, 2011), 296–297.

97. And they had a point, on which see Don E. Fehrenbacher, *The Slaveholding Republic: An Account of the United States Government's Relations to Slavery* (New York, 2001). For Southern influence in Washington, see Alice Elizabeth Malavasic, *The F Street Mess: How Southern Senators Rewrote the Kansas-Nebraska Act* (Chapel Hill, NC, 2017).

98. Earle, *Jacksonian Antislavery*, 66.

99. Brooks, *Liberty Power*, 105–124.

100. *The Voice of New York! Proceedings of the Herkimer Mass Convention of Oct. 26, 1847, with the Speeches of David Wilmot, C. C. Cambreleng, John Van Buren, and Others* (Albany, NY, 1847), 14.

101. Wilentz, *Rise of American Democracy*, 598.

102. *Voice of New York*, 1.

103. John Bigelow, *The Life of Samuel J. Tilden*, vol. 1 (New York, 1895), 118.

104. Samuel Tilden, *The Writings and Speeches of Samuel J. Tilden*, vol. 2, ed. John Bigelow (New York, 1885), 569.

105. Cole, *Van Buren*, 413.

106. Sinha, *Slave's Cause*, 478–490, and Brooks, *Liberty Power*, 129–153.

107. Earle, *Jacksonian Antislavery*, 168. Also see Frederick Douglass, *Life and Times of Frederick Douglass* (Boston, 1895), 343–345.

108. Edward L. Pierce, ed., *Memoir and Letters of Charles Sumner*, vol. 3 (Boston, 1893), 168.

109. William Lloyd Garrison, "The New Political Movement," *Liberator*, July 14, 1848, 2.

110. Earle, *Jacksonian Antislavery*, 10, 171.

111. Joel H. Silbey, *The Shrine of Party: Congressional Voting Behavior, 1841–1852* (Pittsburgh, 1967), 121–136, documents the increasing overlap between the two parties.

112. Cole, *Van Buren*, 381.

113. *Letters and Literary Memorials of Samuel J. Tilden*, ed. John Bigelow (New York, 1908), 120.

114. Roger Taney, *The Dred Scott Decision: Opinion of Chief Justice Taney* (New York, 1860), available at https://www.loc.gov.

115. Lynn, *Preserving the White Man's Republic*, 105.

116. Abraham Lincoln to Anson G. Henry, November 19, 1858, available at https://quod.lib.umich.edu/l/lincoln/.

117. Phyllis F. Field, "Republicans and Black Suffrage in New York State: The Grass Roots Response," *Civil War History* 21.2 (June 1975), 141.

118. On Belmont and the politics of capital, see Sven Beckert, *The Monied Metropolis: New York City and the Consolidation of the American Bourgeoisie* (Cambridge, UK, 2001), 78–97.

119. Cole, *Van Buren*, 425.

3. LIBERATORS

1. For a vivid re-creation, see Freeman, *The Field of Blood*, 217–224.

2. Charles Sumner, *Charles Sumner: His Complete Works*, vol. 8, ed. George Frisbie Hoar (Boston, 1900), 256.

3. Charles Sumner, *The Selected Letters of Charles Sumner*, vol. 1, ed. Beverly Wilson Palmer (Boston, 1990), 307.

4. Sumner, *Complete Works*, vol. 9, 238. The *Tribune* was taking poetic license with Sumner, who started his political life as a recognizable kind of educated northeastern Whig.

5. Sumner, *Complete Works*, vol. 1, 305. Sumner frequently revised his speeches after delivery. When possible, I have checked quotations from his complete works against contemporaneous sources, but there is still no guarantee that the citations exactly reflect the words he used at the time. The substance of his message, however, was remarkably consistent over his career.

6. David Herbert Donald's two-volume biography remains the best source for details on Sumner's life: see *Charles Sumner and the Coming of the Civil War* (New York, 1960) and *Charles Sumner and the Rights of Man* (New York, 1970). A major reconsideration of Sumner is overdue, but for more recent (and more sympathetic) accounts, see Frederick J. Blue, *Charles Sumner and the Conscience of the North* (Arlington Heights, IL, 1994); Anne-Marie Taylor, *Young Charles Sumner and the Legacy of the American Enlightenment, 1811–1851* (Amherst, MA, 2001); and Paul D. Escott, *Lincoln's Dilemma: Blair, Sumner, and the Republican Struggle over Racism and Equality in the Civil War Era* (Charlottesville, VA, 2014).

7. Matthew Karp, "The People's Revolution of 1856: Antislavery Populism, National Politics, and the Emergence of the Republican Party," *Journal of the Civil War Era* 9.4 (2019), 533.

8. Sumner, *Complete Works*, vol. 5, 24–25.

9. On the meanings of "liberal" and "liberalism" in the nineteenth century, see Helena Rosenblatt, *The Lost History of Liberalism: From Ancient Rome to the Twenty-First Century* (Princeton, NJ, 2018), 41–193, and William Selinger and Gregory Conti, "The Lost History of *Political* Liberalism," *History of European Ideas* 46 (2020), 341–354.

10. Sumner, *Complete Works*, vol. 20, 85.

11. Donald, *Charles Sumner and the Coming of the Civil War*, 18.

12. Allen Thorndike Rice, ed., *Reminiscences of Abraham Lincoln by Distinguished Men of His Time* (New York, 1888), 223.

13. Donald, *Charles Sumner and the Rights of Man*, 316.

14. Donald, *Charles Sumner and the Rights of Man*, 324.

15. On Story's life, see R. Kent Newmyer, *Supreme Court Justice Joseph Story: Statesman of the Old Republic* (Chapel Hill, NC, 1985).

16. Sumner, *Complete Works*, 267.

17. Donald, *Charles Sumner and the Coming of the Civil War*, 155.

18. Sumner, *Selected Letters*, vol. 1, 13.

19. Sumner, *Selected Letters*, vol. 1, 95.

20. *Memoir and Letters of Charles Sumner*, vol. 1, ed. Edward Pierce (Boston, 1877), 86.

21. Donald, *Charles Sumner and the Coming of the Civil War*, 82.

22. *Memoir and Letters of Charles Sumner*, vol. 1, 134.

23. *Memoir and Letters of Charles Sumner*, vol. 1, 242.

24. *Memoir and Letters of Charles Sumner*, vol. 1, 173.

25. Sumner, *Complete Works*, vol. 1, 307.

26. Sumner, *Selected Letters*, vol. 1, 407.

27. W. Caleb McDaniel, *The Problem of Democracy in the Age of Slavery: Garrisonian Abolitionists and Transatlantic Reform* (Baton Rouge, LA, 2013), 204.

28. Sumner, *Selected Letters*, vol. 1, 144.

29. Sumner, *Complete Works*, vol. 6, 336.

30. Sumner, *Complete Works*, vol. 3, 138–139.

31. Sumner, *Complete Works*, vol. 2, 239.

32. Sumner, *Selected Letters*, vol. 1, 186.

33. Sumner, *Selected Letters*, vol. 1, 180.

34. Sumner, *Selected Letters*, vol. 1, 186.

35. Sumner, *Complete Works*, vol. 2, 236.

36. Taylor, *Young Charles Sumner*, 227.

37. Sumner, *Complete Works*, vol. 2, 233.

38. *Memoir and Letters of Charles Sumner*, vol. 3, 187.

39. Sumner, *Complete Works*, vol. 6, 331.

40. Sumner, *Complete Works*, vol. 1, 326.

41. Masur, *Until Justice Be Done*, 213–214.

42. *Memoir and Letters of Charles Sumner*, vol. 3, 19; David Lee Child, "John Quincy Adams," in *Homes of American Statesmen: With Anecdotical, Personal, and Descriptive Sketches, by Various Writers* (New York, 1854), 333.

43. Donald, *Charles Sumner and the Coming of the Civil War*, 192.

44. *Memoir and Letters of Charles Sumner*, vol. 3, 259.

45. Sumner, *Selected Letters*, vol. 1, 344.

46. Sumner, *Selected Letters*, vol. 1, 345.

47. Sumner, *Selected Letters*, vol. 1, 453.

48. James G. Blaine, *Twenty Years of Congress*, vol. 2 (Norwich, CT, 1886), 545. David M. Potter, *The Impending Crisis, 1848–1861* (New York, 1976), provides an excellent guide to the politics of the 1850s, although it takes an unduly harsh line on Sumner.

49. Sumner, *Complete Works*, vol. 4, 9.

50. William E. Gienapp, *The Origins of the Republican Party, 1852–1856* (New York, 1987), 98.

51. Richard Malcolm Johnson and William Hand Browne, *Life of Alexander H. Stephens* (Philadelphia, 1878), 286.

52. James A. Morone, *Republic of Wrath: How American Politics Turned Tribal, from George Washington to Donald Trump* (New York, 2020), 107.

53. On the collapse of the Know Nothings, see Tyler Anbinder, *Nativism and Slavery: The Northern Know Nothings and the Politics of the 1850s* (New York, 1992), 162–245.

54. *Congressional Quarterly's Guide to U.S. Elections*, 763.

55. Heather Cox Richardson, *To Make Men Free: A History of the Republican Party* (New York, 2014), 8–9.

56. On the making of the Republican Party, see Eric Foner, *Free Soil, Free Labor, Free Men: The Ideology of the Republican Party Before the Civil War* (New York, 1970); Gienapp, *The Origins of the Republican Party*; Michael F. Holt, "Making and Mobilizing the Republican Party, 1854–1860," in *The Birth of the Grand Old Party: The Republicans' First Generation*, ed. Robert F. Engs and Randall M. Miller (Philadelphia, 2002), 29–59; Christopher H. Achen, "Slavery or Sheep?: The Antebellum Realignment in Vermont, 1840–1860" (paper presented at the Midwestern Political Science Association annual meeting, Chicago, April 2012); and Matthew Karp, "The Mass Politics of Antislavery," *Catalyst* 3.2 (2019), 131–178. On the radicalism of the party's antislavery politics, see James Oakes, *Freedom National: The Destruction of Slavery in the United States, 1861–1865* (New York, 2013); *The Scorpion's Sting: Antislavery and the Coming of the Civil War* (New York, 2014); and *The Crooked Path to Abolition: Abraham Lincoln and the Antislavery Constitution* (New York, 2021). Focusing on Sumner, to my eyes, strengthens the case for the antebellum Republican Party's radicalism. But following him into Reconstruction helps answer a puzzle raised by this interpretation—namely, how the revolutionary ambitions of the party's early years gave way to a more cautious politics in the Gilded Age. For an earlier consideration of this theme, see David Montgomery, *Beyond Equality: Labor and the Radical Republicans, 1862–1872* (New York, 1967).

57. Sumner, *Complete Works*, vol. 6, 122.

58. Sumner, *Complete Works*, vol. 5, 50.

59. Sumner, *Complete Works*, vol. 6, 4.

60. Grinspan, *Virgin Vote*, 167n41.

61. Abraham Lincoln, "Speech at Peoria, Illinois," October 16, 1854, *Collected Works of Abraham Lincoln*, vol. 2, available at https://quod.lib.umich.edu/l/lincoln/.

62. Sumner, *Complete Works*, vol. 4, 83.

63. Stephen W. Angell, "A Black Minister Befriends the 'Unquestioned Father of Civil Rights': Henry McNeal Turner, Charles Sumner, and the African-American Quest for Freedom," *Georgia Historical Quarterly* 85.1 (2001), 27–58.

64. Angell, "A Black Minister," 29–30.

65. On the importance of the slave power as a binding agent for the Republican coalition, see William E. Gienapp, "The Republican Party and the Slave Power," in *New Perspectives on Race and Slavery in America*, ed. Robert H. Abzug and Stephen E. Maizlish (Lexington, KY, 1986), 51–78.

66. *Memoir and Letters of Charles Sumner*, vol. 3, 453.

67. Donald, *Charles Sumner and the Coming of the Civil War*, 288.

68. Donald, *Charles Sumner and the Coming of the Civil War*, 286.

69. Donald, *Charles Sumner and the Coming of the Civil War*, 300.

70. The attack also fed into an increasing sense that the regions were becoming distinct cultures, on which see John L. Brooke, *"There Is a North": Fugitive Slaves, Political Crisis, and Cultural Transformation in the Coming of the Civil War* (Amherst, MA, 2019).

71. Sumner's caning is the exception to the rule about his (slight) neglect by historians. In addition to Joanne B. Freeman's account, cited above, see William E. Gienapp, "The Crime Against Sumner: The Caning of Charles Sumner and the Rise of the Republican Party," *Civil War History* 25 (1979), 218–245; Manisha Sinha, "The Caning of Charles Sumner: Slavery, Race, and Ideology in the Age of the Civil War," *Journal of the Early Republic* 23 (2003), 233–262; and Williamjames Hoffer, *The Caning of Charles Sumner: Honor, Idealism, and the Origins of the Civil War* (Baltimore, 2010).

72. *Memoir and Letters of Charles Sumner*, vol. 3, 486n2.

73. Donald, *Charles Sumner and the Coming of the Civil War*, 347.

74. For Lincoln's biography, with particular attention to his relationship with the antislavery movement, see Eric Foner, *Fiery Trial*.

75. Gienapp, *Origins of the Republican Party*, 375.

76. "Constitutional Union Party Platform of 1860," *The American Presidency Project*, available at https://www.presidency.ucsb.edu. For more on the Constitutional Unionists, including a gentle correction to its typical portrayal as a party of old fogeyism, see Peter Knupfer, "Aging Statesmen and the Statesmanship of an Earlier Age: The Generational Roots of the Constitutional Union Party," in *Union and Emancipation: Essays on Politics and Race in the Civil War Era*, ed. David W. Blight and Brooks D. Simpson (Kent, OH, 1997), 57–78.

77. *Congressional Quarterly's Guide to U.S. Elections*, 764.

78. "Voter Turnout in Presidential Elections, 1828–2016," *The American Presidency Project*, available at https://www.presidency.ucsb.edu.

79. Sumner, *Complete Works*, vol. 7, 33.

80. Sumner, *Selected Letters*, vol. 2, 38.

81. The origins of the Civil War might be the single most debated subject in American historiography. For a summary of the field, see Michael E. Woods, "What Twenty-First-Century Historians Have Said About the Causes of Disunion: A Civil War Sesquicentennial Review of the Recent Literature," *Journal of American History* 99.2 (2012), 415–439. Historians almost univer-

sally agree that slavery was (as Lincoln put it) "somehow, the cause of the war." But the exact meaning of "somehow" still provokes controversy. Two rival schools command significant followings. "Fundamentalists" argue that slave and free states were locked in an irrepressible conflict; "revisionists" insist that the sectional truce was shattered by a combination of chance and political miscalculation. Considering Sumner's career suggests a way to bridge the gap between the two. Politics alone couldn't start a war. As Martin Van Buren pointed out, there were plenty of ways to structure political conflict that wouldn't lead to secession. But the emergence of a major antislavery party focused the energy of the political system on a uniquely divisive subject, like starting a fire by holding a magnifying glass up to the sun. Without the passions generated by mass democracy, it's difficult to imagine an overwhelmingly white North taking up arms to end slavery, or the non-slaveholding Southern majority rising up to defend it. It took a combination of democratic politics and an intractable social divide to spark the Civil War, which is why the precipitating event for the breakup of the union was the election of Abraham Lincoln on the back of a Northern majority.

82. Sumner, *Selected Letters*, vol. 2, 24.

83. Sumner, *Selected Letters*, vol. 2, 131.

84. Sumner, *Selected Letters*, vol. 2, 253.

85. Edward Everett Hale, *Memories of a Hundred Years* (New York, 1902), 191.

86. Sumner, *Complete Works*, vol. 9, 200.

87. Sumner, *Complete Works*, vol. 9, 99, 101.

88. Brooks D. Simpson and Jean V. Berlin, eds., *Sherman's Civil War: Selected Correspondence of William T. Sherman, 1860–1865* (Chapel Hill, NC, 1999), 731.

89. The 1864 rebranding drew on earlier efforts to unite Republicans with pro-war Democrats, on which see John Waugh, *Reelecting Lincoln: The Battle for the 1864 Presidency* (Cambridge, MA, 1997), 6, 20–21.

90. "Republican Party Platform of 1864," *The American Presidency Project*, available at https://www.presidency.ucsb.edu.

91. Elise Lemire, *"Miscegenation": Making Race in America* (Philadelphia, 2002), 116–118.

92. *Abraham Africanus: His Secret Life as Revealed Under the Mesmeric Influence* (New York, 1864); *The Lincoln Catechism, Wherein the Eccentricities and Beauties of Despotism Are Fully Set Forth: A Guide to the Presidential Election of 1864* (New York, 1864), 12.

93. Abraham Lincoln, "Response to a Serenade," *Collected Works of Abraham Lincoln*, vol. 8, available at https://quod.lib.umich.edu/l/lincoln/.

94. Sumner, *Complete Works*, vol. 12, 3–4.

95. Sumner, *Selected Letters*, vol. 2, 279.

96. "What the Abolitionists Want to Do for the Country," *New York Herald*, February 25, 1862, 4.

97. Sumner, *Complete Works*, vol. 12, 196.

98. Sumner, *Selected Letters*, vol. 2, 284.

99. *Memoir and Letters of Charles Sumner*, vol. 4, 237.

100. Sumner, *Complete Works*, vol. 12, 290.

101. *Memoir and Letters of Charles Sumner*, vol. 4, 16.

102. William Herndon and Jesse William Weik, *Herndon's Lincoln: The True Story of a Great Life*, vol. 1 (New York, 1889), 182.

103. Sumner, *Selected Letters*, vol. 2, 297–298.

104. John M. Palmer, *Personal Recollections of John M. Palmer: The Story of an Earnest Life* (Cincinnati, 1901), 127.

105. On Johnson's political strategy, see Eric Foner, *Reconstruction: America's Unfinished Revolution, 1863–1877* (New York, 1988), 248–249.

106. Sumner, *Selected Letters*, vol. 2, 342.

107. Sumner, *Selected Letters*, vol. 2, 359.

108. On Reconstruction broadly construed, see Eric Foner, *Reconstruction*, along with Mark Wahlgren Summers, *The Ordeal of Reunion: A New History of Reconstruction* (Chapel Hill, NC, 2014), and Richard White, *The Republic for Which It Stands: The United States During Reconstruction and the Gilded Age, 1865–1896* (New York, 2017), 23–135. For a suggestive discussion of how the field might evolve, see Thomas C. Holt, "The Future of Reconstruction Studies: Political History," *Journal of the Civil War Era* 7.1 (2017), available at https://www.journalofthecivilwarera.org/.

109. Carl Schurz, "Report of Carl Schurz on the States of South Carolina, Georgia, Alabama, Mississippi, and Louisiana," in *Message of the President of the United States* (Washington, DC, 1865), 20, 45.

110. Hans Louis Trefousse, *Impeachment of a President: Andrew Johnson, the Blacks, and Reconstruction* (New York, 1999), 5.

111. Stephens was blocked from entering the Senate, but he later served in the House and as governor of Georgia.

112. Eric Foner, *The Second Founding: How the Civil War and Reconstruction Remade the Constitution* (New York, 2019), xx.

113. Eric Foner, *Reconstruction*, 314, 352–353.

114. Michael Kazin, *American Dreamers: How the Left Changed a Nation* (New York, 2011), 57; Eric Foner, *Reconstruction*, 352–355.

115. Sumner, *Complete Works*, vol. 18, 7.

116. Sumner, *Complete Works*, vol. 14, 297.

117. Sumner, *Complete Works*, vol. 13, 238.

118. Sumner, *Complete Works*, vol. 14, 229.

119. Montgomery, *Beyond Equality*, 26.

120. Lindert and Williamson, *Unequal Gains*, 142–165.

121. Sympathetically summarized in Richardson, *To Make Men Free*, 25–48.

122. Montgomery, *Beyond Equality*, 30.

123. Sumner, *Complete Works*, vol. 15, 363.

124. Sumner, *Complete Works*, vol. 16, 270.

125. Donald, *Charles Sumner and the Rights of Man*, 346n7. Sumner's support for a speedy return to hard currency set him apart from most Radicals and did the greatest damage to Reconstruction's fiscal viability, on which see Nicolas Barreyre, *Gold and Freedom: The Political Economy of Reconstruction* (Charlottesville, VA, 2015), 194–234.

126. Sumner, *Complete Works*, vol. 14, 308.

127. Sumner, *Complete Works*, vol. 16, 134, 147.

128. *Journal of the House of Representatives of the United States*, 40 Cong., 2 Sess. (Washington, DC, 1868), 463.

129. "Another 'Outrage,'" *New York Times*, March 17, 1871, 4.

130. Ron Chernow, *Grant* (New York, 2017), 699.

131. George F. Hoar, *Autobiography of Seventy Years*, vol. 1 (New York, 1903), available at https://www.gutenberg.org/.

132. Hoar, *Autobiography*.

133. Eric Foner, *Reconstruction*, 484–488.

134. Ulysses S. Grant, *The Papers of Ulysses S. Grant*, vol. 29, ed. John Y. Simon (Carbondale, IL, 2008), 464. Like Sumner, Conkling is overdue for a scholarly reconsideration, but see David M. Jordan, *Roscoe Conkling of New York: Voice of the Senate* (Ithaca, NY, 1971).

135. On Sumner, Grant, and the Dominican controversy, see Nicholas Guyatt, "America's Conservatory: Race, Reconstruction, and the Santo Domingo Debate," *Journal of American History* 97.4 (2011), 974–1000.

136. Octavius Brooks Frothingham, *Gerrit Smith: A Biography* (New York, 1878), 331.

137. Sumner, *Complete Works*, vol. 20, 89, 92.

138. Sumner, *Complete Works*, vol. 20, 85.

139. Donald, *Charles Sumner and the Rights of Man*, 146; *Memoir and Letters of Charles Sumner*, vol. 4, 202.

140. *Memoir and Letters of Charles Sumner*, vol. 4, 370.

141. E. L. Godkin, "'Radicals' and 'Conservatives,'" *Nation*, July 13, 1871, 21.

142. On the Liberal Republicans, see Andrew L. Slap, *The Doom of Reconstruction: The Liberal Republicans in the Civil War Era* (New York, 2006). On the reformulation of American liberalism after the Civil War, see John G. Sproat, *"The Best Men": Liberal Reformers in the Gilded Age* (New York, 1968); Eric Foner, *Reconstruction*, 460–511; Nancy Cohen, *The Reconstruction of American Liberalism, 1865–1914* (Chapel Hill, NC, 2002); and Richard White, *Republic for Which It Stands*, 172–212.

143. Francis Parkman, "The Failure of Universal Suffrage," *North American Review* (1878), 4.

144. Slap, *The Doom of Reconstruction*, 165.

145. Donald, *Charles Sumner and the Rights of Man*, 346n7.

146. Carl Schurz, *Speeches, Correspondence, and Political Papers of Carl Schurz*, ed. Frederic Bancroft (New York, 1913), 312.

147. U.S. Constitution, Amendment XV, §1.

148. Donald, *Charles Sumner and the Rights of Man*, 531.
149. Donald, *Charles Sumner and the Rights of Man*, 553.
150. Sumner, *Selected Letters*, vol. 2, 585.
151. Sumner, *Complete Works*, vol. 20, 173.
152. Sumner, *Complete Works*, vol. 20, 192.
153. Sumner, *Complete Works*, vol. 20, 203.
154. Sumner, *Complete Works*, vol. 20, 203, 253.
155. The censure took place later in the year and was focused on an ostensibly unrelated subject. But its real intent—to punish Sumner for turning against the Republican Party—was obvious. See Donald, *Charles Sumner and the Rights of Man*, 564–568.
156. Donald, *Charles Sumner and the Rights of Man*, 553.
157. Donald, *Charles Sumner and the Rights of Man*, 554.
158. Sumner, *Complete Works*, vol. 20, 267.
159. Donald, *Charles Sumner and the Rights of Man*, 585.
160. Jeremiah Chaplin and J. D. Chaplin, *Life of Charles Sumner* (Boston, 1874), 495.
161. Schurz, *Speeches*, vol. 3, 50.
162. "Address of Mr. Lamar of Mississippi," *Memorial Addresses on the Life and Character of Charles Sumner* (Washington, DC, 1874), 59.
163. Mattie Russell, "Why Lamar Eulogized Sumner," *Journal of Southern History* 21.3 (1955), 376.
164. "Address of Mr. Lamar," *Memorial Addresses*, 65.
165. C. Edwards Lester, *Life and Public Services of Charles Sumner* (New York, 1874), 522–533.
166. David W. Blight, *Frederick Douglass: Prophet of Freedom* (New York, 2018), 557, 605.
167. Lindert and Williamson, *Unequal Gains*, 142–193.
168. Adam Winkler, *We the Corporations: How American Businesses Won Their Civil Rights* (New York, 2018), 113–160.
169. On the overdetermined failure of the Radical Republicans, see Daniel Schlozman, *When Movements Anchor Parties: Electoral Alignments in American History* (Princeton, NJ, 2015), 223–241. For a helpful reminder of the limits of the Reconstruction-era federal state, see Gary Gerstle, "The Civil War and State-Building: A Reconsideration," *Journal of the Civil War Era* 7.1 (2017), available at https://www.journalofthecivilwarera.org/.
170. Sumner, *Complete Works*, vol. 2, 239.

4. ORGANIZERS

1. See William Dean Howells, "Are We a Plutocracy?," *North American Review* 158.447 (1894), 185–196.
2. Thomas M. Norwood, *Plutocracy: Or, American White Slavery; A Politico-Social*

Novel (New York, 1888); Otto Frederick Schupphaus, *The Plutocrat: A Drama in Five Acts* (New York, 1892).

3. Frequency of the word "plutocracy" in the American English corpus, 1850–1900, Google Books Ngram Viewer, available at https://books.google.com/ngrams.

4. Robert J. Gordon, *The Rise and Fall of American Growth: The U.S. Standard of Living Since the Civil War* (Princeton, NJ, 2016), 1–318, documents the effects of this economic revolution. Thomas Piketty, *Capital in the Twenty-First Century*, trans. Arthur Goldhammer (Cambridge, MA, 2014), 92–138, places the emergence of steady economic growth into historical context. On the triumph of the corporation, begin with Adolf A. Berle and Gardiner C. Means, *The Modern Corporation and Private Property* (New York, 1932), and Alfred D. Chandler Jr., *The Visible Hand: The Managerial Revolution in American Business* (Cambridge, MA, 1977). Then see Naomi R. Lamoreaux, *The Great Merger Movement in American Business, 1895–1904* (Cambridge, UK, 1985); Olivier Zunz, *Making America Corporate, 1870–1920* (Chicago, 1990); and Richard White, *Railroaded: The Transcontinentals and the Making of Modern America* (New York, 2011). On the political implications of this shift, Martin J. Sklar, *The Corporate Reconstruction of American Capitalism, 1890–1916: The Market, the Law, and Politics* (Cambridge, UK, 1988), is insightful.

5. Lindert and Williamson, *Unequal Gains*, 173.

6. For a rough estimate of millionaires, see George K. Holmes, "The Concentration of Wealth," *Political Science Quarterly* 8.4 (1893), 592–593. On wages, see Richard White, *Republic for Which It Stands*, 702. And on comparative per capita GDP levels, see Jutta Bolt, Marcel Trimmer, and Jan Luiten van Zanden, "GDP per Capita Since 1820," in *How Was Life?: Global Well-Being Since 1820*, ed. Jan Luiten van Zanden et al. (Paris, 2017), 67.

7. On height and life expectancy, see Richard White, *Republic for Which It Stands*, 478–479.

8. Sean Wilentz, *The Politicians and the Egalitarians* (New York, 2016), 233. For a larger historical perspective, see David Montgomery, "Strikes in Nineteenth-Century America," *Social Science History* 4.1 (1980), 81–104. On the other side of the class divide, see Beckert, *Monied Metropolis*, 207–322.

9. Howells, "Are We a Plutocracy?," 189, 191.

10. "Voter Turnout in Presidential Elections, 1828–2016," *The American Presidency Project*, available at https://www.presidency.ucsb.edu.

11. Charles Postel brings all three movements together in *Equality: An American Dilemma, 1866–1896* (New York, 2019). Also see Elizabeth Sanders, *The Roots of Reform: Farmers, Workers, and the American State, 1877–1917* (Chicago, 1999), and Matthew Hild, *Greenbackers, Knights of Labor, and Populists* (Athens, GA, 2007).

12. Douglas G. Baird, "Money and Art in Edward Bellamy's *Looking Backward*," in *Power, Prose, and Purse: Law, Literature, and Economic Transformations*, ed. Alison LaCroix, Saul Levmore, and Martha C. Nussbaum (New York, 2019), 249.

13. On this "two-and-a-half party system," along with Gilded Age political cul-
    ture more generally, see Mark Wahlgren Summers, *Party Games: Getting,
    Keeping, and Using Power in Gilded Age Politics* (Chapel Hill, NC, 2004).

14. Frances E. Lee, "Patronage, Logrolls, and 'Polarization': Congressional Par-
    ties of the Gilded Age, 1876–1896," *Studies in American Political Development*
    30.2 (2016), 116–217.

15. On the ethnocultural basis of Gilded Age voting patterns, see Richard J. Jen-
    sen, *The Winning of the Midwest: Social and Political Conflict, 1888–1896* (Chi-
    cago, 1971); Paul Kleppner, *The Third Electoral System, 1853–1892: Parties,
    Voters, and Political Cultures* (Chapel Hill, NC, 1979); and Richard Oestreicher,
    "Urban Working-Class Political Behavior and Theories of American Electoral
    Politics, 1870–1940," *Journal of American History* 74.4 (1988), 1257–1286.

16. The current gold standard (as it were) among histories of the Populists is
    Charles Postel, *The Populist Vision* (New York, 2007). Among older works,
    see C. Vann Woodward, *Tom Watson: Agrarian Rebel* (New York, 1938), and
    Lawrence Goodwyn, *The Democratic Promise: The Populist Moment in America*
    (New York, 1976). On Bryan, see Michael Kazin, *A Godly Hero: The Life of
    William Jennings Bryan* (New York, 2006). For a useful corrective to histories
    focused on national politics (including this chapter), see Noam Maggor, *Brah-
    min Capitalism: Frontiers of Wealth and Populism in America's First Gilded Age*
    (Cambridge, MA, 2017), 158–177.

17. Between 1950 and 2020, for instance, the Tories held a majority in the United
    Kingdom for forty-five years, Labour for twenty-five. During the same period
    in Germany, the center-right Christian Democratic Union held power for fifty
    years, the Social Democratic Party for twenty. On both cases, Daniel Ziblatt,
    Conservative Parties and the Birth of Democracy (Cambridge, UK, 2017), is in-
    structive. But the U.S. example is distinctive because of the speed of the coun-
    try's industrialization during the Gilded Age and because Americans already
    had a mature party system when the Germans and British were still making
    tentative steps toward mass politics. On "corporate liberalism"—that is, the
    way progressive reforms served business interests—see, in addition to Sklar's
    Corporate Reconstruction of American Capitalism, Gabriel Kolko, *The Triumph of
    Conservatism: A Reinterpretation of American History, 1900–1916* (New York,
    1963), and James Weinstein, *The Corporate Ideal in the Liberal State, 1900–1918*
    (Boston, 1968). For recent scholarship in line with this chapter's emphasis on
    democratic conservatism, see Julia C. Ott, *When Wall Street Met Main Street:
    The Quest for an Investor's Democracy* (Cambridge, MA, 2011), and Matthew
    M. Heidtmann, "'For the Present Orderly Progress': Congressional Conser-
    vatives in an Age of Reform, 1881–1913" (PhD diss., State University of New
    York at Stony Brook, 2020).

18. Walter Dean Burnham, "Periodization Schemes and 'Party Systems': The
    'System of 1896' as a Case in Point," *Social Science History* 10.3 (1986), 263–
    314. R. Hal Williams, *Realigning America: McKinley, Bryan, and the Remark-*

able Election of 1896 (Lawrence, KS, 2010), and Karl Rove, *The Triumph of William McKinley: Why the Election of 1896 Still Matters* (New York, 2015), also see 1896 as a turning point. Paul Kleppner, *Continuity and Change in Electoral Politics, 1893–1928* (Westport, CT, 1987), pushes the analysis well into the twentieth century. For a contrary perspective, emphasizing the durability of Gilded Age voting patterns, see Allan J. Lichtman, "Political Alignment and 'Ethnocultural' Voting in Late Nineteenth Century America," *Journal of Social History* 16.3 (1983), 55–82. Lichtman is right to argue that the shift in coalitions was more an evolution than a revolution, but, in a closely divided electorate, changes on the margin can have an outsize influence on politics and governance—including, in this case, establishing the template for a lasting majority that broke the Gilded Age's partisan deadlock by reducing (though not eliminating) the salience of ethnocultural conflict in party identification.

19. On McKinley's life, see H. Wayne Morgan, *William McKinley and His America*, rev. ed. (Kent, OH, 2003), and Kevin Phillips, *William McKinley* (New York, 2003).

20. Unlike so many of his peers, Hanna has not been made the subject of a doorstop scholarly biography, but see William T. Horner, *Ohio's Kingmaker: Mark Hanna, Man and Myth* (Athens, OH, 2010); Fred Chester Shoemaker, "Mark Hanna and the Transformation of the Republican Party" (PhD diss., The Ohio State University, 1992); and Thomas Edward Felt, "The Rise of Mark Hanna" (PhD diss., Michigan State University, 1961). Also valuable are Joe Mitchell Chapple, *Mark Hanna: His Book* (Boston, 1904); Herbert Croly, *Marcus Alonzo Hanna: His Life and Work* (New York, 1919); and Thomas Beer, *Hanna* (New York, 1929).

21. Alfred Henry Lewis, "Mark Hanna, McKinley and the Labor Unions," *New York Journal*, August 3, 1896.

22. Chapple, *Mark Hanna*, 20.

23. *Denver Times*, August 6, 1902, box 3, Hanna-McCormick Family Papers, 1792–1985, Library of Congress (hereafter cited as Hanna-McCormick Papers).

24. "Mark Hanna Was Here," *Watertown Times*, box 3, Hanna-McCormick Papers.

25. Croly, *Marcus Alonzo Hanna*, 338.

26. Solon Lauer, *Mark Hanna: A Sketch from Life, and Other Essays* (Cleveland, 1901), 124.

27. On Croly's life and his progressive bona fides, see David W. Levy, *Herbert Croly of the New Republic: The Life and Thought of an American Progressive* (Princeton, NJ, 1985).

28. William Allen White, *Masks in a Pageant* (New York, 1928), 227.

29. "Lincoln Day Oration," *Indianapolis Journal*, February 13, 1901, 2.

30. "Dictated Statement of Hon. James R. Garfield," February 14–15, 1906, box 4, Hanna-McCormick Papers.

31. "Dictated Statement of Peter Cox," July 1905, box 4, Hanna-McCormick Papers.
32. Ron Chernow, *Titan: The Life of John D. Rockefeller, Sr.* (New York, 1998), 29.
33. Chernow, *Titan*, 179.
34. Horner, *Ohio's Kingmaker*, 49.
35. On the revolt against democracy in the Gilded Age, see Keyssar, *The Right to Vote*, 94–138; Michael Perman, *Struggle for Mastery: Disfranchisement in the South, 1888–1908* (Chapel Hill, NC, 2001); and Sven Beckert, "Democracy and Its Discontents: Contesting Suffrage Rights in Gilded Age New York," *Past & Present* 174.1 (2002), 116–157.
36. Louis Galambos, "Technology, Political Economy, and Professionalization: Central Themes of the Organizational Synthesis," *Business History Review* 57.4 (1983), 471–493. For a related argument, see Robert H. Wiebe, *The Search for Order, 1877–1920* (New York, 1967).
37. "Statement of Honorable George B. Cortelyou," April 18, 1906, box 4, Hanna-McCormick Papers.
38. Richard White, *Republic for Which It Stands*, 809.
39. Rove, *Triumph of William McKinley*, 102–103.
40. Morgan, *William McKinley and His America*, 133.
41. Boris Heersink and Jeffery A. Jenkins, *Republican Party Politics and the American South, 1865–1968* (Cambridge, UK, 2020), 128–135.
42. Thomas Collier Platt, *The Autobiography of Thomas Collier Platt* (New York, 1910), 331.
43. Rove, *Triumph of William McKinley*, 156.
44. Croly, *Marcus Alonzo Hanna*, 205.
45. James Ford Rhodes, *The McKinley and Roosevelt Administrations* (New York, 1922), 18.
46. J. Robert Constantine, ed., *Letters of Eugene V. Debs: Vol. 1, 1874-1912* (Urbana, IL, 1990), 120.
47. Michael Kazin, *The Populist Persuasion: An American History* (New York, 1995), 44.
48. "Populist Party Platform of 1892," *The American Presidency Project*, available at https://www.presidency.ucsb.edu.
49. Postel, *Populist Vision*, 173–203.
50. "1896 Democratic Party Platform," *The American Presidency Project*, available at https://www.presidency.ucsb.edu.
51. "Dictated Statement of Hon. C. N. Bliss, Edited," October 30, 1905, box 4, Hanna-McCormick Papers.
52. Richard White, *Republic for Which It Stands*, 846.
53. Chernow, *Titan*, 388.
54. Horner, *Ohio's Kingmaker*, 195–200.
55. Williams, *Realigning America*, 134.
56. "Dictated Statement of Charles Dick," February 10, 1906, box 4, Hanna-

McCormick Papers; Rove, *Triumph of William McKinley*, 287, 336. Though American politics remained highly localized, the McKinley campaign was part of a move toward a more nationalized system, on which see Daniel Klinghard, *The Nationalization of American Political Parties, 1880–1896* (Cambridge, UK, 2010). Republican outreach to former Confederates was also part of a strategy to slam the door shut on the racial politics of the Civil War era, on which see David W. Blight, *Race and Reunion: The Civil War in American Memory* (Cambridge, MA, 2001), and Edward J. Blum, *Reforging the White Republic: Race, Religion, and American Nationalism, 1865–1898* (Baton Rouge, LA, 2007).

57. Williams, *Realigning America*, 123.

58. Williams, *Realigning America*, 138–139.

59. G. W. Steevens, *The Land of the Dollar* (London, 1897).

60. Murat Halstead, *Victorious Republicanism and Lives of the Standard-Bearers: McKinley and Roosevelt* (N.p., 1900), 434–435; "Tin Plate Makers Visit M'Kinley," *Scranton Tribune*, July 4, 1896, 1.

61. Williams, *Realigning America*, 149–150.

62. Horner, *Ohio's Kingmaker*, 210.

63. Mark Hanna to G. T. Thomas, November 5, 1897, box 2, Hanna-McCormick Papers.

64. Mark Hanna to William McKinley, November 15, 1898, Series 1, William McKinley Papers, Library of Congress, available at https://www.loc.gov.

65. For more, see Lamoreaux, *Great Merger Movement*.

66. Heersink and Jenkins, *Republican Party Politics and the American South*, 135–138.

67. Chapple, *Mark Hanna*, 30.

68. "Dictated Statement of William Rush Merriam," undated, box 4, Hanna-McCormick Papers.

69. Chapple, *Mark Hanna*, 44. Despite its innocuous title, the National Civic Federation has played a major role in histories of corporate liberalism, beginning with James Weinstein's *The Corporate Ideal in the Liberal State, 1900–1918*. For a thorough analysis of the NCF, see Christopher Cypher, *The National Civic Federation and the Making of a New Liberalism, 1900–1915* (Westport, CT, 2002).

70. Chapple, *Mark Hanna*, 32.

71. Chapple, *Mark Hanna*, 42–43.

72. Mark Hanna, "Speech Delivered in Central Armory, Cleveland," November 1, 1903, box 3, Hanna-McCormick Papers.

73. Mark Hanna, "Speech Delivered at a Tent Meeting in Cleveland," October 10, 1903, box 3, Hanna-McCormick Papers.

74. Mark Hanna, "Speech of Senator Hanna at the Ohio Republican State Convention," June 3, 1903, box 3, Hanna-McCormick Papers.

75. Eric Rauchway, *Murdering McKinley: The Making of Theodore Roosevelt's America* (New York, 2003), 62.

76. For a brief introduction to Roosevelt's life, see Lewis L. Gould, *Theodore Roosevelt* (New York, 2012). As a work of pure narrative, there is no match for Edmund Morris, *The Rise of Theodore Roosevelt* (New York, 1979).

77. Theodore Roosevelt, *Letters and Speeches*, ed. Louis Auchincloss (New York, 2004), 165. For more on Roosevelt's Southern sympathies, see Adam D. Burns, "'Half a Southerner': President Roosevelt, African Americans, and the South," in *A Companion to Theodore Roosevelt*, ed. Serge Ricard (Malden, MA, 2011), 198–215.

78. Theodore Roosevelt, *Theodore Roosevelt: An Autobiography* (New York, 1922), 56.

79. Roosevelt, *Autobiography*, 77.

80. Roosevelt, *Letters and Speeches*, 86, 671.

81. Roosevelt, *Autobiography*, 86.

82. Roosevelt, *Letters and Speeches*, 160. On Roosevelt's political thought, see Jean M. Yarbrough, *Theodore Roosevelt and the American Political Tradition* (Lawrence, KS, 2014).

83. Morris, *Rise of Theodore Roosevelt*, 69–70.

84. Morris, *Rise of Theodore Roosevelt*, 125.

85. Morris, *Rise of Theodore Roosevelt*, 124.

86. Roosevelt, *Letters and Speeches*, 2–3.

87. Poultney Bigelow, *Seventy Summers*, vol. 1 (New York, 1925), 276.

88. Morgan, *McKinley and His America*, 381.

89. Roosevelt, *Letters and Speeches*, 455.

90. Morris, *Rise of Theodore Roosevelt*, 583, 624.

91. Edmund Morris, *Theodore Rex* (New York, 2001), 112–116.

92. See Thomas G. Dyer, *Theodore Roosevelt and the Idea of Race* (Baton Rouge, LA, 1980).

93. Roosevelt, *Letters and Speeches*, 259. On Roosevelt's persistent fears of race suicide, see Dyer, *Roosevelt and the Idea of Race*, 143–167.

94. Roosevelt, *Letters and Speeches*, 465.

95. "Bliss," Hanna-McCormick Papers.

96. Morris, *Theodore Rex*, 299.

97. Morris, *Theodore Rex*, 95.

98. Heersink and Jenkins, *Republican Party Politics and the American South*, 139–142.

99. Morris, *Theodore Rex*, 310–311.

100. "Senator Hanna," February 16, 1904, *New York Times*, 8.

101. Morris, *Theodore Rex*, 332.

102. For a balanced assessment of Roosevelt's presidential record, see Skowronek, *The Politics Presidents Make*, 228–259.

103. M.P. to J. M. Dickinson, January 1, 1904, Series 1, Theodore Roosevelt Papers, Library of Congress, available at https://www.loc.gov.

104. On Taft's biography, with an emphasis on his record as a reformer, see

Jonathan Lurie, *William Howard Taft: The Travails of a Progressive Conserva-tive* (Cambridge, UK, 2011).

105. Roosevelt, *Letters and Speeches*, 648.

106. The scholarship on progressivism is enormous. For our purposes, it helps to divide the field into three camps: progressivism as a political and intellectual movement, progressivism as a political party, and progressivism as a policy regime. The literature in the first category is by far the largest. Richard Hofstadter, *The Age of Reform: From Bryan to F.D.R.* (New York, 1955), 131–271, is still worth consulting. Daniel T. Rodgers's classic essay "In Search of Progressivism," *Reviews in American History* 10.4 (1982), 113–132, identifies major themes in progressive thought. For subsequent overviews, see Eldon J. Eisenach, *The Lost Promise of Progressivism* (Lawrence, KS, 1994); Michael McGerr, *A Fierce Discontent: The Rise and Fall of the Progressive Movement in America, 1870–1920* (New York, 2003); and Maureen A. Flanagan, *America Reformed: Progressives and Progressivisms, 1890s–1920s* (New York, 2006). On the Progressive Party, see John Allen Gable, *The Bull Moose Years: Theodore Roosevelt and the Progressive Party* (Port Washington, NY, 1978), and Sidney M. Milkis, *Theodore Roosevelt, the Progressive Party, and the Transformation of American Democracy* (Lawrence, KS, 2009). On progressivism as a policy regime, see Stephen Skowronek, Stephen M. Engel, and Bruce Ackerman, eds., *The Progressives' Century: Political Reform, Constitutional Government, and the Modern American State* (New Haven, CT, 2016), and Karen Orren and Stephen Skowronek, *The Policy State: An American Predicament* (Cambridge, MA, 2017). Daniel T. Rodgers, *Atlantic Crossings: Social Politics in a Progressive Age* (Cambridge, MA, 1998), links the American enthusiasm for reform to similar campaigns in Europe, rooting both in the common experience of industrialization. He returns to the importance of political economy—and gently chides recent historians for neglecting it—in "Capitalism and Politics in the Progressive Era and in Ours," *Journal of the Gilded Age and Progressive Era* 13.3 (2014), 379–386. On progressivism and race, the subject of much recent scholarship, see David W. Southern, *The Progressive Era and Race: Reaction and Reform, 1900–1917* (Wheeling, IL, 2005), and Thomas C. Leonard, *Illiberal Reformers: Race, Eugenics, and American Economics in the Progressive Era* (Princeton, NJ, 2016). The so-called Claremont School, depicting progressivism as a fundamental break with earlier American governance, echoes (and in some cases anticipated) much of the literature on progressivism as policy regime. For an introduction, see John Marini and Ken Masugi, eds., *The Progressive Revolution in Politics and Political Science: Transforming the American Regime* (Lanham, MD, 2005).

107. On Roosevelt's relationship to the Progressive movement, see Gable, *Bull Moose Years*, and Michael Wolraich, *Unreasonable Men: Theodore Roosevelt and the Republican Rebels Who Created Progressive Politics* (New York, 2014).

108. Theodore Roosevelt, "Purposes and Policies of the Progressive Party" (Washington, DC, 1912), 29.

109. Roosevelt, *Letters and Speeches*, 630.

110. Roosevelt, *Letters and Speeches*, 669.

111. Roosevelt, *Letters and Speeches*, 664.

112. Paul D. Casdorph, *Republicans, Negroes, and Progressives in the South, 1912–1916* (Tuscaloosa, AL, 1981), 1.

113. Roosevelt was building on earlier organizational work done by Robert La Follette's National Progressive Republican League, on which see William B. Murphy, "The National Progressive Republican League and the Elusive Quest for Progressive Unity," *Journal of the Gilded Age and Progressive Era* 8.4 (2009), 515–543.

114. Milkis, *Theodore Roosevelt, the Progressive Party, and the Transformation of American Democracy*, 3.

115. Genevieve Forbes Herrick, "Mrs. McCormick Fights for Toga as Man to Man," *Chicago Tribune*, April 6, 1930.

116. Kristie Miller, *Ruth Hanna McCormick: A Life in Politics* (Albuquerque, 1992), 47.

117. *Congressional Quarterly's Guide to U.S. Elections*, 777.

118. Edmund Morris, *Colonel Roosevelt* (New York, 2010), 253–254.

119. Miller, *Ruth Hanna McCormick*, 76, 97.

120. Miller, *Ruth Hanna McCormick*, 57.

121. Rebecca Edwards, "Pioneers at the Polls: Woman Suffrage in the West," in *Votes for Women: The Struggle for Suffrage Revisited*, ed. Jean H. Baker (New York, 2002), 90–101.

122. "Million Women Can Vote Now," *Daily Gate City*, June 26, 1913.

123. On Paul, see J. D. Zahniser and Amelia R. Fry, *Alice Paul: Claiming Power* (New York, 2014), and Linda Ford, "Alice Paul and the Politics of Nonviolent Protest," in Baker, *Votes for Women*, 174–188.

124. Miller, *Ruth Hanna McCormick*, 2.

125. "Mrs. M'Cormick Will Oppose 'Militancy,'" *Washington Times*, May 24, 1915, 6.

126. For a comparative analysis of the suffrage movement's success, emphasizing the interplay between activists and elected politicians, see Dawn Langan Teele, *Forging the Franchise: The Political Origins of the Women's Vote* (Princeton, NJ, 2018).

127. Miller, *Ruth Hanna McCormick*, 99.

128. On Harding's roots in Ohio politics, see Randolph C. Downes, *The Rise of Warren Gamaliel Harding, 1865–1920* (Athens, OH, 1970).

129. Kristi Andersen, *After Suffrage: Women in Partisan and Electoral Politics Before the New Deal* (Chicago, 1996).

130. Andersen, *After Suffrage*, 142.

131. On the fall in voter turnout, see Michael E. McGerr, *The Decline of Popular Politics: The American North, 1865–1928* (New York, 1986), and Mark Lawrence Kornbluh, *Why America Stopped Voting: The Decline of Participatory De-*

mocracy (New York, 2000)—the first for a historian's perspective, the second for a political scientist's.

132. Data taken from Harold W. Stanley and Richard G. Niemi, *Vital Statistics on American Politics* (Thunder Oaks, CA, 2015), 4–5, and "2016," *The American Presidency Project*, available at https://www.presidency.ucsb.edu.

133. Miller, *Ruth Hanna McCormick*, 162.

134. Miller, *Ruth Hanna McCormick*, 201.

135. There should be more work on Simmons's fascinating, complex life, but see Andrew Kaye, "Roscoe Conkling Simmons and the Significance of African American Oratory," *Historical Journal* 45.1 (2002), 79–102, and "Colonel Roscoe Conkling Simmons and the Mechanics of Black Leadership," *Journal of American Studies* 37.1 (2003), 79–98.

136. Kaye, "Colonel Roscoe Conkling Simmons," 95.

137. Miller, *Ruth Hanna McCormick*, 163.

138. Miller, *Ruth Hanna McCormick*, 188.

139. Miller, *Ruth Hanna McCormick*, 189.

140. Miller, *Ruth Hanna McCormick*, 164.

141. Miller, *Ruth Hanna McCormick*, 199.

142. "National Affairs," *Time*, April 23, 1928, 12.

143. Miller, *Ruth Hanna McCormick*, 207.

144. "Hearings Before a Select Committee on Senatorial Campaign Expenditures," 71 Cong., 2 Sess. (Washington, DC, 1930), 294.

145. Miller, *Ruth Hanna McCormick*, 223.

146. Philip Kinsley, "Ruth M'Cormick by 200,000," *Chicago Daily Tribune*, April 9, 1930.

147. "Ruth McCormick," *Washington Post*, April 10, 1930, 6.

148. "A Woman's Victory," *New York Times*, April 10, 1930, 23.

149. "Ruth Simms Left $6,068,000," *New York Times*, December 21, 1945, 12.

150. Arthur Evans, "Eyes of U.S. on Illinois Race," *Chicago Daily Tribune*, November 2, 1930, 2; Miller, *Ruth Hanna McCormick*, 232–233.

151. "Party Divisions of the House of Representatives, 1789 to Present," *United States House of Representatives*, available at https://history.house.gov/ and "Party Division in the Senate, 1789–Present," *United States Senate*, https://www.senate.gov.

152. Dennis S. Nordin, *The New Deal's Black Congressman: A Life of Arthur Wergs Mitchell* (Columbia, MO, 1997).

153. On the New Deal as an electoral rejoinder to Mark Hanna's GOP, see Schlozman, *When Movements Anchor Parties*, 49–76. For the making of Roosevelt's coalition, see Kristi Andersen, *The Creation of a Democratic Majority, 1928–1936* (Chicago, 1979).

154. Zachary Karabell, *The Last Campaign: How Harry Truman Won the 1948 Election* (New York, 2000), 76–78.

155. Wayne S. Cole, "The America First Committee," *Journal of the Illinois State*

Historical Society 44.4 (1951), 315. She donated at least $4,000, about $75,000 today.

156. S. J. Woolf, "Dewey's Right-Hand Woman," *New York Times*, February 18, 1940, 127. On the relationship between charisma and mass communication, see Jeremy Young, *The Age of Charisma: Leaders, Followers, and Emotions in American Society, 1870–1940* (Cambridge, UK, 2016), 220–272.

157. Miller, *Ruth Hanna McCormick*, 269.

158. "Gov. Dewey Goes Anti-American," *Chicago Daily Tribune*, September 7, 1943, 16.

159. "Dewey Plans to Go to the Record," *Lawrence Journal-World*, October 7, 1944, 3.

INTERLUDE: THE PARTY OF EVERYONE

1. On the composition of the memo and its role in the 1948 campaign, see John Acacia, *Clark Clifford: The Wise Man of Washington* (Lexington, KY, 2009), 119–150.

2. Clark Clifford, "Memorandum for the President," November 19, 1947, Harry S. Truman Presidential Library, available at https://www.trumanlibrary.gov.

3. See, for example, Paul H. Douglas, *The Coming of a New Party* (New York, 1932).

4. James Q. Wilson, *The Amateur Democrat: Club Politics in Three Cities* (Chicago, 1962). For a recent study of the tight connection between political knowledge and ideological consistency, see Michael Barber and Jeremy C. Pope, "Who Is Ideological? Measuring Ideological Consistency in the American Public," *Forum* 16.1 (2018), 97–122.

5. On McCarthy and American political culture at the height of the Cold War, see David M. Oshinsky, *A Conspiracy So Immense: The World of Joe McCarthy* (New York, 2005), 103–300.

6. On Eisenhower's coalition as harbinger of later Republican gains in the South, see Sean Trende, *The Lost Majority: Why the Future of Government Is Up for Grabs—and Who Will Take It* (New York, 2012), 26–37.

7. After a burst of interest in the 1990s and 2000s, histories of conservatism have fallen somewhat out of fashion. For a fair-minded summary of this scholarship, see Kim Phillips-Fein, "Conservatism: A State of the Field," *Journal of American History* 98.3 (2011), 723–743.

8. The phrase popped up in multiple sites. One possible origin was the *Kentucky Irish American*, on which see Clyde F. Crews, ed., *Mike Barry and the Kentucky Irish American: An Anthology* (Lexington, KY, 1995), 52. On the electoral strategy, see Jonathan Bell, "'We Have Run Out of Poor People': The Democratic Party's Crisis of Identity in the 1950s," in *The Liberal Consensus Reconsidered: American Politics and Society in the Postwar Era*, ed. Robert Mason and Iwan Morgan (Gainesville, FL, 2017), 208–226.

9. Maurice Isserman, *The Other American: The Life of Michael Harrington* (New York, 2000), 188–189.

10. Richard M. Scammon and Ben J. Wattenberg, *The Real Majority: The Classic Examination of the American Electorate—With a New Introduction for the 90's* (New York, 1992), 35–44 (orig. pub. 1970). The political scientist Ronald Inglehart identified a similar shift later in the 1970s, arguing that young people across the United States and Europe were moving toward a "post-materialist" politics, on which see Ronald Inglehart, *The Silent Revolution: Changing Values and Political Styles Among Western Publics* (Princeton, NJ, 1977). More recently, see Benjamin Enke, Mattias Polborn, and Alex A. Wu, "Morals as Luxury Goods and Political Polarization," Working Paper, https://my.vanderbilt.edu /polborn/files/2021/10/Morals_polarization.pdf.

11. Burnham, *Critical Elections*, 141, 169.

12. Burnham, *Critical Elections*, 170.

13. Burnham, *Critical Elections*, 169.

14. Daniel Schlozman and Sam Rosenfeld, "Party Blobs and Partisan Visions: Making Sense of Our Hollow Parties," in *The State of the Parties, 2018: The Changing Role of Contemporary American Political Parties*, ed. John C. Green, Daniel J. Coffey, and David B. Cohen (Lanham, MD, 2018), 32–48.

15. For recent examples, see David Broockman and Christopher Skovron, "Bias in Perceptions of Public Opinion Among Political Elites," *American Political Science Review* 112.3 (2018), 542–563; Peter A. Hall and Georgina Evans, "Representation Gaps: Changes in Popular Preferences and the Structure of Partisan Competition in the Developed Democracies" (paper presented at the Annual Meeting of the American Political Science Association, Washington, DC, August 30, 2019), https://scholar.harvard.edu/files/hall/files /evanshall2019.pdf; Gabor Simonovits, Andrew M. Guess, and Jonathan Nagler, "Responsiveness Without Representation: Evidence from Minimum Wage Laws in U.S. States," *American Journal of Political Science* 63.2 (2019), 401–410; Benjamin I. Page, Jason Seawright, and Matthew J. Lacombe, *Billionaires and Stealth Politics* (Chicago, 2019); David Broockman and Neil Malhotra, "What Do Partisan Donors Want?," *Public Opinion Quarterly* 84.1 (2020), 104–118; and Sarah E. Anderson, Daniel M. Butler, and Laurel Harbridge-Yong, *Rejecting Compromise: Legislators' Fear of Primary Voters* (Cambridge, UK, 2020). The term "overclass" was coined by Michael Lind in *The Next American Nation: The New Nationalism and the Fourth American Revolution* (New York, 1995). You can see the influence of this "overclass" in the structure of this book. Only after I finished the first draft did I realize that all four of the main characters in its second half—Du Bois, Lippmann, Schlafly, and Obama—attended graduate school at Harvard.

16. Kevin Phillips, *The Emerging Republican Majority* (Princeton, NJ, 2015), 267 (orig. pub. 1969).

17. On the decline of class-based voting in comparative perspective, see Terry

Nichols Clark, "The Breakdown of Class Politics," *American Sociologist* 34.1/2 (2003), 17–32; Daniel Oesch, "Explaining Workers' Support for Right-Wing Populist Parties in Western Europe: Evidence from Austria, Belgium, France, Norway and Switzerland," *International Political Science Review* 29.3 (2008), 349–373; Geoffrey Evans and James Tilley, "The Depoliticization of Inequality and Redistribution: Explaining the Decline of Class Voting," *Journal of Politics* 74.4 (2012), 963–976; Maria Oskarson and Marie Demker, "Room for Realignment: The Working-Class Sympathy for Sweden Democrats," *Government and Opposition* 50.4 (2015), 629–651; and Amory Gethin, Clara Martínez-Toledano, and Thomas Piketty, "Brahmin Left versus Merchant Right: Changing Political Cleavages in 21 Western Democracies, 1948–2020," *Quarterly Journal of Economics* 137.1 (2022), 1–48. On the relationship between shifts in electoral coalitions and the ideological center of gravity in parties of the left, see Stephanie Mudge, *Leftism Reinvented: Western Parties from Socialism to Neoliberalism* (Cambridge, MA, 2018).

5. PROPHETS

1. Modern scholarship of Du Bois is written in the shadow of David Levering Lewis's magisterial two-volume biography: *W.E.B. Du Bois: Biography of a Race, 1868–1919* (New York, 1993) and *W.E.B. Du Bois: The Fight for Equality and the American Century, 1919–1963* (New York, 2000). Manning Marable, *W.E.B. Du Bois: Black Radical Democrat* (Boston, 1986), provides a streamlined account of Du Bois's life, with a tight focus on politics. Arnold Rampersad, *The Art and Imagination of W.E.B. Du Bois* (Cambridge, MA, 1976), emphasizes Du Bois's literary work. Edward J. Blum, *W.E.B. Du Bois: American Prophet* (Philadelphia, 2007), brings out the spiritual side of a thinker often depicted as remorselessly secular. Kwame Anthony Appiah, *Lines of Descent: W.E.B. Du Bois and the Emergence of Identity* (Cambridge, MA, 2014), elegantly traces Du Bois's evolving views on race. And Du Bois told his own story multiple times in his career, including at length in two books: *Dusk of Dawn* (New York, 1940) and *The Autobiography of W.E.B. Du Bois* (New York, 1968).

2. Du Bois, *Autobiography*, 394.

3. W.E.B. Du Bois, "Politics," *Crisis*, August 1912, 181.

4. Du Bois, "Politics," 181.

5. W.E.B. Du Bois, "Another Open Letter to Woodrow Wilson," *Crisis*, September 1913, 236.

6. On Wilson's appearance in Du Bois's syllabi, see W.E.B. Du Bois, "From McKinley to Wallace: My Fifty Years as an Independent," in *W.E.B. Du Bois: A Reader*, ed. David Levering Lewis (New York, 1995), 484. Wilson and Du Bois were both published in the March 1901 issue of the *Atlantic*, available at https://www.theatlantic.com.

7. W.E.B. Du Bois, *Dusk of Dawn* (New York, 2007), 118 (orig. pub. 1940). On the explosion of racial rioting during the Red Summer, see David F. Krugler, *1919, the Year of Racial Violence: How African Americans Fought Back* (Cambridge, UK, 2014).

8. Although it's no secret that Du Bois cared about politics, scholars have tended to emphasize either his work as a political theorist or as an activist pushing from the outside, not as an electoral strategist. This chapter tries to weave all three together, beginning from Adolph Reed Jr.'s observation that "Du Bois was one of the very most consistently and resolutely *political* of all twentieth-century black American intellectuals": Adolph L. Reed Jr., *W.E.B. Du Bois and American Political Thought: Fabianism and the Color Line* (New York, 1997), 177. On Du Bois's politics, see, in addition to Reed, Robert Gooding-Williams, *In the Shadow of Du Bois: Afro-Modern Political Thought in America* (Cambridge, MA, 2009); Lawrie Balfour, *Democracy's Reconstruction: Thinking Politically with W.E.B. Du Bois* (New York, 2011); and Charles W. Mills, "W.E.B. Du Bois: Black Radical Liberal," in *A Political Companion to W.E.B. Du Bois*, ed. Nick Bromell (Lexington, KY, 2018), 19–56.

9. "Du Bois Out for Bryan," *Baltimore Sun*, August 28, 1908, 5. On Du Bois's Pan-Africanism, see Wilson Jeremiah Moses, "Africa and Pan-Africanism in the Thought of Du Bois," in *The Cambridge Companion to W.E.B. Du Bois*, ed. Shamoon Zamir (Cambridge, UK, 2008), 117–130. Du Bois's attention to the colonial world was part of a larger tradition among African American thinkers, on which see Nikhil Pal Singh, *Black Is a Country: Race and the Unfinished Struggle for Democracy* (Cambridge, MA, 2004), 38–57.

10. Du Bois, *Dusk of Dawn*, 151.

11. King's fuller assessment of Du Bois's appeal to the Talented Tenth was even more scathing: "a tactic for an aristocratic elite who would themselves be benefited while leaving behind the 'untalented' 90 per cent." Martin Luther King Jr., *Why We Can't Wait* (New York, 2000), 19 (orig. pub. 1964). As is discussed later in this chapter, Du Bois's first impressions of King were equally dismissive. King later adopted a more sympathetic view of Du Bois, on which see Martin Luther King Jr., "Honoring Dr. Du Bois," February 23, 1968, W.E.B. Du Bois Papers, University of Massachusetts Amherst, available at https://credo.library.umass.edu (hereafter cited as Du Bois Papers).

12. Du Bois, *Dusk of Dawn*, 14.

13. W.E.B. Du Bois, "What Is the Meaning of 'All Deliberate Speed'?," in *W.E.B. Du Bois: A Reader*, 419.

14. Du Bois returned to the phrase throughout his life. See, for instance, W.E.B. Du Bois, "The Study of the Negro Problems," *Annals of the American Academy of Political and Social Science* 11 (1898), 1–23; "Marxism and the Negro Problem," *Crisis*, May 1933, 103–104; *Dusk of Dawn*, 29–32; and *Autobiography*, 200–217.

15. W.E.B. Du Bois, "Quarter Centennial Celebration of My Life [fragment]," ca. February 23, 1893, Du Bois Papers.

16. "Great Barrington Briefs: September 29, 1883," in *Du Bois on Reform: Periodical-Based Leadership for African Americans*, ed. Brian Johnson (Lanham, MD, 2005), 8–9.

17. Lewis, *Biography of a Race*, 16.

18. "Great Barrington Briefs," 9.

19. Du Bois, "From McKinley to Wallace," 482.

20. Du Bois, "From McKinley to Wallace," 483.

21. Du Bois, *Dusk of Dawn*, 11.

22. W.E.B. Du Bois, "An Open Letter to the Southern People," 1887, Du Bois Papers.

23. Du Bois, *Dusk of Dawn*, 16.

24. Du Bois, *Dusk of Dawn*, 10.

25. Lewis, *Biography of a Race*, 113.

26. "He Is Young Yet," *New York Age*, June 13, 1891, 2.

27. Lewis, *Biography of a Race*, 102.

28. W.E.B. Du Bois, "The Talented Tenth," in *The Negro Problem: A Series of Articles by Representative American Negroes of Today* (New York, 1903), 33.

29. William Ingersoll, "Oral History Interview of W.E.B. Du Bois by William Ingersoll," May 5 to June 6, 1960, Du Bois Papers.

30. Du Bois, "Quarter Centennial Celebration."

31. On Germany's "socialists of the chair"—the tenured radicals of their era—see Erik Grimmer-Solem, *The Rise of Historical Economics and Social Reform in Germany, 1864–1894* (New York, 2003). For their influence on Du Bois, see Barrington S. Edwards, "W.E.B. Du Bois Between Worlds: Berlin, Empirical Social Research, and the Race Question," *Du Bois Review* 3.2 (2006), 395–424.

32. W.E.B. Du Bois, "The Socialism of German Socialists," 1896, Du Bois Papers. On Du Bois's early engagements with Marxism, see Michael J. Saman, "Du Bois and Marx, Du Bois and Marxism," *Du Bois Review* 17.1 (2020), 34–38.

33. For background, see Michael B. Katz and Thomas J. Sugrue, "Introduction: The Context of *The Philadelphia Negro*," in *W.E.B. Du Bois, Race, and the City: The Philadelphia Negro and Its Legacy*, ed. Michael B. Katz and Thomas J. Sugrue (Philadelphia, 1998), 1–37.

34. W.E.B. Du Bois, *The Philadelphia Negro: A Social Study* (Philadelphia, 1899), 7, 310–311.

35. Lewis, *Biography of a Race*, 195. On Du Bois's contributions to sociology, including his research in Atlanta, see Aldon D. Morris, *The Scholar Denied: W.E.B. Du Bois and the Birth of Modern Sociology* (Berkeley, CA, 2015).

36. Photographs of the exhibit are available at https://www.loc.gov/pictures/collection/anedub/.

37. W.E.B. Du Bois, "Strivings of the Negro People," *Atlantic Monthly*, August 1897, available at https://www.theatlantic.com.

38. W.E.B. Du Bois, *The Souls of Black Folk: Essays and Sketches* (Chicago, 1904), 183, 186.

39. Du Bois, *Souls of Black Folk*, 175.

40. Du Bois, *Souls of Black Folk*, 56.

41. Robert Gooding-Williams, "The Du Bois–Washington Debate and the Idea of Dignity," in *To Shape a New World: Essays on the Political Philosophy of Martin Luther King, Jr.*, ed. Tommie Shelby and Brandon M. Terry (Cambridge, MA, 2018), 19–34, brings out the stakes of this conflict.

42. Du Bois, *Autobiography*, 237.

43. Ingersoll, "Oral History," Du Bois Papers.

44. W.E.B. Du Bois, "The Conservation of Races," in *W.E.B. Du Bois: A Reader*, 25.

45. Ingersoll, "Oral History," Du Bois Papers.

46. Du Bois, *Autobiography*, 222.

47. Du Bois, *Souls of Black Folk*, 212.

48. Lewis, *Biography of a Race*, 333.

49. Ingersoll, "Oral History," Du Bois Papers.

50. Du Bois, *Autobiography*, 222.

51. Lewis, *Biography of a Race*, 316–323, 380–383, 439.

52. W.E.B. Du Bois to Isaac Rubinow, November 17, 1904, Du Bois Papers.

53. *Horizon*, February 1907.

54. *Horizon*, November–December 1908.

55. Louis R. Harlan, *Booker T. Washington: The Wizard of Tuskegee* (New York, 1983), 371.

56. Ingersoll, "Oral History," Du Bois Papers.

57. On the NAACP's founding commitment to integration, see Manfred Berg, *The Ticket to Freedom: The NAACP and the Struggle for Black Political Integration* (Gainesville, FL, 2005), 10–39.

58. Du Bois, *Dusk of Dawn*, 111.

59. "Editorial," *Crisis*, November 1910, 10.

60. "Editorial," *Crisis*, November 1910, 11.

61. Lewis, *Fight for Equality*, 2.

62. W.E.B. Du Bois, "The Negro and Communism," in *W.E.B. Du Bois: A Reader*, 588.

63. "Editorial," *Crisis*, July 1918, 111.

64. Marcus Garvey, "W. E. Burghardt Du Bois as a Hater of Black People," in *Selected Writings and Speeches of Marcus Garvey*, ed. Bob Blaisdell (Garden City, NY, 2004), 111.

65. On Du Bois against Garvey and Stoddard, see Matthew Pratt Guterl, *The Color of Race in America* (Cambridge, MA, 2001), 127–146.

66. T. Lothrop Stoddard, *Re-Forging America: The Story of Our Nationhood* (New York, 1927), 302.

67. *Report of a Debate by the Chicago Forum: Shall the Negro Be Encouraged to Seek Cultural Equality?* (Chicago, 1929), 6.

68. W.E.B. Du Bois, "I Bury My Wife," in *W.E.B. Du Bois: A Reader*, 142.

69. Lewis, *Fight for Equality*, 186–187. Although Jackson began her career at *The Crisis* as Du Bois's assistant, she soon moved into writing regularly for the magazine. She also kept up a good relationship with Du Bois, describing him as a mentor and relying on him for letters of recommendation after she left the job. For an example of the work she put into staying in Du Bois's good graces, see Marvel Jackson Cooke to W.E.B. Du Bois, April 5, 1934, Du Bois Papers. On the complex mixture of feminism and Victorian paternalism running through Du Bois's public work, see Hazel V. Carby, *Race Men* (Cambridge, MA, 1998), 9–44; Farah Jasmine Griffin, "Black Feminists and Du Bois: Respectability, Protection, and Beyond," *Annals of the American Academy of Political and Social Science* 568 (2000), 28–40; and Susan Gilman and Alys Eve Weinbaum, eds., *Next to the Color Line: Gender, Sexuality, and W.E.B. Du Bois* (Minneapolis, 2007).

70. Joel Spingarn to W.E.B. Du Bois, October 24, 1914, Du Bois Papers.

71. W.E.B. Du Bois to Joel Spingarn, October 28, 1914, Du Bois Papers.

72. Lewis, *Fight for Equality*, 230.

73. W.E.B. Du Bois, "How Shall We Vote?," *Crisis*, September 1920, 214.

74. W.E.B. Du Bois, "The Negro and Radical Thought," in *W.E.B. Du Bois: A Reader*, 533.

75. W.E.B. Du Bois, "Russia, 1926," in *W.E.B. Du Bois: A Reader*, 582.

76. W.E.B. Du Bois, "Political Rebirth and the Office Seeker," *Crisis*, January 1921, 104.

77. W.E.B. Du Bois, "The Technique of Race Prejudice," *Crisis*, August 1923, 153.

78. W.E.B. Du Bois, "Marxism and the Negro Problem," in *W.E.B. Du Bois: A Reader*, 541.

79. W.E.B. Du Bois, "The Negro Party," *Crisis*, October 1916, 268.

80. Letter from the League for Independent Political Action to W.E.B. Du Bois, February 28, 1930, Du Bois Papers.

81. W.E.B. Du Bois, "Race Relations in the United States," *Annals of the American Academy of Political and Social Science* 140 (1928), 7.

82. W.E.B. Du Bois, "The Negro Politician," in *Writings in Periodicals Edited by W.E.B. Du Bois: Selections from the Crisis*, vol. 2, ed. Herbert Aptheker (Millwood, NY, 1983), 503.

83. W.E.B. Du Bois to Abram Harris, January 16, 1934, Du Bois Papers.

84. Lewis, *Fight for Equality*, 335–341.

85. W.E.B. Du Bois to George Streator, April 24, 1935, Du Bois Papers. For more on Du Bois's Marxist turn, see Saman, "Du Bois and Marx," 40–48.

86. For contrasting assessments of the effort among European Marxists to push beyond materialism while remaining inside the Marxist tradition, see Perry Anderson, *Considerations on Western Marxism* (London, 1976), and Martin

Jay, *Marxism and Totality: The Adventures of a Concept from Lukács to Habermas* (Berkeley, CA, 1984).

87. Du Bois, *Dusk of Dawn*, 148.

88. W.E.B. Du Bois, *Black Reconstruction in America, 1860–1880* (New York, 1992), 700 (orig. pub. 1935). On the "psychological wage," see Eric Arnesen, "Whiteness and the Historian's Imagination," *International Labor and Working-Class History* 60 (2001), 9–13.

89. For a more nuanced interpretation of the socialist position, see William P. Jones, "'Nothing Special to Offer the Negro': Revisiting the 'Debsian View' of the Negro Question," *International Labor and Working-Class History* 74 (2008), 212–224.

90. W.E.B. Du Bois to George Streator, April 24, 1935, Du Bois Papers.

91. On this generational conflict, see Singh, *Black Is a Country*, 70–83.

92. On Streator and his unhappy stint at *The New York Times*, see Frederick James Carroll, "Race News: How Black Reporters and Readers Shaped the Fight for Racial Justice, 1877–1978" (PhD diss., College of William and Mary, 2012), 140–143.

93. George Streator to W.E.B. Du Bois, April 9, 1935, Du Bois Papers.

94. George Streator to W.E.B. Du Bois, April 18, 1935, Du Bois Papers.

95. George Streator to W.E.B. Du Bois, April 29, 1935, Du Bois Papers.

96. W.E.B. Du Bois to George Streator, April 17, 1935, Du Bois Papers.

97. W.E.B. Du Bois to George Streator, April 24, 1935, Du Bois Papers.

98. W.E.B. Du Bois to George Streator, April 24, 1935, Du Bois Papers.

99. W.E.B. Du Bois to George Streator, April 24, 1935, Du Bois Papers.

100. On *Black Reconstruction*'s place in later scholarship, see Eric Foner, "*Black Reconstruction*: An Introduction," *South Atlantic Quarterly* 112.3 (2013), 409–418. Given the scope of the book's coverage and the speed with which Du Bois wrote, it was perhaps inevitable that *Black Reconstruction* would be an untidy book. He repeated passages verbatim (see, for instance, *Black Reconstruction*, 13 and 184) and plagiarized from at least one other work (Charles H. Wesley's *Negro Labor in the United States, 1850–1925*). On Du Bois's plagiarism, which was not limited to *Black Reconstruction*, see Bonnyeclaire Smith-Stewart, "Hypocrisy in the Life of W.E.B. Du Bois," *Phylon* 51.1 (Fall 2014), 64–66.

101. Du Bois, *Black Reconstruction*, 184–186.

102. Du Bois, *Black Reconstruction*, 591.

103. Du Bois, *Black Reconstruction*, 585.

104. Du Bois, *Black Reconstruction*, 605–606.

105. Du Bois, *Black Reconstruction*, 187.

106. Du Bois, *Black Reconstruction*, 358.

107. Du Bois, *Black Reconstruction*, 16.

108. William MacDonald, "The American Negro's Part in Reconstruction Years," *New York Times*, June 16, 1935.

109. W.E.B. Du Bois, "A World Search for Democracy" (unpublished manuscript, 1937), Du Bois Papers.

110. Du Bois, "A World Search for Democracy."

111. See *Newspaper Columns by W.E.B. Du Bois*, vol. 1, ed. Herbert Aptheker (White Plains, NY, 1986), 28.

112. *Congressional Quarterly's Guide to U.S. Elections*, 783.

113. The sample cities are Chicago, Cincinnati, Cleveland, Detroit, New York, Philadelphia, and Pittsburgh: Nancy J. Weiss, *Farewell to the Party of Lincoln: Black Politics in the Age of F.D.R.* (Princeton, NJ, 1983), 207.

114. Ira Katznelson details the New Deal's accommodations with white supremacy in *Fear Itself: The New Deal and the Origins of Our Times* (New York, 2013), 133–222. For a sympathetic assessment of the Democratic record on civil rights, emphasizing the White House's evolution over the course of the 1930s, see Eric Schickler, *Racial Realignment: The Transformation of American Liberalism, 1932–1965* (Princeton, NJ, 2016), 27–80.

115. *Newspaper Columns by W.E.B. Du Bois*, vol. 1, 274.

116. *Newspaper Columns by W.E.B. Du Bois*, vol. 1, 333.

117. W.E.B. Du Bois, *The World and Africa* and *Color and Democracy* (New York, 2007), 296 (orig. pub. 1945).

118. W.E.B. Du Bois, *Behold the Land* (Birmingham, AL, 1946), 7, 11.

119. Du Bois, *Behold the Land*, 13.

120. W.E.B. Du Bois, "The Talented Tenth: Memorial Address," in *W.E.B. Du Bois: A Reader*, 350.

121. Du Bois, "The Talented Tenth: Memorial Address," 351.

122. W.E.B. Du Bois, "The Revelation of Saint Orgne the Damned," June 8, 1938, Du Bois Papers.

123. *Newspaper Columns by W.E.B. Du Bois*, vol. 1, 195.

124. Gunnar Myrdal, *An American Dilemma: The Negro Problem and American Democracy* (New York, 1944). On the production and reception of Myrdal's work, see Maribel Morey, "The Making of *An American Dilemma* (1944): The Carnegie Corporation, Gunnar Myrdal, and the Unlikely Roots of Modern Civil Rights Discourse" (PhD diss., Princeton University, 2013).

125. W.E.B. Du Bois, "Review: *An American Dilemma: The Negro Problem and Modern Democracy*," *Phylon* 5.2 (1944), 121.

126. Lewis, *Fight for Equality*, 497–498.

127. W.E.B. Du Bois, "The Negro Since 1900: A Progress Report," *New York Times*, November 21, 1948, 267, 269.

128. *Newspaper Columns by W.E.B. Du Bois*, vol. 2, 753.

129. The essay was published after the election but written before. See Letter from *The New York Times* to W.E.B. Du Bois, October 21, 1948, Du Bois Papers.

130. *Congressional Quarterly's Guide to U.S. Elections*, 786.

131. W.E.B. Du Bois, "On Stalin," in *W.E.B. Du Bois: A Reader*, 797; *Newspaper Columns by W.E.B. Du Bois*, vol. 2, 905.

132. W.E.B. Du Bois, "Statement in Opposition to the Military Assistance Act of 1949," in *Contributions by W.E.B. Du Bois in Government Publications and Proceedings*, ed. Herbert Aptheker (Millwood, NY, 1981), 393.

133. W.E.B. Du Bois, "What Is Wrong with the United States?," May 13, 1952, Du Bois Papers.

134. Lewis, *Fight for Equality*, 552.

135. W.E.B. Du Bois, "My Campaign for Senator," in *W.E.B. Du Bois: A Reader*, 787.

136. Lewis, *Fight for Equality*, 547–551.

137. Du Bois, *Autobiography*, 393.

138. Du Bois, *Autobiography*, 394, 395.

139. Du Bois, *Autobiography*, 395.

140. *Newspaper Columns by W.E.B. Du Bois*, vol. 2, 967.

141. For a partial selection of scholarship examining the various tributaries that flowed into the civil rights movement, see Adam Fairclough, *To Redeem the Soul of America: The Southern Christian Leadership Conference and Martin Luther King, Jr.* (Athens, GA, 1987); John Dittmer, *Local People: The Struggle for Civil Rights in Mississippi* (Champaign, IL, 1994); Mary L. Dudziak, *Cold War Civil Rights: Race and the Image of American Democracy* (Princeton, NJ, 2000); Martha Biondi, *To Stand and Fight: The Struggle for Civil Rights in Postwar New York City* (Cambridge, MA, 2003); Glenda Elizabeth Gilmore, *Defying Dixie: The Radical Roots of Civil Rights* (New York, 2008); William P. Jones, "The Unknown Origins of the March on Washington: Civil Rights Politics and the Black Working Class," *Labor: Studies in Working Class History of the Americas* 7.3 (2010), 33–52; Dayo F. Gore, *Radicalism at the Crossroads: African American Women Activists in the Cold War* (New York, 2011); Eric Arnesen, "Civil Rights and the Cold War At Home: Post-War Activism, Anticommunism, and the Decline of the Left," *American Communist History* 11.2 (2012), 5–44; Ben Keppel, Brown v. Board *and the Transformation of American Culture: Education and the South in the Age of Desegregation* (Baton Rouge, LA, 2016); Schickler, *Racial Realignment*, 150–236; and Peniel E. Joseph, *The Sword and the Shield: The Revolutionary Lives of Malcolm X and Martin Luther King Jr.* (New York, 2020), 55–80.

142. Lewis, *Fight for Equality*, 557.

143. On *Brown v. Board* and its legacy, see Clayborne Carson, "Two Cheers for *Brown v. Board of Education*," *Journal of American History* 91.1 (2004), 26–31.

144. Ingersoll, "Oral History," Du Bois Papers.

145. W.E.B. Du Bois to Mahatma Gandhi, February 19, 1929, Du Bois Papers.

146. Mahatma Gandhi to W.E.B. Du Bois, May 1, 1929, Du Bois Papers; "To the American Negro," July 1929, Du Bois Papers.

147. W.E.B. Du Bois, "Crusader Without Violence," in *W.E.B. Du Bois: A Reader*, 361.

148. On King's rise to national prominence, see David J. Garrow, *Bearing the Cross: Martin Luther King, Jr., and the Southern Christian Leadership Council* (New York, 2004), 11–82 (orig. pub. 1986).

149. Du Bois, *Autobiography*, 305.

150. W.E.B. Du Bois, "Will the Great Gandhi Live Again?" in *W.E.B. Du Bois: A Reader*, 360.

151. *The Correspondence of W.E.B. Du Bois*, vol. 3, ed. Herbert Aptheker (Amherst, MA, 1973), 225–226.

152. Du Bois, *Autobiography*, 35.

153. Du Bois, *Autobiography*, 47, 50.

154. Du Bois, *Autobiography*, 52.

155. Historians still debate the total number of lost lives. For details, see Cormac Ó Gráda, "Great Leap into Famine: A Review Essay," *Population and Development Review* 37.1 (2011), 191–202.

156. Du Bois, *Autobiography*, 47.

157. Du Bois, *Autobiography*, 53.

158. Lewis, *Fight for Equality*, 563–564; Kenneth Ray Young and Dan S. Green, "Harbinger to Nixon: W.E.B. Du Bois in China," *Negro History Bulletin* 35.6 (1972), 126–127.

159. Du Bois, *Autobiography*, 406.

160. Du Bois, *Autobiography*, 419.

161. W.E.B. Du Bois to Gus Hall, October 1, 1961, Du Bois Papers.

162. Du Bois to Hall, Du Bois Papers.

163. Martin Luther King Jr., "I Have a Dream," in *A Call to Conscience: The Landmark Speeches of Dr. Martin Luther King, Jr.*, ed. Clayborne Carson (New York, 2001), 82.

164. Charles Euchner, *Nobody Turn Me Around: A People's History of the March on Washington* (Boston, 2010), 180.

165. On Rustin's life, see John D'Emilio, *Lost Prophet: The Life and Times of Bayard Rustin* (New York, 2003).

166. Strom Thurmond, *Congressional Record*, 88th Cong., 1st sess. (August 13, 1963), 14837; D'Emilio, *Lost Prophet*, 191, 348.

167. D'Emilio, *Lost Prophet*, 328.

168. Bayard Rustin, "From Protest to Politics: The Future of the Civil Rights Movement," in *Time on Two Crosses: The Collected Writings of Bayard Rustin*, ed. Devon W. Carbado and Donald Weise (New York, 2015), 125.

169. D'Emilio, *Lost Prophet*, 403.

170. Garry Wills, *Nixon Agonistes: The Crisis of the Self-Made Man* (New York, 1969), 265.

171. Phillips, *Emerging Republican Majority*, 205.

172. Phillips, *Emerging Republican Majority*, 17.

173. Roy Wilkins, "We Want Freedom Now!," in *In Search of Democracy: The NAACP Writings of James Weldon Johnson, Walter White, and Roy Wilkins*, ed. Sondra Kathryn Wilson (New York, 1999), 410.

174. An experience described in Eric Foner, "Drum Major for Justice," *Nation*, November 15, 1993, 579.

6. INSIDERS

1. Ronald Steel, *Walter Lippmann and the American Century* (Boston, 1980), is the best source for information on Lippmann's life. Tom Arnold-Forster, "Walter Lippmann and American Democracy" (PhD diss., University of Cambridge, 2018), does equivalent work for Lippmann's thought, tracking his intellectual development through rigorous investigations of turning points in his career. For other surveys of Lippmann's work, see Benjamin F. Wright, *Five Public Philosophies of Walter Lippmann* (Austin, 1973); D. Steven Blum, *Walter Lippmann: Cosmopolitanism in the Century of Total War* (Ithaca, NY, 1984); and Barry D. Riccio, *Walter Lippmann: Odyssey of a Liberal* (New Brunswick, NJ, 1994). Louis Auchincloss, *The House of the Prophet* (Boston, 1980), brings a fictionalized version of Lippmann to life. For a sample of the response to Lippmann's television debut, see Jack Gould, "TV: Distinguished Bow," *New York Times*, July 8, 1960, 49.

2. The word "pundit" had circulated in the American vernacular since the nineteenth century, but *Time*'s usage solidified the modern meaning. See Eric Alterman, *Sound and Fury: The Making of the Punditocracy* (Ithaca, NY, 1999), 21 (orig. pub. 1992). For TR's praise, see *The Letters of Theodore Roosevelt*, vol. 8, ed. Elting Morison (Cambridge, MA, 1954), 872. On FDR, Eisenhower, and Johnson, respectively, see Steel, *Walter Lippmann*, 300, 480–481, and 548.

3. Steel, *Walter Lippmann*, xvi.

4. It is a telling coincidence that the phrase "and the American Century" appears in the title of Steel's Lippmann biography and the subtitle of volume two of David Levering Lewis's Du Bois biography.

5. Steel, *Walter Lippmann*, 196.

6. Walter Lippmann, "Cassandra Speaking," *St. Louis Post-Dispatch*, April 8, 1947, 23.

7. Arnold-Forster, "Walter Lippmann and American Democracy," 119.

8. Frequency of the phrase "liberal democracy" in the American English corpus, 1900–1950, Google Books Ngram Viewer, available at https://books.google .com/ngrams.

9. *The Essential Lippmann: A Political Philosophy for Liberal Democracy*, ed. Clinton Rositer and James Lare (New York, 1963).

10. On the liberal elite at midcentury, see Katznelson, *Fear Itself*, 367–402; Duncan Bell, "What Is Liberalism?," *Political Theory* 42.6 (2014), 682–715; Anne M. Kornhauser, *Debating the American State: Liberal Anxieties and the New Leviathan, 1930–1970* (Philadelphia, 2015); Steve Fraser, *The Limousine Liberal: How an Incendiary Image United the Right and Fractured America* (New York, 2016), 49–103; and David Ciepley, *Liberalism in the Shadow of Totalitarianism* (Cambridge, MA, 2017). For a perceptive contemporary analysis, see C. Wright Mills, "The Conservative Mood," *Dissent*, Winter 1954, 22–31.

11. The concept of a liberal consensus was put on the historiographical map by Godfrey Hodgson in *America in Our Time: From World War II to Nixon—What*

Happened and Why (New York, 1976). Jefferson Cowie, *The Great Exception: The New Deal and the Limits of American Politics* (Princeton, NJ, 2016), synthesizes a generation of scholarship documenting the fragility of the supposed liberal consensus. For a historiographical overview, see Michael Heale, "Historians and the Postwar Consensus," in *The Liberal Consensus Reconsidered: American Politics and Society in the Postwar Era*, ed. Robert Mason and Iwan Morgan (Gainesville, FL, 2017), 29–51. This chapter's analysis of Lippmann builds on this earlier work, illustrating that even one of the icons of the postwar consensus was a recent and far-from-dedicated convert to the cause. (For a similar approach to John Rawls, another totemic figure in the American liberal canon, see Katrina Forrester, *In the Shadow of Justice: Postwar Liberalism and the Remaking of Political Philosophy* [Princeton, NJ, 2019], esp. 1–139.) But looking at the period through Lippmann's eyes also demonstrates the grain of truth in Hodgson's thesis. Lippmann and his peers believed that the boundaries of respectable debate had narrowed after World War II, especially in economic policy and foreign affairs. And because Lippmann's peers included elected officials, policymakers, and prominent journalists, their views had a disproportionate influence on American life.

12. *Conversations with Walter Lippmann* (Boston, 1965), 14.

13. Walter Lippmann, "Conservative, Liberal, Progressive," *New Republic*, January 22, 1962, 11.

14. Rick Perlstein, *Before the Storm: Barry Goldwater and the Unmaking of the American Consensus* (New York, 2001), 72.

15. *Public Persons: Walter Lippmann*, ed. Gilbert A. Harrison (New York, 1976), 126.

16. *Public Philosopher: Selected Letters of Walter Lippmann*, ed. John Morton Blum (New York, 1985), 4.

17. Jeremy McCarter, *Young Radicals: In the War for American Ideals* (New York, 2017), 5.

18. *Public Philosopher*, 6.

19. Barbara and John Ehrenreich, "The Professional-Managerial Class," in *Between Labor and Capital*, ed. Pat Walker (Boston, 1979), 24.

20. James Weinstein, *The Long Detour: The History and Future of the American Left* (Boulder, CO, 2003), 62.

21. Walter Lippmann, interviewed by Dean Albertson, 1950, Columbia University Oral History Collection, Columbia University.

22. Walter Lippmann, "Two Months in Schenectady," *Masses*, April 1912, 13.

23. *Public Philosopher*, 6–8.

24. *Public Philosopher*, 8.

25. Kenneth E. Hendrickson Jr., "George R. Lunn and the Socialist Era in Schenectady, New York, 1909–1916," *New York History* 47.1 (1966), 31.

26. Walter Lippmann, "On Municipal Socialism, 1913: An Analysis of Problems and Strategies," in *Socialism and the Cities: Essays by Walter Lippmann and Others*, ed. Bruce Stave (Port Washington, NY, 1975), 188.

27. Lippmann, "On Municipal Socialism," 189.
28. Lippmann, "On Municipal Socialism," 189.
29. Lippmann, "On Municipal Socialism," 190.
30. Lippmann, "On Municipal Socialism," 196.
31. Walter Lippmann, *A Preface to Politics* (New York, 1913), 317.
32. Lippmann, *Preface to Politics*, 214, 282.
33. Lippmann, *Preface to Politics*, 283.
34. Lippmann, *Preface to Politics*, 54.
35. Lippmann, *Preface to Politics*, 9.
36. Lippmann, *Preface to Politics*, 244.
37. Walter Lippmann, "The Most Dangerous Man in the World," *Everybody's Magazine* 27 (1912), 100.
38. *Public Philosopher*, 17.
39. Steel, *Walter Lippmann*, 79.
40. On Lippmann's place in his new Progressive milieu, see Brad Snyder, *The House of Truth: A Washington Political Salon and the Foundations of American Liberalism* (New York, 2017).
41. *Public Philosopher*, 29.
42. Graham Wallas, *The Great Society: A Psychological Analysis* (London, 1914).
43. Walter Lippmann, *Drift and Mastery: An Attempt to Diagnose the Current Unrest* (New York, 1914), 36, 45.
44. Lippmann, *Drift and Mastery*, 30.
45. Lippmann, *Drift and Mastery*, 182.
46. Lippmann, *Drift and Mastery*, 136.
47. Lippmann, *Drift and Mastery*, 170.
48. Steel, *Walter Lippmann*, 102.
49. Steel, *Walter Lippmann*, 130.
50. Alfred W. Crosby, *America's Forgotten Pandemic: The Influenza of 1918* (Cambridge, UK, 1989), 206–207.
51. Christopher Capozzola, *Uncle Sam Wants You: World War I and the Making of the American Citizen* (New York, 2008), 10.
52. Robert H. Zieger, *The CIO, 1935–1955* (Chapel Hill, NC, 1995), 9.
53. Walter Lippmann, "Liberalism in America," *New Republic*, December 31, 1919, 150.
54. "Central Authority Is Sapping Blood of Nation from States," *Daily Pantagraph*, October 25, 1924, 20.
55. *Public Philosopher*, 176.
56. Walter Lippmann, *The Phantom Public* (New York, 1925), 155.
57. Walter Lippmann, *Public Opinion* (New York, 1922), 312.
58. Lippmann, *Phantom Public*, 126.
59. Lippmann, *Public Opinion*, 219.
60. Lippmann, *Phantom Public*, 128.
61. "Hoover and Smith So Much Alike in Views, Couldn't Tell 'Em Apart," *Decatur Herald*, August 16, 1928, 6.

62. "The Press: Piano v. Bugle," *Time*, March 30, 1931, 20.

63. Walter Lippmann, "The Press and Public Opinion," *Political Science Quarterly* 46.2 (1931), 163.

64. Lippmann, "The Press and Public Opinion," 164.

65. Lippmann, "The Press and Public Opinion," 164–165.

66. Lippmann, "The Press and Public Opinion," 166.

67. Lippmann, "The Press and Public Opinion," 166.

68. Lippmann, "The Press and Public Opinion," 168.

69. Walter Lippmann, "The Bogey of Public Opinion," *Vanity Fair*, December 1931, 51.

70. *Public Philosopher*, 280–281.

71. Walter Lippmann, "How About Newton D. Baker?," *Boston Globe*, June 29, 1932, 16.

72. *Public Philosopher*, 300.

73. Steel, *Walter Lippmann*, 280.

74. On Lippmann's Keynesian turn, see Craufurd D. Goodwin, *Walter Lippmann: Public Economist* (Cambridge, MA, 2014), 118–170.

75. Walter Lippmann, *The Method of Freedom* (New York, 1934), 28, 59.

76. Lippmann, *Method of Freedom*, 38.

77. Eric F. Goldman, *Rendezvous with Destiny: A History of Modern American Reform* (New York, 1952), 373.

78. Walter Lippmann, "The Voter's Choice," *Asheville Citizen*, September 8, 1936, 2.

79. On Mary and Leon Keyserling, see Landon R. Y. Storrs, *The Second Red Scare and the Unmaking of the New Deal Left* (Princeton, NJ, 2012), 107–176. The major biographical works on Mary and Leon were both written prior to the publication of Storrs's revelatory account, when the Keyserlings were seen as (in the words of Kevin Mattson, writing about Leon) "an old New Deal liberal if ever there was one": Kevin Mattson, *When America Was Great: The Fighting Faith of Postwar Liberalism* (New York, 2004), 143. Although these earlier works understate Mary and Leon's youthful radicalism, they are still valuable on their later careers: Willadee Wehmeyer, "Mary Dublin Keyserling: Economist and Social Activist" (PhD diss., University of Missouri–Kansas City, 1995); W. Robert Brazelton, *Designing U.S. Economic Policy: An Analytical Biography of Leon H. Keyserling* (New York, 2001); and Donald K. Pickens, *Leon H. Keyserling: A Progressive Economist* (Lanham, MD, 2009).

80. Storrs, *Second Red Scare*, 153–154.

81. Leon to Father, November 8, 1932, Keyserling Family Papers, College of Charleston (hereafter cited as Keyserling Papers).

82. Leon to Father, July 15, 1933, Keyserling Papers.

83. Leon to Father, June 25, 1934, Keyserling Papers.

84. Storrs, *Second Red Scare*, 161.

85. Storrs, *Second Red Scare*, 152.

86. Storrs, *Second Red Scare*, 161.

87. Federal Reserve Bank of St. Louis and U.S. Office of Management and Budget, Federal Net Outlays as Percent of Gross Domestic Product, available at https://fred.stlouisfed.org.

88. Walter Lippmann, *The Good Society* (Boston, 1938), 225.

89. Lippmann, *The Good Society*, 210.

90. Lippmann, *The Good Society*, 25.

91. On Lippmann and neoliberalism, see Angus Burgin, *The Great Persuasion: Reinventing Free Markets Since the Depression* (Cambridge, MA, 2012), 55–86, along with Ben Jackson, "At the Origins of Neo-liberalism: The Free Economy and the Strong State, 1930–1947," *Historical Journal* 53.1 (2010), 129–151, and "Freedom, the Common Good, and the Rule of Law: Lippmann and Hayek on Economic Planning," *Journal of the History of Ideas* 73.1 (2012), 47–68.

92. Gary Dean Best, "Introduction," in Walter Lippmann, *The Good Society* (New Brunswick, NJ, 2004), xxxviii–xxxix.

93. Burgin, *Great Persuasion*, 85.

94. Arnold-Forster, "Walter Lippmann," 162.

95. Lippmann, *The Good Society*, 186.

96. Lippmann, *The Good Society*, 226–227.

97. Lippmann, *The Good Society*, 251.

98. On World War II's chastening influence for liberal policymakers, see Alan Brinkley, *The End of Reform: New Deal Liberalism in Recession and War* (New York, 1995), 137–200. This newfound humility in elite circles should not obscure the aggressive role played by the public sector in mobilizing for war, on which see Mark R. Wilson, *Destructive Creation: American Business and the Winning of World War II* (Philadelphia, 2016).

99. *Public Philosopher*, 422.

100. Steel, *Lippmann*, 495. For Lippmann's place in postwar Washington, see Gregg Herken, *The Georgetown Set: Friends and Rivals in Cold War Washington* (New York, 2014).

101. The word "meritocracy" was coined by Michael Young in his dystopian novel *The Rise of the Meritocracy* (London, 1958).

102. Arthur M. Schlesinger Jr., *The Politics of Hope* (Boston, 1963), 145.

103. As Schlesinger put it, "the very success of the older liberalism . . . is the essential cause of its present irrelevance," citing as evidence "a nation with nearly sixty-three million men and women at work, a gross national product of 387 billion a year, business progressive and enlightened, trade unions solid and respectable, minimum wages, maximum hours, and farm-price supports written into the law of the land." See Arthur M. Schlesinger Jr., "The Future of Liberalism: The Challenge of Abundance," *Reporter*, May 3, 1956, 9. Schlesinger was more ambivalent about the retreat from the New Deal's emphasis on class than his rhetoric let on, but a combination of factors—including the shock of Eisenhower's two victories, a desire to stay in step with the Democratic Party, and a disdain for intellectual clichés (even when he believed them)—pushed

him toward qualitative liberalism. On this collection of motivations, see Richard Aldous, *Schlesinger: The Imperial Historian* (New York, 2017), 141–181.

104. Arthur M. Schlesinger Jr., "Where Does the Liberal Go from Here?," *New York Times*, August 4, 1957, 180–181.

105. Arthur M. Schlesinger Jr., "Liberalism," *Saturday Review*, June 8, 1957, 37.

106. Schlesinger, "The Future of Liberalism," 9. On qualitative liberalism, see Mattson, *When America Was Great*, 143–171. For wider-ranging assessments of liberalism's pivot away from the language of class, see Gary Gerstle, "The Protean Character of American Liberalism," *American Historical Review* 99.4 (1994), 1043–1073, and Michael McGerr, "Progressivism, Liberalism, and the Rich," in *The Progressives' Century: Political Reform, Constitutional Government, and the Modern American State*, ed. Stephen Skowronek, Stephen M. Engel, and Bruce Ackerman (New Haven, CT, 2016), 243–263. Strikingly, leftists soon embarked on a parallel search for new agents of change to replace the working class. If liberal professors were the unstated heroes for qualitative liberals, then radical students were the explicit vanguard for the New Left. For a contemporary example, see C. Wright Mills's disavowal of the "labour metaphysic" in "Letter to the New Left," *New Left Review*, September/October 1960, 18–23. On the troubled relationship between the Old and New Lefts, see Maurice Isserman, *If I Had a Hammer: The Death of the Old Left and the Birth of the New* (New York, 1987).

107. Given the later importance of racial justice to liberalism's evolution, it's striking how little attention the concept received from major white liberal intellectuals at the time. Schlesinger, for instance, devoted just a few pages to the subject in *The Vital Center* and happily supported Adlai Stevenson despite the candidate's repeated waffling on civil rights. See Arthur M. Schlesinger Jr., *The Vital Center: The Politics of Freedom* (Boston, 1949), 189–191.

108. Walter Lippmann, *Essays in the Public Philosophy* (New Brunswick, NJ, 2009), 5 (orig. pub. 1955).

109. Storrs, *Second Red Scare*, 171.

110. Leon Keyserling, "Eggheads and Politics," *New Republic*, October 27, 1958, 17.

111. Steel, *Walter Lippmann*, 429.

112. Walter Lippmann, "McCarthy Would Be GOP Dictator," *Decatur Daily Review*, March 2, 1954, 6; Walter Lippmann, "Nightmare in Washington," *Hartford Courant*, May 3, 1954, 8.

113. John Early Haynes, Harvey Klehr, and Alexander Vassiliev, *Spies: The Rise and Fall of the KGB in America* (New Haven, CT, 2009), 174–178.

114. Storrs, *Second Red Scare*, 127–129.

115. Storrs, *Second Red Scare*, 135, 158.

116. "Ho Hum," *Washington Post*, February 12, 1952, 8.

117. Storrs, *Second Red Scare*, 143. With Eisenhower about to take office, both Mary and Leon would likely have been asked to resign, even without the loyalty investigation. But under security regulations adopted by the Eisenhower

White House in April 1953, Mary's record would probably have driven both of them out of government.

118. Storrs, *Second Red Scare*, 170.

119. Perlstein, *Before the Storm*, 217.

120. William F. Buckley Jr., "Our Mission Statement," *National Review*, November 19, 1955, available at https://www.nationalreview.com. To ratchet up the irony, Buckley's positioning—a gadfly taking on an establishment he was ensconced within—recalled nothing so much as a young Walter Lippmann.

121. Walter Lippmann, introduction to *The Chicago Race Riots: July, 1919*, by Carl Sandburg (New York, 1919), iii.

122. Walter Lippmann, "The Right of the Filibuster," *Boston Globe*, February 1, 1938, 14. The column is also excerpted in *The Essential Lippmann*, minus the passage quoted above and the heart of Lippmann's defense of the South. See Rossiter and Lare, *The Essential Lippmann*, 219–220.

123. Walter Lippmann, "Mounting Crisis in Education," *Delta Democrat-Times*, May 21, 1954, 4.

124. *Conversations with Walter Lippmann*, 191.

125. *Conversations with Walter Lippmann*, 155.

126. Walter Lippmann, "Goldwater Puts Himself in Role of 'I Am Only True Republican,'" *Los Angeles Times*, January 8, 1964, A5.

127. Walter Lippmann, "The Primary '64 Mandate," *Nashville Tennessean*, November 8, 1964, 25.

128. Doris Kearns Goodwin, *Lyndon Johnson and the American Dream* (New York, 1976), 154.

129. At least a quarter of Republicans in the House and Senate voted for all but one of the major Great Society reforms. (The Economic Opportunity Act was the sole exception.) Sam Rosenfeld, *The Polarizers: Postwar Architects of Our Partisan Era* (Chicago, 2017), 105.

130. On the Great Society as a retreat from the New Deal's move toward social democracy, see Ira Katznelson, "Was the Great Society a Lost Opportunity?," in *The Rise and Fall of the New Deal Order*, ed. Steve Fraser and Gary Gerstle (Princeton, NJ, 1989), 185–211. Walter Lippmann identified the change in real time. New Dealers, he explained in a 1965 interview, believed "that the amount of wealth in the country was more or less fixed, and that in order to help the poor, or to educate people or to do anything, you had to divide the wealth, take away from the well-to-do and give it either to the government or to the poor." The Great Society, by contrast, assumed that its programs could be paid for by a growing economy, eliminating the need for class conflict: "Nobody is any poorer, everybody's richer." *Conversations with Walter Lippmann*, 220–221. On the Great Society as guardian of the rights revolution, see Sidney Milkis, "Lyndon Johnson, the Great Society, and the 'Twilight' of the Modern Presidency," in *The Great Society and the High Tide of Liberalism*, ed. Sidney M. Milkis and Jerome M. Mileur (Amherst, MA, 2005), 1–49. Julian E.

Zelizer offers an alternative interpretation, emphasizing continuities between the New Deal and Great Society, in *The Fierce Urgency of Now: Lyndon Johnson, Congress, and the Battle for the Great Society* (New York, 2015).

131. Another way of measuring the change in the Democratic coalition is to look at the states where Roosevelt and Johnson performed best. Nine of FDR's ten largest majorities in 1936 came from the South. (The only exception, his tenth-best state, was Nevada.) Only one of LBJ's top ten states—West Virginia—was below the Mason-Dixon line. There was *no* overlap between Roosevelt's and Johnson's highest performing states. Almost the opposite: the five states where Roosevelt did the worst in 1936 (Maine, Vermont, New Hampshire, Massachusetts, and Rhode Island) were some of Johnson's *best* states in 1964. (All but New Hampshire made it into his top ten.) By contrast, Barack Obama's 2008 coalition is a clear descendant of Johnson's majority. Six of Obama's best states were also in LBJ's top ten, including three of the New England states (Vermont, Rhode Island, and Massachusetts) where FDR was least popular. For data on the Johnson and Obama victories, see *Congressional Quarterly's Guide to U.S. Elections*, 790, 801.

132. *Conversations with Walter Lippmann*, 222.

133. *Conversations with Walter Lippmann*, 180.

134. *Taking Charge: The Johnson White House Tapes, 1963–1964*, ed. Michael R. Beschloss (New York, 1997), 313.

135. Wehmeyer, "Mary Dublin Keyserling," 237–246.

136. On the Freedom Budget, see D'Emilio, *Lost Prophet*, 429–439.

137. Rustin, "From Protest to Politics," 128.

138. On resistance to an equal rights agenda from left-wing feminists, see Landon R. Y. Storrs, *Civilizing Capitalism: The National Consumers' League, Women's Activism, and Labor Standards in the New Deal Era* (Chapel Hill, NC, 2000), 46–59, 76–90, and Dorothy Sue Cobble, "Labor Feminists and President Kennedy's Commission on Women," in *No Permanent Waves: Recasting Histories of U.S. Feminism*, ed. Nancy Hewitt (New Brunswick, NJ, 2010), 144–167.

139. For NOW's founding as a repudiation of Keyserling's approach at the Women's Bureau, see Cynthia Harrison, *On Account of Sex: The Politics of Women's Issues, 1945–1968* (Berkeley, CA, 1988), 192–209.

140. Stokely Carmichael (later Kwame Ture) and Charles V. Hamilton cited Rustin by name while dismissing the "myths of coalition": *Black Power: The Politics of Liberation in America* (New York, 1992), 58–59.

141. On the origins and aftershocks of the 1966 midterms, see Andrew E. Busch, *Horses in Midstream: U.S. Midterm Elections and Their Consequences* (Pittsburgh, 1999), 100–106.

142. Walter Lippmann, "The American Promise," *Newsweek*, October 9, 1967, 21.

143. "A New Leader for the Orchestra: Conversation with Walter Lippmann," *New Republic*, December 6, 1967, 21.

144. *Public Persons*, 188.

145. Walter Lippmann, "Historic Party Shift Hinges on Elections in 1968," *Los Angeles Times*, December 17, 1967, 3.
146. Walter Lippmann, "Why Nixon? He Can Be Elected, Could Govern," *Los Angeles Times*, October 6, 1968, F7.
147. Steel, *Walter Lippmann*, 483.
148. Lippmann, "Why Nixon?," 7.
149. Louie Estrada, "Mary D. Keyserling, 87, Dies," *Washington Post*, June 13, 1987, D6.
150. Stephen Goodell, "Oral History Transcript, Leon Keyserling Interview," LBJ Library Oral Histories, LBJ Presidential Library, available at https://discoverlbj.org.
151. Ronald Steel, "The Biographer as Detective," *New York Times*, July 21, 1985, 54.
152. Arnold-Forster, "Walter Lippmann," 204.
153. Mary Blume, "Walter Lippmann at 80: The Hopeful Skeptic," *Washington Post*, May 31, 1970, B3.
154. Henry Brandon, "A Talk with Walter Lippmann, at 80, About This 'Minor Dark Age,'" *New York Times*, September 14, 1969, SM25.
155. Federal Reserve Bank of St. Louis and U.S. Office of Management and Budget, Federal Net Outlays as Percent of Gross Domestic Product, available at https://fred.stlouisfed.org.
156. This pivot to the right on economics is often described as a neoliberal turn, on which see Kim Phillips-Fein, "The History of Neoliberalism," in *Shaped by the State: Toward a New Political History of the Twentieth Century*, ed. Brent Cebul, Lily Geismer, and Mason Williams (Chicago, 2019), 347–362. Accounts of neoliberalism's rise often say little about polarization (and vice versa). The former dominates histories of policy, the latter histories of politics, with less attention paid to how they might relate. For an important attempt to bridge this gap, see Daniel Schlozman and Sam Rosenfeld, "The Politics of Listlessness: Polarization, Neoliberalism, and the Democratic Party Since 1980," Working Paper, October 2020. On uneven polarization, see Daniel Moskowitz, Jon Rogowski, and James Snyder, "Parsing Party Polarization in Congress," Working Paper, July 9, 2019. For a compelling defense of the link between party polarization and economic inequality, see Adam Bonica, Nolan McCarty, Keith Poole, and Howard Rosenthal, "Why Hasn't Democracy Slowed Rising Inequality?," *Journal of Economic Perspectives* 27.3 (2013), 103–124.
157. Steel, *Lippmann*, 599.

7. INSURGENTS

1. "*Firing Line* with William F. Buckley Jr. and Phyllis Schlafly on the New Panama Canal Treaty," Eagle Forum, available at https://eagleforum.org/about/interviews.html.
2. Carol Felsenthal, *The Sweetheart of the Silent Majority: The Biography of Phyl-*

lis Schlafly (New York, 1981), 129. Felsenthal's insightful work is still one of the best accounts of Schlafly's life, but for a more scholarly treatment with comprehensive archival sourcing, see Donald T. Critchlow, *Phyllis Schlafly and Grassroots Conservatism: A Woman's Crusade* (Princeton, NJ, 2005). Schlafly told her own story in a series of biographical interviews, lasting almost fourteen hours, available at https://www2.illinois.gov/alplm/library/collections /oralhistory/illinoisstatecraft.

3. Ruth Murray Brown, *For a Christian America: A History of the Religious Right* (Amherst, NY, 2002), 113.

4. On Schlafly's distinction between the "grass roots" and the "kingmakers," see Phyllis Schlafly, *A Choice Not an Echo* (Alton, IL, 1964), 5–6, 78.

5. *"Firing Line,"* Eagle Forum.

6. On the John Birch Society and its place on the right, see D. J. Mulloy, *The World of the John Birch Society: Conspiracy, Conservatism, and the Cold War* (Nashville, 2014).

7. Ronald Radosh, "Phyllis Schlafly, 'Mrs. America,' Was a Secret Member of the John Birch Society," *Daily Beast*, April 22, 2020, available at https:// www.thedailybeast.com. Images of Schlafly's and Welch's letters are available at https://archive.org/details/schlaflyphyllisandjohnbirchsociety/page/n3 /mode/2up.

8. On populism, see Kazin, *The Populist Persuasion*; Jan-Werner Müller, *What Is Populism?* (Philadelphia, 2016); and Nadia Urbinati, *Me the People: How Populism Transforms Democracy* (Cambridge, MA, 2019).

9. Phyllis Schlafly, *Safe—Not Sorry* (Alton, IL, 1967), 174.

10. On the Old Right, see George Wolfskill, *The Revolt of the Conservatives: A History of the American Liberty League, 1934–1940* (Boston, 1962); Leo P. Ribuffo, *The Old Christian Right: The Protestant Far Right from the Great Depression to the Cold War* (Philadelphia, 1983); Glen Jeansonne, *Women of the Far Right: The Mothers' Movement and World War II* (Chicago, 1996); Eliot A. Rosen, *The Republican Party in the Age of Roosevelt: Sources of Anti-Government Conservatism in the United States* (Charlottesville, VA, 2014); and Joseph Fronczak, "The Fascist Game: Transnational Political Transmission and the Genesis of the U.S. Modern Right," *Journal of American History* 105.3 (2018), 563–588. Although Ruth Hanna McCormick did not belong to the Old Right, she shared its opposition to FDR and to intervening in World War II. The McCormick family's *Chicago Tribune* was also an important voice for the Old Right. On the Old Right's links to postwar conservatism, see David Austin Walsh, "The Right-Wing Popular Front: The Far Right and American Conservatism in the 1950s," *Journal of American History* 107.2 (2020), 411–432. Walsh's emphasis on a conservative populist front joined together by opposition to liberalism, socialism, and communism also captures Schlafly's approach to coalition building.

11. "Against Trump," *National Review*, January 22, 2016, available at https:// www.nationalreview.com.

12. This interpretation of Schlafly's career fits with an ongoing scholarly attempt to move the study of American conservatism beyond a tendency to reproduce an origin story that elite conservatives have long told about their movement—a history as seen from the offices of *National Review*. For related efforts, see Michelle M. Nickerson, *Mothers of Conservatism: Women of the Postwar Right* (Princeton, NJ, 2012); Robert O. Self, *All in the Family: The Realignment of American Democracy Since the 1960s* (New York, 2012); Nicole Hemmer, *Messengers of the Right: Conservative Media and the Transformation of American Politics* (Philadelphia, 2016); George Hawley, *Making Sense of the Alt-Right* (New York, 2017); Corey Robin, *The Reactionary Mind: Conservatism from Edmund Burke to Donald Trump*, 2nd ed. (New York, 2018); and Daniel Schlozman and Sam Rosenfeld, "The Long New Right and the World It Made" (paper presented at the annual meeting of the American Political Science Association, Boston, August 31, 2018). These more recent accounts follow tracks initially laid by Leo P. Ribuffo, "Why Is There So Much Conservatism in the United States and Why Do So Few Historians Know Anything About It?," *American Historical Review* 99.2 (1994), 438–449, and Jean Hardisty, *Mobilizing Resentment: Conservative Resurgence from the John Birch Society to the Promise Keepers* (Boston, 1999). Despite *National Review*'s importance as a gatekeeper on the right, the magazine's own publisher, William A. Rusher, was an early and influential champion of both the Southern strategy and of yoking the right-populist backlash to the conservative movement, creating a new coalition out of "conservative Republicans (broadly represented by Reagan) and conservative Democrats (most of whom have in the past supported [George] Wallace)." See William A. Rusher, "A Marriage of Conservatives," *New York Times*, June 23, 1975, 26.

13. On midcentury St. Louis, with special emphasis on the radical left and far right, see Johnson, *The Broken Heart of America*, 251–336.

14. Felsenthal, *Sweetheart of the Silent Majority*, 41–42.

15. Jason Stahl, *Right Moves: The Conservative Think Tank in American Politics and Culture Since 1945* (Chapel Hill, NC, 2016), 7–46.

16. Felsenthal, *Sweetheart of the Silent Majority*, 71.

17. Felsenthal, *Sweetheart of the Silent Majority*, 77.

18. *Phyllis Schlafly Speaks*, vol. 1: *Her Favorite Speeches*, ed. Ed Martin (Ballwin, MO, 2016), 167.

19. Felsenthal, *Sweetheart of the Silent Majority*, 285.

20. Felsenthal, *Sweetheart of the Silent Majority*, 162.

21. Critchlow, *Phyllis Schlafly and Grassroots Conservatism*, 59.

22. James Reston, "Goldwater Says He'll Run to Give Nation a 'Choice,'" *New York Times*, January 4, 1964, A8.

23. Schlafly, *A Choice Not an Echo*, 6.

24. Schlafly, *A Choice Not an Echo*, 7.

25. Schlafly, *A Choice Not an Echo*, 5, 106.

26. Schlafly, *A Choice Not an Echo*, 107.

27. Schlafly, *A Choice Not an Echo*, 117–118.

28. Fraser, *Limousine Liberal*, 94. Fraser is also excellent on the prehistory of Schlafly's rhetoric, on which see *Limousine Liberal*, 23–47.

29. Stephanie Coontz, *A Strange Stirring: The Feminine Mystique and American Women at the Dawn of the 1960s* (New York, 2011), 145–149.

30. Schlafly, *A Choice Not an Echo*, 9.

31. "Mrs. Phyllis Schlafly Candidate for Congress to Address the Clinton County Young Republicans at Carlyle Thursday," *Breese Journal*, February 19, 1970, 14.

32. On Schlafly's great nemesis, the liberal Republican, see Nicol C. Rae, *The Decline and Fall of the Liberal Republicans from 1952 to the Present* (New York, 1989), and Geoffrey Kabaservice, *Rule and Ruin: The Downfall of Moderation and the Destruction of the Republican Party, from Eisenhower to the Tea Party* (New York, 2012).

33. Critchlow, *Phyllis Schlafly and Grassroots Conservatism*, 145.

34. Schlafly, *Safe—Not Sorry*, 31, 50, 187.

35. Schlafly, *Safe—Not Sorry*, 119.

36. Schlafly, *Safe—Not Sorry*, 8.

37. Schlafly, *Safe—Not Sorry*, 121.

38. Schlafly, *Safe—Not Sorry*, 175.

39. CPI Inflation Calculator, Bureau of Labor Statistics, available at https://www.bls.gov/data/.

40. Felsenthal, *Sweetheart of the Silent Majority*, 200, 206.

41. Felsenthal, *Sweetheart of the Silent Majority*, 203–204.

42. Felsenthal, *Sweetheart of the Silent Majority*, 75.

43. Felsenthal, *Sweetheart of the Silent Majority*, 240.

44. Phyllis Schlafly, "What's Wrong with 'Equal Rights' for Women?," *Phyllis Schlafly Report*, February 1972, available at https://eagleforum.org.

45. Schlafly, "What's Wrong with 'Equal Rights' for Women?"

46. Jane J. Mansbridge, *Why We Lost the ERA* (Chicago, 1986), 44.

47. Critchlow, *Phyllis Schlafly and Grassroots Conservatism*, 224.

48. *Phyllis Schlafly Speaks*, 102.

49. Mansbridge, *Why We Lost the ERA*, 159.

50. Marjorie J. Spruill, *Divided We Stand: The Battle over Women's Rights and Family Values That Polarized American Politics* (New York, 2017), 90.

51. Phyllis Schlafly, "Cultural Conservatism and the Religious Right," in *Big Tent: The Story of the Conservative Revolution—as Told by the Thinkers and Doers Who Made It Happen*, ed. Mallory Factor (New York, 2014), 186.

52. According to the Department of Health and Human Services, 7.1 percent of white children and 49.5 percent of African American children were born out of wedlock in 1975. See *Health, United States, 2006, with Chartbook on Trends in the Health of Americans* (Washington, DC, 2006), 145.

53. Ange-Marie Hancock, *The Politics of Disgust: The Public Identity of the Welfare Queen* (New York, 2004), 51–57.
54. Self, *All in the Family*, 316.
55. Felsenthal, *Sweetheart of the Silent Majority*, 283.
56. Dennis Hevesi, "Mildred Jefferson, 84, Anti-Abortion Activist, Is Dead," *New York Times*, October 18, 2010, available at https://www.nytimes.com.
57. Felsenthal, *Sweetheart of the Silent Majority*, 58.
58. *Schlafly Speaks*, 105.
59. *Schlafly Speaks*, 230.
60. Self, *All in the Family*, 110.
61. Phyllis Schlafly, *The Power of the Positive Woman* (New Rochelle, NY, 1977), 116–117.
62. Felsenthal, *Sweetheart of the Silent Majority*, 26.
63. Phyllis Schlafly, "Ten Years of ERA Is Enough!," *Phyllis Schlafly Report*, April 1983.
64. *Schlafly Speaks*, 225.
65. Mansbridge, *Why We Lost the ERA*, 115.
66. Critchlow, *Phyllis Schlafly and Grassroots Conservatism*, 300.
67. *Schlafly Speaks*, 93.
68. Kathy O'Malley and Hanke Gratteau, "Truth in Labeling . . . ," *Chicago Tribune*, October 8, 1987, available at https://www.chicagotribune.com.
69. Rusher, "A Marriage of Conservatives."
70. R. W. Apple Jr., "Study of 3rd Party for '76 Approved by Conservatives," *New York Times*, February 17, 1975, A12.
71. Ronald Reagan, "Remarks at the Conference Dinner," *Weekly Compilation of Presidential Documents*, January 5, 1981, 329.
72. Schlafly, *Big Tent*, 190.
73. Mansbridge, *Why We Lost the ERA*, 146.
74. "Firing Line," available at https://eagleforum.org/about/ interviews.html.
75. David D. Kirkpatrick, "How a Chase Bank Chairman Helped the Deposed Shah of Iran Enter the U.S.," *New York Times*, December 29, 2019, available at https://www.nytimes.com.
76. Barbara C. Burrell, "Gender, Presidential Elections and Public Policy: Making Women's Votes Matter," *Journal of Women, Politics & Policy* 27 (2005), 31–50; Richa Chaturvedi, "A Closer Look at the Gender Gap in Presidential Voting," Pew Research Center, July 28, 2016, available at https://www.pewresearch.org.
77. Joseph Sobran, "Though the News Media May Revile Her, Phyllis Schlafly Is the Wave of the Future," *Pittsburgh Post-Gazette*, July 10, 1980, A6.
78. Phyllis Schlafly, "U.S. Should Sink the Law of the Sea Treaty," *Phyllis Schlafly Report*, August 1982; Phyllis Schlafly, "Fat Kids: Who's Responsible?," Eagle Forum, September 17, 2003, available at https://eagleforum.org.
79. Schlozman and Rosenfeld, "Long New Right," 56.

80. Laura Ingraham, "My Hero, R.I.P.," *Lifezette*, September 6, 2016, available at https://www.lifezette.com; Ann Coulter, "Phyllis Stewart Schlafly, 1924–2016," *Ann Coulter*, September 5, 2016, available at https://www.anncoulter.com.

81. Amy Larocca, "Political Peroxide," *New York*, August 7, 2017, available at https://www.nymag.com.

82. Critchlow, *Phyllis Schlafly and Grassroots Conservatism*, 270.

83. Anna North, "Phyllis Schlafly, Calendar Girl," *Jezebel*, September 29, 2009, available at www.jezebel.com.

84. Critchlow, *Phyllis Schlafly and Grassroots Conservatism*, 292–295.

85. Laura Blumenfeld, "Schlafly's Son, Out of the Closet," *Washington Post*, September 19, 1992, available at https://www.washingtonpost.com.

86. Mark DePue, "Interview with Phyllis Schlafly," March 29, 2011, Abraham Lincoln Presidential Library, available at https://presidentlincoln.illinois.gov/oral-history/collections/schlafly-phyllis/interview-detail/.

87. Phyllis Schlafly, "Lessons from the Paula Jones Case," Eagle Forum, April 15, 1998, available at https://eagleforum.org; Phyllis Schlafly, "Will We Allow Clinton to Redefine the Presidency?," Eagle Forum, February 11, 1998, available at https://eagleforum.org.

88. Schlafly, "Will We Allow Clinton to Redefine the Presidency?"

89. Phyllis Schlafly, "Buchanan Knows Where the Votes Are," Eagle Forum, February 29, 1996, available at https://eagleforum.org.

90. Phyllis Schlafly, "Where Will the McCain Voters Go?," Eagle Forum, March 22, 2000, available at https://eagleforum.org.

91. Bush's failure to win a majority of the popular vote did not stop Schlafly from defending his legitimacy as president. Like many populists before and since, Schlafly's definition of "the people" could quickly shrink to include her favored section of the public—in this case, rural and working-class white voters who leaned Republican and were given disproportionate weight in the Electoral College. She did, however, believe that the GOP's inability to carry the popular vote was a worrying sign of the party's waning power. For her support of the Electoral College, see "The Way We Elect Our Presidents," *Phyllis Schlafly Report*, December 2000. For her concern about a perennial Republican minority, see Phyllis Schlafly, Ed Martin, and Brett M. Decker, *The Conservative Case for Trump* (Washington, DC, 2016), xix.

92. "In Depth with Phyllis Schlafly," C-SPAN, January 5, 2003, available at https://www.cspan.org.

93. Aman Verjee and Rod Martin, eds., *Thank You, President Bush: Reflections on the War on Terror, Defense of the Family, and Revival of the Economy* (Los Angeles, 2004).

94. Phyllis Schlafly, "The New Political Party Realignment," Eagle Forum, June 25, 1997, available at https://eagleforum.org.

95. Schlafly, "The New Political Party Realignment."

96. Phyllis Schlafly, "Globalism: Enemy of the Middle Class," *Phyllis Schlafly Report*, February 2007, available at https://eagleforum.org.

97. Phyllis Schlafly, "Welfare: Fraud and Failure," *Phyllis Schlafly Report*, February 1996.

98. Phyllis Schlafly, "Constitutional Rights vs. Terrorism Regs," *Phyllis Schlafly Report*, October 2001.

99. Phyllis Schlafly, "Is it Assimilation or Invasion?," Eagle Forum, November 28, 2001, available at https://eagleforum.org.

100. Phyllis Schlafly, "American Citizenship Is Precious," Eagle Forum, October 12, 2005, available at https://eagleforum.org.

101. Phyllis Schlafly, "China Poisons Its Infant Formula," Eagle Forum, September 26, 2008, available at https://eagleforum.org.

102. Phyllis Schlafly, "Whatever Happened to Informed Medical Choice?," *Phyllis Schlafly Report*, February 1999; Phyllis Schlafly, "Follow the Money on Vaccines," Eagle Forum, September 5, 2001, available at https://eagleforum.org.

103. See Joseph Scotchie, *Revolt from the Heartland: The Struggle for an Authentic Conservatism* (New York, 2002); Samuel Francis, "The Paleo Persuasion," *American Conservative*, December 16, 2002, available at https://www.theamericanconservative.com; Timothy Shenk, "The Dark History of Donald Trump's Rightwing Revolt," *Guardian*, August 16, 2016, available at https://www.theguardian.com. On right-wing anticapitalism, see Peter Kolozi, *Conservatives Against Capitalism: From the Industrial Revolution to Globalization* (New York, 2017).

104. Phyllis Schlafly, "Where Do We Go from Here?," *Phyllis Schlafly Report*, November 2008.

105. Sarah Palin, "She Went Down Swinging!," Facebook, September 5, 2016, available at https://www.facebook.com/sarahpalin/posts/she-went-down-swinging-phyllis-schlafly-may-she-rest-in-peace-iconic-heroic-no-o/10154517217468588/.

106. Phyllis Schlafly, "The Republicans' Call to Arms," September 5, 2008, available at https://eagleforum.org.

107. Phyllis Schlafly, "Singing Heil Obama in New Jersey," October 2, 2009, Eagle Forum, available at https://eagleforum.org.

108. Phyllis Schlafly, "Obama's 'New World Order,'" *Phyllis Schlafly Report*, March 2009.

109. On the Tea Party, a movement after Schlafly's heart if ever there was one, see Theda Skocpol and Vanessa Williamson, *The Tea Party and the Remaking of Republican Conservatism* (New York, 2013).

110. Phyllis Schlafly, *Who Killed the American Family?* (Washington, DC, 2014), 145.

111. Schlafly, *Who Killed the American Family?*, 214.

112. Phyllis Schlafly, *A Choice Not an Echo: Updated and Expanded 50th Anniversary Edition* (Washington, DC, 2014), 260.

113. David Weigel and Jose Del Real, "Phyllis Schlafly Endorses Trump in St. Louis," *Washington Post*, March 11, 2016, available at https://www.washingtonpost.com.

114. Phyllis Schlafly, "The Establishment Looks for 'Plan B,'" *Phyllis Schlafly Report*, October 2015.

115. "Top Conservative: Trump Is 'Last Hope for America,'" *WND*, December 20, 2015, available at https://www.wnd.com.

116. "Phyllis Schlafly Endorses Donald Trump at a Rally in St. Louis, MO. (3–11–16)," YouTube Video, available at https://www.youtube.com.

117. Matthew Boyle, "Audio File: Phyllis Schlafly Rallies Tens of Thousands Nationwide to Her Side as She Defends Against Internal Coup Efforts," *Breitbart News*, May 19, 2016, available at https://www.breitbart.com.

118. Schlafly, Martin, and Decker, *Conservative Case for Trump*, 49, 55.

119. Libby Nelson and Dara Lind, "Sarah Palin's Rambling Endorsement of Donald Trump, Annotated," *Vox*, January 21, 2016, available at https://www.vox.com.

120. Julia Hahn, "Phyllis Schlafly: National Review Is Not the Authority on Conservatism," *Breitbart News*, January 23, 2016, available at https://www.breitbart.com. On Hahn, see Andrew Marantz, "Becoming Steve Bannon's Bannon," *New Yorker*, February 5, 2017, available at https://www.newyorker.com.

121. Schlafly, Martin, and Decker, *Conservative Case for Trump*, 88, 92.

122. Schlafly, Martin, and Decker, *Conservative Case for Trump*, x.

123. Phyllis Schlafly, "Trump Battles the Globalists of Both Parties," *Phyllis Schlafly Report*, August 2016.

124. "Hardcover Nonfiction," *New York Times*, September 25, 2016, available at https://www.nytimes.com.

125. Reena Flores, "Donald Trump Attends Funeral of Conservative Icon Phyllis Schlafly," CBS News, September 10, 2016, available at https://www.cbsnews.com.

126. "Trump Speaks at Campaign Donors Dinner," CNN, January 19, 2017, available at http://transcripts.cnn.com.

127. Kevin McDermott, "As Ed Martin Tries to Claim Phyllis Schlafly's Legacy, PR Firm Tries to Get $130K It Says It's Owed," *St. Louis Post-Dispatch*, September 27, 2017, available at https://www.stltoday.com.

128. Eunie Smith, "Poll Shows Voters Demanding Conservative Agenda," Eagle Forum, September 7, 2017, available at https://eagleforum.org/publications/press-releases; "Presidential Approval Ratings—Donald Trump," Gallup, accessed July 2, 2019, available at https://news.gallup.com/. On the Republican Party's consolidation behind Trump, see Paul Pierson, "American Hybrid: Donald Trump and the Strange Merger of Populism and Plutocracy," *British Journal of Sociology* 68 (2017), S105–S119.

129. Kaveh Waddell, "The Exhausting Work of Tallying America's Largest Protest," *Atlantic*, January 23, 2017, available at https://www.theatlantic.com.

130. Timothy Williams, "Virginia Approves the E.R.A., Becoming the 38th State to Back It," *New York Times*, January 16, 2020, available at https://www.nytimes.com.
131. Elizabeth Warren, *A Fighting Chance* (New York, 2014), 2.
132. Elizabeth Warren, "What Is a Women's Issue? Bankruptcy, Commercial Law, and Other Gender-Neutral Topics," *Harvard Women's Law Journal* 25 (2002), 55.

8. POLITICIANS

1. David J. Garrow, *Rising Star: The Making of Barack Obama* (New York, 2017), 403. A monumental feat of research, Garrow's is the most illuminating of the many books that have been written on Obama. David Remnick's earlier biography, *The Bridge: The Life and Rise of Barack Obama* (New York, 2010), remains a valuable resource. On the ideas that informed Obama's early politics, see James T. Kloppenberg, *Reading Obama: Dreams, Hope, and the American Political Tradition* (Princeton, NJ, 2010); Thomas J. Sugrue, *Not Even Past: Barack Obama and the Burden of Race* (Princeton, NJ, 2010); and Stacey Marlise Gahagan and Alfred Brophy, "Reading Professor Obama: Race and the American Constitutional Tradition," *University of Pittsburgh Law Review* 75.4 (2014), 495–581. Edward McClelland, *Young Mr. Obama: Chicago and the Making of a Black President* (New York, 2010), explores the influence of Obama's adopted hometown on his later career. The three memoirs Obama has published (with a fourth to come, as of this writing) all reward study, including for the ways they differ from one another: Barack Obama, *Dreams from My Father: A Story of Race and Inheritance* (New York, 1995); Barack Obama, *The Audacity of Hope: Thoughts on Reclaiming the American Dream* (New York, 2006); and Barack Obama, *A Promised Land* (New York, 2020).
2. Barack Obama and Robert Fisher, "Outline—Transformative Politics: Paper for Law and Society," manuscript in author's possession. On their plans for turning the manuscript into a book, see Garrow, *Rising Star*, 432–434. They also considered titling it "Promises of Democracy: Hopeful Critiques of American Ideology."
3. Barack Obama and Robert Fisher, "Race and Rights Rhetoric," manuscript in author's possession. Although Obama was an unusually talented defender of this class-based strategy, he was far from its only champion. By the early 1990s it was closely associated with the political scientist Charles V. Hamilton—the same Charles V. Hamilton who, with his coauthor Stokely Carmichael, cast a doubtful eye on "the myths of coalition" in *Black Power*. After the reversals of the Nixon years, Hamilton came around to a position quite similar to Rustin's, with an agenda focused on "deracializing" political debate by appealing to the material concerns of the Black and white working class. See Charles V. Hamilton, "Deracialization: Examination of a Political Strategy," *First World*

(1977), 3–5. The legal scholar Derrick Bell, with whom Obama would later cross paths at Harvard, argued in a much-cited 1980 article, "The interest of blacks in achieving racial equality will be accommodated only when it converges with the interests of whites": Derrick Bell, *"Brown v. Board of Education and the Interest-Convergence Dilemma," Harvard Law Review* 93.3 (1980), 523. As will be discussed later in this chapter, by the time Obama was enrolled at Harvard, the sociologist William Julius Wilson was garnering considerable attention for his electoral defense of "race-neutral policies": William Julius Wilson, *The Truly Disadvantaged: The Inner City, the Underclass, and Public Policy* (Chicago, 2012), 155 (orig. pub. 1987), and "Race-Neutral Policies and the Democratic Coalition," *American Prospect*, Spring 1990, 74–81. Meanwhile, Black politicians, including Jesse Jackson in his two presidential campaigns, were running on platforms that owed a clear debt to Hamilton's "deracialization" strategy. For a dubious assessment of "deracialization" written around the period when Obama was working on "Transformative Politics," see Robert Smith, "Hammering at the Truth," *Transition* 54 (1991), 90–103. Sheryll D. Cashin (an acquaintance of Obama's from Harvard Law School) offers a more favorable interpretation, tracing a through line from Rustin to Bell, in "Shall We Overcome? Transcending Race, Class, and Ideology Through Interest Convergence," *St. John's Law Review* (2005), 253–291. For a thoughtful consideration of the young Obama's place in the debates over deracialization, see Richard Johnson, "Hamilton's Deracialization: Barack Obama's Racial Politics in Historical Context," *Du Bois Review* 14.2 (2017), 621–638. On Black politics in the generation before Obama's national debut in 2004, see Frederick C. Harris, *The Price of the Ticket: Barack Obama and the Rise and Decline of Black Politics* (New York, 2012), 3–69, 137–169. Claude A. Clegg III, *The Black President: Hope and Fury in the Age of Obama* (Baltimore, 2021), carries this story through Obama's time in the White House. And for an illuminating discussion of Hamilton's shifting tactics, see Charles V. Hamilton and Frederick C. Harris, "A Conversation with Charles V. Hamilton," *Annual Review of Political Science* 21 (2018), 21–27.

4. Barack Obama and Robert Fisher, "Plant Closings: Creative Destruction and the Viability of the Regulated Market," manuscript in author's possession.

5. Barack Obama, "Obama Rallies Columbia, Missouri," Real Clear Politics, October 30, 2008, available at https://www.realclearpolitics.com/.

6. On increasing economic inequality, see Thomas Piketty, Emmanuel Saez, and Gabriel Zucman, "Distributional National Accounts: Methods and Estimates for the United States," *Quarterly Journal of Economics* 113.2 (2018), 553–609. On polarization, see Drutman, *Breaking the Two-Party Doom Loop*, 107–122. And on frustration with the political system, see "Public Trust in Government: 1958–2019," Pew Research Center, April 11, 2019, available at https://www.pewresearch.org. As these citations indicate, my focus in this chapter (and throughout the book) is on domestic politics—not because Obama's foreign

policy was less historically significant but because, as is usually the case, American voters in the Obama years cared more about the home front. In 2012, for example, a Pew Research Center study found that "terrorism" and "foreign policy" ranked eighth and ninth in voters' priorities, putting them behind "economy," "jobs," "health care," "education," "budget deficit," "taxes," and "Medicare." See "For Voters, It's Still the Economy," Pew Research Center, September 24, 2012, available at https://www.pewresearch.org.

7. Obama re-created the scene in *Dreams from My Father*, 149. On Wisconsin Steel, see R. C. Longworth, "It's Almost Over for Wisconsin Steel Plant," *Chicago Tribune*, June 24, 1985, available at https://www.chicagotribune.com.

8. Ivor Lensworth Livingston, *Handbook of Black American Health: The Mosaic of Conditions, Issues, Policies, and Prospects* (Westport, CT, 1994), 323–324; Heather Little, "Toxin Shock," *Chicago Tribune*, January 15, 1995, available at https://www.chicagotribune.com.

9. Hiram Fong (Republican) and Daniel Inouye (Democrat), both Asian American. The other nonwhite senator was Joseph Montoya of New Mexico. See "Ethnic Diversity in the Senate," United States Senate, available at https://www.senate.gov.

10. Obama, *Dreams from My Father*, 50; Garrow, *Rising Star*, 68–69.

11. Obama, *Dreams from My Father*, 97.

12. Obama, *Dreams from My Father*, 50.

13. Garrow, *Rising Star*, 543.

14. Garrow, *Rising Star*, 124.

15. Garrow, *Rising Star*, 144.

16. On the antipolitical politics of community organizing, see Sanford D. Horwitt, *Let Them Call Me Rebel: Saul Alinsky, His Life and Legacy* (New York, 1989), and Aaron Schutz and Mike Miller, eds., *People Power: The Saul Alinsky Tradition of Community Organizing* (Nashville, 2015).

17. On Washington, see Gary Rivlin, *Fire on the Prairie: Harold Washington, Chicago Politics, and the Roots of the Obama Presidency* (Philadelphia, 2012).

18. Barack Obama, "Political Race/s," in *Who's Afraid of a Large Black Man?*, ed. Michael Wilbon (New York, 2006), 36 (orig. pub. 2005).

19. Obama, *Dreams from My Father*, 142.

20. Allison Pugh, "New Head of Harvard Law Journal Wants to Be Part of U.S. Change," *Rochester Democrat and Chronicle*, April 16, 1990, 3B.

21. Obama, *A Promised Land*, 18.

22. Wilson, *The Truly Disadvantaged*, 155.

23. Garrow, *Rising* Star, 286. Ironically, Obama also cited Wilson in an essay defending the importance of community organizing: Barack Obama, "Why Organize? Problems and Promise in the Inner City," *Illinois Issues*, August/September 1988, available at https://www.lib.niu.edu.

24. Obama, *Dreams from My Father*, 276.

25. Robert Granfield and Thomas Koenig, "The Fate of Elite Idealism: Accom-

modation and Ideological Work at Harvard Law School," *Social Problems* 39.4 (1992), 322. On the culture at Harvard Law School during Obama's time as a student, also see Robert Granfield and Thomas Koenig, "Learning Collective Eminence: Harvard Law School and the Social Production of Elite Lawyers," *Sociological Quarterly* 33.4 (1992), 503–520.

26. Obama, *Audacity of Hope*, 114.

27. Garrow, *Rising Star*, 424.

28. Not everyone appreciated Obama's penchant for synthesis. One student remembered, "He would raise his hand and say 'I think what my colleagues are trying to say if I might sum up,' and we'd be like 'We can speak for ourselves— shut the fuck up.'" Garrow, *Rising Star*, 341. Mitch McConnell would have a similar reaction, on which see Mitch McConnell, *The Long Game: A Memoir* (New York, 2016), 185, 209–210.

29. Derrick Bell, *Faces at the Bottom of the Well: The Permanence of Racism* (New York, 2018), xxi (orig. pub. 1992).

30. Garrow, *Rising Star*, 446.

31. Obama, *Dreams from My Father*, 437.

32. Garrow, *Rising Star*, 392.

33. Barack Obama and Robert Fisher, "Race and Rights Rhetoric."

34. R. J. Reinhart, "George H. W. Bush Retrospective," Gallup, December 1, 2018, available at https://news.gallup.com.

35. Obama, "Why Organize?"

36. Obama and Fisher, "Race and Rights Rhetoric."

37. Obama and Fisher, "Plant Closings."

38. Obama and Fisher, "Race and Rights Rhetoric."

39. Obama and Fisher, "Race and Rights Rhetoric."

40. Obama and Fisher, "Race and Rights Rhetoric."

41. Obama and Fisher, "Race and Rights Rhetoric." They also noted the significance of the "optimism of the average American—I may not be Donald Trump now, but just you wait."

42. Obama and Fisher, "Race and Rights Rhetoric."

43. McClelland, *Young Mr. Obama*, 109.

44. Obama, *Dreams from My Father*, 25.

45. Hank De Zutter, "What Makes Obama Run?," *Chicago Reader*, December 8, 1995, available at https://www.chicagoreader.com.

46. De Zutter, "What Makes Obama Run?"

47. De Zutter, "What Makes Obama Run?"

48. "Election Results for 1996 Primary Election, Illinois Senate, District 13 (Democratic Party)," Chicago Democracy Project, available at http://chicagodemocracy.org.

49. Adolph Reed Jr., *Class Notes: Posing as Politics and Other Thoughts on the American Political Scene* (New York, 2000), 13.

50. Bob Roman, "A Town Meeting on Economic Insecurity," *New Ground*,

March–April 1996, available at https://www.slideshare.net/tradeequity/new
-ground-45-chicago-dsa.

51. Garrow, *Rising Star*, 597.
52. Garrow, *Rising Star*, 610.
53. Garrow, *Rising Star*, 41.
54. Obama, *Audacity of Hope*, 240.
55. Garrow, *Rising Star*, 850, 876.
56. "Election Results: 2004 General Primary," Illinois State Board of Elections, available at https://www.elections.il.gov/.
57. Rich Miller, "Barack Obama Wins Big," *Capitol Fax*, March 25, 2004.
58. "Interview: David Axelrod," *Frontline*, October 14, 2008, available at https://www.pbs.org/wgbh/frontline/.
59. "Galesburg, Illinois Population" and "East St. Louis, Illinois Population," Census Viewer, available at https://www.censusviewer.com.
60. Michelle Obama, *Becoming* (New York, 2021), 216 (orig. pub. 2018).
61. "Paperback Best Sellers," *New York Times*, February 13, 2005, available at https://www.nytimes.com.
62. Jonathan Alter, "The Audacity of Hope," *Newsweek*, January 3, 2005, available at https://www.newsweek.com.
63. Daniel Libit, "Won't You Be My Mentor?," *Politico*, March 30, 2009, available at https://www.politico.com.
64. Remnick, *The Bridge*, 429.
65. Remnick, *The Bridge*, 445.
66. Remnick, *The Bridge*, 444.
67. Obama's consistency was more impressive than his originality. Most of his analysis of what ailed American democracy was popularized by E. J. Dionne Jr., *Why Americans Hate Politics* (New York, 1991). Although Obama drew a stark contrast between his politics and Clintonian triangulation, the former president cited both Dionne and William Julius Wilson as key influences, on which see Bill Clinton, *My Life* (New York, 2004), 339 and 366. By 2004, the Harvard political scientist Theda Skocpol had spent more than a decade insisting that universal policies could provide a politically sustainable basis for a redistributive program, a position that she acknowledged was built on a foundation laid by William Julius Wilson. See, for example, Theda Skocpol, "Targeting Within Universalism: Politically Viable Policies to Combat Poverty in the United States," in *The Urban Underclass*, ed. Christopher Jencks and Paul E. Peterson (Washington, DC, 1991), 411–436. There were also clear parallels between Obama's program and Elizabeth Warren's near-simultaneous endorsement of gender-neutral economic reforms that would in practice deliver much of their benefits to poor and working-class women. And Obama's emphasis on the transformative consequences of incremental change fit with liberal conventional wisdom of the aughts, as seen in works like Matt Miller, *The Two Percent Solution: Fixing America's Problems in Ways Liberals and*

Conservatives Can Love (New York, 2003); Jeffrey D. Sachs, *The End of Poverty: Economic Possibilities for Our Time* (New York, 2005); and Richard H. Thaler and Cass R. Sunstein, *Nudge: Improving Decisions About Health, Wealth, and Happiness* (New Haven, CT, 2008).

68. Obama, *Audacity of Hope*, 28.

69. Obama, *Audacity of Hope*, 114.

70. Obama, *Audacity of Hope*, 247.

71. Obama, *Audacity of Hope*, 248.

72. Obama, *Audacity of Hope*, 232.

73. Obama, *Audacity of Hope*, 268.

74. Obama, *Audacity of Hope*, 40.

75. Julie Bosman, "Obama's New Book Is a Surprise Best Seller," *New York Times*, November 9, 2006, available at https://www.nytimes.com.

76. Joe Klein, "The Fresh Face," *Time*, October 15, 2006, available at https://www.time.com.

77. Brian Stelter, "Following the Script: Obama, McCain, and 'The West Wing,'" *New York Times*, October 29, 2008, C1.

78. David Brooks, "Run, Barack, Run," *New York Times*, October 19, 2006, A27.

79. Jacob Weisberg, "The Path to Power," *Men's Vogue*, September 2006, 223.

80. Mark Penn, "Weekly Strategic Review on Hillary Clinton for President Committee," *Atlantic*, March 19, 2007, available at https://www.theatlantic.com.

81. On Obama's fundraising in 2008, see Joshua Green, "The Amazing Money Machine," *Atlantic*, June 2008, available at https://www.theatlantic.com, and Jose Antonio Vargas, "Obama Raised Half a Billion Online," *Washington Post*, November 20, 2008, available at https://www.washingtonpost.com.

82. On Wright's impact, see Brian McKenzie, "Barack Obama, Jeremiah Wright, and Public Opinion in the 2008 Presidential Primaries," *Political Psychology* 32.6 (2011), 943–961.

83. Barack Obama, "A More Perfect Union," in *We Are the Change We Seek: The Speeches of Barack Obama*, ed. E. J. Dionne Jr. and Joy-Ann Reid (New York, 2017), 63.

84. Mayhill Fowler, "Obama: No Surprise That Hard-Pressed Pennsylvanians Turn Bitter," *Huffington Post*, April 11, 2008, available at https://www.huffingtonpost.com.

85. Ed Pilkington, "Obama Angers Midwest Voters with Guns and Religion Remark," *Guardian*, April 14, 2008, available at https://www.theguardian.com.

86. Kathy Kiely and Jill Lawrence, "Clinton Makes Case for Wide Appeal," *USA Today*, May 8, 2008, available at https://www.usatoday.com.

87. For Virginia's and Kentucky's returns, see Paul R. Abramson, John H. Aldrich, and David W. Rhode, *Change and Continuity in the 2008 Elections* (Washington, DC, 2010), 32. On perceptions of Obama among white voters in the 2008 primary and general election, see Todd Donovan, "Obama and the White Vote," *Political Research Quarterly* 63.4 (2010), 863–874. However debatable the

importance of racism was at the time of the 2008 primary, the issue was clarified in 2016, when rural and blue-collar whites turned from Clinton to Bernie Sanders, suggesting that her earlier popularity had more to do with having a Black candidate to run against. On the changing racial demographics of Clinton's coalition, see John Sides, Michael Tesler, and Lynn Vavreck, *Identity Crisis: The 2016 Presidential Campaign and the Battle for the Meaning of America* (Princeton, NJ, 2018), 113–117.

88. "A Liberal Supermajority," *Wall Street Journal*, October 17, 2008, available at https://www.wsj.com.

89. "Palin's Speech at the Republican National Convention," September 3, 2008, available at https://www.nytimes.com.

90. "AP Poll: Whites Help McCain to Slim Lead," NBC News, September 12, 2008, available at https://www.nbcnews.com.

91. Jeff Zeleny and Adam Nagourney, "Obama's Tone Sharpens as Party Frets," *New York Times*, September 12, 2008, available at https://www.nytimes.com. On the campaign's outreach to voters who were potentially skeptical about a Black president, see Sasha Issenberg, *The Victory Lab: The Secret Science of Winning Campaigns* (New York, 2013), 296.

92. On the 2008 Obama coalition, see Abramson, Aldrich, and Rhode, *Change and Continuity in the 2008 Elections*, 56–79. On the evolution of Loudoun County, see "Loudoun on Election Day: A Battleground No More," *Loudoun Now*, November 2, 2020, available at https://loudounnow.com/.

93. *Federal Elections 88: Election Results for the U.S. President, the U.S. Senate, and the U.S. House of Representatives* (Washington, DC, 1989), 13.

94. Abramson, Aldrich, and Rhode, *Change and Continuity in the 2008 Elections*, 60.

95. Barack Obama, "A New Era of Responsibility," in *We Are the Change We Seek*, 100.

96. Tim Alberta, *American Carnage: On the Frontlines of the Republican Civil War and the Rise of Trump* (New York, 2019), 43.

97. Micah Sifry, "Obama's Lost Army," *New Republic*, February 9, 2017, available at https://www.tnr.com.

98. On Congressional polarization, see Christopher Hare and Keith T. Poole, "The Polarization of Contemporary American Politics," *Polity* 46.3 (2014), 411–429.

99. Brian Abrams, *Obama: An Oral History 2009–2017* (New York, 2018), 52.

100. Eric Cantor, "What the Obama Presidency Looked Like to the Opposition," *New York Times*, January 14, 2017, available at https://www.nytimes.com.

101. Bob Woodward, *The Price of Politics* (New York, 2013), 80 (orig. pub. 2012).

102. Abrams, *Obama: An Oral History*, 78.

103. On the Obama administration's response to the Great Recession, see Noam Scheiber, *Escape Artists: How Obama's Team Fumbled the Recovery* (New York, 2012); Adam Tooze, *Crashed: How a Decade of Financial Crises Changed the World* (New York, 2018), 276–313, 449–470; Eric Rauchway, "Neither a De-

pression nor a New Deal: Bailout, Stimulus, and the Economy," in *The Presidency of Barack Obama: A First Historical Assessment*, ed. Julian E. Zelizer (Princeton, NJ, 2018), 30–44; and Reed Hundt, *A Crisis Wasted: Barack Obama's Defining Decisions* (New York, 2019), 125–243. For the political backdrop, see Theda Skocpol, "Obama's New Deal, Tea Party Reaction, and America's Political Future," in Theda Skocpol et al., *Obama and America's Political Future* (Cambridge, MA, 2012), 1–89.

104. Obama, *A Promised Land*, 397. According to Obama, his political team believed that his comments about Gates did more damage to his standing with white voters than any other event in his presidency. But Obama was already well below his postinaugural highs by the time he weighed in on the Gates controversy, suggesting that it accelerated a decline that was already in progress.

105. Ashley Fantz, "Obama as Witch Doctor: Racist or Satirical?," CNN, September 17, 2009, available at https://www.cnn.com.

106. Skocpol and Williamson, *Tea Party*, 78.

107. On the causes of the Democratic rout, see James Campbell, "The Midterm Landslide of 2010: A Triple Wave Election," *Forum* 8.4 (2010), 1–17.

108. In one sign of how quickly the political culture shifted, Bob Woodward's *The Price of Politics*—a book-length postmortem on the grand bargain, published in 2012—does not mention either Donald Trump or Bernie Sanders.

109. "Text of Obama's Remarks on His Birth Certificate," NBC News, April 27, 2011, available at https://www.nbcnews.com.

110. Abrams, *Obama: An Oral History*, 215.

111. Christopher Hayes, *Twilight of the Elites: America After Meritocracy* (New York, 2012), 236.

112. Barack Obama, "I Am Here to Say They Are Wrong," in *We Are the Change We Seek*, 175, 180–181.

113. "Obama Complains About 'Fat-Cat Bankers,'" Reuters, December 11, 2009, available at https://www.reuters.com; "Obama Doesn't 'Begrudge' Dimon, Blankfein over Pay," Reuters, February 10, 2010, available at https://www.reuters.com.

114. Woodward, *Price of Politics*, 47–49.

115. Woodward, *Price of Politics*, 52.

116. Morton Keller, *Obama's Time: A History* (New York, 2015), 77.

117. David Axelrod describes the scene in *Believer: My Forty Years in Politics* (New York, 2015), 445–446.

118. Axelrod, *Believer*, 447.

119. "Transcript: President Obama's Convention Speech," NPR, September 6, 2012, available at https://www.npr.org.

120. Henry Gomez, "Obama Campaign Says Romney 'Not One of Us' in Response to Ohio Coal Country Commercials," *Cleveland*, September 23, 2012, available at https://www.cleveland.com.

121. Ronald Brownstein, "Obama Buoyed by Coalition of the Ascendant," in *Annual Editions: American Government 09/10*, ed. B. Stinebrickner (New York, 2010), 141–143.

122. Dan Balz, "Obama's Coalition, Campaign Deliver a Second Term," *Washington Post*, November 7, 2012, available at https://www.washingtonpost.com.

123. Michael Shear, "Demographic Shift Brings New Worry for Republicans," *New York Times*, November 7, 2012, available at https://www.nytimes.com. Although far from universally accepted within the GOP, the argument received the imprimatur of the Republican National Convention in a hundred-page election autopsy urging the party to adapt itself to a younger and more racially diverse electorate. For an example of the contemporary reaction, see John Dickerson, "The GOP's Anguished Attempts at Reinvention," CBS News, March 19, 2013, available at https://www.cbsnews.com.

124. An early exception was Sean Trende, "The Case of the Missing White Voters," *Real Clear Politics*, November 8, 2012, available at https://www.realclearpolitics.com.

125. On Obama's 2012 coalition, see Paul Abramson, John Aldrich, Brad Gomez, and David Rhode, *Continuity and Change in the 2012 Elections* (Washington, DC, 2015), 115–126; Nate Cohn, "How the Obama Coalition Crumbled, Leaving an Opportunity for Trump," *New York Times*, December 23, 2016, available at https://www.nytimes.com.

126. "Remarks by the President on Economic Mobility," Barack Obama White House Archives, December 4, 2013, available at https://obamawhitehouse.archives.gov.

127. Devin Dwyer, "Obama Says GOP 'Fever' on Taxes May Break in a Second Term," ABC News, June 1, 2012, available at https://abcnews.go.com.

128. Obama, *A Promised Land*, 478.

129. Dan Pfeiffer, *Yes We (Still) Can: Politics in the Age of Obama* (New York, 2018), 192.

130. For a sympathetic overview of Obama's record, see Julian E. Zelizer, "Policy Revolution Without a Political Transformation: The Presidency of Barack Obama," in *The Presidency of Barack Obama*, ed. Julian E. Zelizer (Princeton, NJ, 2018), 1–10.

131. Noam Scheiber, "Get Rich or Deny Trying," *New Republic*, April 15, 2013, available at https://newrepublic.com/.

132. Michael Shear and Gardiner Harris, "With High-Profile Help, Obama Plots Life After Presidency," *New York Times*, August 16, 2015.

133. "Fox's Hasselbeck Knocks Obama's 'Class Warfare' Speech: 'He *Is* the System' He Created," *MEDIAite*, December 5, 2013.

134. Gerry Boehme, *How Hamilton Made It to the Stage* (New York, 2019), 57.

135. Barack Obama and Marilynne Robinson, "President Obama and Marilynne Robinson: A Conversation—II," *New York Review of Books*, November 19, 2015, available at https://www.nybooks.com.

136. Michael Paulson, "'Hamilton' Raises Ticket Prices: The Best Seats Will Now Cost $849," *New York Times*, June 8, 2016, available at https://www.nytimes.com.

137. Matt Flegenheimer, "$2,700 for Hillary Clinton at 'Hamilton'? That Would Be Enough," *New York Times*, July 12, 2016, available at https://www.nytimes.com.

138. Life expectancy offered one marker of how difficult it was becoming to compare relative privilege. According to a popular definition of racism developed by the geographer and social theorist Ruth Wilson Gilmore, "racism, specifically, is the state-sanctioned or extralegal production and exploitation of group-differentiated vulnerability to premature death": Ruth Wilson Gilmore, *Golden Gulag: Prisons, Surplus, Crisis, and Opposition in Globalizing California* (Berkeley, CA, 2007), 28. During the Obama years, however, the racial gap for life expectancy declined as the educational gap rose. "Education," concluded the economists Anne Case and Angus Deaton, "is now a sharper differentiator of expected years of life between 25 and 75 than is race." Unsurprisingly, racial differences persisted. Expected life span was highest for college-educated white people and lowest for non-college-educated Black people. But African Americans with a BA had a higher life expectancy than whites without a degree—a gap that opened up in the Bush era and then expanded significantly under Obama. The key change that took place around 2010 was that life expectancy began to fall for *both* white and Black people without college degrees. Meanwhile, it continued rising for both white and Black people *with* college degrees. And because most Americans don't graduate from college, overall life expectancy for both races fell. See Anne Case and Angus Deaton, "Life Expectancy in Adulthood Is Falling for Those Without a BA Degree, but as Educational Gaps Have Widened, Racial Gaps Have Narrowed," *Proceedings of the National Academy of Sciences of the United States of America*, March 2021, available at https://www.pnas.org.

139. See Pfeiffer, *Yes We (Still) Can*, 173, and Ben Rhodes, *The World as It Is: A Memoir of the Obama White House* (New York, 2018), xvii. On the interweaving of racial attitudes and partisan identity during the Obama presidency, see Michael Tesler, *Post-Racial or Most-Racial: Race and Politics in the Obama Era* (Chicago, 2016).

140. On Black Lives Matter and the Obama administration, see Peniel Joseph, "Barack Obama and the Movement for Black Lives: Race, Democracy, and Criminal Justice in the Age of Ferguson," in *The Presidency of Barack Obama*, ed. Julian Zelizer (Princeton, NJ, 2018), 127–143. For a more severe assessment, see Keeanga-Yamahtta Taylor, *From #BlackLivesMatter to Black Liberation* (Chicago, 2016), 135–152. In a sign of the shifting political climate, William Julius Wilson modified his earlier approach to "race-neutral" coalition building, arguing that Obama's 2008 campaign—specifically, the Philadelphia address on race—pointed the way toward a program that recognized

the need for race-specific policies without alienating white voters. See William Julius Wilson, *More Than Just Race: Being Black and Poor in the Inner City* (New York, 2010), 141–143, and "Q&A: Revisiting Race-Neutral Politics," *American Prospect*, March 9, 2011, available at https://prospect.org.

141. "Race Relations," Gallup, available at https://www.news.gallup.com.

142. Abrams, *Obama: An Oral History*, 341.

143. Though Obama did not officially endorse Clinton until after Sanders's campaign had run aground, his preference was obvious. See, for instance, John Cassidy, "Why Is President Obama Embracing Hillary Clinton Now?," *New Yorker*, January 26, 2016, available at https://www.newyorker.com. On Sanders's primary coalition, see Sides, Tesler, and Vavreck, *Identity Crisis*, 117–119, 123–127. On Sanders himself, see Matthew Karp, "The Long Shot," *Nation*, May 7, 2019, available at https://www.thenation.com.

144. "President Barack Obama," *WTF with Marc Maron*, June 22, 2015, available at http://www.wtfpod.com.

145. Obama, *A Promised Land*, 602.

146. Jennifer Epstein, "Pre-Game, Obama Spars with O'Reilly," *Politico*, February 2, 2014, available at https://www.politico.com.

147. Kiely and Lawrence, "Clinton Makes Case for Wide Appeal."

148. "Election 2016: Primary Results," *New York Times*, available at https://www.nytimes.com.

149. Jim Geraghty, "Chuck Schumer: Democrats Will Lose Blue-Collar Votes but Gain in the Suburbs," *National Review*, July 28, 2016, available at https://www.nationalreview.com.

150. Jon Favreau, "Why Electing Hillary in '16 Is More Important Than Electing Obama in '08," *Daily Beast*, February 26, 2016, available at https://www.thedailybeast.com.

151. Amy Chozick, "Hillary Clinton Calls Many Trump Backers 'Deplorables,' and G.O.P. Pounces," *New York Times*, September 10, 2016, available at https://www.nytimes.com.

152. "Transcript: President Obama's Democratic National Convention Speech," *Los Angeles Times*, July 27, 2016, available at https://www.latimes.com.

153. Obama, *Dreams from My Father*, 231.

154. Obama, *Dreams from My Father*, 50.

155. Lynn Sweet, "Obama, 50 Years After March on Washington: 'We Are Not Trapped by the Mistakes of History,'" *Chicago Sun-Times*, November 19, 2013, available at https://chicago.suntimes.com.

156. Barack Obama, "What Our Democracy Demands," in *We Are the Change We Seek*, 327.

157. The comparison might have occurred to Obama. His postpresidential memoir, *A Promised Land*, offered a much more upbeat assessment of Washington's legacy. "Despite the roadblocks, Chicago changed on his watch," Obama wrote, citing more equitable city services, fairer assignments of city jobs, and

increased attention to diversity in the business community. "Above all, Harold gave people hope," Obama concluded. "It wasn't so much what he did as how he made you feel." Obama, *A Promised Land*, 17.

158. Christine J. Walley, *Exit Zero: Family and Class in Postindustrial Chicago* (Chicago, 2013), 4.

159. Elizabeth Svoboda, "Life and Death After the Steel Mills," *Sapiens*, October 18, 2017, available at https://www.sapiens.org.

160. William Wan, "At the Housing Project Where Obama Began His Career, Residents Are Filled with Pride—and Frustration," *Washington Post*, January 8, 2017, available at https://www.washingtonpost.com.

161. Jackie Gu, "The Employees Who Gave Most to Trump and Biden," *Bloomberg*, November 2, 2010, available at https://www.bloomberg.com.

162. Obama, *Audacity of Hope*, 40.

163. Michelle Darrisaw and Elena Nicolaou, "Here Are All of Barack and Michelle Obama's Netflix Projects," *Oprah Daily*, February 9, 2021, available at https://www.oprahdaily.com/.

164. Michael Shear and Kate Kelly, "Obama Balances Civic-Minded Side with the Lure of a $400,000 Speech," *New York Times*, April 26, 2017, available at https://www.nytimes.com.

165. Lynn Sweet, "Obama Foundation Raises $232.6 Million in 2017, Best Year Ever," *Chicago Sun-Times*, August 9, 2018, available at https://chicago.suntimes.com.

166. Barack Obama, "Nuclear Option," *Congressional Record* 151.43 (2005), available at https://www.congress.gov; "Read the Full Transcript of Obama's Eulogy for John Lewis," *New York Times*, July 30, 2020, available at https://www.nytimes.com.

167. Jonathan Allen and Amie Parnes, *Lucky: How Joe Biden Barely Won the Presidency* (New York, 2021), 112, 224–225.

168. "Transcript: Barack Obama's DNC Speech," CNN, August 20, 2020, available at https://www.cnn.com.

CONCLUSION: THE ROAD TO FREEDOM

1. On Babbitt's life, see "The Journey of Ashli Babbitt," *Bellingcat*, January 8, 2021, available at https://www.bellingcat.com; Peter Jamison, Hannah Natanson, John Woodrow Cox, and Alex Horton, "'The Storm Is Here': Ashli Babbitt's Journey from Capital 'Guardian' to Invader," *Washington Post*, January 10, 2021, available at https://www.washingtonpost.com; and Ellen Barry, Nicholas Bogel-Burroughs, and Dave Philipps, "Woman Killed in Capital Embraced Trump and QAnon," *New York Times*, August 23, 2021, available at https://www.nytimes.com.

2. "Journey of Ashli Babbitt," *Bellingcat*.

3. "Journey of Ashli Babbitt," *Bellingcat*.

4. David Corn, "Sponsors of the Pre-Attack Rally Have Taken Down Their Websites. Don't Forget Who They Were," *Mother Jones*, January 12, 2021, available at https://www.motherjones.com.

5. Dan Spinelli, "A List of the Lawmakers Who Joined Pro-Trump Crowds on the Day of the Capitol Riot," *Mother Jones*, January 16, 2021, available at https://www.motherjones.com; Fredrick Kunkle, "Trump Supporter in Horns and Fur Is Charged in Capitol Riot," *Washington Post*, January 9, 2021, available at https://www.washingtonpost.com; Matthew Rosenberg and Ainara Tiefenthäler, "Decoding the Far-Right Symbols at the Capitol Riot," *New York Times*, January 13, 2021, available at https://www.nytimes.com.

6. Robert Pape, "What an Analysis of 377 Americans Arrested or Charged in the Capitol Insurrection Tells Us," April 6, 2021, available at https://www.washingtonpost.com.

7. "Journey of Ashli Babbitt," *Bellingcat*.

8. Karoun Demirjian, "Acting Capitol Police Chief: More Than 10,000 Rioters Came onto Capitol Grounds and More Than 800 Breached the Building," *Washington Post*, February 25, 2021, available at https://www.washingtonpost.com.

9. Rachael Bade and John Wagner, "GOP Candidate Poses with Rifle, Says She's Targeting 'Socialist' Congresswomen," *Washington Post*, September 4, 2020, available at https://www.washingtonpost.com; Catie Edmondson, "Marjorie Taylor Greene's Controversies Are Piling Up. Republicans Are Quiet," *New York Times*, January 29, 2021, available at https://www.nytimes.com.

10. "Congress and the Public," *Gallup Historical Trends*, available at https://news.gallup.com.

11. Paul Schwartzman and Josh Dawsey, "How Ashli Babbitt Went from Capitol Rioter to Trump-Embraced 'Martyr,'" *Washington Post*, July 30, 2021, available at https://www.washingtonpost.com.

12. Jack Healy, "These Are the 5 People Who Died in the Capitol Riot," *New York Times*, February 22, 2021; Nicholas Bogel-Burroughs and Evan Hill, "Death of QAnon Follower at Capitol Leaves a Wake of Pain," *New York Times*, May 30, 2021, available at https://www.nytimes.com; Peter Hermann, "Two Officers Who Helped Fight the Capitol Mob Died by Suicide. Many More Are Hurting," *Washington Post*, February 12, 2012, available at https://www.washingtonpost.com.

13. "Statement of Concern," *New America*, June 1, 2021, available at https://www.newamerica.com.

14. Jonathan Elliot, ed., *The Debates, Resolutions, and Other Proceedings, in Convention, on the Adoption of the Federal Constitution*, vol. 1 (Washington, DC, 1827), 221.

15. Nick Salvatore, *Eugene V. Debs: Citizen and Socialist* (Urbana, IL, 1982), 325.

16. Russell Baker, "Capital Is Occupied by a Gentle Army," *New York Times*, August 29, 1963, 1.

17. On organizing the March, see William P. Jones, *The March on Washington: Jobs, Freedom, and the Forgotten History of Civil Rights* (New York, 2013), 163–200.

18. Jones, *March on Washington*, 181.

19. Jones, *March on Washington*, 190.

20. Murray Kempton, "The March on Washington," *New Republic*, September 14, 1963, 19.

21. Rosalind Rosenberg, *Jane Crow: The Life of Pauli Murray* (New York, 2017), 267.

22. Malcolm X, *The Autobiography of Malcolm X* (New York, 1964), 278.

23. Jones, *March on Washington*, 203.

24. Jones, *March on Washington*, 202.

25. Lerone Bennett Jr., "Masses Were March Heroes," *Ebony*, November 1963, 119.

26. D'Emilio, *Lost Prophet*, 403.

Acknowledgments

I woke up the morning after the 2016 election convinced that I needed to write a book about . . . something. Edward Orloff shepherded me through the early steps of figuring out what that book should look like, and then he placed me under the editorial guidance of Alex Star. If you're the kind of person who reads the acknowledgments section of books like this one, then you have probably heard of Alex before. I'd heard that stuff too—"dream editor," "world-class adviser," "a real-life version of the wise mentor from a Joseph Campbell–style monomyth." To which I can now say: Yup, it's all true. Ian Van Wye kept me on track with just the right balance of velvet glove and iron fist. Maxine Bartow cleaned up my typos, solecisms, and other linguistic felonies, all without making me feel like an absolute dummy.

Without institutional backing, there would be nothing for Alex and company to work their magic on. This book took shape while I was an Andrew W. Mellon Postdoctoral Fellow in the Humanities at Washington University in St. Louis. It's a mouthful of a title that I give in full so that I can thank Joe Loewenstein, director of WashU's Interdisciplinary Project in the Humanities, for encouraging me to take this project on and then moving bureaucratic mountains to make it possible.

After I decamped for Washington, D.C., Awista Ayub and Clark Reeves found space for me at New America while Angus Burgin arranged for me to keep a foot in academia at Johns Hopkins. Then the history department at George Washington University brought me back into the university full-time. I could not imagine kinder or more supportive colleagues. Daniel Schwartz provided the logistical backing that allowed me to balance teaching and writing. Steve Brady, Sara Matthiesen, and Trevor Jackson gave me the junior faculty survival guide. Without GW's crack administrative team—Sam Nora, Michael Weeks, and Evelyn Williams—I'd still be locked out of my office. There might be academics out there in the world who are luckier than I am, but I haven't found them.

I've been lucky, too, in the opportunities I've had to test-drive the ideas here. Talks at Harvard Business School, the Johns Hopkins Seminar on the History of American Capitalism, and the Columbia University seminar on twentieth-century politics and society all sent me scurrying back to the keyboard for rounds of frantic revising. So did my students at WashU and GW, especially the undergraduates in my seminar on the history of American democracy since 1776.

Speaking of revising—and with apologies for the segue—it's time for a word about editors. This book exists in the first place because David Wolf and Jonathan Shainin at *The Guardian* let me take a deep dive into the intellectual prehistory of Trumpism back in the summer of 2016. I worked through my arguments in essays for David Marcus at *The Nation*, Laura Marsh at *The New Republic*, and Toby Lichtig at *The Times Literary Supplement*. And I had these opportunities only because of John Palattella, whose advice and example are in my head every time I write.

Then there's the help that only friends can give—in particular, friends who are experts in subjects that you're navigating for the first time. Lee Drutman, Sam Moyn, and Eric Arnesen read through chapters when the drafts were still in their awkward adolescence. Michael Kazin and Michael Lind did the same and then folded their advice into a yearslong conversation about democracy's past, present, and future. David Garrow offered generous, comprehensive, and astonishingly prompt support as I steered my way through Obama World, including vouching for me with Rob Fisher. Mark Fisher (no relation) introduced me to what twenty-first-century scholarship has to say about the Ancient Greeks.

I owe special thanks to the two brave souls who waded through an entire draft of the book. You could say that Daniel Schlozman is a walking version of *The Almanac of American Politics*, except he also has the soul of an activist and the intellectual range of a millennial Robert Dahl. It's almost enough to make me wish I'd been a political scientist—except that Eric Foner continues to remind me of why there's no beating history. Once again, his advice on matters big and small made me look smarter and wiser than I deserve.

So do my fellow Dissentniks. Natasha Lewis, Nick Serpe, Flynn Murray, Lyra Walsh Fuchs, and Joshua Leifer made the magazine run while I disappeared into working on this book. They are brilliant, humane, and—most important for me—forgiving. Lyra also gave the manuscript one of her characteristically meticulous fact checks, for which I am particularly grateful. I've run up a considerable debt to this entire group over the years, and I look forward to settling my tab.

But I owe even more to my family. Doraikannu and Leelavathi Regunathan swooped in when emergency called, pandemic be damned. Carolyn and Emma Shenk are the very best. Meg Hawco—or, as I call her, "Mom"—shaped this book in ways that I only now realize. You could tell the story of the New Deal coalition's breakdown just by looking at her extended clan. I won't do it, because I love them all too much: Sarah, Jim, Maggie, and Sammy Gilligan; Ted and Patrick Hawco; Tim and Cynthia Hawko; and Mary Ann, Kenny, and Beth Hyland. But, really, you could.

And that brings me to the family I helped make: my wife, Renu Regunathan-Shenk, and our sons, Nikhil and Adi. You three are my world. I wrote this book because you deserve a better one. But for now I'm looking forward to spending more time in this one with you.

Index

Page numbers in *italics* refer to illustrations.

abortion, 256; *Roe v. Wade*, 282
Adams, Charles Francis, 73–75, *74*
Adams, John, 21, 51, 56
Adams, John Quincy, 28, 37–38, 46, 51–56, 58, 68, 73, 75, 320; in election of 1828, 55–56, 67; Sumner and, 90
AFL-CIO, 246, 347–49
African Americans, 22–23, 63, 71, 103–104, 167, 225, 258, 268, 296, 298, 304–305, 346, 349; Barnburners and, 71; Black Codes and, 103; Black Lives Matter and, 329–30, 333; Black Power and, 248, 249; civil rights and equality for, *see* civil rights; Constitution and, 26; Democratic Party and, 158, 166, 172, 210, 331, 333, 346; Du Bois and, *see* Du Bois, W.E.B.; FDR and, 196, 197; freedmen, 50, 101, 103–104, 193, 194; Freedom Budget and, 246; illegitimacy rates among, 273; interracial marriage and, 49, 50, 62–63, 99, 185; Jefferson on, 23–24; life expectancy and, 421*n*138;

Lincoln and, 65*n*, 93; Madison and, 23–25; McCormick and, 155, 158; in multiracial coalition, 302, 309, 310, 312, 330, 332, 346; in New York City, 49, 50; Obama and, 314–19; Obama and Fisher on, 306–308; Paulding and, 62; in Philadelphia, 179; politicians and elected officials, 104, 136, 305; Populists and, 131–32; Reconstruction and, 103; Republican Party and, 132, 133, 142, 148, 159, 171, 172, 179, 183, 189, 346; Rustin on, 209–10; segregation and, *see* segregation; slavery of, *see* slavery; Smith on, 24; Sumner and, 84, 89, 93–94, 101, 104, 106, 111–12, 114–15; Theodore Roosevelt and, 141–42, 144–46, 148; violence against, 63, 103, 107, 116, 172, 226, 244; voters, 104, 121, 132, 155, 157–58, 171–74, 177, 188–89, 196, 203, 312, 346; voting rights for, 49–50, 71, 77, 93, 103–105, 108, 111, 117, 127, 129–30; Whigs and, 65*n*; white supremacy

African Americans (*cont.*)
   and, 10, 22, 65, 71, 73, 77, 83, 116,
   166, 190, 194, 197, 202, 203, 210,
   243, 244, 260, 303; Wilson and,
   301–302; World War I and, 185
Ailes, Roger, 280
Albany Regency, 48–49, 52, 55
Alien and Sedition Acts, 37
Alinsky, Saul, 300, 301, 331
Altgeld Gardens, 298, 301, 304, 334,
   336, 339
America First Committee, 160
American colonies, 16, 17, 22
American Dilemma, An (Myrdal),
   198–99, 203
American Enterprise Institute, 260
American Federation of Labor, 136
American Party, 92
American Philosophical Society, 24
American Protective Association
   (APA), 129
American Revolution, 16–18, 23, 30,
   33, 40, 45, 46, 60
Americans for Democratic Action
   (ADA), 239, 248
Ames, Fisher, 31
Antifederalists, 28–30, 33–35, 41, 345
aristocracy, 9, 17, 19, 20, 28, 47, 48, 64,
   69; Constitution and, 28; democracy
   and, 27; natural, 21–22, 25–26, 28,
   29, 35, 51, 56, 83; white, 70
Aristotle, 21
Articles of Confederation, 17, 18
Atlanta, Ga., 182
Atlanta Constitution, The, 182
Atlantic Monthly, 172, 180
Audacity of Hope, The (Obama), 314, 316,
   325, 329, 332, 338
Axelrod, David, 314, 325

Babbitt, Ashli, 341–43, 346
Bachmann, Michele, 280
Back-to-Africa movement, 185

Baker, Newton, 225, 230
Bakewell, Claude, 260–61
bank, national, 51, 57, 76, 116;
   Hamilton and, 32, 33, 40, 57; Jackson
   and, 61, 62, 76, 78
banks, 61–62, 306; failures of, 128;
   Republican Party and, 132
Bannon, Steve, 289, 290
Barnburners, 71–73, 75
Bell, Derrick, 303, 305, 413*n*3
Bellamy, Edward, 120–22
Belmont, August, 78
Bennett, Lerone, 349
Bentley, Elizabeth, 241
Benton, Thomas Hart, *66*, 91, 138
Biddle, Nicholas, 51
Biden, Joe, 5, 292, 337, 338, 343, 344
Bigelow, Poultney, 139
Bill of Rights, 31–32, 34
Bismarck, Otto von, 176
Black Lives Matter (BLM), 329–30,
   333
Black Majesty (Vandercook), 187
Black Reconstruction in America (Du Bois),
   193–94, 392*n*100
Bliss, Cornelius, 132
Booth, John Wilkes, 102
Bowman, Jamaal, 342
Breitbart News, 289
Bright, John, 98
Brooks, David, 313, 316
Brooks, Preston, 81, 83, 95–96
Brown, Lewis, 260
Brown, Michael, 330
Brown, Pat, 248
Brownstein, Ronald, 326
Brown v. Board of Education, 90, 203,
   243
Bryan, William Jennings, 148, 156,
   183, 313; Debs and, 131; in election
   of 1896, 121–23, 130–32, 134, 136,
   137; in election of 1900, 137
Buchanan, Pat, 282, 286, 288, 310

Buckley, William F., Jr., 243, 289; Schlafly's debate with, 255–59, *257*, 278

bureaucracy, government, 122, 145, 153, 161, 162, 232, 235–37, 239, 262, 277, 345

Bureau of Labor Statistics, 179, 183

Burke, Edmund, 83

Burnham, Walter Dean, 167, 169

Burr, Aaron, 38, 46; in duel with Hamilton, 39, 47

Bush, Cori, 342

Bush, George H. W., 251–52, 281, 304, 320

Bush, George W., 282, 283, 328, 409*n*91

Bush, Jeb, 288

Butler, Andrew, 95

Butler, Pierce, 22

Byrd, Robert, 314

Calhoun, John, 50, 54–55, 58–60, 63, 67–69, 91; death of, 76; Jackson and, 55, 58; slavery and, 58–59, 62, 68, 69; South and, 54–55, 58–59, 76; Van Buren and, 54, 59–60, *66*

Cantor, Eric, 321

capitalism, 10, 57, 59, 78, 89, 105, 116, 117, 120, 121, 122, 131, 220–21, 224, 239, 244, 260, 271, 315; democracy and, 135; Du Bois's views on, 174, 190–92, 194, 195, 197, 207; industrial, 120, 127, 128; labor and, 134–36; Lippmann's views on, 229; "money power," 57, 59, 61, 62, 69, 70, 73, 78, 89, 105, 110, 116, 131; Republican Party and, 122

Capitol, January 6 attack on, 5, 342–44, 346, 347

Capozzola, Christopher, 226

Caribbean, 108

Carnegie Corporation, 198–99

Carter, Jimmy, 256, 278–79

Cass, Lewis, 73, 95

Catholics, 58, 65, 121, 128, 129, 132, 135, 165, 263, 273

Chase, Salmon, 88

Chase Manhattan Bank, 256, 266, 278–79

Chicago, Ill., 298, 300–301, 308, 312, 327

Chicago Tribune, 110, 147, 161

China, 205–206, *206*, 262, 285, 289, 346

Chinn, Julia, 62

Choice Not an Echo, A (Schlafly), 259, 264–67, *264*, 279

Christianity, 38, 88, 166, 174, 274, 285

Churchill, Winston, 241

CIO (Congress of Industrial Organizations), 159, 196

civil rights, 49, 50, 59, 73, 83, 103, 104, 106, 111–13, 115, 116, 129, 144, 162, 166, 167, 200*n*, 203, 217, 246, 252, 289, 295, 299, 304, 305, 310, 349; backlash against, 243–44; Democratic Party and, 196, 203, 346; Du Bois and, 168, 171, 172, 174, 188, 193, 211; King and, *see* King, Martin Luther, Jr.; liberalism and, 211, 401*n*107; Lippmann and, 243–45; March on Washington, 208–11, 297, 310, 320, 335, 347–50, *349*; Republican Party and, 203, 346

civil service, 111

Civil War, 4, 5, 98–101, 104–106, 110, 114–17, 122, 127, 128, 134, 345, 347; slavery as cause of, 372*n*81

Clare Boothe Luce Policy Institute, 280

Clay, Henry, 68–69, 91

Cleveland, Grover, 130, 132, 133

Clifford, Clark, 163

Clinton, Bill, 281, 282–84, 317, 320

Clinton, Hillary, 317, 318, 322, 329, 330, 333, 418*n*87; "basket of deplorables" remark of, 333–34

coalitions, 6–8, 10, 11, *352nn*6,7, 353*n*19

Cold War, 199, 200, 200*n*, 203, 217, 238, 241, 242, 246, 261–63, 266, 268

Colton, Calvin, 65

communism, 165, 209, 217, 232–34, 239–40, 257, 260; Cold War and, *see* Cold War; Du Bois and, 174, 192, 195, 199–200, 202, 207, 208; Keyserlings and, 242; McCarthyism and, 165, 217, 241–43, 252, 262; Schlafly's views on, 261, 262, 263, 265, 268

Confederacy, 54, 92, 98, 103, 104, 137, 289, 347

Congress, U.S., 19, 20, 34, 36, 104, 128, 164, 321; anti-slavery gag rule in, 62, 69, 87; House of Representatives, 20, 30, 151, 164; Senate, 26, 30, 151, 164–65

Conkling, Roscoe, 108–10, 116, 139

conservatism, 167–69, 232, 243, 248–50, 255, 260, 279–82, 293, 302, 308, 314, 322, 406*n*12; blue-collar, 262; conservative Democrats, 216, 406*n*12; democratic, 122, 123, 127–28, 150; paleoconservatives, 286; populist, 258, 331; Republican Party and, 167, 406*n*12; Schlafly and, 255, 258, 260, 262, 263, 266–68, 277, 280–82, 286, 287, 289, 290, 292; Trump and, 288–91

Conservative Case for Trump, The (Schlafly), 289, 290

Conservative Political Action Committee, 280

Constitution, U.S., 8–9, 13, 14, 17, 21, 22, 27–29, 35, 38, 39, 46, 51, 54, 57, 87, 88, 208, 296, 338, 347, 353*n*17; aristocracy and, 28; Bill of Rights in, 31–32, 34; critics of, 13, 28; Fifteenth Amendment to, 111; Fourteenth Amendment to, 116, 139; Nineteenth Amendment to, 122, 150, 151; ratification of, 13, 16, 27–29; slavery and, 26, 94, 101

Constitutional Convention, 18–20, 22, 23, 25–27, 31, 77

Constitutional Union Party, 96–97, 99

Constitution of Liberty, The (Hayek), 236

Continental Congress, 15, 16

Conway, Kellyanne, 280, 290

Coolidge, Calvin, 153

Cori, Anne Schlafly, 288–89

coronavirus pandemic, 4

corporations, 116, 120, 128, 135, 139, 161, 224, 278, 315, 328

Cortelyou, George, 128

cotton, 51–52, 89

Coulter, Ann, 280

Council for National Policy, 280

Crawford, William, 53

Crisis, The, 171, 172, 184–88, 190, 204, 208, 391*n*69

Crockett, Davy, 45, 65

Croly, David Goodman, 125

Croly, Herbert, 125–26, 223

Cromwell, Oliver, 138

Cronkite, Walter, 216

Cruz, Ted, 288–89

Czolgosz, Leon, 137

Daily Mail, 134

Davis, Frank Marshall, 299

Debs, Eugene, 131, 136, 151, 153, 171, 172, 174, 183, 233, 345, 348

Declaration of Independence, 17, 85, 98, 101, 104, 208

democracy, 6–11, 15, 20, 39, 41, 84, 117, 120, 127, 128, 153, 171, 172, 217, 283, 292, 308, 311, 315, 344, 350, 353*nn*17,19; abolition, 193, 208, 347; ancient, 20, 29; aristocracy and, 27; capitalism and, 135; crisis of, 344–46; Du Bois's views on, 172–77, 181, 184, 187, 189, 190, 193–96, 198–200, 203, 207, 211; elections and, 20–21, 38; golden line between rulers and ruled in, 4, 6; liberal, 215–16, *215*,

304; Lippmann's views on, 227–30; Obama's views on, 295–97, 314, 316, 338, 341, 416n67; political parties and, 43–44; pure (direct), 20, 21, 29, 145, 175, 219; representative, 21, 305, 357n36; Schlafly on, 264; slavery and, 23, 58, 70, 88, 372n81; social, 159, 164, 246

democratic conservatism, 122, 123, 127–28, 150

democratic elite, 6–9, 12, 14, 15, 21

Democratic National Committee, 78, 321

Democratic National Convention, 230, 313, 334, 338–39, *339*

Democratic-Republicans (Republicans), 14–15, 35–40, 44, 46, 48–54, 56

Democratic Socialists of America, 310, 342

Democrats, Democratic Party, 5–6, 10, 11, 82, 90, 93, 96–98, 105, 112, 116, 121, 122, 128, 131, 132, 148, 161, 162, 163–66, 195, 201, 216–17, 227–29, 238, 244–45, 249, 252, 292, 296, 304, 305, 309, 314, 318, 319, 323, 327, 332–33, 336–38, 344, 403n131; African Americans and, 158, 166, 172, 210, 331, 333, 346; Barnburners, 71–73, 75; Bryan and, 121, 122, 130–31; in Chicago, 300, 301; civil rights and, 196, 203, 346; conservative, 216, 406n12; in election of 1864, 99–100; FDR and, 159, 164, 168, 196, 210, 245, 292; gender gap and, 279, 291; Great Society and, 244; Hanna and, 133; Hunkers, 71, 73; Jacksonian (the Democracy), 5, 7, 10, 44, 45, 54–58, 61–78, *66*, 82, 85, 88, 89, 95, 102, 123, 153, 164, 345; Johnson and, 245, 337; Keyserlings and, 234, 251; liberalism and, 167, 252, 400n103; Lippmann and, 238; in New York, 63, 71–75; Obama and,

297, 301, 310, 312–16, 318, 319, 321, 324–26, 334–37; partisanship and, *see* partisanship and polarization; Populist fusion with, 121, 131, 132; progressivism and, 166; Schlafly and, 256, 277; slavery and, 68, 71–72; in South, 10, 70–75, 129, 165, 196, 200, 245, 320, 337; Trump and, 291; working class and, 232, 240

Deneen, Charles, 157–58

Denver Times, 124

Depression, Great, 5–6, 17, 158–59, 162, 164, 190, 194, 229, 231, 238, 241, 259, 293

De Priest, Oscar, 157–59

Dewey, Thomas, 159–62

Dickens, Charles, 83

Dissent, 11

Dole, Bob, 281

Dominican Republic, 108

Douglas, Paul, 189, 200n

Douglas, Stephen, 77, 95

Douglass, Frederick, 73, 75, 81, 83, 93, 101, 114–15

Dreams from My Father (Obama), 308–309, 313, 334

Dred Scott v. Sandford, 76

Drift and Mastery (Lippmann), 224

Du Bois, Burghardt, 182

Du Bois, Nina, 182

Du Bois, W.E.B., 7, 168–69, 171–211, 214, 215, 218, 219, 297, 299, 310, 345; Atlanta University position of, 171, 179, 183–84, 190, 199; autobiography of, 207; *Black Reconstruction in America*, 193–94, 392n100; capitalism as viewed by, 174, 190–92, 194, 195, 197, 207; in China, 205–206, *206*; civil rights movement and, 168, 171, 172, 174, 188, 193, 211; communism and, 174, 192, 195, 199–200, 202, 207, 208; *The Crisis* and, 171, 172, 184–88, 190,

Du Bois, W.E.B. (*cont.*)
204, 208, 391*n*69; death of, 208, 211;
and death of son, 182; democracy
as viewed by, 172–77, 181, 184, 187,
189, 190, 193–96, 198–200, 203, 207,
211; Douglas and, 189, 200*n*; early
life of, 175–76; education of, 176–79;
FDR and, 195–97, 215; Gandhi
and, 204; in Germany, 178–79; in
Ghana, 174, 207, 208; indicted as
foreign agent, 202, 211; Jackson and,
185–87; King and, 173, 203–204,
388*n*11; liberalism and, 168, 172,
174, 183, 192–94, 211; Marvel and,
185–87, 391*n*69; Marxism and,
190–91, 194, 205; NAACP and, 171,
184–87, 190, 199, 200, 207, 208,
211; *The Philadelphia Negro*, 179;
philandering of, 185–87; politicians
disdained by, 175*n*; racist letters
received by, 205; Reconstruction as
viewed by, 176, 193–94; "A Search for
Democracy" manuscript of, 194–95;
Senate campaign of, 200–202, *201*;
separatist approach taken by, 174,
190; socialism and, 171, 172, 174,
178, 183, 187, 188, 190–93, 195, 197,
202, 205, 207; *The Souls of Black Folk*,
172, 181, 182, 211; statistical charts
of, 179–80, *180*; Stoddard and, 185,
186; Streator and, 192–93; Talented
Tenth and, 171, 173, 179, 183, 193,
198, 202, 312, 388*n*11; Washington
and, 181–84, 190; Wilson endorsed
by, 172, 174, 187, 207; world travels
of, 194–95, 205–207
Dukakis, Michael, 281, 320
Dunham, Madelyn, 299
Dunham, Stanley, 299, 307
Dunne, Edward, 150

Eagle Forum, 272, 280, 281, 288, 290,
291, 342

economic inequality, 61, 78, 94, 162,
168, 293, 295, 297, 325–28, 332
Einstein, Albert, 202
Eisenhower, Dwight D., 165, 166, 217,
238, 257, 263, 266, 315, 346, 400*n*103,
401*n*117; Lippmann and, 213
elections, 9, 11, 14, 16, 29, 353*n*17;
democracy and, 20–21, 38;
presidential, *see* presidential elections;
see also voters
Electoral College, 21, 26, 36, 97, 148,
409*n*91
Emerging Republican Majority, The
(Phillips), 165, 210–11
Emmanuel, Rahm, 322
Equal Rights Amendment (ERA), 151,
248, 250, 270, 291
Ervin, Sam, 277
Essays in the Public Philosophy
(Lippmann), 239
eugenics, 198
Everett, Edward, 95
Exit Zone (Walley), 335

Fabian Society, 219, 243
Fair Employment Practices Committee,
196
family, 273, 274, 276, 282, 285, 290,
293; illegitimacy and, 273, 285
Favreau, Jon, 333
Federalist Papers, The, 13–14, 32, 34
Federalists, 14, 15, 29, 36–41, 44,
48–54, 64
Federal Reserve, 148
Feminine Mystique, The (Friedan), 266
feminism, 150, 248–50, 252, 255–56,
271–76, 285, 291, 292
Fessenden, William Pitt, 105
financial crisis of 2008, 286, 319;
stimulus and, 322
Firing Line, 255, 256, 278
Fisher, Robert, 295, 296, 304–308
Fisk, Theophilus, 63

Floyd, George, 5
Ford, Betty, 274
Ford, Gerald, 253, 269, 277
Ford, Henry, 266
Ford Foundation, 253
Fortas, Abe, 234
Fortas, Carol, 234
founders, 9, 20–22, 36, 56, 83, 345
Franklin, Benjamin, 16
Freedom Budget, 246–49
Free Soil Party, 72, 73, *74*, 75, 77, 88, 90, 91
French Revolution, 34, 36
Freneau, Philip, 35
Freud, Sigmund, 191, 205
Friedan, Betty, 248; *The Feminine Mystique*, 266
Friedman, Milton, 233
Friedman, Tom, 313
Fukuyama, Francis, 304, 305
Furman, Jason, 322

Gandhi, Mahatma, 204
Garfield, James A., 126–28
Garfield, James R., 126
Garrison, William Lloyd, 75, 83, 87, 88
Garvey, Marcus, 185
Gates, Henry Louis, Jr., 322, 419*n*104
gay people, gay rights, 252, 268, 271–72, 281, 282, 312, 327
General Theory of Employment, Interest, and Money, The (Keynes), 231
Germany: Du Bois in, 178–79; Nazi, 237
Ghana, 174, 207, 208
Gilded Age, 7, 116, 119, 122, 123, 140, 153, 215, 232, 321, 370*n*56, 377*n*17, 378*n*18
Gilmore, Ruth Wilson, 421*n*138
Gingrich, Newt, 284
globalists, 283–86
Godkin, E. L., 109
Goldwater, Barry, 244, 248, 259, 264–67, 282, 289

Gompers, Samuel, 136
Good Society, The (Lippmann), 235–36
Gramsci, Antonio, 191
Grant, Ulysses S., 106–108, 113, 128, 131, 134; in election of 1872, 110, 113; Ku Klux Klan and, 107, 111; Sumner and, 107–109, 111
Great Depression, 5–6, 17, 158–59, 162, 164, 190, 194, 229, 231, 238, 241, 259, 293
Great Recession, 4
Great Society, 224–25, 227, 244, 246, 267, 298, 322, 402*n*130
Greeley, Horace, 83, 110, 112, 113
Greene, Marjorie Taylor, 342–43
Gulf War, 283, 304
Guyatt, Nicholas, 23

Hahn, Julia, 289, 290
Haiti, 37, 86
Hamilton, 328–29, 333
Hamilton, Alexander, 9, 13–16, 18, 22, 28–36, 38–41, 225, 228, 329, 358*n*52; at Constitutional Convention, 19–20, 26–27; in duel with Burr, 39, 47; early life of, 16; Madison and, 15, 16, 30, 33–35; on manufacturing, 32, 360*n*86; national bank of, 32, 33, 40, 57; on representative democracy, 21, 357*n*36
Hamilton, Charles V., 412*n*3
Hamilton, William, 358*n*52
Hamiltonians, 15, 35, 39, 41, 48, 51, 57, 69, 76
Hanahan, Tommy, 277
Hanna, Mark, 7, 123–28, *124*, *125*, 135–37, 150, 153–55, 159, 224, 229, 258, 297; appearance and character of, 125–26; business of, 126, 127; Croly's biography of, 125–26, 223; death of, 142–43; Democrats and, 133; foreign policy views of, 140–41, 153; health problems of, 142; McKinley and, 123,

Hanna, Mark (*cont.*)
  127, 129, 130, 133, 135, 140; as
  National Civic Federation president,
  136; as plutocrat, 123, 124, 126;
  Republican National Convention
  and, 143–44, *143*, 185; Republican
  Party and, 123, 127–28, 130, 132,
  133, 135–37, 142–44, 161, 162, 164,
  168, 195, 292, 345; Rockefeller and,
  126–27; Roosevelt and, 140–43, 145,
  146; in Senate, 135, 136
Hanna, Ruth, *see* McCormick, Ruth
  Hanna
Harding, Warren, 151, 153, 154
Harriman, Averell, 262
Harrington, Michael, 166, 209
Harrison, Benjamin, 128
Harrison, William Henry, 65–67, 96;
  death of, 67
Hart, Albert, 177
Hasselbeck, Elisabeth, 328
Hawaii, 298–99
Hayek, Friedrich, 233, 235–37, 260
Hayes, Rutherford B., 128
health care, 301, 305, 312, 315, 322, 327
Hearst, William Randolph, 123, 229
Helms, Jesse, 277
Hemings, Sally, 358*n*52
Herndon, William, 102
Higgins, Dallas, 273
Hillbilly Elegy (Vance), 329
Hillquit, Morris, 219–20
Hitler, Adolf, 200
Hoar, George, 107
Hobart, Garret, 137
Hoover, Herbert, 156, 159, 161, 164,
  166, 189, 238, 265; in election of
  1928, 228
Horizon, 183
Horton, Willie, 281
Hose, Sam, 182
House of Representatives, 20, 30, 151,
  164

House Un-American Activities
  Committee, 241
Howells, William Dean, 120
Humphrey, Hubert, 249
Hunkers, 71, 73
Hunt, Nelson Bunker, 280

immigrants, 58, 92, 121, 128–29, 131,
  132, 135, 153, 155, 225, 285–87, 327;
  Trump and, 287–89
Indians, 57, 62, 63, 65, 66, 73, 89;
  Sumner on, 94*n*
industry, 94, 120, 127, 128–29, 134,
  144, 164, 235, 237, 238, 377*n*17
Ingraham, Laura, 280, 289
Iran, 278–79
Iraq, 283, 312, 317
Irish immigrants, 58, 92

Jackson, Andrew, 43, 44, 51, 53, 55–58,
  60–62, 65, 73, 333; bank war of,
  61, 62, 76, 78; Calhoun and, 55,
  58; in election of 1828, 55–56, 67,
  75; "money power" and, 57, 59, 61,
  69, 70, 73, 116; slavery and, 57; Van
  Buren and, 53, 55, 56, 58, 60, 61, 69
Jackson, Marvel, 185–87, 190, 208,
  391*n*69
Jacksonian Democrats (the Democracy),
  5, 7, 10, 44, 45, 54–58, 61–78, *66*,
  82, 85, 88, 89, 95, 102, 123, 153,
  164, 345
James, William, 177, 218
James II, 64
Jay, John, 14
Jefferson, Mildred, 273
Jefferson, Thomas, 4, 5, 15, 18, 21, 26,
  30, 32–41, 44, 52, 83; *Notes on the
  State of Virginia*, 23; race and slavery
  and, 23–24, 358*n*52
Jeffersonians, 37–38, 41, 44, 46, 48,
  52–54, 56, 69, 77
John Birch Society, 256–57, 263–64, 280

Johnson, Andrew, 99, 102–104, 116, 169; impeachment of, 106; Lincoln and, 102; Sumner and, 102, 103, 106
Johnson, Cheryl, 336
Johnson, Hiram, 157
Johnson, Lyndon, 210, 244–45, 247–48, 251, 297, 298, 319, 347, 403n131; Democratic Party and, 245, 337; Keyserlings and, 245–49; Lippmann and, 213, 245, 247, 249
Johnson, Richard Mentor, 62–63, 65n
Jung, Carl, 147

Kansas-Nebraska Act, 95
Kempton, Murray, 348
Kennedy, John F., 217, 245, 297, 347, 348
Kerry, John, 312–13
Keynes, John Maynard, 226, 231–32, 235
Keyserling, Leon, 233–35, 239–40, 242, 245–47, 249–51, 401n117
Keyserling, Mary Dublin, 233–35, 239–40, 242, 245–51, 274, 401n117
Khrushchev, Nikita, 251
King, Coretta Scott, 204n
King, Martin Luther, Jr., 173, 203–204, 208, 210, 246, 297–99, 310, 348, 349; Du Bois and, 173, 388n11
Kissinger, Henry, 256, 278, 284
Know Nothings, 92
Korean War, 199, 241, 262
Ku Klux Klan (KKK), 107, 111, 227, 266, 273, 274

labor, 105, 106, 120–22, 124, 129, 132, 216; capital and, 134–36; organized, 136, 161, 163–66, 246, 248, 296, 314, 322, 349; strikes, 226; see also working class
La Follette, Robert, 147, 153
Lamar, Lucius, 114
Lamont, Thomas, 229
Landon, Alf, 159

League of Nations, 153, 284
League of Women Voters, 151
Le Diplomate, 3–4
Lehman, Herbert, 160
Lewinsky, Monica, 281
Lewis, David Levering, 186–87
Lewis, John, 196
liberal democracy, 215–16, *215*, 304
liberalism, 83, 109–13, 117, 163, 166–69, 197–99, 218, 226–28, 234, 235, 238, 246, 248–49, 305, 308, 309, 314, 331, 347, 349; civil rights and, 211, 401n107; consensus in, 216–17, 247, 252–53, 315; Democratic Party and, 167, 252, 400n103; Du Bois and, 168, 172, 174, 183, 192–94, 211; elites, 166–69, 258, 262; Great Society and, 244; Keyserlings and, 240, 247, 250, 252; liberal Republicans, 110, 111, 116, 216; Lippmann and, 215–16, 218, 226–32, 235–37, 239, 240, 247, 250–53; McCarthyism and, 241; Obama and, 303, 314, 315, 325, 335; pro bono, 303, 314, 325; qualitative, 239, 240, 244, 401n103; quantitative, 249; Schlafly and, 261, 279, 289; Schlesinger and, 238–39, 400n103; Sumner and, 83–85, 110; women's issues and, 292
Lichtman, Allan J., 378n18
Lieber, Francis, 113
Lieberman, Joe, 313
life expectancy, 421n138
Lincoln, Abraham, 44, 65n, 77, 92, 93, 101, 102, 104, 127, 128, 144, 159, 244; assassination of, 101–102, 114; in election of 1860, 96–97, 99, 134; in election of 1864, 98–100; Emancipation Proclamation of, 98, 144; Johnson and, 102; pamphlets on, 99, *100*; slavery and, 98, 372n81; Sumner and, 84, 97–98, 101–102
Lincoln, Robert, 102

Lippmann, Walter, 7, 168–69, 213–53, *214*, 257, 258, 265, 297, 305, 345; anticommunism as viewed by, 241; capitalism as viewed by, 229; death of, 253; democracy as viewed by, 227–30; Democrats and, 238; *Drift and Mastery*, 224; *Essays in the Public Philosophy*, 239; FDR and, 213, 215, 230–32, 250; *The Good Society*, 235–36; Great Society and, 224–25, 227, 402*n*130; Hayek and, 235–37; Johnson and, 213, 245, 247, 249; Keynes and, 226, 231–32, 235; liberalism and, 215–16, 218, 226–32, 235–37, 239, 240, 247, 250–53; *The Method of Freedom*, 231, 238; New Deal and, 231–38, 250, 402*n*130; *New Republic* and, 223–26; at *New York Herald Tribune*, 229, 230; at *New York World*, 227, 229; Nixon as viewed by, 250; *The Phantom Public*, 227; *A Political Philosophy for Liberal Democracy*, 216; *A Preface to Morals*, 227; *A Preface to Politics*, 222; progressivism and, 223–26, 247; *Public Opinion*, 227; Republicans and, 219, 243, 244; socialism and, 218–24, 226, 229, 232, 241, 252; on socialism versus progressivism, 221, 240, 247, 249; Theodore Roosevelt and, 213, 219, 223; "Today and Tomorrow" column of, 215, 231; Wilson and, 225–27
Longfellow, Henry Wadsworth, 86
Looking Backward (Bellamy), 120–22
Louisiana Purchase, 52
Luce, Henry, 213
Lunn, George, 220, 221
lynching, 182, 183, 196, 204, 243

Maclay, William, 32
Madison, James, 9, 14–16, 18, 28–41, 44, 46, 51, 339; appearance and
character of, 15–16; in congressional campaign against Monroe, 30–31, 40; at Constitutional Convention, 18–20, 25–27; early life of, 15; Hamilton and, 15, 16, 30, 33–35; race and slavery and, 23–26, 358*n*52
Malcolm X, 299, 348
Mansbridge, Jane, 271–72
Mao Zedong, 206, *206*
March on Washington for Jobs and Freedom, 208–11, 297, 310, 320, 335, 347–50, *349*
marriage: Du Bois on, 198; interracial, 49, 50, 62–63, 99, 185
Marshall, Thurgood, 199, 203
Marshall Plan, 199, 239
Marx, Karl, 191, 193, 207, 222
Marxism, 190–91, 194, 205, 220–21, 224, 234
Masses, The, 220, 226
Matthews, Chris, 313
McCain, John, 282, 286, 319
McCarthy, Joseph, 241, 242, 266
McCarthyism, 165, 217, 241–43, 252, 262
McCormick, Medill, 147–50, 157, 161; death of, 152
McCormick, Ruth Hanna, 146–61, *152*, 258, 261, 262, 345; African Americans and, 155, 158; death of, 161; Dewey and, 159–61; foreign policy views of, 153, 155, 157, 158, 160; marriage to Medill McCormick, 147; marriage to Simms, 159; Medill's death and, 152; 1928 congressional campaign of, 154–57; 1930 Senate campaign of, 157–59; Simmons and, 155; *Time* feature on, 156, *156*, 157; wealth of, 158; women's suffrage and, 149–51
McHenry, Patrick, 321
McKinley, William, 128–30, 136, 144, 161; assassination of, 137, 139;

in election of 1896, 122–23, 127,
129–35, 137, 380n56; in election of
1900, 137; Hanna and, 123, 127, 129,
130, 133, 135, 140; Republican Party
and, 122–23, 128–30, 132–35; South
and, 129–30
Meaney, George, 349
media, 4, 163, 217, 281, 310
meritocracy, 238, 302
Messina, Jim, 321
Method of Freedom, The (Lippmann),
231, 238
Mexican-American War, 71
Michels, Robert, 227
Mill, John Stuart, 236
Miranda, Lin-Manuel, 328–29
miscegenation, 99, 125, 185
Missouri Compromise, 52
Mitchell, Arthur, 159
"money power," 57, 59, 61, 62, 69, 70,
73, 78, 89, 105, 110, 116, 131
monopolies, 236, 306, 328
Monroe, James, 30, 39, 40, 51, 54;
in congressional campaign against
Madison, 30–31, 40
Moon Illustrated Weekly, The, 183
Morgan, J. P., 124, 142
Morris, Gouverneur, 138
Morris, Thomas, 69–70
Mugwumps, 127
multiracial coalition, 302, 309, 310,
312, 330, 332, 346
Murray, Pauli, 348
Muslims, 286, 288, 289
Myrdal, Gunnar, *An American Dilemma*,
198–99, 203

NAACP, 196, 203, 208, 347; Du Bois
and, 171, 184–87, 190, 199, 200, 207,
208, 211
Nation, The, 109, 185
National American Woman Suffrage
Association (NAWSA), 150

National Civic Federation, 136, 380n69
National Federation of Republican
Women, 263, 267, 272, 275
National Organization for Women
(NOW), 248, 249, 292, 348
National Review, 243, 255, 257, 277,
289, 406n12
National Woman's Party, 188
Native Americans, *see* Indians
NATO, 199, 241
neoliberalism, 236, 253, 310, 311, 346
New Deal, 5, 6, 123, 159, 162, 168,
195–97, 199, 210, 216, 217, 247,
249–51, 258, 260, 262, 299, 314, 319,
347, 400n103; coalition of, 163–69,
210, 252, 295, 296, 307, 345; Great
Society and, 244; Keyserlings and,
234–35, 240; Lippmann and, 231–38,
250, 402n130; McCarthyism and,
241; Schlesinger and, 238, 239
New Left, 249, 252, 268
New Republic, The, 185, 223–26, 234,
348
Newsweek, 313
New York City, 38, 63; African
Americans in, 49, 50
New York Globe, The, 175, 176
New York Herald, 101
New York Herald Tribune, 229, 230
New York Journal, 123
New York State, 29, 45–46, 48, 52, 71,
75, 77; constitutional convention
in, 49–50; Democrats in, 63, 71–75;
voting requirements in, 49–50
New York Times, The, 91–92, 105, 143,
158, 160, 169, 192, 194, 199, 200,
211, 217, 229, 258, 290, 313, 316,
328, 347
New-York Tribune, 82, 110
New York World, 99, 227, 229
Niagara Movement, 183
Nietzsche, Friedrich, 222
9/11 terrorist attacks, 285, 286

Nixon, Richard, 217, 250, 268–69, 284
Nkrumah, Kwame, 207
Notes on the State of Virginia (Jefferson), 23
nuclear weapons, 217, 256, 262, 263, 266

Obama, Barack, 5, *5*, 7, 164, 286, 292, 295–339, 341, 345, 347; African Americans and, 314–18; *The Audacity of Hope*, 314, 316, 325, 329, 332, 338; in Chicago, 298, 300–301, 308, 327; as community organizer, 300–302, 309, 313, 327, 334, 336; congressional campaign of 1999, 311; democracy as viewed by, 295–97, 314, 316, 338, 341, 416*n*67; Democratic National Convention address of 2004, 313; Democratic National Convention address of 2020, 338–39, *339*; Democratic Party and, 297, 301, 310, 312–16, 318, 319, 321, 324–26, 334–37; *Dreams from My Father*, 308–309, 313, 334; early life of, 298–99; father of, 309; Fisher and, 295, 296, 304–308; Gates incident and, 322, 419*n*104; "guns and religion" remark of, 318, 333–34; at Harvard Law School, 286, 295, 302–304, 314, 336; Illinois Senate campaign of, 308–11; liberalism and, 303, 314, 315, 325, 335; mother of, 299, 301, 309, 310, 335, 336; multiracial coalition and, 302, 309, 310, 312, 330, 332; presidency of, 321–28, 331–35; presidential campaign of 2008, 316–21; presidential inauguration of, 320, *320*; *A Promised Land*, 422*n*157; reelection of, 324–27; Republican Party and, 316, 317, 319, 321, 323–28; Schlafly and, 286–88; Senate campaign of, 312; as senator, 314; "Transformative Politics," 295,

296, 304–308, 312, 314, 315; Trump and, 323–24, 334; working class and, 307, 318
Obama, Michelle, 304, 308, 312, 313, 338
Obamacare, 322, 327
Ocasio-Cortez, Alexandria, 331, 342
Occupy Wall Street, 324, 325, 330, 333
O'Donnell, Gladys, 275
Ogle, Charles, 64, 67
Ohio, 69
oligarchy, 8, 21, 44, 48, 51, 57, 78, 89, 120, 187–88, 194, 197, 227
Owen, Ruth Bryan, 156

Paine, Thomas, 86
Palin, Sarah, 286, 289, 319
Panama Canal, 141, 256, 259, 289
Paris World's Fair, 179–80
Partisan Leader, The (Tucker), 43, 362*n*9
partisanship and polarization, 11, 14–15, 40, 167–69, 252, 258, 268, 278, 291, 292, 296, 297, 316–18, 321, 329, 330, 332, 334, 345, 346
Patriot Act, 283
Paul, Alice, 150, 151, 188
Paulding, James Kirke, 62, 67
Pearl Harbor, 160, 237, 265
Penn, Mark, 317
People's Party (Massachusetts), 98
People's Party (Populists), 121–23, 131–32, 135, 145, 177, 347
Percy, Charles, 277
Perot, H. Ross, 284
Pfeiffer, Dan, 327
Phantom Public, The (Lippmann), 227
Philadelphia, Pa., 179
Philadelphia Negro, The (Du Bois), 179
Phillips, Kevin, 165, 169, 210–11
Phillips, Wendell, 102
Pierce, Franklin, 78
Pinckney, Charles, 19, 22
Platt, Thomas, 130

Plessy v. Ferguson, 136

Plouffe, David, 319, 323–24

plutocracy, 119–20, *119*, 123, 159, 215, 324; Hanna and, 123, 124, 126

political machines, 48–49, 52–53, 139, 140, 153, 154, 159, 160, 163, 165, 168, 261, 345

political parties, 6, 35, 43–44, 48; democracy and, 43–44; partisanship and, *see* partisanship and polarization; slavery issue and, 52; third, 120, 121; two-party system, 6, 96, 120, 121, 127, 131, 154

Political Philosophy for Liberal Democracy, A (Lippmann), 216

Polk, James K., 69, 71, 72

populism, 8, 10, 57, 58, 89, 136, 158, 161, 168, 169, 250, 251, 258, 262, 297, 331, 333, 344, 346, 347

Populists (People's Party), 121–23, 131–32, 135, 145, 177, 347

Power of the Positive Woman, The (Schlafly), 275

Pravdin, Vladimir, 241

Preface to Morals, A (Lippmann), 227

Preface to Politics, A (Lippmann), 222

presidency, 20

presidential elections, 21, 26; of 1796, 37; of 1800, 37–38, 56; of 1824, 51, 53; of 1828, 55–56, 67, 75; of 1840, 63–67, 69, 86, 96; of 1844, 69, 72; of 1848, 73–75, 77, 88; of 1860, 96–97, 99, 134; of 1864, 98–100; of 1872, 110–13; of 1892, 128, 131; of 1896, 121–23, 127, 129–37, 380n56; of 1900, 127; of 1912, 147–49, 153, 171–72; of 1920, 151; of 1924, 153; of 1928, 228; of 1932, 230–31; of 1936, 195–96; of 1948, 163; of 1968, 250; of 2008, 316–21; of 2016, 290, 337; of 2020, 337, 342–44

Pressman, Lee, 234

Price, Mary, 241

Price, Melvin, 261–63

Progressive Party (1912), 146–49, 153, 161

Progressive Party (1948), 200

progressivism, 145–46, 148, 221, 243, 250, 251, 302, 305, 307, 316, 328, 345; Democrats and, 166; Lippmann and, 223–26, 247; scholarship on, 382n106; socialism versus, 221, 240, 247, 249

Prohibition, 153, 155, 158, 227

Promised Land, A (Obama), 422n157

property rights, 106

Protestants, 58, 110, 121, 129, 163, 273

Public Opinion (Lippmann), 227

Publius, 13, 15, 18, 28–30, 32–35, 37, 41, 79, 296; *The Federalist Papers*, 13–14, 32, 34

Publius Valerius, 13

Pugh, Allison, 295

Pullman Company, 131

Puritans, 83, 84

race, *see* African Americans

radio, 160

railroads, 116, 131

Randolph, A. Philip, 347, 348

Rankin, Jeannette, 149

Reagan, Ronald, 6, 248, 267, 268, 273, 277–81, 284, 286, 326, 335, 345, 406n12

realigners, 7–8, 10, 11; guardians, 13–41; insiders, 213–53; insurgents, 255–93; liberators, 81–117; organizers, 119–62; partisans, 43–79; politicians, 295–339; prophets, 171–211

realignments, 7, 10

Reconstruction, 5, 101, 103, 108, 110, 111, 116–17, 347, 374n125; Du Bois's views on, 176, 193–94; Sumner and, 105, 112, 113, 116–17

Reed, Adolph, Jr., 310

Republican National Committee, 130

Republican National Convention, 143–44, *143*, 159, 185, 263, 266, 283, 286, 289, 319

Republicans (Democratic-Republicans), 14–15, 35–40, 44, 46, 48–54, 56

Republicans, Republican Party, 5, 7, 11, 44, 77, 95–97, 103–109, 112, 115–17, 121, 122–23, 128, 134–35, 147, 148, 151, 153–55, 158, 159, 161–62, 164–65, 167, 201, 211, 216, 228, 229, 238, 239, 244, 248, 251, 266, 267, 269, 270, 279, 296, 323, 326, 327, 344, 370*n*56; African Americans and, 132, 133, 142, 148, 159, 171, 172, 179, 183, 189, 346; capitalism and, 122; civil rights and, 203, 346; the Combine, 129; conservatism and, 167, 406*n*12; Du Bois on, 193–94; as emerging majority, 165, 210, 211, 250; formation of, 76, 81, 92; funding for, 132, 251; gender gap and, 279, 291; Great Society and, 244; Hanna and, 123, 127–28, 130, 132, 133, 135–37, 142–44, 161, 162, 164, 168, 195, 292, 345; liberal, 110, 111, 116, 216; Lippmann and, 219, 243, 244; McKinley and, 122–23, 128–30, 132–35; National Union Party, 99; Obama and, 316, 317, 319, 321, 323–28; partisanship and, *see* partisanship and polarization; populism and, 297, 331, 344; Populist fusion with, 132; Progressive, 146–49, 153; Radical, 83, 98, 101, 103–105, 109, 174, 193, 194, 374*n*125; Schlafly and, 258, 260, 263, 265–70, 275, 277, 281–84, 286, 289–90, 409*n*91; slavery and, 92–95, 122; in South, 129, 132, 142, 162, 165, 166, 250; Stalwarts, 108, 110; Sumner and, 81–84, 92, 93, 95–96, 98, 101, 104, 107–109, 112, 116, 122, 123, 164, 345; Theodore Roosevelt and, 139–42,

144, 146, 161, 345; Truman and, 163; Trump and, 287–88, 290–91, 333, 334; women and, 150–52, *152*

Revels, Hiram, 104, 111

Revolutionary War, *see* American Revolution

Richmond Junto, 52

Ritchie, Thomas, 52, 53

Road to Serfdom, The (Hayek), 236

Roberts v. City of Boston, 90

Robins, Raymond, 149

Rockefeller, David, 256, 278–79

Rockefeller, John D., 120, 126–27, 132, 256

Rockefeller, Nelson, 268

Roe v. Wade, 282

Romney, Mitt, 287, 325, 326

Roosevelt, Alice, 147

Roosevelt, Eleanor, 234

Roosevelt, Franklin Delano, 5–6, 159, 161, 163, 166, 195–97, 216, 217, 230, 233, 259, 265, 307, 315, 403*n*131; African Americans and, 196, 197; Democratic Party and, 159, 164, 168, 196, 210, 245, 292; Du Bois and, 195–97, 215; in election of 1932, 230–31; in election of 1936, 195–96; Keyserling and, 234; Lippmann and, 213, 215, 230–32, 250; New Deal of, *see* New Deal; Schlesinger and, 238, 239; World War II and, 237

Roosevelt, Theodore, 137–47, 150, 153, 154, 157, 297, 324; African Americans and, 141–42, 144–46, 148; becomes president, 137, 139–40; in election of 1912, 147–49, 153, 171, 172; family background and early life of, 137–39; foreign policy of, 140–41; Hanna and, 140–43, 145, 146; inner circle and, 138, 140, 146; Lippmann and, 213, 219, 223; McCormicks and, 147–49; progressive movement and, 145–46, 148; Republican Party and,

139–42, 144, 146, 161, 345; Sumner
    and, 139
Roosevelt, Theodore, Sr., 137, 139
Rowe, James, 163
Rubin, Robert, 284
Rush, Bobby, 311
Rusher, William A., 277, 406n12
Russell, Richard, 245
Rustin, Bayard, 208–11, 246, 248, 296,
    297, 301, 320, 338, 347–50, 412n3

St. Louis Globe-Democrat, 267, 269
Sanders, Bernie, 297, 327, 330–31, 333,
    337, 338, 418n87
Santayana, George, 218
Santo Domingo, 108
Scammon, Richard, 166–67
Schlafly, Andrew, 286, 290
Schlafly, Fred, 261
Schlafly, John, 281, 290
Schlafly, Phyllis, 7, 255–93, 297, 342,
    345, 409n91; anticommunism of,
    261, 262, 263, 265, 268; Buckley's
    debate with, 255–59, *257*, 278; cancer
    and death of, 259, 288, 290; *A Choice
    Not an Echo*, 259, 264–67, *264*, 279;
    congressional campaigns of, 261–63,
    269–70, 275; conservatism and, 255,
    258, 260, 262, 263, 266–68, 277,
    280–82, 286, 287, 289, 290, 292; *The
    Conservative Case for Trump*, 289,
    290; conspiracies as viewed by, 265;
    Democratic Party and, 256, 277;
    early life of, 259–60; Equal Rights
    Amendment and, 255, 256, 270–74,
    276–78, *276*; feminism and, 271–76,
    285; globalists as viewed by, 283–86;
    Goldwater and, 259, 264–67;
    marriage of, 261; nationalism of,
    284–87; Obama and, 286–88; *The
    Phyllis Schlafly Report*, 268, 270–72,
    280, 281, 285, 290; *The Power of the
    Positive Woman*, 275; Republican

Party and, 258, 260, 263, 265–70,
    275, 277, 281–84, 286, 289–90,
    409n91; Trump and, 259, 287–90,
    293; Warren compared with, 291–92
Schlesinger, Arthur M., Jr., 238–40,
    400n103, 401n107
Schumer, Chuck, 333
Schurz, Carl, 103–104, 111, 114
segregation, 50, 90, 111, 136, 182, 190;
    Brown v. Board of Education and, 90,
    203, 243; integration, 243; Jim Crow,
    10, 50, 116, 136, 153, 154, 166, 172,
    176, 181, 182, 188, 189, 196, 197,
    315, 345, 348, 353n17
Seidenberg, Ivan, 325
Senate, 26, 30, 151, 164–65
September 11 terrorist attacks, 285, 286
Shaw, George Bernard, 219
Sherman, John, 98–99
Sherman, William Tecumseh, 99
Shipley, George, 269
Simmons, Roscoe Conkling, 155
Simms, Albert, 159
skeleton-key histories, 10
Skocpol, Theda, 416n67
slavery, 15, 22–26, 44, 50, 57–58,
    61, 68, 76, 77, 92, 111, 117, 176;
    abolitionists and, 24, 26, 60, 62, 63,
    68–70, 73, 75, 81, 82, 86–95, 98–102,
    109, 116, 139, 345; Calhoun and,
    58–59, 62, 68, 69; as cause of Civil
    War, 372n81; Congressional gag rule
    and, 62, 69, 87; Constitution and, 26,
    94, 101; cotton market and, 51–52;
    decline in, 49, 51, 52; democracy and,
    23, 58, 70, 88, 372n81; Democrats
    and, 68, 71–72; emancipation and,
    24, 49, 50, 52, 81, 85, 87, 89, 98, 105;
    Emancipation Proclamation and, 98,
    144; end of, 99, 112; expansion of, 52,
    68, 71–73, 75, 87, 94, 95; Hamilton
    and, 25; Jackson and, 57; Jefferson and,
    24, 358n52; Lincoln and, 98,

slavery (*cont.*)
372*n*81; Madison and, 25, 26,
358*n*52; Missouri Compromise
and, 52; political parties and, 52;
Republicans and, 92–95, 122;
Roosevelt on, 137; "slave power" and,
69–70, 73, 75, 76, 89, 94, 95, 97, 101,
102, 106, 109, 116, 117; Smith on,
24–25; South's economic strength
and, 70; Sumner and, 81, 82, 86–95,
97–102, 103, 105, 106, 110, 112, 117;
three-fifths clause and, 26, 38, 70,
87; Van Buren and, 46, 59, 62, 70–71,
77, 78
Slavery in the United States (Paulding), 62
Smith, Adam, 105–106, 235
Smith, Al, 228
Smith, Melancton, 28, 345
Smith, Samuel Stanhope, 24–25, 358*n*52
Sobran, Joseph, 279
social democracy, 159, 164, 246
socialism, 136, 161, 166, 209, 219–20,
224, 232–34, 238, 240, 242, 249,
261, 263, 286, 297, 347; Du Bois
and, 171, 172, 174, 178, 183, 187,
188, 190–93, 195, 197, 202, 205, 207;
Lippmann and, 218–24, 226, 229,
232, 241, 252; progressivism versus,
221, 240, 247, 249
Souls of Black Folk, The (Du Bois), 172,
181, 182, 211
South, 54–55, 57, 58, 60, 61, 76, 93,
94, 104–106, 111, 112, 121, 176,
181, 225, 260, 372*n*81; Calhoun
and, 54–55, 58–59, 76; Confederacy,
54, 92, 98, 103, 104, 137, 289, 347;
Democrats in, 10, 70–75, 129, 165,
196, 200, 245, 320, 337; economic
strength of, 61, 70; impact of votes
in, 197, *197*; McKinley and, 129–30;
planter class in, 33, 38, 52, 55, 61,
63, 69, 70, 73, 76, 78, 97, 102–103,
111, 116, 117, 188, 194; Republicans

in, 129, 132, 142, 162, 165, 166,
250; secession of, 97, 101, 372*n*81;
Theodore Roosevelt and, 145–46
Soviet Union, 241, 262, 266, 304; Cold
War and, *see* Cold War; Du Bois and,
184, 187, 200, 202, 205, 207
Spain, 141
Spanish-American War, 141
Spanish flu, 226
Spingarn, Joel, 187
Stalin, Joseph, 200, 238, 241, 262
Standard Oil Company, 120, 127, 132,
256
states' rights, 20, 26, 46, 58, 117, 266
Steffens, Lincoln, 219
Steinem, Gloria, 274
Stephens, Alexander, 92, 104
Stevenson, Adlai, 163, 166
Stewart, Dadie, 259
Stewart, John, 259
Stoddard, Lothrop, 185, *186*
Story, Joseph, 39, 85–86, 90
Strategic Arms Limitation Treaty, 256
Streator, George, 192–93
Sumner, Charles, 7, 75, 81–117, *82*,
169, 193, 296, 302, 372*n*81; Adams
and, 90; African Americans and, 84,
89, 93–94, 101, 104, 106, 111–12,
114–15; Brooks's assault on, 81, 83,
95–96; civil rights bill of, 111–13,
115, 116; Conkling and, 108–10,
139; "The Crime Against Kansas,"
83; currency and, 106, 374*n*125;
death of, 113–15, *115*; early life of,
84; Grant and, 107–109, 111; health
problems of, 113; Johnson and, 102,
103, 106; Lamar's tribute to, 114;
law career of, 86, 90; as liberal,
83–85, 110; Lincoln and, 84, 97–98,
101–102; marriage of, 85; on Native
Americans, 94*n*; Reconstruction and,
105, 112, 113, 116–17; Republican
Party and, 81–84, 92, 93, 95–96, 98,

101, 104, 107–109, 112, 116, 122, 123, 164, 345; Roosevelt and, 139; Santo Domingo annexation and, 108; selected for the Senate, 90–91; slavery and, 81, 82, 86–95, 97–102, 103, 105, 106, 110, 112, 117; Story and, 85–86, 90; Van Buren and, 86

Sumner, Julia, 91

Supreme Court, U.S., 76, 85, 115, 116, 169, 290–91; *Brown v. Board of Education*, 90, 203, 243; *Dred Scott*, 76; Obama on clerking at, 304; *Plessy v. Ferguson*, 136; *Roe v. Wade*, 282

Sweezy, Paul, 234

Taft, Robert, 259, 262, 266

Taft, William Howard, 144–48, 171, 172, 183, 266

Talented Tenth, 171, 173, 179, 183, 193, 198, 202, 312, 388*n*11

Taney, Roger, 76

taxes, 26, 38, 106, 110, 131, 262, 269, 277, 283, 305, 315, 323, 324, 328

Taylor, Zachary, 75, 87

Tea Party, 287, 322–23, 342

Tecumseh, 63

television, 160, 165, 213, 217, 258, 281

Texas, 67–69, 72, 87

Thomas, Norman, 195, 233, 242

Thompson, Bill, 157

Thurmond, Strom, 200, 209, 268

Tilden, Samuel, 72

Time, 156, *156*, 157, 213, 229, 316

Tocqueville, Alexis de, 47, 175

Treasury Department, 30, 32–34

Truman, Harry, 163, 199–200, 239, 241, 245, 262

Trump, Donald, 4, 5, *5*, 11, 287–88, 292, 311*n*, 329, 337, 341, 342; Capitol attacked by supporters of, 5, 342–44, 346, 347; elected president, 290, 337; immigration and, 287–89; Obama and, 323–24, 334; Republicans and,

287–88, 290–91, 333, 334; Schlafly and, 259, 287–90, 293; women's opposition to, 291

Turner, Henry McNeal, 94

Tyler, John, 67, 68

United Nations, 260

Upshur, Abel, 68

urbanization, 94

vaccination, 285

Van Buren, Abraham, 46, 89

Van Buren, John, 72, 88

Van Buren, Martin, 7, 43–79, *47*, 65, 66, *74*, 83, 129, 296, 345, 372*n*81; appearance and character of, 45, 48, 60; banks and, 61–62; books written by, 76, 77; Calhoun and, 54, 59–60, *66*; early life of, 45; in election of 1840, 63–67, 69, 96; in election of 1844, 69, 72; in election of 1848, 73–75, 88; homes of, 64, 67, 76; Jackson and, 53, 55, 56, 58, 60, 61, 69; Jacksonian Democracy and, 44, 45, 54–58, 61–78, *66*, 123, 164; Johnson and, 62–63; law career of, 47–48, 86; political career of, 45, 48, 82; slavery and, 46, 59, 62, 70–71, 77, 78; spending by, 64; Sumner and, 86; Texas statehood and, 68–69, 72, 87

Vance, J. D., 329

Vandercook, John, 187

Van Ness, William, 47

Vietnam War, 247–50

Village Voice, The, 310

Virginia, 4, 15, 29, 30, 33, 34, 38, 39, 41, 52, 305, 319, 333

voluntary associations, 120

voters, 345; African American, 104, 121, 132, 155, 157–58, 171–74, 177, 188–89, 196, 203, 312, 346; participation rates of, 16–17, 38, 40, 43–44, 66, 97, 120, 127, 153–54, *154*,

voters (*cont.*)
  157–58; Southern, impact of, 197, *197*; women, 154, 157–58
voting rights: for African Americans, 49–50, 71, 77, 93, 103–105, 108, 111, 117, 127, 129–30; restrictions on, 49–50, 104, 127, 154, 181; for women, 50, 105, 122, 131, 133, 149–51, 154, 158, 161

Wallace, George, 250, 277, 284, 406*n*12
Wallace, Henry, 200
Wallas, Graham, 219, 224
Walley, Christine, 335–36
Wall Street Journal, The, 319
Ward, Chester, 266
War of 1812, 39, 40
Warren, Elizabeth, 291–92, 327, 338, 416*n*67
Washington, Booker T., 142, 155; Du Bois and, 181–84, 190
Washington, George, 15, 16, 18, 30–32, 34, 36, 37, 40–41
Washington, Harold, 300–301, 309, 331, 334–35
Washington Daily News, 160
Washington Post, The, 158, 242, 326, 336
Wattenberg, Ben, 166–67
Wayne, John, 269
Wealth of Nations, The (Smith), 105–106, 235
Weber, Max, 178
Webster, Daniel, 91
Welch, Robert, 257
welfare, 166, 167, 216, 238, 244, 260, 262, 273
Wells, H. G., 219
Western expansion, 52, 57, 67–68, 71–73, 75, 87, 94, 95
West Wing, The, 316
Weyl, Nathan, 234
Weyl, Walter, 234

Weyrich, Paul, 280
Whigs, 64–68, *66*, 71, 73, 75–78, 82, 87–89, 90, 92, 93, 95–98, 109, 134
White, William Allen, 126
Wilkins, Roy, 190, 208, 211
Willkie, Wendell, 260
Wilmot, David, 71, 75
Wilmot Proviso, 71
Wilson, James Q., 165, 261
Wilson, William Julius, 301, 307, 310*n*
Wilson, Woodrow, 148, 153; Du Bois's endorsement of, 172, 174, 187, 207; Lippmann and, 225–27; World War I and, 225–26
Wisconsin Steel, 298, 304, 335–36
women, 57, 65; Equal Rights Amendment and, 151, 248, 250, 270, 291; feminism and, 150, 248–50, 252, 255–56, 271–76, 285, 291, 292; Republican, 150–52, *152*; Trump opposed by, 291; voters, 154, 157–58; voting rights for, 50, 105, 122, 131, 133, 149–51, 154, 158, 161; working-class, 248; in work force, 174, 282, 285, 292; World War I and, 150
Women's Bureau, 246–48
Women's March, 291
Women's National Democratic Club, 239
working class, 183, 192–93, 198, 210, 216, 234–35, 252, 282, 296, 297, 319, 326; Democratic Party and, 232, 240; Obama and, 307, 318; white, 165–67, 188, 192, 204, 297, 307, 318–20, 329, 409*n*91; women, 248; *see also* labor
Works Progress Administration, 197
World Court, 153, 155, 157, 158
World War I, 150, 151, 158, 225–26, 230; African Americans and, 185
World War II, 160, 198, 203, 209, 210, 237, 260, 262, 266; Pearl Harbor, 160, 237, 265
Wright, Jeremiah, 317

Illustration Credits

All images not included below are in the public domain.

Page 156: Time USA, LLC

Page 186: W.E.B. Du Bois Papers, Robert S. Cox Special Collections and University Archives Research Center, UMass Amherst Libraries

Page 197: Oxford Publishing Limited

Page 201: W.E.B. Du Bois Papers, Robert S. Cox Special Collections and University Archives Research Center, UMass Amherst Libraries

Page 206: W.E.B. Du Bois Papers, Robert S. Cox Special Collections and University Archives Research Center, UMass Amherst Libraries

Page 214: Walter Lippmann Papers, Manuscripts and Archives, Yale University Library

Page 257: Firing Line Broadcast Records, Hoover Institution Library & Archives

Page 264: Phyllis Schlafly Revocable Trust

Page 349: Minnesota Historical Society

A NOTE ABOUT THE AUTHOR

Timothy Shenk is an assistant professor of history at George Washington University. The coeditor of *Dissent* magazine, he has written for *The New York Times*, *The Guardian*, the *London Review of Books*, *The Nation*, *The New Republic*, and *Jacobin*, among other publications. He has been a Mellon postdoctoral fellow at Washington University in St. Louis and has received fellowships from the National Endowment for the Humanities, the American Council of Learned Societies, and New America. He lives outside Washington, D.C.